Irrevocably Yours

Paperback ISBN: 9798386105013
Hardcover ISBN: 9781088096291

A Publication of *Tall Pine Books*
119 E Center Street, Suite B4A | Warsaw, Indiana 46580
www.tallpinebooks.com

| 1 23 23 20 16 02 |

Published in the United States of America

Irrevocably Yours

Where Two Become One

Dawn Horsfall

To Jesus Christ and His Bride; The Church

If any part of this book has any bit of religion, legalism, or law, I want you to know that is not my intent. Please understand that I continue to grow in Kingdom realities. This book was simply the beginning of my journey of coming out of religious tradition and being born again. This is what God gave, to me, for the church as a starting place to come out of the system of religion and into freedom and Truth. I know there will continue to be greater revelations and more books to come as I continue to grow and learn about His Kingdom realities.

Contents

Why "Irrevocably Yours?"

I HAVE LEARNED that being a Christ Follower is much different than calling myself a "Christian." And the Lord has given me a compelling desire to share all I have learned about this matter with you. We can learn and know a lot of things about being a Christian, but we do not walk it out in the fullest measure we are called to by Jesus Christ. Sometimes we do not know how to. We are told a certain thing like, "deny yourself" and then we do not understand what that looks like or how to do it. The desire and design for this book is to help you understand the "how to's," and give you examples of what it looks like to actually be doers of the Word and not hearers only thereby deceiving yourselves (James 1:22-25). What it means to be a disciple.

The Lord has brought me on this journey of becoming a Christ follower in Word and in deed, and not just in word only (by saying I am a Christian and not acting like one). Holy Spirit teaches and reveals Truth. He leads and guides us. And where the Spirit of the Lord is, there is freedom (2 Corinthians 3:17). I have experienced first-hand living this life of freedom. By surrendering to Holy Spirit, following Him, and denying my-self (the self-life), which has made me free from me. It does not mean trials and tribulations are gone. It does mean God changes our perspective, in the midst of them, from being self-centered to being Christ-centered.

Self is our biggest enemy because self is controlled by satan. Can you imagine living free from frustration, annoyances, despair, discouragement, anger, jealousy, insecurities, defeating thoughts, and believing lies? It is possible! In fact, we have been made free and yet we live in bondage. When Jesus said, "It is finished" that is exactly what He meant. He accomplished everything on that old rugged cross. There is nothing left for Him to do. It is now up to us to respond. We are to have the faith to believe it and receive it as Truth. Then we will walk in the reality of it. We will walk in the freedom that is already ours. That has already been bought and paid for by the blood of Jesus Christ.

I know some of you when you read "believe it and receive it" you already shuddered. You immediately thought of the "name it and claim it" era. This is not that! This is not a believe it to receive it for your own selfish gain and desires. This is believe God's Word so you can receive it for your spiritual freedom. We can only receive and walk in what we believe is true of His Word. If we do not believe it, we will never receive it (Mark 11:22-24 & Matthew 21:21-22).

Have you ever heard the story of the man who is sitting in a prison cell? He is in despair because he is stuck in prison. Cut to the scene of Jesus crucified. What Jesus did on the cross broke every chain of bondage and opened every prison door. Yet the man remains in prison because he is stuck in his own finite mind of not being able to believe it is true. Because he does not believe it, he cannot receive the freedom that he has. He could walk right out of that door, instead he remains sitting in the prison cell. With his chains broken, door wide open, and a slave's mind stuck in the bondage of his own thoughts and not the Truth.

When Jesus was crucified so was our own flesh, and the self-life, we get stuck living in. Why do we have such a hard time believing this when it is written throughout Scripture? In Galatians 2:20 He tells us we have been crucified (past tense) with Christ. In Galatians 5:24, He says those who are Christ's have crucified the flesh (past tense). And in Romans 6:6-8, our old man was crucified with Him, he who has died, has been freed from sin, now if we died with Christ, we believe we will also live with Him (all past tense).

My heart's desire is for us all to live in this freedom. To live in such peace and joy that is indescribable through Christ. This is not some fairytale story or Hallmark movie; it is real Life. It is His Word. I am a walking, breathing, experience of this. Am I perfect? Not yet (smile). However, God's aim (therefore it is my aim) for my entire life is that it is no longer

I who lives but Christ lives in me (Galatians 2:20). Christ in me is perfect. My prayer is you will read the book in its entirety to discover the Truth the Lord has for you, to live this life of freedom and transformation.

I promise you, when you follow the Lord, it will be your best life ever. We do not have to wait "to get to heaven" to live that kind of life. We were created to walk out heaven here on earth. Jesus prayed to our Father (Matthew 6:10) "Your Kingdom come. Your will be done ON EARTH AS IT IS IN HEAVEN." The King lives inside of us. That makes us the carriers of His presence and His Kingdom here on earth. We are the conduits, His vessels, of His will being done here on earth. Thereby we bring heaven to earth. By faith we bring the unseen world into the seen.

Jesus came that we would have life and have it MORE abundantly (John 10:10). I like to look up definitions, to receive what the word is really saying to me. The definition of abundantly according to *Merriam-Webster Dictionary* is, "Existing or occurring in large amounts." Other descriptions are (to include the Greek meaning from *Strong's Concordance*), exceedingly, beyond measure, overflowing, a quantity as to be considerably more than what one would expect or anticipate, excessive. This is not just what is waiting for us in heaven. This is the life He came to give us here and now. And it is the abundant life ONLY He can give. How many do you know who are living this kind of life, right now? This kind of life, He said, He came to give us?

At this time, I will release a warning statement. I may get repetitive. I may say things over and over within a chapter and even repeat it in several chapters. There are a few reasons for this. Repetition is good. We repeat things over and over to learn them. Repetition in learning helps us to remember and to know them. In repetition we will be transformed. Another reason repetition may happen is because a lot of these subjects overlap. The same thing may be discussed in several chapters because it applies to the process in each of those chapters. I am not oblivious to the fact of repeating myself. At times it is intentional. Other times it is just plain necessary so we will KNOW Truth that makes us free (John 8:31-32).

It is my recommendation to not speed read through the book. It is written to be an interactive book and a study guide. Designed to help you know how to live the life of following Jesus. Prayerfully it is a tool that will help lead you and guide you in your own personal relationship with Him and transformational journey. This is not a "quick fix" guide but a daily life surrendered manual.

There will be my own personal journal entries that were written as I journeyed this road. There will be questions asked, for you to honestly reflect on, to understand where you are at. There will be practical examples of what this life looks like. How to apply it to your life and your own relationship with Jesus. There will be prayers to pray. The prayers are intended for you to have an intimate exchange with Jesus. The definition of intimate according to *Merriam-Webster Dictionary* is, "Marked by a warm friendship developed through long association." *Oxford Languages* describes intimate as, "Closely acquainted, familiar, involving very close connection, detailed or thorough knowledge of someone."

Take time with the prayers. Don't just repeat them quickly and move on but think about what you are saying. May these prayers be a commitment to Jesus and an exchange of Love. There will be Bible verses referenced throughout that will not always be fully written out. Having a Bible on hand is highly recommended. This is purposefully done for you to be able to study it for yourself. Open your Bible, read it, and eat the Bread of Life!

I also want to take time to answer the question some of you may have about the title of this book, why "Irrevocably Yours?" Let us first look at the definition of irrevocably. From *Oxford Languages* it is, "Not able to be changed, reversed, or recovered; final." Some other definitions use the words; unable to be repealed or annulled, not to be revoked or recalled. Another way we can say this is; to be done in such a way that it cannot be undone.

"Yours," is more specifically Jesus'. I am His, in such a way that it cannot be or will not be undone, changed, reversed, repealed, revoked, or recalled. I am Irrevocably His. In other words, "I am Irrevocably Yours, Lord."

The idea of something being done in such a way it could not possibly be undone was a great gift of solace to me. Especially in a world and, dare I say, even in the church that does not take commitment seriously. They so easily break covenant with one another. People who are largely consumed with themselves (their own self-will, self-fulfillment, selfish desires, selfish pursuits, and even their own self-preservation). Where generally much is left undone and promises are often broken, this profound word "Irrevocably," was what Jesus was forming in my life. It became an anchor for my soul.

Understanding the transformation Holy Spirit was taking me through would never be reversed by Him. The change happening inside of me would never be undone. God's covenant with me could never be annulled or revoked and His promises to me would never be broken or recalled. Being Irrevocably His, was my hope, my Truth, and my greatest comfort. This is what I could cling to on so many long, hard, and dark days in my journey.

Jesus has drawn me to Himself, in such a way, that this cannot be undone either. He will do this for you as well. We are His bride after all. The one He is coming back for, to marry. The whole Bible culminates on our wedding day at the marriage supper of the Lamb (Revelation 19:1-9). This book is intended to help the bride of Christ to be ready when our Bridegroom, King Jesus, returns for His bride. A bride that is without spot or wrinkle, that we should be holy and without blemish before Him (Ephesians 5:27).

In Hosea 2:14, God says, "Behold, I will allure her, and bring her into the wilderness, and speak tenderly to her." Allure means to powerfully attract. The journey we, as Christ Followers, should all be on is one of Him powerfully attracting us to Himself. In this place where He has allured us, He wants to speak tenderly to us so we will enter into an intimate relationship with Him. A relationship He very much desires to have with each one of us

From this intimate relationship with Him, we will surrender our lives to Him completely. So that we can be transformed by His Love, and be transformed into His Love, which is His Image, because God is Love. Through transformation we take on the identity of Christ, (what I call Godentity). When we live from His Godentity we know who we are, and we will bring heaven to earth. By being just as Jesus in this world (1 John 4:17).

Others will recognize His Love in us. Drawing them in, so they will experience Jesus in a powerful and profound way. By this encounter they will surrender their all to Him and be changed forever. So, they can be just as Jesus in this world. This would be called making disciples and advancing the Kingdom of God here on earth.

Our mission has always been more than making sure we get to heaven. Please do not get me wrong, heaven is most definitely where we want to be for eternity, but what do we do until our bodies expire? We are not to be saved and then just sit here and wait. Our mission, Jesus has given us, is to make disciples (Matthew 28:19-20). However, we cannot make disciples until we ourselves have become one first.

In Luke 14:33 Jesus says, "So likewise, whoever of you does not **forsake all that he has** cannot be My disciple." The definition of forsake according to *Merriam-Webster Dictionary* is, "To renounce or turn away from entirely." This would mean surrender all that you have and all that you are to Him and turn away from everything else. This is the first step of discipleship; <u>forsake all</u>. How often do we teach this to the church? How do we do this, and what does it look like to do so? We will take the time to learn these things throughout this book.

Jesus also says in John 8:31, "If you **abide in My Word**, you are my disciples indeed." Abide means to stay, remain, dwell, continue in, or adhere to. Jesus is saying IF you adhere to My Word, IF you remain faithful to all I am teaching you, IF you continue to dwell in Me, this proves you are My learned ones (disciple) who follow Me indeed (Christ Followers). They are the ones who adhere to Jesus' Word and direct their lives by it. It is not a casual attitude towards His Word. It is complete obedience to His Word. And those who obey Him, it is proof they Love Him (John 14:15).

Lastly Jesus says, in Matthew 16:24, "If anyone desires to come after Me, let him deny himself, and take up his cross, and follow Me." How many of us are living crucified to the self-life? Being transformed by His Word, and becoming His Word? Becoming like Christ in every situation, thereby "<u>Following Him</u>?"

We are not here just to wait to get to heaven when we die, a physical death, but we are alive to have heaven inside of us. Can you imagine living heaven here on earth every day of our lives? We can because it is Christ in us. Truly this is the best life ever!

Lord, this is ALL for You and for Your glory! May You be magnified! Your Kingdom come, Your will be done on earth as it is in heaven!

Irrevocably Yours,

Dawn Horsfall (AKA Sunshine)

Picture drawn by Hannah Isham.

James 1:14-15, "But each one is tempted when he is drawn away by his own desires and enticed. Then, when desire has conceived, it gives birth to sin; and sin, when it is full-grown, brings forth death."

CHAPTER 1

Death of Me; The Unveiling

I WAS DYING. I was dying on the inside. I was dying from a sickness that was in my soul and I was in an Intensive Care Unit (my living room to be exact). This was not clinically diagnosed but Holy Spirit diagnosed. "Lord, how did I get here?" I wanted to live again. I knew what it was like to have the passion of Holy Spirit inside of me transforming me like wildfire. This passion and fire had been quenched long ago. Holy Spirit was still there with me, but He was like an old debit card I had deactivated, and I could no longer access my funds. This would be how my soul got to the place of being bankrupt.

I knew what it was like to have the all-consuming Love of Jesus pulsating through my veins and how His Light would shine through me. The smile, the laugh, the glisten in my eyes, I had them all and now the smile, the laugh, the glisten, they were long gone. How I missed those days of old. Being alive, feeling the passion. Now my life had been sucked out of me. I could barely breathe I was suffocating inside. I desperately needed my lifeline, Jesus, to come and save me. "Help me!" Was all I could say in the weakest of whispers.

Flatline.... I died. On December 10th, 2018, my soul had died. And in that moment, Jesus came to my rescue with a vengeance only He can have. Nothing can tame the Lover of my soul when my soul is caught in death's grip. There was no stopping Him. He took the paddles of His defibrillator (which would be His Loving and healing hands) in that Intensive Care Unit, where I was laying, and He was restarting my heart, so I could live.

"Clear!" And although it felt as if this was truly the end, with what was happening in my family now. "Clear!" My life was being completely torn apart, yet once again. "Clear!" I had an underlying sense this was His redemption plan for my life. "Clear!" His rescue of me was my only comfort, which was otherwise a time of devastation, confusion, and absolute heartbreak. "Clear!" He came into my darkness, wrapped His arms around me, and snatched me out of that slimy pit I was in and said, "My beloved, My chosen one, My precious daughter, will not be left here for dead. Breathe!!" In one swooping breath, I breathed in the breath of Life. As I laid there in His arms, while He held me so very close to Him, all I could do was gaze into His Ever-Loving eyes of fire. With tears flowing down my face, I whispered, "You saved me!"

How does someone go from having such passion, exuberance, and being so full of Life to dead on the inside? What is the culprit when this happens? Holy Spirit tells us clearly what it is.

> **James 1:14-16** "But each one is tempted when he is drawn away by <u>his own desires</u> and enticed. Then when desire has conceived, <u>it gives birth to sin</u>; and sin, when it is full grown, <u>brings forth death</u>. Do not be deceived, my beloved brethren."

Here is the recipe for death. This is how satan (whom I also refer to as the enemy, the devil, or demon) gets us. he distracts us with meaningless pursuits. he entices us to chase after our own desires. When we chase after our own selfish desires, we cannot live in God's desires. His desires for us are His plans for us. This is our created purpose. When I chased after my own desire, I left the path of my intended purpose and entered the slow fade to the death of my soul. Life as I knew it was over. Holy Spirit even warns us "DO NOT BE DECEIVED My beloved."

We are deceived if we think what we want for our lives is better for us than what God wants for our lives. Let me tell you; Father knows best! When we believe lies, we are defenseless. We will get caught in the lie's tangled web. Think about what happens to insects when they get caught in a spider's web. They are defenseless, they die, and become food for the spider. Sounds exactly how satan operates. For he is the father of lies and he spins the webs that entrap us.

"Then when desire has conceived it gives birth to sin." All disobedience to God is sin. And my disobedience to God is what led me to the Intensive Care Unit. When we are disobedient to God, we are walking in a different direction than what He would have us go. We, in our disobedience, are walking away from Him and His ways which are the only ways of true Life. If we are disconnected from our only source of Life, we die. The body cannot live without a beating heart.

This does not mean He leaves us, that is not what I am saying. The Bible (I also will refer to as His Word and the Scriptures) is very clear that He never leaves us. But it does mean that in our sin we disconnect ourselves from Him. He has not left us, but we have left Him. It is no different than in any other close relationship. We can be in a room with this person, even very close in proximity, and still be very disconnected from them. It does not mean they are not there sitting right next to us. It does mean something is off, something is not right, something is missing, something has interrupted our connection.

We cannot walk down two paths at the same time. Just like we cannot go left and right at the same time or forward and backwards at the same time. We cannot walk with God in obedience at the same time we walk away from God in disobedience. It is one or the other. If Holy Spirit tells us to go right and we go left, we cannot say we are following Him and His way.

We make the choice of which way we are going every minute of every day. His way or our own way. Proverbs 14:12 (ESV) "There is a way that seems right to a man, but its end is the way to death." It was God's mercy and grace that got me out of the place I found myself in and brought me off the path that led to death. But it is my obedience to Him that will keep me where He wants me, and on the path that leads to Life.

God tells us in Deuteronomy 30:15-20, to choose this day life or death. To live in obedience to God is to choose life. To live in disobedience (sin) to God is to choose death. Understand that this is His Word and His promise for us, one or the other will happen (life or death), depending on the choices we make. God tells us to choose this day. Then He even gives us the answer for this pop quiz when all of life's testing happens, verse 19 He says to us, "Choose life!" To give you the New Testament reference, John 14:15 (NLT) Jesus says, "If you Love Me, obey My commandments." We are to obey His Word and what He tells us to do in His Word.

Considering all of this, it is very clear I had made some very wrong choices. I was to the point of death. I had chased after my own desires and by choosing my own desires, I was choosing death. Matthew 16:26, "For what profit is it to a man if he gains the whole world (or gains all his own desires) and loses his own soul? Or what will a man give in exchange for his soul?" Every sin, and any desire apart from God's purpose for us, will lead to a death of the soul or a physical death.

I can honestly say now, and I pray this helps save so many of you from a path of destruction, NOTHING is worth exchanging for your soul. Nothing is worth that kind of pain and agony or that kind of death. To be fully alive physically and yet dead on the inside, it is a horrible place to be and a horrible way to live. The walking dead is a real thing, I now know! Trust what the Word of God says is True. If you choose your own desires your soul will die, or you will physically die, it is just a matter of time (James 1:14-16 & Romans 7:11).

It was my lack of surrender that got me there. And it was a snare and a stronghold of satan, along with my lack of knowing Truth, that led to wrong choices I made. Hosea 4:6, "My people are destroyed for lack of knowledge...." Oh, what a tangled web the enemy weaves... and we get caught in it. When, God's ways are so simple. Not necessarily always easy but they are simple. It is as simple as Jesus saying, "Follow Me," so we follow Him. Below are lyrics from the song "Charming One" by The Waiting:

"So, I followed the deceiver, too blind to discern.
But deception was a teacher, and a brutal way to learn.
That I should have turned myself around and run.
you were a charming one."

We must always remember, satan only comes to steal, kill, and destroy. To stop the advancement of the Kingdom of God in us. He has been trying to do this in my life for a long time. I have had a few near-death experiences where satan has tried to get me out of the way. Out of his way.

There was a car accident when I was a teenager. I was sitting in the middle seat of a pick-up truck, with no seat belt on, and the truck hit a tree. I flew into the windshield. My friend's dad had gone later that day to see the truck at the accident site. When he came back to where I was at, he looked at me with eyes wide open, and almost as white as a ghost. He basically said there is no way that I should be alive, it is only by the grace of God I was. satan could not take me out and he did not win, God did! Then when I was 20, I almost died after a simple outpatient surgery. I was getting my gallbladder taken out. When I should have been home that same day, I ended up unconscious in ICU (literally this time) for 3 days. Once I awoke, I found myself hooked to a machine to help me breathe and my family gathered around me. I was in the hospital for 7 days, then I was released. satan did not win, God did! Later in life, my 2 boys and I were in a serious car accident. T-boned right on my side, the driver's side, and all 3 of us walked away. People around us were amazed. They were not expecting us to get out of that car. They said it was a miracle. satan did not win, God did!

Then there were many emotional adversities in life. When my sister died suddenly in a car accident, satan still did not win. When my dad died suddenly from a stroke, satan did not win. When my teen-age son decided, he did not want to live with me anymore and went to live with his dad, satan did not win. Through 2 divorces, satan did not win. Through other personal hardships, many strongholds, addictions, and many, many, many flat-out wrong choices I made (did I say MANY?), satan did not win. Over the years pieces of my heart had been taken, stolen, given away, crushed, torn apart, and ripped out. Repeatedly ripped out. And God has so carefully kept me in His Ever-Loving hands through it all.

satan TRIED to destroy my life first, many times and through many tragedies. Also, through many dark nights of the soul. At times I hardly thought I would make it. But you see the devil had to try, because there was a very good chance, he would destroy me in the process and stop me from advancing God's Kingdom. So, he took his chances, and they backfired every time. satan tries because he fears we will become the living and breathing Word of God. It is God's Word the enemy is terrified of. he is terrified of us who believe the Word of God to be true and who know our authority in it. satan fears the possibility of us saying, "Yes Lord, I will go, send me!" he fears us exposing his kingdom of darkness. But all his attempts to take me out, only gave me a greater tenacity to destroy the works of hell. he could not have me.

I have a dear friend that has spoken this to me, "satan has seen your films." Just like a football coach will watch footage of an opposing team's previous games. This is done to see where the other team is weak. To spot gaps, to see where one can penetrate to gain the upper hand, to win the game. The enemy is a watching demon. he knows our struggles. he knows where we are weakest. In 2014, he knew exactly what to do to try to take me out for good, so he attacked right where I was weakest. Before we get to that, we must go back in time first. To view a portion of my films.

I was married previously for 15 years to someone with whom I thought I would spend the rest of my life with. When he walked away in 2011, I was devastated (that is putting it lightly), I thought my life was over. My world came crashing down and I did not know how I was going to make it through. There was a thick blanket of heaviness over me. I was so alone, broken, and even embarrassed to face people. The pain was more than I could bear. It was an extremely difficult road to walk and there were many times I had asked God to take me. I would not take my own life, but I prayed many times that God would take my life for me, "Please take me home now." But God had different plans for me.

During that time was when I really started getting serious about my relationship with God. I started to draw very close to Him and to understand what a relationship with Him truly looked like. I find all too often we do not know how to have a relationship with Him, we are very flippant about it. We forget He is a Holy God, and instead of reverence for Him, we approach Him as if He is our "Genie in a bottle." When we need something, we will come to Him. We rub the lamp so He will show up and grant us our request. Then the rest of the time we leave the lamp sitting on a shelf with Him in it.

Sure, we may go to church and read His Word, but this does not mean we have a relationship with Him. This leads to lukewarm Christianity. Which Christ says He will vomit you out of His mouth if you are lukewarm (Revelation 3:16). And yet this is where most Christians are. That was the state I was in until my world came crumbling down in every way in the summer of 2011. This was the beginning of my transformation.

By 2014, I was going strong with Jesus. He had done truly amazing things in my life. How He had healed my heart and brokenness after my divorce was absolutely astounding. He had given me a new life and I was on fire. However, there was this one area I could not surrender to Him completely. I was trying to surrender, and He was working with me on it. But I never made it to the place of full surrender at that time.

My particular weakness was that I wanted a relationship. I desired to marry again. I did not want to be alone for the rest of my life. I wanted to know He had a good, godly, man for me. I wanted a marriage that would be a powerhouse for His Kingdom. More than anything (at that time) I wanted to believe there was someone out there that could love me. I wanted an intimate relationship with someone. Never fully understanding at that point in my life the most intimate relationship I could ever have would be with Jesus, the Lover of my soul, my Bridegroom King. This was an area I did not know Truth in.

Instead of God giving me confirmation of <u>this</u> plan, "my plan" for my life, He revealed to me in one quick moment I was to remain single, for a period of time. He wanted me to focus my attention on writing this book. Here-in was His desire for me. This was His plan for me. When He showed me, I immediately had peace about it.

Then the enemy was quick to grab ahold of the thoughts and the feelings of my flesh that were not dead yet. He penetrated the area where I was not fully surrendered to God. The thought of not having a husband to share my life with, this relationship I so desired, tormented me. Literally, I would go into weeping fits. I wanted to have a man to love me, a man who would not leave me. Someone to care for me through thick and thin. Someone who could care enough to stick around. I did not want to be "alone."

When all of this flooded over me, I cried, and I cried, and I cried. The other thoughts and questions the enemy planted in my mind, "Oh no, how long is this going to take?" "I am not a writer; this could take forever." "Am I going to be single for another 10 years?" "The rest of my life? Ugh!!!"

Where I first had peace, I was now filled with dread. The enemy had me gripped with fear. In letting this go would I ever have someone to share life with? Would I ever receive what I so desired? I could not trust God with this part of my life. Everything else, but not this. It became very clear this was my "Isaac" I needed to lay on the altar of sacrifice and allow God to provide for me, just as He did for Abraham (Please read Genesis 22:1-19). To completely let go of it. To sacrifice my desire so He could birth His desires in me. So, He could have His way.

I knew this, and through many days and many tears I tried to lay the desire down on the altar and completely let go of it, time after time I tried, to no avail. I would lay it down, but then I would always pick it back up again. The fear was so strong. The lies were so many. And not that wanting these things were wrong, it was simply not God's timing for any of them to happen in my life... yet.

God was wanting me to have this relationship with Him. He wanted me to know who He is. He wanted me to choose to make Him first in my life. He wanted to be my only desire. He wanted me to know how to have this intimate relationship with Him. He wanted me to trust Him, obey Him, and follow Him. I now know, in hindsight, if He would have brought someone into my life at that time I would have been swept away with the guy. Never having my relationship with Jesus where it needed to be... of utmost importance and my solid foundation. There was still much growing I needed to do. To be fully devoted to Him first and foremost before anyone else or anything else.

He was asking me, "Are you willing to kill your desires?" God had promised Abraham a son and then told Abraham to offer that son as a sacrifice. To give His promise back to Him. He essentially asked Abraham, "Are you willing to kill your promise?" Because otherwise the promise God has given, or the desires we have could become idols to us. The promise can mean more to us than the Promise Giver.

Needless to say, I never made it to the altar. This would be like Abraham making that journey with Isaac, as the sacrifice, then turning around and going back a mile. Starting the journey again and then stopping to dig a well. Starting again and then stopping to rest. Never making it to the place, God had told him to go, to build the altar for his sacrifice. The crazy thing is, I knew! I knew if I could just get to the altar, lay this desire down, raise the knife to kill it, God would have said, "Stop! Now I know you fear Me, since you have not withheld your desire from Me." However, that was not my story.

In that instant, in 2014, satan knew exactly what to do in my weakness. He had seen my films. So, he plots, saying, "I know, I will bring someone into her life to entice her and draw her away. She is already struggling with being single, wanting to be loved by a man, and she is lonely. She wants a relationship, and this is the perfect distraction to get her off course. To keep her far away from God's plan for her life and keep me in control." So, this is what he did. And I was just as much a pawn in this evil game he was playing.

<u>**I chose**</u> to chase after that carrot he was dangling in front of me. It was my own desire he was enticing me with, of wanting a relationship with someone. However, this was a relationship that was never meant for me. While being distracted with this, now was the opportune time for him to feed me more lies.

It is confounding to look back and see how deceived I was. To think that I thought I could not trust God with my life. To think that I thought I was better off to control it myself, which ultimately was having satan control it. To think that I thought God did not know what was best for me. To think that I thought someone else could make me happy. To think that I thought this relationship was okay to be in. Ugh is a good word to use here. The lies, the web, I was stuck. I could not see Truth at the time.

In all my journals and writings, looking back (hindsight), I can see where God was warning me time and time and time again. "Do not do this!!!!" "This is not My plan for you!" 7 times to be exact. And yet I could not see the truth of the matter at all while I was steeped in it. When all was said and done, I ended up on a 5-year detour from God's path for my life. I had traded God's best for my own desires. And I could not even recognize it at the time.

I was being manipulated by the master manipulator. Deceived by the father of lies. I was completely blinded and satan's plan was working. Because of the lies I believed; I was going in a direction God NEVER intended for me to go in. I was completely defenseless. Like the scripture says in James 1:14-16, I chased after my own desires, which was having a relationship, and when desire had conceived it gave birth to sin.

I became disobedient (sin) to God and His plan for me to remain single for a period of time. Then fornication (sin) entered the relationship. This became a stronghold in my life. There is a reason God tells us to not have sex outside of marriage, in fact, many reasons. One of the most beautiful things God created, is the sacred union of husband and wife and the marriage bed to not be defiled (Hebrews 13:4). It is not to be done flippantly among people. Treated as if it doesn't matter. While saying, "everybody's doing it," "that is such an 'old school' way of thinking," or "but we 'love' each other." We must trust God knows what is best. We are to obey what He says in His Word to do! Remember? Choose Life! Flee fornication is what He tells us in 1 Corinthians 6:18. Please read through verse 20.

I knew what I was doing was wrong. I was convicted of this. I knew I could not keep fornicating and then ask for forgiveness and yet continue to sin. This was not a true repentant heart. But this pattern continued. It was slowly killing me. At the time I didn't know Truth that would make me free. Because I didn't know Truth, I tried to break free from this pattern on my own, but I couldn't get out of it. Self can never free you from self. However, where the Spirit of the Lord is there is freedom (2 Corinthians 3:17).

If I would have submitted to God, the devil would have fled (James 4:7). Since I was going against God instead of submitting to Him, I could not escape the stronghold. I was stuck. I was blinded. And by now, I thought I was doing the right thing by talking this person into getting married. Let me tell you, when you force things to happen, when you are living deceived, your world is going to crumble so quick you will not know what hit you. If **you** have to make it happen, it is not God.

In 2016 we were married. I was with a person I was never meant to be with and in a place, I was never meant to be. When this happens, it is a miserable spot to be in. And it will take its toll on you and everyone else around you. Back to James 1:14-16, "When sin is full grown it brings forth death." I will say this next line again because it is so crucial for you to understand. Because of the lies we believe; we will end up going in a direction God NEVER intended for us to go in.

I was forging my own path, with this marriage. And for my remaining time here, I would endure the depths of hell on earth and the biggest tug of war over my soul I would ever physically experience in my life. The devil dragging me one way to deep dark pits of woundedness and ugliness. Where the pain, resentment, rejection, hatred, and anger would fester and grow. And then Holy Spirit gently drawing me back the other way towards the Light and to Life. Trying to teach me how to Love and live free from it all. Back and forth, back and forth this would go.

This would go on for almost 3 long years. You may say, "Oh honey, 3 years is not that long." Let me tell you, it felt like eternity, being in a place that was not meant for me. I was in a marriage where I was so alone. The exact thing I did not want to be, I was. I have never felt more alone in my entire life than I did during this period of time. All the while slowly fading and suffocating inside. Slowly dying. I had a friend say to me, "I just wanted to shake you and say, 'Dawn, where are you? Come back!!'"

When I was laying on my living room floor in what I would call my ICU room (described at the beginning of this chapter), exactly 2 months before this in October of 2018, Holy Spirit was calling me close to Him. I answered that call with, "Yes Lord." When that 2-month period came (October & November 2018), Holy Spirit had given this word to me; "Sequester." I knew in an instant what that meant. I immediately thought of a jury that gets sequestered. There is no interaction with the outside world. They cannot be distracted or influenced by what other people are saying. They have a mission and a focus, to get a job done. Holy Spirit had a mission to get a job done with me and He needed my undivided attention.

He spoke to me about anchoring myself in Him. "Anchor yourself to My voice, anchor yourself to the Truth that I will show you, anchor yourself to My Love," He would say to me. I was being sequestered to marinate in His Love for me. His Love, His Love, His Love. To remain steadfast and anchored in knowing His Love for me. He was infusing me with Hope.

Hebrews 6:17-19, "Thus God, determining to show more abundantly to the heirs of promise the immutability of His counsel, confirmed it by an oath, that by two immutable things, in which it is impossible for God to lie, we might have strong consolation, who have fled for refuge to lay hold of the hope set before us. This hope, we have as an anchor of the soul, both sure and steadfast, and which enters the Presence behind the veil."

I wrote in my journal, "His Love will carry me through the journey ahead." I had NO idea at that time, the journey ahead, was going to entail another divorce, but my Father knew. He was preparing me and steadying me. He knew the "sequester" was the calm before the storm. He knew there were going to be a lot of lies exposed. He knew there would be some very difficult things to work through (with having 2 divorces now). He knew 42 years' worth of deception would be unveiled. He also knew through all of this I would receive the greatest deliverance of all. I would finally be free from me. I would finally receive the freedom, for which He has already paid the highest price. With every chain broken, I would know this Truth of being free and I would walk in it.

He pulled me in so close to Himself to prepare me, to hold me, to steady me. Because He knew 2 months later, I would be in that ICU room, on my living room floor, with my life falling apart once again. He knew I was going to need everything He was giving me for the journey ahead. What He was doing was reenforcing me, giving me a supply from which to draw. That when I continued with Him through the storm of life I had more than enough to get to the other side. By being anchored to Him, I would not drift away. I am not saying it was easy; because it was hard, and painful. However, I never quit pressing into Him and He gave me everything I needed to get through.

In my living room, where I would sit and meet with Him most every day during my second marriage, He met me there. He gave me His ring, He covered me with His robe and carried me away in redemption. With eyes of fire, and a voice like thunder, and a mighty hand, He saved me from the miry clay, the sinking sand, the slimy pit I was suffocating in. Thank You Jesus for saving me.

In summary, I had lived a life where I had chased after my own desires, followed after lies, and didn't realize it. That is the thing about deception, you believe lies as truth, and you do not know any better. The father of lies (satan) uses deception to keep us imprisoned. He comes to steal, kill, and destroy. To live deceived, it steals our identity, our joy, and our peace. To live deceived, it kills our purpose and our testimony (while we are in that place). To live deceived, it will destroy our lives and leave us for dead. The deadliest thing we can do is to unconsciously live a lie. I know, I was there.

We must **know** the Truth that will make us free (John 8:32), so we will never be deceived. We will know Truth in relationship and by having intimacy with Jesus. To know Him. Not just to know about Him but to personally know Him. We will know Truth when we read the Word of God. Not to just read but allow Holy Spirit to teach us and transform us by the renewing of our mind. We will know Truth and not be deceived ever again when we are **fully surrendered** to Jesus Christ, and we live with the flesh crucified. When the flesh is completely dead, we will do what God tells us to do. This is called obedience! In other words, we will only do the will of our Father.

What the enemy intended for evil, drove me into the arms of the only One who would never choose someone else over me. Never reject me. Never betray me. Never leave me. Never fail me. Never run away from me. The only One who is never changing, not broken, or weak. The only One whose vows will never be broken. The One who keeps covenant forever. The One who keeps every single one of His promises. And there in His arms, only there, did I find everything I was searching for my whole life. Love that lasts forever and to know I am beautiful to the One who matters most. satan's attempt to break me helped make me instead.

I am living, breathing, proof God never gives up on us. I am so thankful beyond words Holy Spirit won the tug of war over my soul and Jesus came to rescue me from a terrible life I had created by being disobedient to Him. The rescue-mission? **He saved me from my-self.** For that, I am eternally grateful! This is what we all need, is to be saved from ourselves. Self cripples us. No, more than that, it destroys us and eventually kills us. Our self-life is controlled by satan and thereby self is our own worst enemy.

December 10th, 2018 was the moment in time I was all in! Finally, fully surrendered to Him so He could have His way in me. It has been the best, the greatest, and most glorious decision I have ever made. From that moment on, my life has been radically changed. It was said to me how quickly I came to Life; how noticeable it was once the surrender had taken place. My prayer is that you will be inspired by Holy Spirit to radically give it all up in full surrender. Do not take one baby step at a time. Don't waste time by doing it that way. No, dive all in, headfirst, and say, "Lord, I am Irrevocably Yours!"

2 Corinthians 3:16, "Nevertheless when one will turn to the Lord, the veil will be taken away." And as a husband removes the veil of his bride on their wedding day, the veil of deception that is over our lives, will be removed when we turn and face Jesus, our Bridegroom King, and give Him our all. This is the greatest unveiling.

"Charming One" by The Waiting: (Parenthesis added)
"I saw You shamed upon a cross, wounded and naked on that tree.
You counted everything a loss, gave every bit of it to me.
So, when all the other suitors come, so cleverly disguised.
They will find me clinging to Your arm, and gazing in the eyes
that holds a passion that can never be undone.
You (Jesus), are The Charming One."

Journal Entry 12/25/2018:

I could hear my Lord say to me, "I Love you, My Sunshine. You can stop searching now. You have everything you need in Me. I will not hold anything good back from you. There is no need to feel shame because when you look to Me, you are radiant. There is no need to feel "less than," because I choose you. The Great I Am has chosen you, Sunshine, my beautiful one, to be with Me forever. Now and forever more in this great romance. Come and rest in My arms of Love. Let Me hold you close. Lay your head on My bosom and feel My heartbeat for you. Listen to My heart sing over you. No one can Love you better than Me. You do not ever have to wonder if you are losing My attention, because My attention is always on you. I give you all of Me. I have the best plan for your life. I will never leave you. I am faithful to you forever. There will never be any love that is greater than My Love for you. I make everlasting covenant with you. My vows to you will never be broken. I rejoice over you. And My rejoicing over you does not last for only a moment. Neither does it come and go on a whim. But My rejoicing over you lasts for all eternity. I do not have to Love you, Sunshine, I want to Love you. I choose you."

Isaiah 62:5, As the bridegroom rejoices over the bride, so do I, your God, rejoice over you.

My response: "Oh, Jesus sweet Lover of my soul, it has always been

You calling me home. It has always been You, the One holding me. It has always been You, speaking tenderly to me. It has always been You, the One Loving me perfectly. It has always been You, that has stayed by my side. It has always been You, saying I am worth it, that I am worth dying for. Otherwise, You would have never given Your life for me. It has always been You, that has wanted my heart. It has always been You, that has pursued all of me. And it is from this place of knowing I am fully Loved that I know who I am, and I know whose I am, and I can find rest for my soul." **End of journal entry.**

PRACTICAL APPLICATION:

Now it is time to think and apply this to your life.

1. What is your "Isaac?" What is it that needs to be laid on the altar of sacrifice?
2. What has the potential of becoming an idol to you? Or what currently is an idol?
3. What sin is it that keeps you entangled? That keeps you from surrendering all. That keeps you blinded and deceived because you have not turned fully to face only Jesus Christ.
4. What fears or thought processes are keeping you to live in disobedience to God?
5. What are the other suitors that have come to steal you away from your One true Love, your first Love, Jesus? Is it unforgiveness? Is it worry or fear? Is it anxiety? Is it doubt? Is it insecurity? Is it addiction? Is it other relationships and people? Is it sexual immorality of any kind, fornication, lust, adultery, pornography, impure thoughts? These are only a few examples. Keep in mind, anything that does not lead you to the Lord, leads you away from Him.

Take time to think, and pray, and write down the things that need to be removed from your life. And as we go through this book you will understand how to remain free once and for all.

A PRAYER TO PRAY:

"Father, here am I. I repent and turn to You. I give to You all my failures, all my mistakes, all my disobedience, all my sin, all the disappointment I have had in myself, all the regret, all of the shame. I lay it all down at the foot of the cross and leave it there. These are not my burdens to carry. I do not want to pick these things back up again. I change my way of thinking and I turn to You. I know You have forgiven me. You have thrown all these things into the sea of forgetfulness. The amazing thing that is so hard for me to comprehend, is from all this mess I have made, from all these ashes, You will bring forth beauty. You take all these dead places, inside of me, and You breathe Life into me. You work all things together for good, because I Love You and I am called according to Your purpose. You redeem all the shattered pieces of my life and make me brand new. I cling to You. I want to know You. I want to trust You with my life completely. To know Your plan for me is good. No, actually, it is great! Your plan is the very best plan for my life. I thank You for it. And I thank You for the Death of Me, In Jesus name, Amen!"

Joel 2:25-26, You will restore to me the years that the locusts have eaten.... And I will eat in plenty and be satisfied and praise the name of You Lord my God that has dealt wondrously with me and I will never be ashamed.

This picture is provided from the internet.

John 17:3, "And this is eternal life, that they may know You, the only true God, and Jesus Christ whom You have sent."

CHAPTER 2

Knowing The Lover of My Soul

RELATIONSHIP

"LORD, WE COME to You when we need something. We come to You when our lives are falling apart, and when we are broken. We come to You with our lists of desires, wants, what we think we need, and what we really do need. When all You have ever wanted, since the beginning of creation, is to be with us. Your desire has always been to have our hearts. Not just our "laundry" lists. You want us to know You, to really know You. And even though we reject You time and time again, You continue to reach out to us. You comfort us. You meet with us. You are merciful to us. We walk away from You, yet You still draw close to us. What kind of Love is this?

You want a relationship with us, and we want things. We want what You can give us. We want Your blessings. We want Your healing. We want You to fix it, whatever "it" may be. How often do we just want You? How often do we come to You because we simply Love You? How often do we trample over Your heart, as You extend it to us, just to get what we want or "need?" Yet, You continue to give, and You give, and You give. You continue to pursue us. Even when we look the other way. Your Love is relentless. Lord let this be a turning point in our lives, that our unrelenting selfishness will end here. May a new chapter begin in many lives. Where we long to really know You, the Blessed Lover of our souls. It is Your Loving-kindness, and goodness that leads us to repentance (Romans 2:4). In the name of Jesus, Amen."

How many times have we fallen to our knees in need? We need a miracle, so we go and sit in the sanctuary of where we gather on Sunday's, or kneel in the hospital chapel, or fall on our bedroom floor and pray. We cry out to God to save our loved one. We cry out to God to save our marriage. We cry out to God to save our job. We cry out to God to heal our sickness or terminal illness we just got diagnosed with.

I am not saying that crying out to God is wrong because crying out to Him **is** our **only** answer. The issue is we cry out to God as though He is our genie in a bottle. When we need something, we take the bottle off the shelf, rub it, and "poof" He appears. He is to grant us our 3 wishes, and then we sit Him back on the shelf until the next time we need something. We know we need Him, but do we really Love Him? Do we know how to Love Him? When was the last time you ever went to Him for nothing else but to be with Him? To sit with Him. To Love on Him.

Yet maybe it is we pray every day. We have a relationship with Him as best as we know how. But how well do we know God our Father, Jesus Christ the Son of God, and Holy Spirt the Spirit of God, when 90% of our approach to Him is "problem" and "needs" driven? Instead of being driven from a place of knowing Him, from relationship, from Love? Can we truly call our Blessed Trinity (Father, Son, and Holy Spirit) the Lover of our souls? Do we really know Him that intimately?

The definition of intimate according to *Merriam-Webster Dictionary* is, "Marked by a warm friendship developing through long association." *Oxford Languages* describes intimate as, "Closely acquainted, familiar, involving very close connection, detailed or thorough knowledge of someone." Can we honestly say we have this kind of relationship with the Trinity? Do we grow everyday knowing Him more today than yesterday? Or are we satisfied with the "best that we know how to" relationship we currently have with Him?

Here is the pivotal chapter. Everything hinges on this. All of life will be meaningless, pointless, and empty without having an intimate relationship with the Blessed Lover of your soul.

1.   First and foremost, we are here, in this world, for relationship

with our Father. Intimate, close relationship. This is the greatest commandment. You shall Love the Lord your God with ALL your heart, with ALL your soul, with ALL your strength, and with ALL your mind, and your neighbor as yourself. Do this and you will live (Luke 10:27-28). Jesus died to bring us back into unbroken and unhindered relationship with God our Father. Jesus paid it all so our sin would be removed, and we could be reconciled to God as a son or daughter. If we do not have a nurtured, solid, and growing relationship with Him then we will not be able to do anything else in the following chapters. Because everything we are, do, say, think etc. is to reflect God's image to the world.

2. Which is another reason we are here, is to be a reflection of Jesus Christ. Be imitators of God as dear children. And walk in Love, AS Christ also has Loved us and given Himself for us (Ephesians 5:1-2). Let us learn from Jesus how to be in relationship with Him and with others that will be a true, holy, and pure representation of Him to all the world.

3. And by this we will then be able to make disciples of all the nations (Matthew 25:18-20). Which some of you are aware is another reason we are here, but not the only reason. The other two must come first. We cannot make disciples unless we are a disciple first.

By knowing Jesus intimately is how we become this representation of Him. We become what we behold, by the power of Holy Spirit who transforms us (2 Corinthians 3:18). Here is where everything comes to life. Everything changes in intimacy with the Lover of my soul. When I behold Him and see His beauty, when I see His Love for me it changes everything. My Love for Him then changes everything. This Love we share together changes the way I think, see, hear, feel, speak, and believe. It changes the way I treat people. It changes the way I respond to people. It changes the way I handle challenging situations that may arise. It changes the way I act and what I do. It changes the things I think upon.

His Love transforms everything about me. Transformation has its own chapter in this book, but I want to take a moment here to emphasize the importance of knowing the Trinity's Love for you. Because there is a big gap in saying flippantly, "Yea I know Jesus Loves me," to "I have experienced this Love of Jesus and I KNOW Jesus Loves me. I know His Love personally."

A prayer I prayed all the time in the beginning of my intimate relationship with the Lord was, "Father, I need Your Love for me to get from my head to my heart. I know You Love me in my head, with my mind, I have this head knowledge of Your Love. But I need, I want, to know Your Love for me in my heart. In the depths of my soul, with all that I am, I want to know and experience Your Love that surpasses knowledge" (Ephesians 3:17-19).

I would pray this day in and day out all while pursuing Him. I had to be intentional to not quit if I could not feel His Love or when I felt like it was not happening fast enough. Because on the magnificent day when that prayer manifests, and He floods your heart with the experience of His Love, yep you guessed it, it changes everything. I feel like I have said this already (smile). I repeat because it is so important for you to know. Knowing His Love changes everything.

THE BLESSED TRINITY

Now, I want to take a moment to talk about the Trinity because I will intertwine them throughout this book. Even though the wonderful Trinity are One they are three persons in One. Each One has their specific role in our lives. Much like a car. You have one car, yet different parts in the car have their different functions for the car to run properly. We are a good example of this ourselves. We are one person, yet we have a body, a soul, and a spirit. We are spirit, which possesses a soul, and lives in a body. They each have their specific function in our lives. However, we are one person.

For me, I grew in Love with the Trinity differently and at different points. I am not saying this will be the same for everyone, only, this is how it happened for me. A beautiful thing about our Creator is, He made each one of us unique, to have our very own special relationship with Him. Truths revealed throughout this book are Truths to be applied to your own individual relationship with Him. Now, I am in Love with each person of the Trinity alike. Each One is magnificent to me. But to share some of my journey as I am led to, I will start at the beginning.

When I first ran to the Lord, in my season of dire need, it was 2011. I was the perfect example of what I mentioned in the first part of this chapter. I had a relationship with Jesus as best as I knew how but there was no deep and meaningful intimacy with Him. I would read my Bible, pray the Scriptures, and then give Him my "to do" list. I would run to Him when I was in trouble, or when I needed help and then go about my life as "usual" the rest of the time.

By this point He had already, so mercifully, brought me through many other tragedies that had happened in my life, so I knew Him as my Rock. He was the only thing in my life that would never change. He was my constant. When 2011 rolled around my life was falling apart, and I felt like it was over. With everything being in upheaval in my marriage, and my family being destroyed, I knew I could run to Jesus. I was so broken and hurting, I seriously needed Him. I knew I would not make it through this life-altering time without Him.

I came to Jesus in desperate circumstances. Pouring out my hurt and my sorrow to Him. Pouring out my heart to Him endlessly. Giving Him all my cares and concerns. Even though I came to Him completely broken and in much need, I learned how to have an intimate relationship with Him during this time. I talked with Him all the time. I also had a secret place I met with Him (I speak more about the secret place later). Such a sweet place it was and continues to be! It brings me to tears just thinking about it. I would be in there for hours on end. My boys (a 10- and 12-year-old at the time) knew when I was in there, I was getting what I needed, and mama would be okay. I asked Jesus questions. I would sit and be still with Him. I would be alone with Him, just to be near Him. I would listen to Him speak to my heart. And He would hold me tight in His peace. Sitting with Jesus was the purest form of comfort I could have. He was the calm in my storm.

At that time, I was still in a process of gaining a right understanding of who God was. I was still unsure about coming to God for anything. However, it was easy for me to come to the One who had died for me. Who gave His Life as a sacrifice for me. The only One who had Loved me with such perfect and selfless Love. He is my Savior and I Loved Him immensely for saving me. He is my Healer. Which I needed His healing desperately for my shattered soul. He is my Redeemer and my Restorer. I undoubtedly needed His redemption and restoration in my life. He was hundreds of other things to me and for me. Everything I needed Him to be, He was. Oh, how I Love Jesus, and I am eternally grateful for who He is!

Along the way I started learning the Truth about who God really is. He is not the tyrant I thought He was, as I was growing up. He is not the Father I would never be able to please. And no, this is not because "that was how my dad was." It is because as a child growing up, the God of the Old Testament scared me. I did not understand Him any way other than, He was a God of wrath, and He was hard to please. He had so many "rules to follow" and there was just no way I could keep them all to make Him happy.

As I read the Bible for myself, **personally**, my eyes were opened to who He really is. He is the most patient, generous, merciful, faithful, Loving, Father. The list could go on for all of eternity, of His infinite goodness. And my understanding of Him grew. At a certain point on my journey, in the middle of all the heartache and pain, I just really wanted my Abba, my Daddy.

I would imagine crawling up into His lap and allow Him to hold me, many, many, many days, and nights. I would focus my attention on Him, until His arms around me, were as real as hugging you. I would talk to Him intimately, as He was my good, good Father. I Loved Him immensely for choosing to create me and being my Daddy. For wanting me. For taking care of me. For never giving up on me. For His never-ending faithfulness to me. For an infinite number of things, He was to me...He is... "I Am." Oh, how I Love God my Father, and am eternally grateful for who He is!

Now, I knew Holy Spirit. I knew Him as my Comforter and my Helper. I knew Him as the power of God inside of me (and yet, I didn't fully understand the fullness of His power for a long time). I knew Him as the giver of the gifts He had given me. Then I started to really know Him more personally. How He is the One who transforms me. He is the One who **does the work** of making me like Christ. He is the One who was taking all the ashes of my life and making something beautiful. He is the One resurrecting me. He is the One taking me from a caterpillar and turning me into a butterfly. He is my cocoon where the transformation happens.

When I finally surrendered everything over to Him and lived crucified to my flesh once and for all, I knew I needed Holy Spirit to have all of me. I could not do this. I knew I could not, because I tried for many long and hard years, and I failed. I had come to Love Holy Spirit immensely for being the Strength in my weakness. For being my Helper. For being my Comforter. For being my Transformer (♫"more than meets the eye," ♫ most of you will get that. Smile). For transforming me into the likeness of Jesus. For being my very Best Friend. Oh, how I Love Holy Spirit and am eternally grateful for who He is!

Pursuing Him

To <u>know</u> the Lover of our soul is the most exciting relationship we can ever have. The definition of exciting according to *Oxford Languages* is, "Causing great enthusiasm and eagerness." We often equate excitement to the likes of adrenaline rushes, thrill seeking adventures, things we are looking forward to doing and experiencing. I want to say, we are to be the most eager in our pursuit of Jesus. We are to have more enthusiasm about our relationship with Jesus than anything else in this world.

Our relationship with Him is more exciting than your favorite hobbies or sports gatherings. More exciting than the next cell phone upgrade, the newest video game that comes out, or up and coming movies that will be premiering. More exciting than the next concert we go to, or celebrity we get to meet. More exciting than the most extravagant vacation we can take. Yes, even more exciting than going to Israel. More exciting than a first date or the new boyfriend/girlfriend we have. More exciting than our wedding day. More exciting than having children.

To <u>know</u> the Lover of our soul, more and more, should be the most exciting and intimate relationship we could ever have. Lyrics in a song I heard Steffany Gretzinger sing are, "You can Love me more in one moment than all the other lovers could in a lifetime." Selah (meaning to pause). Whenever I will use the word "Selah" it will be for you to stop. Really think about something, what is being said, and ponder it. So, Selah, really think about the Truth of the statement Steffany made! We need to know that no one can Love us more than Jesus. And a quote by Samuel Rutherford; "Oh, woe, woe to the fools who run by Christ to other lovers."

Our response to this kind of Love Jesus has for us should be a Love for Him that far outweighs any other love we have ever had for anybody else. To Love Jesus more than our child. Yes, even our spouse. Our relationship with Him is to be more intimate than the relationship we have with our spouse. I know these can be some very new concepts to some of you, but I urge you to continue to read on.

Do you realize we can go to Sunday services, pray, read our Bibles, memorize Scriptures, do Bible studies, even teach the Bible studies ourselves, preach sermons, do miracles in the name of Jesus, and still not <u>know</u> Him? We are only going through the motions. We think we know Him, but what we really know is A LOT **about** Him (please read Matthew 7:21-23). Knowing about Jesus does not save us. The devil knows all about Jesus and he knows Jesus is Lord, but he will not be saved and in heaven.

satan is fully convinced that he can get us going to Sunday service, lifting our hands, praising God, doing miracles, but never know the Father in relationship. satan wants our minds to be so messed up that we have a form of godliness (doing all the religious things) but denying the power thereof (2 Timothy 3:5). It would be good for us to realize that being a pastor, serving in a ministry, and being a praise and worship leader as we sing our songs to Him, will not change our disposition or motive of our heart, but knowing Jesus will. We are not to serve Him and listen to songs about Him but fail to be with Him. We should not let knowing about Him take the place of knowing Him. So how is it, we can have a real, personal, and intimate relationship with Him and not just know about Him?

HIS PRESENCE

It is established in His presence. There is nothing better than the constant awareness of His presence. It is Life, joy, peace, rest, strength, wisdom, Truth, every single good thing. We are to dwell in His presence which will change everything (Psalm 91:1 KJV). Not just visit Him from time to time, but to dwell. To abide/dwell in Him is a constant communion with Him. Our abiding in Him will result in a deeper relationship with Him. It is to rest in Him. It is to live in Him, and He in us. This makes us One with Him. By being One with Him, we will know how to pray and know how to walk in Love. We will be His Light to the world. He will reveal things to us.

We will hear His voice and we will know His voice (John 10:1-5). Knowing His voice comes by being in relationship with Him. Because of this relationship another's voice we will not follow. We will not run away with a stranger thinking it is our Father. However, many do not know His voice because they do not draw near to Him and dwell in His presence. Again, this is a remaining in Him, not just a visit with Him.

Invest time in the Lord's presence with no agenda and no need for immediate answers. Not just coming to Him with all our "problems," but to be with Him, talking with Him. Talking with Him is no different than how you would talk to your best friend. Tell Him about your day, your thoughts, your mood, and where you are struggling. Talk to Him about the character flaws that need to be transformed. Where you are having a hard time to Love someone as Jesus Loves them. Or having a hard time forgiving someone and letting go. These are all things we need to talk to Him about more than anyone else.

Other ways to simply be with Him are to sit with Him, wait on Him, and be still in His presence. His presence brings peace to the storm. His presence brings calm to the chaos. His presence cultivates Love without even trying. There is no forcing it, it just comes. When I sit with Him, and make Him my focus, His Love overflows in my heart every time. Then His perfect Love casts out all fear (1 John 4:18). There is freedom in His presence (2 Corinthians 3:17). And in His presence, we will come to know Him personally. He will reveal Himself to us (John 14:21). He will show us things (Jeremiah 33:3). He will speak to us (John 10:27-28).

If you have an overactive mind, one that is constantly going, thinking, moving, and may get easily distracted, this may take some training to be still. However, with God all things are possible. When you sit to be with the Lord and your mind wanders, begin to tell Him how wonderful He is. Bless His holy name. Pour your adoration upon Him. Keep praising Him. Thank Him for the cross and start listing off everything He accomplished, for you, on it. This gets me every time! As I am before Him full of emotion and in awe.

For Example: Thank You for saving me. Thank You for freeing me. Thank You for my flesh being crucified with You. Thank You for reconciling me. Thank You for restoring me. Thank You for bringing me back into relationship with our Father. Thank You for healing me. These are just a few to get you started.

In this atmosphere, of thanksgiving, praise, and adoration, you can feel your mind being able to focus solely on Him and you can sit and be still. If your mind wanders again, continue to pour your affection on Him. Thank Him for His goodness, and you may be able to sit a little longer to wait on Him. The point is not to give up and say, "Well, my mind wanders all over the place, I can't do this!" Be intentional with this and you will be able to work the time up from 30 seconds to 1 minute to 20 minutes to an hour, and so on.

Bask in His presence. It is the beauty of being with Him. Near to Him in intimacy. When we bask in His presence we will become like Jesus, because we become what we behold (2 Corinthians 3:18). We can never carry out our assignment or calling in life (being one with Jesus), if we do not become like Him. We only become like Him in His presence, in intimacy, in communion, in the renewing of our mind, by the transformation power of Holy Spirit.

His presence also frees us from the heavy burden of needing to have anything else. The "need" of recognition, affirmation, accolades, praises of men, and things of this world. This is all garbage compared to knowing Him (Philippians 3:8). When we are in His presence, just to be near to Him, He will consume us. What we value in life will shift when we give Him all our attention. We can only have our hearts and attention tied-up in other things or focused on other people when they are not fully given to Him. His presence is so simple, where His yoke is easy and the burden light (Matthew 11:25-30). He says, "Come to Me."

The Secret Place

Now, I know, we never leave His presence (Psalm 139:7-8). In fact, He is inside of us. We do not need to meet with Him in a certain place, in order to be with Him. Nor do we need to go and "seek His presence," to be with Him. He is here! Always with us. However, we do want to seek to be alone with Him. A one on one, kind of presence. This is where intimacy is created. Even though I gave the definition of intimacy earlier, it is important to know what it looks like in our relationship with Jesus. Intimacy is what happens when we are **alone** with Him, behind closed doors, in secret. We can call this our prayer closet or room (Matthew 6:6), or the secret place. Wherever it is, it is meant to be our private place to go and pray and to be with Him.

Psalm 91:1, "He who dwells in the secret place of the Most High shall abide under the shadow of the Almighty." "Dwell" in Hebrew is to sit down, in quiet, to remain, habitation, to settle, and to marry... wow! Those are just to name a few things that *Strong's Concordance* lists. "Secret" is a cover, hiding place, protection. "Abide" is to stay permanently, continue, dwell, endure, remain, and tarry. Now re-read that Scripture using some of the different descriptions and see how powerful that verse is. For instance: "When I make my habitation in the hiding place of the Most High I will stay permanently under the shadow of the Almighty." Selah!

I heard it said of Susanna Wesley that her secret place was in her chair with her apron over her head. And when her 10 children saw this, they knew she was not to be disturbed unless it was an emergency. You can literally make your secret place anywhere with Him. Wherever your secret place is, it is intended to be your place of intimacy with Him. Where you intentionally pour your affection onto Him. Where tender words will be exchanged. Where a personal relationship will be created from this interaction. Where His will is conceived within you.

Nevertheless, we have taken the term prayer closet and only utilize it as a place to go and do our daily regimen. We go there to pray, read our Bible, and do our devotional. Where very often we get stuck in the rut of religious routine, and we walk out of that space as empty or shallow as we went in. We have not put any focus in to just being with Jesus and Loving Him. We have not taken the time to sit, talk, listen, and wait on Him (Psalm 27:14).

Just because we read about someone does not mean we know them personally. Just because we ask someone to solve all our problems and give us what we want or need, does not mean we Love them. Just because we are in the same room as someone does not mean we recognize them; they could still be a stranger to us.

When we are in Love with someone, it is because we have taken the time to know the person. Our prayer closet is where we get to know Jesus. Interact with Him, and converse with Him. We need this secret place to get ourselves face-to-face with God (Psalm 27:8-9), through His Word and communion. Communion definition by *Oxford Languages*, "The sharing or exchanging of intimate thoughts and feelings, especially when the exchange is on a mental or spiritual level."

Do You Know Him? – In Truth

Do you KNOW who it is that Loves you? Do you know this Lover of your soul? He is the One who Loves you the most intimately. Who Loves you more deeply. Who Loves you the most passionately. Who Loves you more completely and unconditionally **than any other person** could ever love you. He Loves you to wholeness. He Loves you to healing. He Loves you to freedom. There is no other love that can compare to the Love of Jesus. His Love is never changed by your moods. His Love is never altered by your performance. The King of the Universe wants to talk with you. Your Bridegroom King wants to be with you.

Do you know this Jesus who Loves you so immensely? Because there is an extremely deep void to only knowing about Jesus and knowing Jesus personally. Most of the time, we end up ignoring Him only to go through our religious traditions. We say we believe in Jesus (to get to heaven), we go to church, we read our Bible, and we say a prayer. We do the "Jesus things" very well, but this does not mean we know Him. Why do we not know Him personally?

A large reason is because we run to everyone else. Sure, we will go to God with our prayer request. But do we really have faith He will do anything with it? Do we trust Him for the answer? Do we know He will take care of us? This trust depends entirely on our understanding of the One with whom we speak. We must know we are putting our requests in the hands of the One who is omnipotent Love, and most of the time we do not know this. We do not trust Him because we do not know Him.

Since we do not know Him this way, we instead run to pastors, spouses, friends, any other relationship that is close to us. Any input from anyone else, instead of waiting on God to reveal Himself to us. This reveals that God is not enough for us. We get impatient with Him. So, we consume ourselves with everything else rather than God. We go and seek out sermons, books, the "mantra" prayers that someone told us to say in a particular situation, therapists, etc. We absorb ourselves into any effort of human nature to try to figure it out. We want to get the answer we are looking for and to get what we so desperately "need."

I am not suggesting these things are all wrong. It is that we are so filled with these things and pre-occupied with them, to where there is no room for God to come in and take possession of us and show anything of Himself to us. If there is any weakness in the body of Christ it is that we do not know the God, we have. People want what is comfortable and familiar, in everyone else and everything else. In what they can physically see and hear. It would be good for us to stop running to anything else and sit alone with God. What we need is to have a healthy, personal, and intimate relationship with the Lover of our soul.

To have this kind of relationship we must know who He is in Truth. Expelling any lies we may have heard or "known," or thought about Him. We cannot come up with the full picture of God based solely on a couple of books of the Bible. Until we see Jesus as the entire volume of the Bible, we do not see God rightly. Jesus IS God in the flesh (John 14:9).

The Pharisees thought they knew God and then Jesus shows up standing right in front of them and they do not even recognize Him as God. Their wrong perspective, their wrong theology, their wrong understanding of who God was, kept them from embracing the True and Living God that was right before their eyes. The enemy will try to twist our view of God. We need to remember Jesus Christ is God revealed, period. What you see in the life of <u>Jesus is who God is</u> for they are One. God cannot be anything outside of who Jesus is. God cannot be anything outside of His nature and He is Love.

When we really know someone who is completely good, excellent, caring, Loving, and perfect in every way, we are comfortable to draw close to that person. When we draw close to that person, we can then trust them. When we can trust that person, we will become intimate with them. When we are intimate with that person, we know we can share the most private details of our lives with them. We can entrust all the affairs of our lives to them. They are our "go to," person for all things. This "go to" person, in our lives, is to be Jesus. Not our spouse, our parents, or our best (human) friend, but Jesus.

DO YOU KNOW HIM? – IN INTIMACY

More than anything God wants to have this kind of close and personal relationship with us, His children. I want to make this more personal for a moment. The Creator of the Universe wants to have an intimate relationship with you to the extent that He created you. You did not create yourself. Even your parents could not create you on their own. He has known you since before the foundations of the world. Let this really sink in. Did you ask to come into this world? God did not have to create you. He wanted to. He wanted you!! He chose to have you, so He brought you into existence. He knows you more intimately than anyone could ever know you.

He knows exactly how to Love you perfectly. He is the only One who can do this. Yet, we will settle for crumbs from other people. We want their approval, we want their words of affirmation, we want their love, we want their attention. We want these things so we can feel something, anything. "A fix," even if it is for just a moment. When Jesus can give us the whole cake, why do we settle for only crumbs that will never completely satisfy? Jesus says, take My Love, take My approval, take My acceptance, take My attention, here have it all.

Our relationship with Jesus is to be our fulfillment. Only He can satisfy our souls and our longings. We need His touch to make our hearts race. And intimacy with Him to be our source of Life, Love, and true Joy. His Words of affirmation are what we need to rely on, not words from any other person. His Words and His Love burned, seared, and branded into our souls.

If we only understood that when we KNOW God's Love, when we have intimacy with Him, we will have the greatest fulfillment of life ever possible (Psalm 16:11). If we could believe this with all our hearts, we would with ultimate joy give up everything that tries to separate us from Him! Instead of escaping into the world and its ways. Where we are too busy pursuing other things in life that do not matter. Talking about everything not of importance instead of what is eternal. Never understanding an intimate relationship with God is what will change everything in our lives. Before we know it, God is just something "to do" if we are not busy with something else. We give Him our leftovers and call it "good enough." The more other things rise in our lives the more disconnected we will feel from Jesus.

There are many reasons why to many of us, intimacy with Him feels like a burden:

1. In our fast-paced world we find it difficult to sit still and wait on Him. We try it for 2 minutes and then we are off, on to the next thing.
2. Intimacy with Jesus seems to be unnatural to us. We do not know how to have this kind of relationship with Him. We have never even heard of it before now.
3. We do not know it is possible. We have not had an example of this kind of relationship lived out before us or even talked about.
4. We find it hard to enter this kind of relationship with someone we cannot physically see, hear, or touch, so He gets dismissed. We are in such a world that lives by what we see. "We have to see it to believe it." "We have to see it to feel it." And what we see most of the time is an illusion. It is only what people want us to see. It is by faith we enter this relationship with God, and He in return WILL make Himself known to us.

Psalm 16:11, "You will show me the path of life; In Your presence is fullness of joy; At Your right hand are pleasures forevermore." I want you to let this Scripture really sink into your soul. Hear what He is saying. In God's presence is the **fullness of joy**. At His right hand (being near to Him) are pleasures forevermore! Jesus is at His right hand, and we are seated in Christ in the heavenlies (Ephesians 2:6).

But here we are, looking for fullness, fulfillment, and pleasure in ALL the **wrong** places. We look for these things in the world, in other people, and in ourselves. And then we become gravely disappointed each time we do not find fulfillment in any of these places. We may find momentary pleasure, but it does not last, it is only a temporary fix. Knowing the Love of Christ is what will give us fullness. It is only His Love, that will give us the fullness of God (Ephesians 3:19).

KNOWLEDGE VS. KNOWING

I heard a quote from Mark Batterson, "Every Christian knows that God loves him or her. Unfortunately, that fact remains a tenant of the mind. And until it gets into your heart, it remains information. Once it gets in your heart, it results in transformation."

There are so many truths we know (with our mind). I know people who can quote the Bible all day long, yet they are mean and cold hearted. Their lives do not reflect the Truth they are speaking of. Have they become Love? People who can only quote the Word of God and do not live it are not transformed (James 1:22 they are hearers of the Word and not doers, deceiving themselves). They have all the head knowledge or information just as the Pharisees did without allowing Truth to penetrate their hearts. We have become conditioned to practice religion. Making it more of a habit instead of seeking true intimacy with Jesus by experiencing Him; a heart experience.

The Lord impressed upon me one time and said, "If you have been in My Word just to know what I can do for you, and not to know Me, you are wrong." Needless to say, this stopped me in my tracks. I was reading His Word initially to see how He could get me through my difficult situation. How He could save my marriage. He corrected me and thankfully I listened.

A lot of people read the Word of God looking for the answer to their problems. They read for knowledge (intellectual purposes) to puff themselves up. They scour His Word to "prove a point," or from the "bless me, bless me, bless me," mentality of "what can You do for me, God?" They know all the Scriptures that pertain to their particular situation, but do not have relationship with Him. They do not know Him, and who He is. There is a distinct difference in reading the Word of God to get something from Him or reading His Word to know Him. When we read His Word in relationship with Him, we can see Him Fathering us. We can know His Father's heart.

I cannot tell you how many times I have heard the Scripture quoted, "My people are destroyed for lack of knowledge," Hosea 4:6. And most of the time it gets referenced to knowing His Word, an intellectual knowledge. People get destroyed because they do not know what God's Word says, is what I would hear people saying. What we see if we read Hosea 4:1, is "there is no faithfulness or steadfast love, and no knowledge of God in the land." The Scripture means that people do not know Him. Essentially what is said is, "My people are being destroyed because they do not know Me."

Yes, I understand we get to know Him through His Word. But how many times are we reading His Word for our own benefit and not to know Him at all? We get informational "knowledge" to bless us or puff us up and walk away still not knowing Him, still getting destroyed. If we intellectually "know" His Word but do not become it, then we are missing the point.

We give a tithe because that is what the Bible says to do **for our** storehouses to be filled to overflowing. Did we do it for our own blessing or because we Love Him and we want to know Him more? <u>We obey Him because we Love Him (John 14:15), not because we want to get something from Him.</u>

We cover motives of the heart in the Detox chapter, so keep reading (smile). If we know our Father, rightly know Him, we will not be destroyed for lack of knowledge. Ephesians 1:17, "God of our Lord Jesus Christ, the Father of glory, give to us the spirit of wisdom and revelation **in the knowledge of You.**" This is to know Him. Not just to have information about Him.

Understanding Relationship

To understand how to come into this knowledge of Him through a close and personal relationship, let us take a look at earthly relationships. Eventually it will be the other way around as it should be. Where we can look at our intimacy with Jesus and allow that to be the example for our earthly relationships. But I know a lot of us are not in the place to do that just yet. We have not known how to enter an intimate relationship with the Lover of our soul. So, we are going to learn how.

First, we will look at what a personal, intimate, relationship is not:

1.   This kind of relationship is not created by ignoring someone and only seeing them once a week, let's say, on Sundays. If you only

saw your spouse once a week, would you say that you would draw closer together?

2. It is not casually saying "Hi" to someone every now and then. Even if it is a "Hi" and "Bye" every day, but there is no other kind of meaningful interaction or communication.

3. You do not create an intimate relationship with someone by only speaking with them for 5 minutes a day. Or by reading about them for 10 minutes a day. Then putting them aside, and not giving them another thought until the next morning or evening.

4. Intimacy with someone is not created with only one person involved. Intimacy is not created with only a one-way conversation. You do not create an intimate relationship with someone by only asking them for things and then never listening to what they have to say.

When you are in Love with someone, you are consumed with that person. All you can do is think about them. All you want to do is be with them. You look at your phone 100 times a day to see if they have texted you or called. If they have texted you, you then proceed to read those texts over and over and over. All you want to do is talk with them. You are giddy and excited when you think about them.

This is exactly how it should be with the Lover of your soul and even more so. You should be consumed with Him. Thinking about Him constantly. Being giddy and excited about Him. Running to your prayer closet to be alone with Him. Reading His texts (The Bible), He has written to you, 100 times over. Face timing Him. Snap chatting Him. Talking with Him all day long (pray without ceasing).

Pray without ceasing is simply an ongoing conversation with Him. Think about it. He is with us always and never leaves us, so we can talk with Him all day long. While we are at the grocery store picking out apples. When we are waiting in line to buy shoes. When we are driving. When we are working. When we are eating. When we are exercising. When we are happy and excited about something. When we are hurting or broken about something. When we are confused. When we need answers.

He is to be our Best Friend who we talk with about everything. He should be our first call always never our last resort. A dear friend of mine says, "Run to the Throne not the phone." This does not mean we cannot talk with others and seek wise counsel as He leads us to. However, it does mean He needs to be the first One we go to about all things, always.

Drink coffee with Him. Laugh with Him. He has a sense of humor, He is funny! When I do something silly or find something funny, we laugh together. I know He Loves my quirkiness. He is the only One that can be with us constantly, we might as well enjoy His company. Jesus should be the most important Friend, Lover, and Companion we have.

We have largely allowed the world to form our ideas of what a relationship looks like and what intimacy is. This must change. We need to look to Jesus to show us how we are to be. Who we are to be. What we are to do. How we are to act. He must be our example of Love in all things. Not the "entertainment" industry in their movies, TV shows, music videos, and lyrics to their songs. These have all had their negative impacts on our outlooks and perspectives on what relationship, intimacy, and True Love is.

In addition, we all too often keep our lives separated. We have our Christian life, our Christian friends, and our Christian appearance. We have our work life, our work friends, and our work appearance. We have our social life, our social friends, and our social appearance. And finally, our home life and all that entails, the good, the bad, and the ugly.

We praise Him on Sunday morning, then we give our spouse the silent treatment on the way home. We talk inappropriately with our co-workers on Monday. We freak out and yell at our kids on Tuesday. We get annoyed with people and have attitudes towards them. Then we go out on Friday to have a few drinks (or more) to wash our "troubles" away. We get together with friends to complain about everything "wrong" in our lives. We pray when we need something, and we "try" to give God 5 minutes of our day in a devotional every morning. We sing to Him and Dance for Him, again on Sundays, but we do not know Him. Because if we did, we would never do all these other things.

Then we repeat the cycles. With no real relationship with Him. No intimacy with Him. And wonder why we cannot get out of the rut we are in. And why "life is a grind." We must understand this separation of our lives does us no good. 1 Corinthians 10:31, "Whether therefore you eat, or drink, or **whatever** you do, do ALL for the glory of God." There is unspeakable comfort in this; in that it turns **all of life** (the kitchen, the laundry room, the office, the soccer field, the gym, the school, the PTA meetings, the social gatherings, EVERYTHING) into awareness of His continual presence. It also sets our thoughts to only glorify Him in all of it.

We do not divorce Him from our Christian life on Sundays, or our ministries, or the mission field. So, why do we divorce Him from our everyday life? Our businesses, our homes, our social lives, are each as equally important to be done in awareness of His Presence as the other. What a privilege and honor to continually be in His presence. That we are so connected to Him we are One with who He is. That we can be One with His heartbeat in ALL we do.

To Know Him

John 17:2-3 says, Jesus gives eternal Life to as many as the Father has given Him. Jesus says, "and this is eternal Life, that they may KNOW YOU, the only true God, and Jesus Christ whom You have sent." To know Him is the real definition of eternal Life. Yet, we have reduced eternal Life to only "getting into heaven." Please do not get me wrong, to be where God is for eternity is definitely a BIG deal. It is where we all want to be forever. However, when we make getting to heaven our only goal and focus, we miss the true blessing of what eternity is all about. And that is knowing Him. The Lover of our soul. Our Bridegroom King. The One we were created for. Who we will marry and be with for all of eternity.

Let us not just want and focus on what He has to "offer" (getting to heaven), or all His many benefits (Psalm 103:2). But let our desire and focus be, to KNOW HIM, to know His heart. If we do not know Him what He has to offer us will be handled improperly anyway. We will not know how to take care of the gifts He has given us. Know Him not for what He can do for you but for who He is.

Now how is it that we get to know someone? I can sum it up in one word, nearness. We draw near to the person we want to know. We draw near to them by being with them. Investing time with them. (Side note: I prefer "invest" as it has a more positive connotation. In contrast "spending" has a more negative connotation. As in "spending" time with someone). Investing time with them in a group of friends. Investing time with them alone. We draw near to them by communicating with them. Asking questions, spilling our heart out to them, and listening to what they have to say. We draw near to them by being interested in them. We want to know their desires. We want to know their likes and dislikes. We want to know what makes their heartbeat. What is their passion? In drawing near to someone, we get to know everything about them.

How do we discover all we can about God? Jeremiah 29:13 says, "You will seek Me and find Me, when you search for Me with ALL your heart." This means we must search For God. And not just search, but with ALL our heart. Not just part of our heart, "half-heartedly." We are to search out the things of God, the heartbeat of God. We are to search the Scriptures. And when we do this with all our heart, we will find Him. We will know Him. The following are some examples of searching the scriptures.

To know Him is to know His heart. He is gentle and humble in heart, Matthew 11:28-30. Jesus essentially says, "Come to Me and I will do the rest." He has always intended for this to be a relational journey with Him, "Come to Me." For me to be able to walk unhindered towards Him. Nothing standing in the way. Nothing standing in between. We are as close to God as we choose to be. What He desires is our heart. Let us come to give Him our devotion, not to pay homage to Him. We are to pursue intimacy with Jesus over the things of Jesus. Pursue the Giver not the gifts.

To know Him is to know His ways. Exodus 33:13, Moses said, "I pray, if I have found grace in Your sight, show me now Your way, that I may know You and that I may find grace in Your sight..." This tells me if I know God's ways, I will know Him. Now I want to search the Scriptures to find His ways. A reminder, Jesus Christ, and the life He lived is God revealed to us (John 14:8-9). So, let's look in the Scriptures to see the way Jesus walked through every situation.

To know Him is to know His delight. Jeremiah 9:23-24, "Thus says the LORD: 'Let not the wise man glory in his wisdom, let not the mighty man glory in his might, nor let the rich man glory in his riches; But let him who glories glory in this, that he understands and knows Me, That I am the LORD, exercising loving-kindness, judgement, and righteousness in the earth. For in these I delight,' says the LORD." As we search the Scriptures, we will know what He delights in and what He does not delight in, and this will be important to us as we grow in Love with Him.

Now, we all know there are different levels to knowing someone. Which determines how close we are to them.

1.   We may know of or about someone, but we have never met this person ourselves. We may hear so much about this person it may seem like we know them. However, until we have been with them personally, we still only know about them, and we do not know them.

2. There are the ones we may see occasionally. And when we do we exchange pleasantries and small talk, but this is the extent of it. We know them to a certain degree. Typically, these are considered acquaintances. The ones we say "Hi" to as we pass by.

3. Then there are ones we may know a little more about. We talk to them more frequently but still keep them at an arm's length away. This could be co-workers or ones we see on a more regular basis. We may meet for a coffee every now and then and engage in "small talk."

4. Then there are the friends we know intimately. We know everything about them. And they know everything about us. These are the ones we have invested a lot of time with. We have had endless conversations and we can say we know them intimately.

Where are you at in knowing the Lover of your soul? As Christ followers we should know Him in intimacy, #4. Maybe it is, we do not even desire to have this kind of intimacy with Jesus. The lack of desire would be because we do not really know who He is. If we truly knew who He was then we would be running to our secret place, closing the door with excitement, to be alone with Him. Receiving direct enjoyment from Jesus. Beholding His wonderful face.

We cannot reflect Jesus to others when we are not looking at Him ourselves. This means we must get to know who He is on an extremely deeper level. As a culture we are most proficient in surface relationships. Take Facebook for instance, we have 800 friends! How many of these "friends" do we know intimately? As Christ followers we must want this to change and not allow this kind of casualness into our relationship with Jesus.

To create this deeper relationship with Him we must have a hunger for Him. To create a hunger for Him we have to be with Him. You know how God's Kingdom and the kingdom of this world operate exactly opposite of each other? Well in the world's kingdom to create hunger you do not eat. In God's Kingdom to create hunger you eat more. The more you eat of Jesus, who is the Bread of Life, the hungrier you will be for Him. The more you invest time with Him intimately the more you will want to be with Him. The more you are with Him, the more excited you are to be there and the more in Love with Him you will grow. Great will be the return on your investment.

You may say you are hungry. But how hungry are you when you choose

5 other things over going to be alone with him? How hungry are you really? Say it is your day off, you have no plans, and you have no other obligations. You have several other things you can do. You have some of your most enjoyable hobbies to choose from, or your most favorite places to go, or simply the things to do that are FUN. Do you choose Him over any of those things? I am not saying those things are "wrong," but when we persistently choose them over Him? Oh, that we would hunger and thirst for more of God as if our life depends on it, because our life does depend on Him completely.

PRACTICAL APPLICATION:

I want to give some very practical examples of how to enter intimacy and get to know the Lover of your soul:

1. <u>First</u>: Before getting out of bed in the morning be aware of His presence with you. As soon as you open your eyes may He be the first One you greet with a holy kiss. Tell Him how much you Love Him. Engage in intimate conversation with Him. Psalm 90:14 "Oh, satisfy us early with Your mercy; That we may rejoice and be glad ALL our days." Give Him thanks for this day that He has made. For only He can make a day. Give Him thanks for the breath that is in your lungs. Acknowledge the Lord, before you acknowledge anyone else. May He be first.
2. <u>Communicate</u>: When you read your Bible, do not just read your particular scripture or devotional for the day, and be done. Robotically going through the motions. Read His Word to know Him and knowing Him will transform you. When you read, talk to Him. Ask Him questions. Ask Him to give you revelation of Himself through what you are reading. Apply the scripture to yourself personally. If it is something you see you do not have, ask Holy Spirit to grow that in you. Converse with Him as you read His Word.

For Example: Philippians 2:3 "Let nothing be done through selfish ambition or conceit." This is not the whole verse, but I am going to stop right here and talk to The Lord about this. "Holy Spirit, do this in me! I surrender myself to You. Remove every bit of selfish ambition and conceit that may be in me. Even in the hidden places where I do not see it or recognize it as such. I do not want this in me at all. Thank You for taking this from me as I surrender it to You. And if it rears its ugly head, I ask You to convict me and correct me. This will not rule over me and I know You will uproot every last bit of it out of me, thank You!"

Now back to the verse, "but in lowliness of mind let each esteem others better than himself." Now I talk to Him again. "In humility, Jesus, I surrender to You and I give You all of me. Give me eyes to see others as You see them. That I will never see myself as better than anyone else, but I will esteem others better than myself. Holy Spirit, I cannot do this in and of myself, but You can do this in me. I am asking for You to do it as I surrender to You. Transform me into Your Word, Jesus is Your Word. Thank You for doing all these things in me. I trust it is so. I Love You, Holy Spirit, I cannot live life without You. In Jesus' precious, beautiful, and mighty name Amen!"

This is communicating His Word with Him. Doing this will do two amazingly drastic things. First it WILL transform your life because when you pray His Word to Him, His Word does not return void (Isaiah 55:11). It will perform what it has been sent forth to do. Second it WILL bring you into an intimate relationship with Him by communing with Him in His Word.

3. Communion: Another practical thing to do to enter into a more intimate relationship is to take communion regularly. At one point I was taking communion every day. I would take time to meditate on Jesus, the cross, and what He did for me. I would envision my flesh being crucified with Him (Galatians 2:20). Dying to the self-life. Praising Him, thanking Him, talking with Him about it. Tears streaming down my face. Singing to Him. However I was led. But I would do this every day. This helped to bring me into the place of intimacy with Jesus. And if I ever feel it waning, this intimacy, I will return to daily communion.

4. Wait: Say to Him, "Holy Spirit, here am I, have all of me and take full possession of me," then wait. The Lover of your soul is longing to have you for His own. Take time to be still before Him without saying one word. We need to learn how to simply sit in silence before Him. Habakkuk 2:20, "The LORD is in His holy temple. Let all the earth keep silence before Him." We must learn how to be quiet to hear what He has to say. And even if He does not speak let us wait more earnestly and intensely upon Him. Lamentations 3:25, "The LORD is good to

those who wait for Him, To the soul who seeks Him." God will shine into your heart and reveal Himself to the waiting soul. He will make Himself a reality to you.

5. Time: We prove the value we attach to things by the time we devote to them. To walk in perfect fellowship with God, we cannot do this, without investing our time with Him. We take time for everything else. We will devote overtime to our careers. An athlete will devote seasons of time to their sport and even in their off season they are still in training. How much time do we spend on social media getting so wrapped up in other people's lives, watching TV shows, movies, binge watching Netflix, or playing video games? And do we think without investing time, we can find close fellowship with God? It is Holy Spirit who can work in us such a yearning, that we will give up worldly pleasures, to invest more time with Him. The Lover of our soul is worth our time. Sell all you have to buy the treasure of knowing Jesus. The Pearl of great price is worth everything.

6. Worship: To humble ourselves before the Lord. To bow before our King, the King of the Universe, in reverence. Worship Him in awe and adoration. I will tell Him how wonderful He is. How worthy He is to be praised. It is amazing how you will feel your heart fill to overflowing as you lift Him high. How you will begin to see Him rightly as you exalt His name. "Lord, You are so beautiful to me. You are glorious in all Your ways. Majestic, Holy, Lovely, I Love You and I worship You." There is something about worshipping Him that draws us in, and we cannot help but pour our Love upon Him.

7. Remember: We will draw into a closer and more intimate relationship with Him as we remember His faithfulness. OFTEN, I will look back on my life and recount all the times He was the only One there for me. The many nights in my room crying to Him (not just crying but sobbing uncontrollably). Knowing He was holding me all the while. All the times of talking to Him. All the questions I asked Him. He was the One that was there for me and the only One that could answer me. Even if He did not answer my questions, it was being there with Him in that moment that mattered most. Remembering how He came through for me in every season. How He rescued me from destruction. How He saved me from myself! How He delivered me from sick and destructive patterns I had. How He Loved me and was so merciful to me. How He was so patient with me. The list can go on forever. How-

ever, when I recount these events, it reminds me of His faithfulness. I cannot help but to grow more in Love with Him and praise Him for all He has done. When I look back on His faithfulness, I know I can trust Him with all of me. And I only long to know Him more.

Ask yourself the following questions. They may help you to remember what He has done for you, and then worship Him. For He is worthy!!!

1. How did He change your life?
2. What did He save you from? (Example: Any bad decisions you made where He saved your life, saved your marriage, saved your job? Etc.)
3. What did He deliver you from? (Example: Any addictions or strongholds He has delivered you from?)
4. What has He rescued you from? (Example: Prison, car accidents, tragedies, sickness, or disease?)
5. What has He done in your life, in your children's life, in your family?

UNMET EXPECTATIONS

This is where you may be thinking to yourself, "He has done none of these things for me." You may not be able to recount His goodness to you. I understand some people are in this place. If you are then I encourage you to recount and remember that He died for you. If you feel He has done nothing else for you, He has changed your eternal destination. He has saved you, delivered you, and rescued you. Jesus took on the most brutal death ever known to man FOR YOU. Start here at the cross, and worship Him! Because He is worthy!

It is important for me to point out also, not to allow any unmet expectations you may have placed on God to create for you a wrong identity of God and a wrong theology about God. Because of what you thought He was going to do or how He was going to do it. The problem is we take our circumstances, apply the Word of God to them, and expect that we know how God is going to move or do something. Then when it does not happen exactly how we thought it was going to, we create an idea about God that is wrong about Him.

Suddenly, we are hurt by God and offended with Him. Our offense is not because of who God is but because we looked at Him wrong. We thought about Him wrong. We expected something our own way and it has nothing to do with who He really is. Now we build doctrine around our own circumstance and outcomes rather than around the nature of God, who He really is, and the Word of God. God cannot do anything outside of His nature and He is good, and He is Love (1John 4:16).

Wrong theologies about God come from unmet expectations and our own error. Proverbs 19:3 (NLT) says, "People ruin their lives by their own foolishness and then are angry at the Lord." And because God did not move as we expected Him to or thought He would, in our time of need, now we are disappointed, discouraged, and we resent God for it. We do not realize it is not because of God but because of a method we applied and outcomes we created in our own minds. <u>My life experiences should never have the right to define who God is</u>. He has already defined Himself through Jesus Christ's Life lived (John 14:7-11). Jesus came to show us who the Father is and always has been (Hebrews 1:3). The enemy likes nothing more than to distort our view of a Loving Father into someone who has "disappointed us" and "didn't come through" for us.

If there are things that did not turn out the way you expected or even the way the Lord says they will according to His Word, we are never to point the finger at God but to look to ourselves. Ask Him the hard questions... "What can I do differently?" "Where can I grow in this?" "How do I become more like You through this?" "I may be missing something Lord, show me what it is." "Reveal Yourself to me in this." "Make me more like You." We are the ones who are to **grow up into Him** in all things (Ephesians 4:11-15). God is NEVER to blame. No matter how "wronged" we may feel.

For Example: When I was going through the pain and tragedy of my first divorce in 2011, my heart broke into a million pieces. In one instant my world stopped. Yet, I believed God would save my marriage. I had faith for my family to be back together. To end our marriage, our family, was the last thing I wanted. I never dreamed this would happen. I do not want to come across as completely innocent in this matter either. I had done many things to hurt this man I was married to. Mainly in the way I had treated him. And at that time in my life, I was a hard person to live with. I was broken. We had many good times as well as many difficult times. Like it says in Proverbs 19:3 (NLT), people ruin their lives by their own foolishness.

My divorce had taken about a year before it was finalized in June of

2012. Now I had the divorce papers in hand, but I continued to stand in faith. In November of 2012 my ex-husband had come back wanting to try to make it work. Yay! Praise the Lord, my prayer was answered! However, he had turned away from God by this time and I was very close to God. Because of this we had many disagreements especially in what was taught and talked about with our boys. I was not completely dead to myself (I had not understood dying to the self-life in its fullness), so I was handling the situation the best I knew how at the time. But now, here we are not married, we are not together in Christ, and we are unequally yoked. Also, his heart was invested somewhere else and that ran its course.

God honored my faith by bringing us back together. He gave me what I had been asking for. Although it did not work out for many reasons. I could have created many different theologies about God based off my circumstances. I could have defined God in a whole new way based on my experience. I could have been disappointed in God. Because quite frankly it did not turn out how I had expected it to. I did not have the outcome I had wanted. I could have blamed God because He can do anything right?! Then why didn't He save my marriage??

For a time satan tried to get me to go down those roads and to entertain those thoughts. However, praise the Lord, I did not stay there. I am not saying going through it was easy because it was HARD. But here on the other side where I have complete healing, I see how God carried me through the whole way. He never left me or forsook me. And I could never blame Him for things that happen in this life, in this fallen world. We have a very real enemy who is against us and any advancement of the Kingdom of God. We have foolish choices we make with our own free will; it is called self-will. satan will try to distort our Father any way he can to try to bring us to discouragement and disappointment in Him. We must be diligent in continuing to know who our good, good, Father is in Truth. And never allow our experiences to define Him.

PERSONAL RELATIONSHIP

It is important to understand my relationship with Jesus does not work exactly the same as your relationship with Him. I am only talking about our personal relationship with Him here. I am not referring to Biblical Truths and His order of doing things. He has order in His Kingdom that will always remain constantly and consistently the same.

For Example: We are all to obey Him. This does not change from person to person. From relationship to relationship.

However, with our own personal relationship with Him, He has made us each to function differently with Him. He has placed within each one of us something specific to us that touches His heart. When He created us, He put it in us for us to find it. What it is He gave us to touch His heart with. Once we find what it is that touches His heart, we then give it back to Him, pouring it out onto Him. And it becomes a continuous circle and flow of Him pouring into us and we pour back onto Him. And because of this specific thing, special to you, of what touches His heart you will function with Him and interact with Him differently than I do. He delights in you. Yes, in YOU.

For Example: It could be the way you talk to Him. There could be a specific thing you say that makes Him smile. It could be your sense of humor. You may share an inside joke with Him, and you both laugh every time you think about it. It could be your appreciation of nature. It could be the way you dance for Him. (This is a good example right here. Because I am NOT a dancer! But it certainly is a special moment we laugh about when I try, smile.) It could be the pictures you draw for Him. It could be the song you sing or play to Him. I understand there are a lot of people who have these different giftings and ways to worship Him. Yet, there is something specific within you that is only for you and the Lord, and it touches His heart every time.

Take the helpful tips and general ideas that are shared and apply it to your own relationship with Him. Do not try to change how He created you and how your relationship with Him is to work, by trying to make it look exactly like someone else's relationship with Him. That is a beautiful thing about Him, He created each one of us differently. We each have a very personal and unique relationship with Him. Keep it that way! While still applying the applications shared.

Furthermore, God is a gentleman. He will pursue you, but He does not push Himself on you. He does not force anything. He rarely will come barging through your barricades you have built and so strategically placed all around yourself. He will draw on your heart until it is an invitation you give to Him to come near, and He will respond. James 4:8, Draw near to Him. His response, and He will draw near to you. Matthew 7:7-8, seek Him. His response, you will find Him. If you knock, His response, the door will be opened. He will draw us to Himself with Loving kindness. He will pursue us. But He will never force Himself on us.

Nevertheless, once we have given Him the invitation He will come in with a holy vengeance and break down every wall and barricade that has kept us from Him. If we come to Him in absolute surrender, He will obliterate and destroy everything in us that needs to go. Are you allowing Him access or are you pushing Him away and ignoring Him?

In Song of Solomon (or Song of Songs) chapter 5 it speaks of the obstacles the bride (the church) must overcome as she searches for Jesus, her Bridegroom. She gives all she has to find Him. She is beaten and bruised and yet there is a hunger in her that says, "I will not stop, I will go beyond what is comfortable, I will do whatever it takes to have Him." The people ask her what it is about Him that makes Him better than all the other lovers. The bride goes on to describe His magnificent beauty. There are those who are reading this who have not seen His beauty for themselves. It is such a picture of what can happen in the church today. We have been in the Sunday services, the meetings, the conferences, and going to all the activities, but we have not seen His beauty for ourselves.

It is in a very real and personal relationship with Jesus, in intimacy, in the secret place, and being alone in His presence, where we will see and know His beauty. Like I mentioned before the more we are aware of Him and alone with Him the hungrier we will be for Him. When this happens everything changes and we will no longer desire things that are not of Him, for Him, or from Him. We will only want what glorifies Him in our lives. Let our search and pursuit for Him be with passion. Fierce and relentless, like SOS chapter 5. That we always have a burning heart for more of Him in our lives and our desire is to know Him.

We cannot have passion or be full of life when we do not know the Source of all life. And anything apart from God is lifeless, it is without a heart. Within a heart that burns for Him is where it turns from, ho hum, "I should pray," or "I have to read my Bible." To the excitement of, "I need to pray!" and "I must read my Bible! I will do whatever it takes to have Him!" Not just robotically reading our daily devotional and praying our self-centered prayers, then going about our day doing our "own thing." But being alone in His presence in reverence and awe. Completely humbling ourselves. Emptying ourselves before Him. Asking Him to fill us and be our everything. To be consumed and absorbed in His Love.

The Tough Times

One last thing I want to touch on. When we are in trials. When we are in what seems like an impossible situation. When we are hurting so bad and do not feel we can make it. When we are so confused as to what is happening and why. When He feels so far away and so distant. I want you to know I understand these places. I have been through all these arid lands. I know for some of you it may be your natural instinct to pull away from Him and blame Him. I beg of you, do not. He is the only One who can get you through this. No, you may not get all your questions answered. Yes, you may be angry. However, this is when you need to press into Him and not let go no matter what. Do not put the blame on Him and do not run away from Him. He can handle whatever it is you are feeling.

Do not believe the lies of satan. satan likes to direct our issues to God to get our eyes off him. So, we will make our "issue" with the Lord. he only wants to tear us apart from God. Do not allow him to wear you down. To tear you apart. Keep holding on to Jesus. Your redemption story is unfolding. You will see God's power move if you keep holding on. Do not let go of Him because He will never let go of you. Do not give up on Him because He never will give up on you. It is never He that is unfaithful. It is us who do not remain faithful. It is never His Word that is not true. It is us who quit and then say it is not true.

In these times we cannot afford to turn away from Him. We must press hard into intimacy with Him, especially when we do not feel like it. We will have to be very intentional about it. And to know, no matter what, He is good. He is good! HE IS GOOD! If you do not know His goodness, you will, if you press into Him and do not turn away. I promise you, He is good, no matter what you face.

We are to be people of faith, perseverance, endurance, and steadfastness. We are to stand until the enemy quits. We do not quit. We are to stand (Ephesians 6). Continue to speak His Word in intimacy with Him until we have encountered Him in this place. Until we know His Word is true from deep within us. We may have to speak it through tears. We may have to speak it through trembling. But we keep speaking it until we are strengthened by Him in our inner beings. Until we know it to be true in the depth of our soul. Until our faith is in Him and Him alone and we know we can trust Him no matter what is happening in the natural realm.

During such times as these, never let go. With everything you have (it can be the weakest of grips, barely hanging on) cling to Jesus. He will prove Himself faithful. I promise you He will! Because only He is the Lover of your soul.

Deeply understand this as well; if He does nothing else for you in this lifetime, He died for you. If He were to never give one more blessing, He saved you from the pit of hell. And that is MORE than enough.

No matter what is going on we are to say, "Yet I will rejoice in the LORD; I will take joy in the God of my salvation" (Habakkuk 3:18). As Cody Carnes sings, "Jesus, You don't owe me anything." Do not get so worldly minded, and so discouraged in the earthly things that you lose sight of eternity and what He has already done for you. Do not believe discouragement is "normal." The Kingdom of heaven doesn't even know what that is.

JOURNAL ENTRY 9/14/2019:

I woke up this morning pleading with God to encounter me in a new way. I have felt stuck. I am pursuing Him, but I do not "feel." I do not feel joyful. I do not feel passion. More than anything I am sad, lonely, and distant. I cry every day and I do not know fully as to why. I just slept 10 hours and yet wake up feeling exhausted. I am not excited to be with You, Lord. I want to be, everything within me wants to be yet I am not. I want to see You. I want to feel You. I want to experience You like Psalm 16:11, "You will show me the path of life; in Your presence is fullness of joy; at Your right hand are pleasures forevermore." Yet, I am not here. I am stuck. However, I keep chasing after You even when I do not feel like it or I do not "feel" You.

After writing this I had dozed off to sleep and when I was awakened it was to this impression upon me, "When you seek Me, you will find Me, and I reward those who **diligently** seek Me." I felt the silent and gentle nudge, "Keep on, do not stop. Keep on, for <u>I Am your reward</u>." **End of journal entry.**

Luke 10:41-42, "And Jesus answered and said to her, 'Martha, Martha, you are worried and troubled about many things. But ONE thing is NEEDED, and Mary has chosen that good part, which will not be taken away from her." (Please read the whole encounter, Luke 38-42.) We must catch the magnitude of this. JESUS SAYS, the ONE THING NEEDED is HIM. Not rushing around only doing ministry. Not rushing around taking care of this thing or that. Not being worried, troubled, and frustrated. But one thing is needed: Jesus. Take the time to sit at His feet and Love on Him. Take the time to be with Him. Take the time to listen to Him. Take the time to know Him. These are most effectively accomplished alone with Him in intimacy (behind closed doors). From this place everything else will flow. From this place you will take Him into your daily life, activities, and duties.

JOURNAL ENTRY 7/8/2020:

I was starting to panic today. I had much to accomplish and wanted to get started. It had to do with writing this book. It was work for Him. It was what He had called me to do. I would still be with Him while doing it. However, He spoke to me and said, "You will accomplish more in the day after being intimately alone with Me. You will accomplish very little if you do not have this time with Me." I stopped and just sat with Him. Then later this very day I was listening to the leader of Jesus Image. His name is Michael Koulianos, he said this, "When we are looking for direction, He is looking for affection. Direction flows from affection. While we want Him to tell us what to do, He wants us to be with Him. And while we are with Him, He tells us what to do." Selah. **End of journal entry.**

A PRAYER TO PRAY:

"There is none upon earth I desire besides You, Lord. Let everything else fade away right now. The things of earth grow strangely dim in the light of Your presence. Nothing else matters. No one else can compare. In Your presence is fullness of joy. You are what gives me fullness of joy and pleasures forevermore, not anything else in this world and not anyone else in this world. Why would I ever trade what is temporary for what is eternal?! Only You can satisfy. Not seeing someone. Not vacations. Not conversations. These are temporary moments of happiness, brief moments of life, but they only leave me wanting more and cannot fully satisfy as You do.

Holy Spirit, take me deeper. Teach me and show me true Love and intimacy. The kind of Love and intimacy that is far beyond what any other person can give me. I want to know the depths and heights of this kind of relationship with You. I want to know You, Father, Son, and Holy Spirit. Really know You. Rightly know You. I want You to be the Love of my life. I want to encounter You in a way that changes me forever. To be One with You. Overwhelm me so I will never be the same again. And make me a vessel overflowing with Your Love, mercy, grace, faithfulness, and goodness. So, I can pour it out onto others. I invite You to come and be the Lover of my soul. In Jesus name, Amen."

FIVE TAKE AWAYS + BONUS ONE

1. All of life is meaningless without having an intimate relationship with Jesus.
2. Knowing Jesus and becoming One with Him is the highest purpose of our lives.
3. Knowing God rightly and in Truth will be our greatest success. Not by knowing some false god we created from an outcome of our circumstances.
4. Knowing Jesus is our reward and the true definition of eternal life.
5. We can know a lot about Him but not really know Him personally. We get to know Him through His Word and in His presence. In intimacy and the secret place.
6. My life experiences should never have the right to define who God is.

Picture drawn and created by Darby Horsfall

Psalm 68: 6, "… the rebellious dwell in a dry land."
Psalm 18:30, "As for God, His way is perfect…"

Chapter 3

Absolute Surrender

I FINALLY ARRIVED. Praise God, I arrived! It was a long journey. It was a painful journey. It was much of a <u>self-inflicted</u> journey. Yet I arrived. "Arrived where?" You may ask. It is the place of peace, with no strife. It is the place of plenty, with no lack. It is the place of rest, with no toiling. It is the place where you are free from striving. It is the place where you are free from stress. It is the place where you do not work in your own power anymore. It is in the place called, End Of Me. I was finally here at the end of myself. I had no more great ideas. I had no more great attempts. I was done trying. I was done having to know what was going to happen next. I was done "having to know" anything at all for that matter. I had wandered in the wilderness for 40 plus years to get here, going in circles. Hmmm, sounds familiar... I have heard this story before.

The Israelites. Oh yes, the Israelites. We will shake our heads in dismay at them. We will wonder why they could not just listen and follow directions. "Would you stop complaining and thank God for taking care of you, already?" "Why would you want to go back to Egypt?! Back into captivity??? Can you just enjoy being free?" And the idols they made. "Come on, what were you thinking?!" We will remain shocked that an 11-day journey to their destination, took 40 years. "You guys, 40 years, really?! Why would you doubt God???" People! Get it together!"

And yet here we are today, history repeats itself. I know because I traveled 40 years in the wilderness. Not obeying God. Doing my own thing. Then complaining about how my life was going. Remaining in captivity to sin. Putting everything else before God (creating idols). Then doubting Him. Doing this over, and over, and over. Until I had finally arrived at the End of Me. I was standing on the highest summit overlooking the place called the Promise Land. What is the "Promise Land?"

In the day of the Israelites, God says in Joshua 24:13, it was the land He had given to them where they did not have to labor, cities given to them they did not have to build, vineyards and orchards they did not have to plant. In our day we can very much consider the Promise Land, our "Promised Life" in Christ Jesus. It is the Life where we do not have to labor. It is not by our own works. It is nothing we can do of ourselves or for ourselves, except surrender.

All we must do is fully surrender our lives and accept the finished work that has already been done for us and in us (Galatians 5:1, Galatians 2:20, Romans 6:6-8, these are only a few examples). Seems too good to be true, right? Well, it is true! This is the Gospel of Christ; this is the Good News!

All we have to do is, by faith, receive everything that has been accomplished for us through Jesus Christ. Then we will walk in the freedom that is already ours. However, we can and will only receive what we believe, through faith (John 1:11-12, Matthew 21:21-22, Mark 11:22-24). Faith brings the unseen into the visible realm (Hebrews 11:1). Faith brings what is already done in heaven to earth. Your Kingdom come Your will be done on earth as it is in heaven (Matthew 6:10). Read all of Hebrews 11 and see everything faith does.

Appendix A in the back of the book will outline this life of faith.

Our enemy was defeated 2,000 years ago by the death and resurrection of Jesus Christ. We already have victory over everything through Christ. Over every sin, every addiction, every bit of the flesh. Self has been conquered. The flesh was crucified with Christ (past tense, Galatians 2:20). Now we need to be transformed in the renewing of our mind (Romans 12:2) and the Truth will make us free (John 8:32). We will experience this life of freedom by our faith that brings the Truth of God's Word into the physical realm.

Every battle has already been won. We **stand,** against the schemes of the devil (Ephesians 6). Standing in the victory and freedom Jesus already paid the price for us to have. Our only fight is the fight of faith (1 Timothy 6:12). Believing our every need is already provided for. We do not have to worry about tomorrow (Matthew 6:33-34). Where we can cast every care (1 Peter 5:7). And we are free to live for Him. We are free period (2 Corinthians 3:17 & John 8:36). We are not bound to ourselves and thinking for ourselves. Our chains have been broken and the prison door opened! Receive the finished work and walk as the free person you are! This is the Promised Life!

This is our land flowing with milk and honey. Instead of land given to us, its freedom that has been given to us. Instead of vineyards we do not have to plant, we grow fruit planted by Holy Spirit. A Promised Life where I do not have to labor and toil for righteousness but where Jesus has finished the work and has made me righteous. Everything has been accomplished.

Today I rejoice. This day I celebrate. I celebrate as I stand on the highest mountain overlooking the beautiful land flowing with milk and honey, my Promised Life. I took the hard way to get here. I took the long way, much like the Israelites, but by the grace of God I am here. I do not recommend the route I took. In fact, I write to you now to encourage you to take God's path. Take the one where He has cleared the way for you already. It is smooth over there; it is level ground (Isaiah 26:7 ESV). He has made a wide path for you so your feet will not slip (Psalm 18:36). Where His footsteps are your pathway (Psalm 85:13). It will take you less time to get to the destination. Surely not 40 years!

Do not take the path I took. It was the path God never intended for me to take. I was forging my own way. Traveling down a road that was never leveled or cleared. Where I was stubbing my toes on rocks. Climbing over trees that had fallen across the way. Tripping over debris, scraping my knees, and falling flat on my face. I was mangled when I arrived. I may have been tattered, torn, bruised, and beaten, yet I assuredly arrived at the End Of Me.

There was one thing left to do and that was to give Him my absolute surrender. Total abandonment of myself to dive into total trust in Him. This is His plan for us. And He always led me to this fork in the road my entire life, where I would have to choose. However, I have always chosen the wrong way. You know the way with the big "Danger; Do Not Enter" sign on it. I always took the road called "My Way" ... and it was a painful way to go!!! When we choose to follow Him, this is a one-way street called "His Way Only."

My thick headedness finally cracked. I saw the ashes of my life for what it was, a complete mess, and I gave it all to Jesus. It was the best choice I ever made. His ways are greater, and His thoughts are higher than our own (Isaiah 55:8-9). His plan for our life is far greater than what we could come up with. DO NOT think for a moment that you know better than He and take your life into your own hands. Going your own way.

Most of the time we see the way that is easiest, but God knows the way most beneficial. What we see as a "problem," will be what God is using to build us, to grow us, and move us into our future. But we see the "problem" and immediately think, "Short cut! I want a short cut around this! Get me outta here!" While we frantically search for the easiest way out, we must understand God's plan for our life is bigger than what we can see in front of us. We must surrender to Him and His way.

SURRENDER ALL: WHAT IT MEANS

"I Surrender all" is one of those phrases that can become a cliche, to us Christians. We know the song word for word. We sing it with a boisterous voice and with enthusiasm, but do we mean it? Do we know what we are saying? Do we really surrender ALL? Or do we surrender our lives to so many other things? So many other things and God too? Have we surrendered to Him some? A little bit? Any at all? Do we comprehend what "surrender all" entails? Let's look at the beauty of what absolute surrender means.

It means completely letting go of what I held on to, so tightly to, for so long, ALL of me. Surrendering my will of what I want. Surrendering my ideas on how I think things should be. Surrendering my decisions of what I think I should do or anyone else should do for that matter. It is to surrender all my thoughts, my words, my actions, my attitudes, my relationships, my heart, my emotions, ALL OF ME. We do not even realize how tightly we are holding onto all these things until we completely let go and we can finally breathe again.

I surrender all means cutting all ties that attached me to every bit of myself. Being tied to self-reliance (AKA independence), self-preservation, self-defense, self-awareness, self-confidence, self-fulfillment, selfish pursuits, and selfish desires. I surrender all means cutting all the strings that attached me to anything or anyone else. Areas where I was attached to any person, place, or thing. Allowing Holy Spirit to take all those severed ties and strings and bind ALL of me to ALL of Him, instead. To bind my wandering heart to thee (Psalm 119:9-16).

Where we are unquestionably, undoubtedly One. I am bound to Him alone. His will is my will. He governs my decisions. He captivates my thoughts. He guards my mouth and the words I speak are His. He directs my actions. He overtakes my attitudes, so I am nothing but Love. He guides my way. He is first in every area of my life and in all my relationships. He overwhelms my heart. He aligns my emotions and my desires to His emotions and His desires. He is my world. He is my only addiction.

Some of you may think I am being extreme. You may have never heard of this before. You may not even know what this looks like to **not** be attached to yourself. I can hear it now, "Independence is good. The one person I can rely on is myself. I was always taught to be self-confident. What is wrong with that?" Jesus never taught us to be independent or to be or have "self" anything. He taught us to be completely dependent on Him and to deny our-self (John 15:5 & Matthew 16:24).

You may not know what it looks like to not be attached to anyone else. You may be saying, "I have a spouse, I have children, I have a family, and what about my friends? Am I to cut all these people out of my life?" This is not what I am saying. The point is God is to have ALL of us and then He leads us in ALL our relationships and endeavors. When we make Him our One and Only everything else comes under His umbrella.

We are all too often given more to the people in our lives than to the Lord. We say God is first or all that we want, **but is He really**? It was a difficult thing for me when I had to come to grips with this question. "Is He really ALL I want? Is He really ALL I need?" When I stared those questions square in the face and had to give an honest "no" answer, I knew things needed to change. I was desperate for that to change.

Oswald Chambers in *My Utmost for His Highest* says this, "There is only one relationship that matters, and that is my personal relationship to a personal Redeemer and Lord. Let everything else go, but maintain that at all costs, and God will fulfill His purpose through my life."

Everything about our lives must flow from our relationship with God! It is so easy to make someone or anything else an idol. We must cut all ties and make Jesus our One and Only. Then He can take our lives and be in us and through us everything we need, everything our relationships need, everything our jobs need, and everything our futures need. Not only is this the way God has designed it, but it is also the most beautiful of ways (no surprise here). Our relationships become more vibrant because they are not revolving around each other or ourselves but the Lord only! When He has all of me then I can accurately impact others. Because He is the One in me, the One working through me, and it is not me at all (Galatians 2:20).

For Example: "Because You, Lord, have all my attention, You cause me to be attentive to others. You show me how to care for them. Because You, Lord, have all my heart, You then fill my heart with good things. And out of the good things in my heart flows goodness to others (Matthew 12:35). Because You, Lord, have all my Love, You then show me how to Love and become Love to everyone around me. Because You, Lord, are my One desire, You then fill my heart with the purest of desires, which are Your desires. Because I seek first (and dare I say "only") Your Kingdom and Your righteousness, You then add all these things unto me. Therefore, I will not worry about tomorrow (Matthew 6:33-34). Because You, Lord, are all I need. You supply all my needs according to Your riches in glory, in Christ Jesus (Philippians 4:10-20 ESV). I do not **need** anything from anyone else. Will you give to me through others? Of course, You will, and You do. But it is not that I need anything from them. It is that I rely on You to supply however You wish to supply. Also, You will show me how to give to others who are in need."

I now understand, this life is not about me, myself, and I (the self-life). It is all about Jesus and I becoming One. It is about us, the bride of Christ, being ready for our wedding day (Revelation 19:7). Life is all about Jesus and His bride. He came and gave His life for us. That is a really BIG deal! We must be EXTREMELY precious, valuable, important, and worthy (we were worth His Life, we were worth dying for). And now our lives are to be lived in absolute surrender and obedience to Him. To be lived for His glory and for His name.

Our job is to surrender all, be in intimate relationship with Him, and through faith He will do the rest to the praise of His glory. Please read all of Ephesians chapter 1. It is easy to get off track when we take our eyes off Him and off living for Him alone even for a second. Jesus is our only answer for everything. And should we ever look outside of Him, for anything, we will be deceived and led astray every time.

Should we ever think this life is all about us (living life for ourselves in selfishness), just keep reading Ephesians chapter 1 over and over. Notice all the, "in Him's," "according to's," and "to the praise of **His** glory's," as it will be worded in the NKJV. Ephesians 1:18 says, that you may know what is the hope of **His calling**. Not your calling but His calling. What **He** has called you to do. Not what you think you should do. This chapter should really put it in perspective for us. It is all about our life lived **IN HIM** not our own life lived for our own personal gains, pleasures, or purposes.

He created us for Love and to become Love. He created us to have an intimate relationship with Him. He created us for His purpose not what we think we want to do. He created us to be the image of Christ in this world. He created us to be disciples for the souls of men. This life is not our own, it is His. Are you willing to lay it down? Not for any other reason but to serve Him, to Love Him, to worship Him, to respond to Him, to bring Him glory for His name's sake?

"Jesus, this life is all about You and I being One. Then becoming One with the rest of Your body. And for us to get ready for our wedding day. This life is not all about my selfish life, pleasures, or desires! I surrender all."

Once we get to the End Of Me it is freedom. Until we surrender all, all is not okay. It is not okay for one part of me to be given over to anything else. God is jealous for all of me. I am to hold nothing back from Him. Therefore, God may be all to me, in me, and through me. Where I do not rely on myself or anyone else but the Lord. Where I allow Him to take His rightful place in my heart and my life.

Give up everything to follow Him. Everything is God's anyways (Psalm 24:1). Everything comes from Him. For Him to work through it. Then to be given back to Him in surrender (Romans 11:36). Our relationships (children, spouse, family, and friends), our finances, our jobs, our homes, everything is on loan from God for us to have stewardship over. To include our own lives. In surrender, we are giving back to Him what was never ours in the first place. Our life was always meant to be God's. Our life was never our own to be lived however we wanted. This is a deception of the enemy where he has kept us in bondage. Is there anything you are holding on to that you need to surrender?

LIVING THE SELF-LIFE

If we are Christians, it is no longer "my life," it is Christ's life lived in me (Galatians 2:20). **It is His life!** This life was never ours to keep. It was never ours to try to manage. It was never ours to try to manipulate and control. We were created **for Him**, and in all things, He is to have preeminence (Colossians 1:16-18). But because of this self-life we are drowning in, the life we are supposed to deny (Luke 9:23), we have made life all about us instead of Jesus.

We fill our lives with everything but Him and then wonder why it all falls apart. We wonder why we feel empty. We feel empty because we have filled our lives with meaningless pursuits. We have not enriched who God created us to be by seeking fulfillment in Him and Him alone. We seek the pleasures of this world, the desires of the fallen flesh, and think we will be happy with these things. Such as alcohol, drugs, cigarettes, partying, sex, gambling, cars, sports, shopping (buying the next bigger and better thing). We get addicted to any of the above, also to our electronics, TV shows, and yes even relationships, the list can go on of the addictions we have.

We look to other things or other people to meet our needs, wants, and desires; financially, emotionally, and physically. When that doesn't work, we move on to the next person or thing. Thinking there was something wrong with the last one and that it will be different this time. The problem is these will never bring you fulfillment. You cannot find fulfillment outside of Jesus.

When we go to the things of this world to try to satisfy us, it leaves us wanting more. So, we keep going back to get our momentary fix. Our moment of happiness. Our moment of enjoyment. When we go to Jesus to satisfy us, He leaves us wanting more. So, we keep going back to Him to get our eternal fix. Our eternal happiness. Our eternal enjoyment. There is a big difference here.

When we go to Jesus, even though we want more, He truly does satisfy and satiate. In His presence is fullness of joy and pleasures forevermore. True joy and pleasures not just mirages that never satisfy. When we keep going to Him it is the path of wholeness, completeness, and healing. Taste and see that the Lord is good.

When we continue to go to the world, sin, other people, addictions, etc. it leaves us even more incomplete and broken. Never being fulfilled. We are constantly chasing illusions, thinking we are good, happy, and whole when it is the furthest thing from the Truth. And we cannot even see it!!

When we drink deep of Him in true intimacy, we will never thirst for the things of this world again. We will see how superficial it is. We will abhor the world and sin. All we will want is more of Him. The deeper we go in Jesus the more we desire Jesus. The deeper we go in sin the more we desire sin. This is a matter of Life or death, you choose.

We are created to be an empty vessel for Him to fill, to do His will, not our own. We will be filled with Holy Spirit to the extent we are emptied of ourselves. Self and Holy Spirit cannot occupy the same space. Whatever we hold on to are areas that will continue to be governed by ourselves and NOT by Holy Spirit. Whatever we keep for ourselves, we are on our own with.

Whatever addictions, whatever control, whatever worries, whatever part of our past, whatever selfish thoughts, ways, desires, whatever offenses, and unforgiveness, these are all to be handed over to Him. So, He can have His way in us. Let it all go. Completely emptied of self. There is nothing else to hold on to, only Him. Give it all over to Holy Spirit and see what His fullness can and will do in your life.

How many of you live day to day struggling to get through? The only reason why we think life is "tough" or that it is a "grind" is because we are consumed with thinking about self. We live without His order of things. We want to use God to help us in our own agendas and endeavors and to bless us in what we are doing instead of letting Him lead us to bless us in what HE is doing. We make life all about "ME." The reason it becomes tough, and a grind is because we are working against the grain of our created purpose in God. We are trying to live under our own control, according to our own will, our own desires, or what we think is best and then have Him "bless" it.

Some may ask, "How would living in my own will and desires ever be tough or a grind?" It may seem like it is fun, the best life ever, and full of freedom. "I get to do what I want, right? How bad is that?" Those are all mirages, false images, the enemy would have you believe. They are traps set to destroy you. Living life this way can never satisfy. Just as the mirage of water in the desert will never satisfy the one who is thirsty. Only Jesus can satisfy. Plain and simple. Our God given design was never to live for ourselves.

Who I am today and who I continue to grow to be has come from the place of surrender. Instead of continuing to fight God to have my way I surrendered to Him. The only fight I have now is the good fight of faith (1 Timothy 6:12). I stopped fighting everything else. I stopped fighting against the only One who could help me and cause me to win every time against my enemy. I have given Jesus everything and He has made me who I am. Full of peace, joy, Love, kindness, patience, understanding, freedom, victory, authority, etc. I will not go back. I will not go back to who I was before, but yet, I will go back if I begin to do things my own way again. If my zombie self is resurrected... Yikes!

You see, my way of doing things or the world's way of doing things only led to destruction, death, pain, and misery. I broke and shattered my life. Thankfully, God was there to pick up the pieces. He is now gently unfolding His masterpiece in me. He has much more to do so I have resigned to getting myself out of the way and just let Him do it. Because quite frankly, I like me for the first time ever. Only because I am seeing Christ in me more and more and more. It is not my-self I like; it is Christ in me, and He looks beautiful! He does amazing work. I, on the other hand, do not do amazing work. Nor does the world, society, or other people who do not live in Christ.

We will live our lives for ourselves and think we are happy to do so. However, we will wake up a week, or a month, or years later and realize we are miserable. And yet we will continue to cycle through life this way. We do the same thing over and over and over thinking it will be different. Just because we may have a different job, a different spouse, a different home, or we live in a different state, does not mean it will be different. It will not be different until we absolutely surrender our lives to Jesus, and He changes everything. He gives us a life worth living. Only He can do this, not a new job, spouse, home, etc.

We end up in messes living for ourselves. We are miserable because we live for ourselves. Then we cannot even see it is for this reason we are miserable! We are good at passing the buck of our misery onto anyone or anything else, especially onto our spouses, other relationships, and even God. Please read James 3:13-18. James 3:16 says, "for where envy and self-seeking exist, confusion and **every** evil thing are there." Selah! Every evil thing is found in selfishness! Do not blame God or anyone else!

Pleasing self is the greatest sin and destruction of man. Yes, you can track it all the way back to the Garden of Eden. satan challenged what God had said (Genesis 3:4) and challenged Eve's identity (Genesis 3:5). Ultimately it was pride, which stems from selfishness, as to why the fruit was eaten. If she had not thought about herself or what God might be "holding back from her," but kept her eyes on the Lord, she would have been okay. But she looked to the tree and desired the wisdom of it and ate of the forbidden fruit of her own desire. Selfishness led to our fall.

It is imperative to understand our lives will always come to destruction when we are living outside of His will and living for self. Every other kingdom built will crumble to dust. Only what is built on Jesus will remain. If He is not in it, it will fail (Psalm 127:1-2). All things apart from Him are meaningless pursuits. Yet we have spent most of our lives wasting them away by living for ourselves and what we want. All the while trying to be good, happy, and useful doing it.

Every time we do something to please our self (living for the flesh) we are denying Christ. When instead, we are to deny ourselves and live in Christ. We cannot live for the flesh and live in Christ at the same time. We live life thinking we can live in both worlds, our own and His. We have never made the distinction it is one or the other. It cannot be both. IT CANNOT BE BOTH.

When we realize our life is what it is because of our own decisions and way of doing things, we are quick to surrender all to Him. More than likely, we are quick because we have made a complete mess. When we get to this point it radically changes our lives because we do not ever want to go back to the place of desolation from which we came. It is a dry and weary place to be. Most of the difficulty we have in life is from a lack of surrender. If we acknowledge God in ALL our ways then He WILL direct our paths (Proverbs 3:1-8). If we are living life any old way we want, we are only acknowledging ourselves and a way that seems right to a man will only lead to death (Proverbs 14:12-14).

JOURNAL ENTRY:

I cannot fix this mess I am in. I cannot do this apart from You. Jesus, I need You. I am letting go of everything I have EVER known, so You can lead me into the unknown. As I sit here crying, I release my tight grip off everything. I repent of all I have been holding on to. I repent of my selfishness and arrogance. I repent for going my own direction. I am so thankful You know the way from here. All I have to do is follow You. I repent for holding back from You. I lay it all down at Your feet, Jesus. Please come sit in this mess with me right now and be my comfort. Meet me where I am at and be everything I need. Be my Truth. Please come into the chaos that is my life right now. Be my Prince of Peace. Bring peace and order to this storm. Silence the voice of the enemy. Silence the voice that is trying to hold me in bondage. May Your voice, Father, be the only One I hear. Cheering me on to get my fight of faith back. To get out of the mess and stand. **End of journal entry.**

Maybe you are at the other end of the spectrum where everything is going great. You have lived your own life for quite some time now and everything is "good!" There have not been any major catastrophes. Because all is going "well" there is an illusion of everything being "just fine." "Why fix what ain't broke," right? But if you are hearing what He says and not doing it, it is only a matter of time before it all crumbles down, <u>and great will be its fall</u> (please read Matthew 7:24-27 & Psalm 127:1-2). We are to have **entire** dependence on our Father, just as Jesus did. Do not be dependent on your own ways.

THE CARE-FREE/WORRY FREE, LIFE OF REST

When we truly surrender all, we will not have a care in the world. I know a lot of you had a twinge of disagreement with that statement. I heard a lot of you gasp and ask, "How could she say that?" Now hear me out. Because in surrender we cast **the whole** of our cares upon Jesus (1 Peter 5:7). According to *Strong's Concordance* the Greek meaning for cast means to <u>throw upon</u>. *Dictionary.com* says cast is to throw or hurl, to throw off or away. When we cast something away from us and upon someone else it is no longer ours. We have **cast** it. Then we trust He is taking care of the cares we have cast to Him. Because He cares for us.

He has given this life to us so we can trust Him to maintain it through to the end. It is extremely easy to cast all my cares onto Him, the One, who gives me my all. We do not need to micromanage God. He is more than capable to handle our lives and every care or concern we have. Do we think we are more "spiritual" if we carry our cares and concerns around with us? When we have supposedly entrusted them to our Father?

It is almost as if we are trying to show them off, when in fact, let's get rid of them. It is not show and tell time to see who has the biggest burden to carry or the largest grudge to hold. While comparing our scar stories. It is not impressive it is only burdensome. So why do we carry around our cares, concerns, burdens, grudges, and hurts when we were never meant to carry them? In absolute surrender we are to leave in His care, moment by moment, all our cares, all our concerns, all our burdens, all our struggles, our everyday life, in short everything. We are to immediately take these things to the throne of grace. Let it out, let it go, and cast it to Jesus. Receive His healing for the hurt and receive His peace over it all.

If you delegate (cast onto) someone who you know is completely dependable to do something, do you trust they will do it? If you know it is someone who will get it done, then you do not have to think about it one more second. You have entrusted it in the care of a trustworthy person. You do not have to be anxious about it, you can have peace. You do not have to check up on it. It is out of your hands of responsibility and into theirs. You can let it go and move on with no worry or concern about it. This is exactly how we should be with Jesus. No, even more so! <u>When a believer really trusts Him, they cease to worry</u>. We can say, "Lord, I know You are taking perfect care of this, I will not want for anything (Psalm 23)."

JOURNAL ENTRY:

I feel uncovered not wearing a care in the world. It feels like I should be wearing something. I have many things I care about but I have cast them all to You, Father. And even though I feel bare, I am so secure. I am free. Free from worry. Free from anxiety. Free from trying to figure anything out.... FREE! **End of journal entry.**

The carefree life also causes us to live in a constant state of peace where we do not "need a vacation" or "need to just get away." Nothing against vacations. But if we live every day surrendered to Jesus and following Holy Spirit then we go where He leads us. We go when He leads us. We are in perfect peace and flow. By casting our cares onto Him we are free to follow (to follow Him wherever He may go...smile).

Instead of striving every day to fix this. Go there for that. Put out fires here. Try to make something happen over there. Then be so exhausted because we have done everything in our own strength, without following the leading of Holy Spirit. Now we "need a vacation to just get away from it all." The carefree life is a state of constant rest. Resting in the Lord and trusting Him. It does not mean we do nothing; it means we seek Him and wait on Him to do anything. Even then, when we are surrendered, He is the One who does the work through us. We are simply His vessel. He lives in me and through me!

To enter this interior life of continual rest we must be completely surrendered to Jesus. We follow Him with total abandonment and utter faith. Imperatively we need to let go and drop it into God's very capable hands, there is no other way. When I encourage younger adults "to just do it, surrender now," it is to save years of weariness from striving to do it on your own. To save you from the pain and heartache of where your own decisions and ways of doing things will lead you. Do not go down that road! DANGER!!!

I refer to this as the self-inflicted fire or in other words, "pain!" Self-inflicted fire can be avoided. When you have abandoned yourself to the Lord, He will maintain His authority in your soul. From here on you do not, in any sense, belong to yourself. But it is precisely here you can find rest. Rest assured He has you. Stay away from doing it yourself and getting burned.

In the book of Joshua, the Israelites **never lost a battle** <u>when they were with God and living in obedience to Him.</u> In fact, they were guaranteed the victory every time. There were battles where men lost their lives yet they still won in the end. As it is with us! In the sweet rest of faith, we can trust it is all taken care of in the hands of Jesus. We may lose some things along the way. We may lose lives of those who are close to us. However, our greatest comfort is we have Jesus. He will guide us. He will keep us. He will be everything it is we need. He has already defeated the enemy. So, when the battle, trial, or tribulation comes to us, while we are in it, we can rest knowing we have Jesus to be our defense, our refuge, our comfort, our guide, and our strength. Rest in the victory that is already ours through Christ. It is finished! We have won.

Trusting Him

When we relinquish people or situations to the Lord, we give Him the opportunity to work as He sees fit. It is not our job to try to control or manipulate. Our part is to surrender to Him continually and daily. Starting each day in sweet submission. God's part is to work to do the thing that has been entrusted to Him. When we trust, the Lord works, and much is accomplished. This means we can pray and leave it there in His hands. Do not walk away with it. If you find you do, take it back and leave it with Him as many times as you need to. Every act of trust makes the next less difficult. Before long trusting Him is as natural as breathing.

With my life or the life of my loved ones in the hands of Jesus I can cast my cares upon Him for He cares for me. In return I do not have to carry the cares of mine, of others, or of this world. They are not mine to carry. I have handed them over to the One who is my Life. My soul is now in a safe haven of green pastures and still waters with goodness and mercy following me all the days of my life (Psalm 23). We are to unwaveringly persevere in the face of every obstacle and every tribulation. Walking through the valley of the shadow of death fearing no evil because He is with us. He who trusts in the Lord mercy shall surround him (Psalm 32:10).

There are 2 things that are diametrically opposed, more than oil and water, and that is worry and trust. When we worry it is proof, we do not trust. When we really trust, we will cease to worry about what we have trusted God with. Some think this is impossible to not worry, but it is not. We are to surrender it to Him by casting it upon Him. Now we are to trust Him with it and stay in faith. Taking it even a step further, when we do this, we do not have to think about it anymore. Because we have given it to someone who is completely trustworthy.

In Matthew 6:25-34 Jesus tells us 3 times DO NOT WORRY. In verses 33-34, He specifically tells us to seek first the Kingdom of God and His righteousness, and all these things shall be added to you. THEREFORE, do not worry... If we find ourselves worrying; seek His Kingdom and His righteousness. Camp out in this section of Scripture for awhile until it becomes the Truth we know that makes us free.

Hannah Whitall Smith wrote a book called *The Christian's Secret of a Happy Life*. By the time the book was published in 1875, 3 children of hers had already died (at the ages of 5, 18, & a stillborn). Eventually it was 4 altogether (the 4th being 11 when she died). She had many other trials and tribulations in her marriage and life besides the tragedy of the death of her children. Her life was not "easy," yet she knew who her enemy was, and she knew who her God was, and she trusted God relentlessly. Our lives are not carefree because they are perfect and without trial. They are carefree because we know the God we have in the middle of the fiery furnace. I want to share an excerpt from her book, which I highly recommend reading (emphases and underline added).

"Thy will be done. We mean the giving up of all liberty of choice. We mean a life of inevitable obedience. To a soul ignorant of God, this may look hard. But to those who know Him, it is the happiest and most restful of lives. He is our Father, and He loves us, and He knows just what is best, and therefore, of course, His will is the very most blessed thing that can come to us under all circumstances. I do not understand how it is that satan has succeeded in blinding the eyes of the Church to this fact. But it really would seem as if God's own children were more afraid of His will

<u>than of anything else in life;</u> His lovely, lovable will, which only means loving-kindnesses and tender mercies, and blessings unspeakable to their souls. <u>I wish I could only show to everyone the unfathomable sweetness of the will of God</u>." WOW!!

ANYTHING WE HOLD ONTO

It is so sad a lot of us struggle most of our lives to get to the point of absolute surrender. If we get there at all. When it is the absolute best place for us to be and it is so simple here! We give Him our lives and we obey Him, that's it! Instead, we give over to Him small areas at a time. Only to find out everything we are struggling to lay down is that which will eventually kill us anyway. Either physical death or death of our soul. Because everything we are holding on to is still rooted in self and self kills. It does not make one bit of sense and yet this is where we are stuck. As if our way is better than His. We continue to live deceived. My hearts cry is for people to be free.

When we make the decision to believe in Jesus Christ as our Savior, thereby committing our life to be a Christ follower, we are to submit to Him immediately and never look back. Not hem and haw and say, "Here is my family but You cannot have my social life." Jesus said to Matthew (Matthew 9:9) "Follow Me" and Matthew, a tax collector, **arose** and followed Him. With Simon Peter and Andrew, they were fishermen, and Jesus said to them (Matthew 4:19-20) "Follow Me," and they **straightway** left their nets and followed Him. With intentionality and immediacy, the disciples left what they were doing to follow Jesus Only. As with us we should be all in with immediacy. Straightway leaving selfishness and the world behind.

But I would venture to say most of us start out halfheartedly following Him saying, "God, I want You to take care of my health, family, and finances but I definitely want to keep my social life for myself (and all that entails). My future, I can handle that as well (I like the plans I have). And I will keep the attitudes of my heart (such as bitterness, unforgiveness, anger, jealousy, worry, selfishness, pride, etc.)." We give Him certain areas of our lives to have Him take care of and we hold on to the rest. We hold on to the motives of our heart, "our rights," and our emotions of the flesh.

We do not leave everything at once to follow Him. We try to control what He can have of us and how much He can have. When we do this, we will find it will take most of our lives to completely surrender to Him.

Which to remind you is our land that flows with milk and honey, peace, joy, rest, and abundance. Just like the Israelites in the wilderness.... the journey is much shorter than we think. The reality is we drag the journey out way longer than it needs to be. Wasting a good portion of our lives just poking along with our surrender.

In any area where we have made the decision to hold on to something (for any number of fleshly reasons which we will go over some of these later) it is fair game for the enemy. We can easily be deceived. It becomes nearly impossible to find the mind of God in a matter of something we are holding on to. It can be the smallest, tiniest of corners that is not surrendered. It can be the most "insignificant" things in our lives we hold on to. Or it can be things that are the most detrimental to our lives. <u>Anything not surrendered is now open season for satan to have his way.</u> Therefore, we must purpose in our hearts to surrender and obey the Lord in every respect and every aspect of our lives.

We do not realize all we are holding on to in our own power. Everything we are trying to control. Until we completely let go of everything and we feel like we can fly. We are as light as a feather with the weight lifted off. It is freedom. We no longer have our own plan or our own agenda. We are completely submitted to Him. We have total trust in who He is and His plan for our life. And while we wait for the fruits of this transformation to grow in us, we daily surrender to Him. We are to trust Him with our life, with everything, in complete obedience to Him!

There is a statement, "hold on loosely," are we to hold onto anything but Jesus at all? I don't think so. When I tenaciously hold onto something (even if it is loosely) the question needs to be asked if I love this person or thing or idea or ideal more than God? Is my desire more for this than for God?

When I was not fully surrendered to Holy Spirit and I held on to my own wants and desires, I struggled immensely. It was an easy target for satan to hit me. Bullseye, he got his arrow of fear in me telling me I would be alone for the rest of my life. I was so easily deceived in what was not surrendered to Jesus. From there I took my own way what I wanted to do, and it was my failure and my own demise.

It was nothing but ugly and 100 degree burns all the way down that road. (Is there such a thing as 100-degree burns? Um yes!) Oh, sure doing my own thing had the illusion of being fun, carefree, and good for a time but it was far from the reality of what it was. It turned out to be hell on earth. The idea of it was great the reality of it was hell. But isn't that satan's objective? Getting our attention, distracting us, and alluring us away from God? To allure us with our own desires. With the illusion of fun, carefree, good, and pleasurable? It should have been of no surprise to me that I got burned. When God tells us specifically that sin (any disobedience to Him) leads to death (Genesis 2:17, Romans 6:16, & 7:5).

The things you do selfishly may be fun for the moment, but they will leave you craving, wanting more, and you will still be empty in the long run. If you keep trying to search for fulfillment and seek for fun outside of God, you will remain void. I have been through it. I have tried it. I filled my life with everything else and a little of God too and it fell apart many different times. It flat out does not work, and it will never work that way. Because our whole purpose for being created BY Him, is FOR Him. But until you choose Him, you will be chasing after optical illusions that your enemy has put into place to try to destroy you, distract you, and make you think "this is what life is all about." He is a liar. Always has been always will be.

My Stubborn-Life: Hitting Rock Bottom

I heard someone's testimony one time they said, "I have given my life – DONE!!" Just that one statement hit me. By now I had surrendered (given) my life to Jesus probably at least 100 times or more at this point. I could not understand why I kept coming back to the same place. Why didn't I have a "DONE" experience? My question, "How many times do I have to keep giving my life away?" Holy Spirit's response, "As many times as you keep taking it back."

This was a **difficult** lesson for me to learn. I spent a lot of long and grueling years here. I realized there were a couple reasons I kept taking it back and coming around full circle. One was because I did not trust God, so therefore, I was not fully surrendered to Him. And secondly my flesh was still alive. I had not fully received the death of myself that was accomplished on the cross (Romans 6). Instead, my-self was still very much alive. My-self always wanted to have a say and thought I knew better than God. Once you realize your-self was crucified with Christ on the cross, then it cannot speak anymore. When self is dead it cannot have a say, and it must completely let go.

I am a firm believer it does not always have to be that one has to "hit rock bottom" in order to surrender. You can do it. Just do it!! However, for me, I did. I was a very stubborn, hardheaded, and self-willed individual. In my stubbornness I had to learn a lot of things the HARD way. I have realized my stubbornness in my own hands is detrimental. However, "stubbornness" in His hands is perseverance. And it gives me a resolve, a steadfastness, a never give up mentality. And with that resolve for His use, I stand strong in the Truth I now know. Praise God He is showing me how to utilize this for His Kingdom.

As of late, I have been stubbornly obedient to God. Living Life the way He intended me to live. Taking my stand in what I know to be true of His way of doing things, His way of living, according to His Word. And it has been beautiful, peaceful, literally carefree, and such a blessed Life. I am grateful for the steadfastness God has put in me for His use. It has given me the resolve to keep moving forward. To not quit. It has given me the perseverance to keep fighting in faith. To stay in surrender to Him. To never give up.

Whereas being stubbornly disobedient to God, living life the way I wanted to live, and having to learn things the hard way was ugly, painful, messy, and a cursed way to live. That was the way that led to the death of my soul. Been there, done that, and I do not ever want to go back!!! Once I hit my rock bottom, I truly was at the End Of Me and my ways. I had absolutely no problem surrendering at that point. I was done. I mean SO DONE! I finally trusted Jesus more than I ever trusted Him in my entire life. I finally trusted Jesus more than I trusted myself (Ugh)!

Because of everything I have been through and everything He has shown me to be true I trust Him with my life completely. If I stay surrendered to Him, He will work it all out and I do not have to. He has proven Himself faithful to me, repeatedly. Even through all my "mess ups." Now, out of my Love for Him, I want to be obedient to Him and do what I know He says to do. Knowing everything He tells me is only for my good. His Word is the guideline for His very best Life for me. I will stay faithful to Him.

My rock bottom was the point of no return. Now I am very hardheaded and stubbornly surrendered to Him. When I finally made it to the End Of Me, I truly understood the necessity of absolute surrender and complete obedience to Jesus. The importance of denying myself and living the crucified life. We all think we know what is best for us in our lives. We all fall prey to this lie of satan. And from this lie we will go in directions God never intended for us to go in. There is no way on God's earth we could ever know what is best for our lives apart from seeking Him. Only God knows what is best for us. Because He is the One who created us for His purpose. He knows the plan. He knows the way.

Obstacles We Face

We are going to go over some of the obstacles to absolute surrender. These are only a few examples of what will hold us back from entering the Promised Life of Freedom in Christ:

1. <u>Self</u>: The first and foremost issue we have is that we are not living dead to self. We do not live the crucified Life. We are riddled with the self-life. We want to obey certain things of God but to be perfectly obedient to Him is not appealing to us. Our flesh always wants to have a say in what we do, how we do it, or what we don't do. We cannot surrender to self and God at the same time. In all things we are choosing one or the other. We are choosing to follow our flesh or to follow Holy Spirit. Self must die.

2. <u>Risk</u>: As if complete abandonment to Jesus without any reserve is too much to ask for and too great a risk for us. We consider absolute surrender as a task that is not "manageable" for us to do. As if our managing of our situations is better than what God can do, so we choose to rely on ourselves. Therefore, we consider surrender too "risky" and a "risk" most of us are not willing to take. Sadly, when it is no risk at all. We have everything to gain in the life of surrender and living One with Christ.

3. <u>Fear</u>: We have a fear God will not come through for us <u>the way we have planned</u>. So, we decide to take things into our own hands. Which puts our self-will in overdrive to "do something." This is called self-confidence. We simply cannot let go or do not want to. We trust ourselves to handle it more than we trust God to. We may not trust His plan for our future and that causes fear. We may not like His plan. We think His plan and what He is doing is not good enough. Again, as if we know how to do it better than He. Do you know how absurd this sounds? Yet, this is what we are saying and thinking when we do not leave it in God's hands, and we try to

figure it out for ourselves. Why would you ever want something He doesn't want for you or have in mind for you? Do not rely on your own plans and ideas you have made up along the way without even realizing it. Because when we are not fully surrendered, we will be deceived by our own thoughts. There is only one way to do something, and it is His way! Every time. Do not fear His plan for it is the very best plan for your life.

4. <u>Trust</u>: We do not trust God. Even if He has to walk us through a tragedy, only He knows beginning to end. Only He knows how to do that! We are to trust Him (Psalm 121:7-8 & Romans 8:28). Let us learn to say, "Lord, no matter what happens in life, I know You have the very best for me! As I want the best for my children, would I intentionally bring them harm? NO! And am I a better parent than You?? NO! Your plan for my life is Your perfect, good, and Loving plan for my life. You will get me through any tragedy I may face. I will be still and know You are God. You are with me, and You are my refuge (Psalm 46:10-11)!! I will stand in Your ways. I will see and ask where the good way is, and I will walk therein, and I will find rest for my soul (Jeremiah 6:16)."

Sidenote: We have a very real enemy who brings tragedy in our lives. He comes to steal, kill, and destroy. We have our own self-will (ruled by satan) that makes decisions that will cause trial and tribulation. The enemy enjoys nothing more than for us to blame God for what is happening or has happened so we will not trust Him or run to Him. If there is tragedy that has happened, I am not saying this was God's plan or path for you. What I am saying is He is the only One who can walk you through that tragedy and yes even heal you completely I will commit my way to the LORD, trust also in Him, and He will bring it to pass (Psalm 37:5). This means we Trust Him with His plans for our lives. If the Lord wants you to have it, He will not let you miss it. If it is His plan for You, He will make it happen. Otherwise, you are just trying to force something to happen that you want. And it is your plan and your desire you are chasing after and not His. When we let go and allow the Lord to work, He will either bring it together or it will be taken out of our lives. By us letting go and trusting Him we will know His plan instead of forcing something to happen.

5. <u>Uncertainty</u>: Uncertainty will cause us to be afraid of the unknown, making us vulnerable. As a whole we do not like vulnerability. We will begin to have anxiety over the not knowing. It then becomes our life's mission to know all things. I call this the "I need to know" syndrome. I need to know how this is going to turn out. I need to know what they are going to do. I need to know what is going to happen next. I need to know what they are thinking. I need to know this, and I need to know that. Now we are compelled to try to control things. If I can orchestrate it, then I can control it (theoretically). If I can manipulate it, then I will know what will happen next (theoretically). As we let go and abandon all to Him we will see our trust in Him gets rooted deeper. And all we really "need to know" is He is good, He is God, and He is Love and that is enough for us to trust Him with all things. We need to keep our focus on Him and not on the people around us, the current circumstances, or the outcomes. Corrie Ten Boom says (emphasis added), "Never be afraid to trust an unknown future to a KNOWN God."

6. <u>Control</u>: All these lead to one main underlying problem and obstacle.... control. We want to control everything about our lives, our future, and even those around us. Thinking that if we control it, we have got it under control. What we have control over are the choices we make, our very own free will. Will we obey Jesus or not? We have control over the words of our mouth (and the prayers we pray). Will we line our words up with His Word or not? We have control over our own faith. Will we believe His Word and trust God with our lives or not?

It is easy to think we have given up control when we have not. We are still trying to figure it out in our own minds. It is easy to think we are completely trusting the Lord when we are not. Our concern and worry are a dead giveaway. These two things can be very subtle deceptions. Especially for those who try to control everything, everyone, the outcomes, and their tomorrows.

When what we think, do, and say are no longer aimed at controlling our circumstances, our results, our future, or other people, we are able to be in the present moment. The present moment is the only thing we have any real say about. This moment is what matters. We might as well pay attention to it and what we are going to do with it. Not to be stuck in some distant future or past.

For Example: I wanted to marry again. I needed to surrender this to God and trust His plan for my life. However, I could not. If He would have told me "You will marry again." If He would have just told me what point A to point B would look like, then I would be good and have joy to carry on. I could have trusted Him with it. Because I would have known the outcome. I would not have had the fear of the unknown. Fear of possibly being single for the rest of my life. But He was not telling me what I wanted to hear. I did not know what His plan was. He did not give me all the details and that made me vulnerable and uncomfortable.

satan used this to create fear in my stubborn and self-willed mind. I was uncomfortable with not knowing. I was vulnerable in not knowing. So, I took things into my own hands. Trying to figure it out and work it out. I was so gripped with fear, and I did not trust God. It makes me sad to even say that right now. How could I NOT trust God?!?! Because to doubt the Lord is to doubt His character. At that time in my life, I obviously did not know His character and who He was/is.

Andrew Murray's last words right before he went to be with the Lord, "God is worthy of trust." Once you surrender ALL and KNOW the God you have, you will no longer think about what He is doing, what He is going to do, or how He is going to do it! You simply trust Him with everything implicitly. Trust is no longer an "issue." You trust Him with your life.

REPENTANCE

In absolute surrender there also must be genuine repentance. And in genuine repentance there will be absolute surrender. These two go together. Repentance is to change your mind, change your thinking, a reversal, and go in the opposite direction. Repentance is a turning to God and by this act of turning to God you are, as a result, turning away from sin.

In true repentance there is a godly sorrow and repulsiveness to stepping back into the flesh and into sinful ways. Much like two magnets. On two sides there is an attraction and on the other two sides there is a repulsion. We are to be so attracted to Jesus on one side, and on the flip side be so repulsed by sin that we do not want it in our lives anymore. In fact, the repulsion is so strong you cannot push the two magnets together.

When we truly repent and fall into the arms of Jesus, in surrender, He will show us who we are in Him and how to live Life in Him. But until the moment of true repentance and surrender we will continue in our own way of life. A life we have created for ourselves, however false it may be, we are totally content to stay there.... YUCK!

Face the ugliness for what it is, UGLY, and fall to your face before Him. This is what makes it true repentance. You are genuinely sorrowful for what you have done. The life you have lived apart from Jesus. "Bring forth fruit of your repentance" (Matthew 3:8). If your outward behavior (fruit) does not reflect your inner decision to turn to Jesus and accept Christ as your Savior, then there is no evidence of repentance. There is no real fruit. The change in your behavior is for fruit and for your own good. Not for your acceptance. This change is called the NEW life Jesus has for you. Where you are to look like Him.

Jesus says to "Follow Me" so that means it can be done. This does not mean only in His ways and miracles but in His character as well. We are to follow Him in all His ways **and** in all of who He is. We can actually live as Jesus lived. This will take the power of the surrendered life to Holy Spirit to do the work in us. Surrender is not you doing the work. It is when I stopped trying to change me, putting all my own effort into it, and surrendered to Holy Spirit, that He could move in and change me. He could then do what He does best, resurrect that which is dead into something beautiful and bring forth the fruit of my repentance.

HOLINESS

We are to humbly come before His throne of grace and lay down our lives at Jesus' feet. This is something He has shown me is to be a daily routine until it is our automatic way of life. We are to humbly surrender our lives to Holy Spirit every morning, emptied of ourselves, and allow Him to transform us. Give Him everything and do not hold anything back. One of the biggest lessons I learned was I cannot change me, only He can. I tried, and my efforts to achieve holy living only resulted in failure, with much frustration, and grief.

The Spirit of God is a holy Spirit. Holiness is the work of Holy Spirit to deliver us from the power of sin, guilt, and shame (Romans 8:13-14), and to produce in us the fruits of holiness. We are to leave this in His hands to do the work. However, this holiness can only result in our daily surrender and daily obedience to the leading of Holy Spirit. We are to walk in the Spirit and not in the flesh (Galatians 5:16-17). Holy Spirit can come in, rule, and give grace to pass through all hardship without sinning (Romans 6:22). Our body is the temple of Holy Spirit, it is to be holy in things (1 Corinthians 6:19-20). We are to be holy as He is holy (1 Peter 1:16).

Holy in the Greek means, sacred, physically pure, morally blameless, consecrated, and a saint. Holiness is to characterize our life every moment of every day. Holy is to be separated to God for His possession (1 Peter 2:9). We are to live as Christ in this world and what was Christ's life characterized with? Holiness. He gave Himself completely for God's Kingdom and His glory. We cannot chase after the things of this world and eternal things at the same time. We were created for His purposes and not our own agenda.

Do you desire your own agenda, your own desires, your own will, more than you desire God? Are you willing to lay it all down at the altar? Leave it all, if so required? Do you believe His ways are higher and His thoughts for you are higher? His purpose for your life greater than your own? If you want to live in the joy of Holy Spirit, you must ask yourself, "Am I willing to surrender everything that is sinful, even that which appears to be "good?"

THE YIELDED-LIFE

We will struggle when we are outside of the will of God. Because the fruits of Holy Spirit are in direct contrast with the acts of sinful nature. The flesh wars against the Spirit. If we want to live a Holy Spirit filled Life, we cannot do it if we are not yielded to Him. We cannot do it of our own will power. We must have God's will power. We will have the greatest strength when we have the indwelling of Holy Spirit and He can only operate in the yielded life.

We cannot live a Holy Spirit filled Life if we are living a double life. So many of us live one way on Sunday's and another way at home, the workplace, or at school. It is one or the other. We are either Spirit led or self-led. Spirit filled or full of self. When we are His we cannot continue to be a part of the world (James 4:4-10).

The Word of God can only go so far as the yielded life is to Him and His ways (1 Corinthians 3:1-3). The deeper our commitment (yieldedness) goes the more He will reveal to us. Are we all in or are we only halfway in? And He can only reveal to us on the level we understand. Are we shallow or are we deep? We can receive as much of Him as we want. And we will be able to receive His Word to the extent we are yielded to Him.

We will find it hard to hear God's voice when we have not completely yielded our lives **fully** to Him. When there is mixture in our life (any part of the flesh) we cannot hear the Lord clearly. We think the Lord is doing something other than what He is really doing. We cannot make sense of anything, and we cannot hear Him.

For Example: I thought He was telling me it was ok to marry someone when He was clearly not telling me to do that. I can say "clearly" now because as I looked back in all my journaling, I saw each time where He was telling me, "NO!" But I was so deceived in the area that was not surrendered to Him. I could not hear Him clearly. His voice was muffled.

In order to hear God clearly, we must be **fully** yielded to Him. Not holding back even a tiny corner because that is still a small crack in the door for satan (Ephesians 4:25-32). Where we are submitted to God, the devil flees (James 4:7). Where we are not submitted to God, the enemy does not flee. he has a legitimate place, full access, free reign, and an open bullseye.

Where we are not surrendered to Jesus, we will end up looking for answers elsewhere. We will be deceived and led astray every time. "Jesus, You are our answer for everything; health, wholeness, relationships, finances, etc. We do not need to run to anyone else looking for 'answers' or to anything else to find 'answers.' We only need to look to You Lord!"

How yielded are you to Him? You can tell this by the way you live your life. Are you carnal (led by flesh) or spiritual (led by Holy Spirit)? Do you alter your life to live according to the Word of God or do you try to alter the Word of God to fit your life?

His Lordship

Coming to Jesus is more than just a "ticket" to heaven. Coming to Jesus is giving our ALL to Him. We accept Christ as our Savior to get to heaven, but we never make Him Lord over our lives. And there is an extreme difference. Too many of us only want to take the life insurance policy He has to offer. But we do not want to give Him our lives in full surrender making Him Lord over us. Lord means a person who has authority, control, or power over us. A master, chief, or ruler.

How many people never make Jesus their Lord and then can walk away from their "faith?" They may say things like, "Jesus was real to me." "I talked to Him." "I believed." People can say a lot of things that sound right. However, He was not Lord of their lives. He was just a sort of helper. When there was trouble, they came to Him. When they sinned, they asked Him for forgiveness. When they were in darkness, they cried out to Him. But they more often lived according to their own will and never made Jesus the Ruler of their lives.

When you know Jesus in an intimate relationship, you can NEVER walk away from Him. Once you truly know Him. **Never.** He is too good. You must come to the place where it is more than feeling and emotion. And decide to follow Him no matter what. No matter what happens in life He is your Lord, your Master, the One who has all authority over you. The One you are completely dependent on just as He was with Our Father (John 5:19).

Lordship decides who is in charge and who we trust. People can know He IS Lord and still not yield to Him, making Him Lord. We can delay our destiny because of our stubbornness of not wanting to yield and be led. To make Him Lord of your life it means surrender and submission to Him. We both cannot rule our lives. We know He is Lord when He is the only Ruler. The only One who has any say.

We are to present our bodies a living sacrifice, holy, acceptable, to God, which is our reasonable service (Romans 12:1). It does not say to only offer Him a hand or a mouth or a foot, but our entire body. This means we do not only give Him part of us or some of us. Jesus, the sacrificial Lamb was a complete offering (not in part). What did Jesus hold back from us? Extremely nothing. He spared not Himself. How can I give back to Him anything less than all of me? We know He is Lord when we have given Him all of us. Is Jesus Lord over your life? Jesus, Lord no matter what?

And if He asked you to walk away from it all today, I mean everything, would you? Or would you argue and justify why that couldn't' possibly be the Lord. Would you give up all the kingdoms you have built? Your business portfolio? All the identities you have made for yourself? Your family? Your fame? Would you give them up for Him right now if He asked you to? Would you sell all you have and give it to the poor to follow Him (Matthew

19:16-30)? Until you can honestly answer "yes" there is more surrender and letting go that needs to happen. What you build with your own hands will fail. It will not last. It will crumble to the ground. What you give to the Lord and allow Him to build will stand forever. We know He is Lord when we have given Him everything.

JESUS OUR REWARD

Our job is to surrender. We can even serve Jesus for selfish gain or with wrong motives if we are not surrendered to Him. We will serve Him to get something from Him. Or we will serve Him because it is what we should do, from a place of obligation, it is not from a place of Loving Him. Self is wickedly deceitful.

We have people that say, "If I follow Jesus, I will get (fill in the blank); healing, joy, peace, prosperity, all the blessings I can get." Instead of, "If I follow Jesus, I will get Jesus!!!" Jesus should be our One and Only heart's desire. I must say by default we receive all those things because that is who Jesus IS. But we should never make those things our pursuit. Jesus is to be our pursuit, and our heartbeat. By remaining in continual fellowship with Him. Jesus is the ultimate, highest, and most beautiful reward we will EVER receive. Jesus is the more abundant Life that He came to give (John 10:10).

Thomas Merton says, "When we live superficially.... we are always divided and pulled in many directions. We find ourselves doing many things that we do not really want to do, saying things we do not really mean, needing things we do not really need, exhausting ourselves for what we secretly realize to be worthless and without meaning in our lives."

Isaiah 55:2 ESV, "Why do you spend your money for that which is not bread, and your labor for that which does not satisfy?"

PATIENCE

James 1:4, "Let patience have its perfect work, that you may be perfect and complete, lacking nothing." We hear all the time, "Oh no, don't pray for patience." What a deception! Do you honestly hear what this verse tells us? When patience has its perfect work in us, we will be **complete** and **lacking nothing**!!! Pray for patience people! Pray for patience! Sure, we will get tested. Sure, things will come at us. However, we are also to be dead to the flesh. The testing will not disrupt a dead person.

Don't get discouraged and don't throw in the towel. Don't talk yourself out of what God is doing in your life just because you bump into a testing and an expression of weakness. Rejoice that you see it for what it is. Rejoice that Light is in your life and that God is increasing you and growing you. Don't take one big step backwards and condemn yourself saying, "I should know better by now." Don't talk like that, that is deception.

Be patient with the process of absolute surrender! When I was surrendering selfishness to Holy Spirit, I wanted all of it gone immediately. I could not stand it anymore. I did not want one bit of it. For about a week in my quiet times I would say to the Lord crying, literally crying, "You know I don't want this, I hate it. I have been giving it to You and it is still here. Take it, take it, take it, I DO NOT WANT IT." There were a few things He showed me during the next few weeks:

1. "Your way right away, has got to go." Which oddly enough even in wanting something good so badly, this was selfish. Therefore, even in surrendering to Holy Spirit I was still trying to insist He go faster and do it my way, "I want this gone NOW!" See how deceitful and wicked self is and how it can be masked so "cleverly?"
2. I was always striving for the next thing. I had a perfectionist mindset of myself. I had to be better and better and better. I expected more of myself. In which He responded to me with,
3. "Just enjoy being Mine." I must admit when I heard this, I stopped. I responded, "I do not even know how to do that! Please show me how! Show me how to enjoy being Yours!" Where I was striving for more transformation to take place, He was saying to me, "Rest in Me. Find joy in being with Me. Be content in being with Me. Just be with Me."

JOURNAL ENTRY:

"Rest in My Love for You," is what the Lord said when I realized I was back in striving mode, performance mode. Just wanting things to happen and be done already. Thinking I am not where I "should be," feeling like a failure. How did I get back here, being my own worst critic again?

The struggle with; being Yours without having to prove a thing. Having high expectations of myself then not living up to them. You say to me, "Stop striving, just surrender, and rest in My Love for you."

The struggle with; being Yours without having to do everything perfectly. Do I know You will not leave me if I am not perfect? You say to me, "Stop striving, just surrender, and rest in My Love for you."

The struggle with; being Yours in my weakness. Not covering up for them, trying to hide them, being embarrassed by them, and pretend they are not there. You say to me, "Stop striving, just surrender, and rest in My Love for you."

The struggle with; being Yours in failures. To not condemn myself and beat myself up. You say to me, "Stop striving, just surrender, and rest in My Love for you."

The struggle with; being Yours and receiving You freely without doing something for You. You say to me, "Stop striving, just surrender, and rest in My Love for you."

The struggle with; being Yours and believing I could be Loved this way. Even if I don't know how to fully Love in return. You say to me, "Stop striving, just surrender, and rest in My Love for you."

The struggle ends here. I will focus solely on the enjoyment of being Yours. Without having to prove a thing. Without having to be perfect. Without being embarrassed of my weaknesses. Without condemnation. Without having to "do" anything for You. Without fully knowing how to Love You in return. I will experience Your Love that is poured in my heart (Romans 5:5). This will be my common everyday enjoyment! Just to be Yours! I will stop striving, I surrender all, and I rest in Your Love for me! **End of journal entry.**

GIVE HIM ALL

The world tries to mold us and tell us what we need to do to succeed. The world will try to put us in a box. Do not let what the world says define you. Submit to God and surrender your ways to His ways. He is perfect. God will place you where He wants you. There is no box for God. He is limitless. Your life is divinely planned, divinely led, and divinely in His hands (Proverbs 3:5-6). You will not have to work at living life at all. God does not do things in part but in full (Jeremiah 2:5-9, 11).

It is time we give Him what He deserves and that is our all or nothing. He gave us His everything. He did not hold anything back from us. Why do we think it is okay for us to hold some of ourselves back from Him? Love the Lord your God with ALL your heart (not part), ALL your mind (not part), ALL your soul (not part), ALL your strength (not part). There are too many "part timers" today! They want the miracles, they love His gifts, but not the life He is calling them to live.

Nothing but full surrender will satisfy Him. Love gives all and must have all in return. As a bridegroom rejoices over his bride, so does He rejoice over you (Isaiah 62:5). When we are married to someone and utterly in Love with them, do we keep one foot in the door and the other foot out? Waiting for something better? Of course not! Do we only give our spouse part of us? Of course not! (At least we shouldn't!) Why is it any different with the Lover of our soul, our Bridegroom King, the One we are betrothed to, and will marry one day?

If we are not in constant communion with Jesus, how can we stay in the place of sweet surrender giving Him our everything? If we wake up in the mornings and walk out the door without being in communion with Jesus, then we are walking out the door surrendering ourselves to the world. What are we waking up to in the morning and saying, "Here am I?" If it is not Jesus, in time alone with Him, in surrender, in His Word, then it is the world.

Who do you want to be surrendered to? A Loving Father or a ruthless enemy? Silly question, I know! Yet day after day we wake up and walk out the door and say, "Here am I" to our ruthless enemy because we have not been with Jesus in communion and surrender. Give Him your all! Do not let the enemy have any of it! Do not allow him a foothold!

I am here to give you hope. Hope for yourselves. Hope for your children. Hope for your grandchildren. Hope for anyone you know, watching them "throw" their lives away. Anyone you are standing in faith for, for them to turn their lives around and surrender. The Lord got through to me and I know He can get through to them. Have faith.

This could be you if you struggle through life day in and day out, now is the time to be made free from this vicious cycle! Give Him everything and be done with living your way. The Lord is patient, and kind, and oh so faithful!

PRACTICAL APPLICATION:

1. In surrender, we sometimes feel the "worst" habit we have, or the

addiction must be the first to go and we make it our main goal. We fail in our own power to quit doing those things. We must give over in surrender our attitudes, thoughts, responses, our actions, everything. The Lord spoke this to me one day, "You cannot take "this" into the future I have for you. If you want My best for your life, give it all up for Me."

I was a smoker. Every time I tried to quit on my own (and I was so determined to) I would fail. I decided I was going to give it over to the Lord. Even while I was having a cigarette, I would pray for Holy Spirit to remove the desire to smoke from me. You see, I wanted to smoke, I enjoyed it. I wanted to quit because I wanted to be an accurate representation of Jesus to the world. Not having to rely on a substance for anything. I also wanted to keep the temple where the Lord dwells pure. And now God was asking me to give it up. Yet, I really needed Holy Spirit to remove the desire from me.

I needed to continue, by faith, to know this was already defeated. To walk in faith by handing it over to Holy Spirit to have His way in me. Every time something went "wrong" I needed Him to be who I ran to and not a cigarette. I needed Him to transform me in every way regarding smoking. The way I thought about it, my desire for it, even the "need" for it. And He did. But it was not anything I could force myself to do. He had to do the work in me. My job was to be intentional and faithful in surrendering it to Him every time (no matter how long it took). One day I woke up and the desire was not there. I was done smoking. I will say it took me awhile to be around people who smoked. When I was, I would have emotional struggles with it. That environment would be difficult for me, however, in time that went away as well. Now I can be around them and it does not bother me at all.

I had a hard time with this concept for a long time, all my life really, because in my mind I was the one making the decision to smoke so I was the one who had to make the decision to not smoke. I am the one lighting up this cigarette then I must be the one to stop lighting it. Makes sense, right? I could not understand where the power was and that it was in my surrender to Holy Spirit to do the work. I can admit I felt pretty stupid smoking and praying at the same time. However, I did it. Every single time I would ask Him to take it from me until one day it was gone.

For me this did not happen overnight, but it can. It can happen whatever way the Lord so chooses. The manifestation of our freedom from an addiction, a bad habit, wrong thought patterns, etc. doesn't only have to happen how it happened for me. This was only a way to show you an example of what surrender will look like. You follow the Lord with what He is showing you. He may show you some things you have to do differently. The key is to surrender to Him, listen to Him, and obey what He is saying to do.

2. Another Example: I go to be alone with Holy Spirit behind closed doors genuine and sincere, and I am really worried about something. I simply talk to Him about it. I do not beat up on myself. I do not say how stupid I am because I know I am not supposed to worry. My conversation with Him will look like this:

"Father I know in Your Word You say to me not to worry about anything and what will worry add to my life? I am asking You Holy Spirit to bring me to a deeper revelation of who You are. I evidently have worry because I do not fully trust You. Holy Spirit please reveal to me Your Truth, in Love. I humbly surrender to You. I choose to live crucified to worry, I do not want it at all. I want to trust You completely and not think twice about it. I empty myself of all of me so You can fill me with all of You. Teach me how to cast all my cares onto You and know in the depths of my heart how much You care for me. To trust You are taking all these cares and providing a way. Thank You for doing this in me. For there is no fear in Love and Your perfect Love casts out fear and he who fears has not been made perfect in Love (1John 4:18). Lord, perfect me in Love! In Jesus name, Amen."

Then I trust He is doing the work I have given Him to do. God will maintain authority in my soul if I <u>remain submitted to Him</u>. He will indeed. It may not change overnight, and I do not know how long it will take. However, every time worry comes back, I give it right over to the Lover of my soul. My job is to surrender, trust, listen, and obey. His job is to do the transformation in me. One day I will recognize that I have not worried in a day, a week, in over a month and realize it is gone. Completely gone. I am full of faith and Love and not worry.

I want to also add to this, the more we dwell in intimacy and relationship with our Lord, the more we will know Him. When we know Him for who He is we will then find it is not hard to trust Him to take care of every part of us. Psalm 55:22, "Cast your burden on the LORD, and He shall sustain you; He shall never permit the righteous to be moved." We can do all things through Christ who strengthens us (Philippians 4:13). Without Him we can do NOTH-ING. We cannot, only He can. Lay down everything you have been carrying at His feet. Your life will be radically changed once you surrender ALL and do not hold onto anything.

3. Another important thing to address is knowing how to follow Him. He says if we acknowledge Him in all our ways, He will direct our path (Proverbs 3:5-8). But how do we know the direction He is leading us? There are several things He will do; it is not cookie cutter and the exact same for everyone. However, there are common denominators we can depend on.

A) We go to His Word. We see what His Word says about a matter, and He will lead us by His Word.

B) We must be fully surrendered. Say we go into prayer about a job. Should we take this one? Or this one? So, we ask Him for His direction. But if we never fully surrender our will, feelings, and thoughts to Him, we will go into prayer and walk away with all our own reasons why God would surely have us go with "this one" because "it is so obvious." However, a way that seems right to a man will lead to death (Proverbs 14:12). We must be fully surrendered to accurately hear Him and know where He is leading us. We must empty ourselves of all our own thoughts, ideas, and reasoning. Deny our flesh. Do not allow to be led by our flesh and surrender to Him.

C) We wait if we do not hear from Him right away, we wait until we do. If we feel rushed into a decision and we do not have the answer yet, we wait! We do not make a move without Him. The enemy will always try to pressure us into something, the Lord will not. Always bringing every thought into captivity into the obedience of Jesus (2 Corinthians 10:5). When we do not wait on Him for an answer, we will walk away and forge our own path. Where He has not gone before us and cleared the way.

D) He will bring us confirmations through various ways. Whether it be from wise counsel, or a friend. It could even be in a dream. However, I know He will bring us confirmation if we ask (Judges 6:36-40).

JOURNAL ENTRY:

No one has ever died for me except for Jesus. No one has ever gotten beaten and whipped beyond recognition for me with flesh torn apart hanging from His body, except Jesus. No one has taken all this kind of injustice for me, being completely innocent and then dying for me so I could be reconciled to God and be made completely free. Jesus paid it all for me. So, I choose, not "I have to" no, I choose to give Him all of me…. this is Love. And He has given me so much more than I could ever imagine. So, I will gladly give Him my life and I will follow Him.

I will give everything up for You Lord. Although I must admit what I have to give You is broken, severely broken. I give You this shattered unrecognizable life of mine. Please put me back together as is pleasing to You. Father, I come to You broken hearted, yet I know in all things you work for the good of those who Love You and are called according to Your purpose (Romans 8:28). You can do immeasurably more than all I can ask for or imagine according to Your power that is at work within me (Ephesians 3:20). I lay my requests before You and wait in expectation (Psalm 5:3). For You perform wonders that cannot be fathomed and miracles that cannot be counted (Job 5:9).

Give me what I need to be who You created me to be. Father, You will give me what I need each and every day. You are more than enough. Out of this suffering, You will make something beautiful. What I lost to the world's ways and to the enemy's lies, what seems far beyond repair, in Your mercy, You redeem and make brand new. You can take the broken pieces in Your hand and make me whole again! Holy Spirit, I pray You teach my soul to soar. Train me in Your Holy ways Lord! There is NOTHING like Your Love! You have never rejected me or will ever reject me. You will never leave or abandon me! I will not think upon what the enemy is doing or has done, what he is saying or has said, because it is all lies. If it is not from You, my Father, and in line with Your Truth, it is ALL lies, and I WILL NOT believe it! I will not worry, for it only leads to evil (Psalm 37:8). My God can move the mountains. He is mighty to save! I will not let my mind think upon the days of old. I will not wish for those days to come back. For I was not living in Your fullness I was living in my-self. I will think upon what You do, for You are doing a new thing, it will spring forth and I will see it (Isaiah 43:18-19). **End of journal entry.**

A Prayer to Pray:

"Jesus take my thoughts and make them Your thoughts. Open the eyes of my understanding. Lord Jesus, take my ways and make them Your ways. For Your ways are higher than my ways. Help me to walk in complete obedience to You. Jesus take my heart and make it Your heart in me. I want to Love the way You Love, overcoming death and darkness. Jesus, take all my desires and make them Your desires. You are the One I desire and seek after. I want to be filled with the desires of Your heart. Lord, I need You to order every single step of my life, so I do not make a move without You.

Lord, I know I have choices to make, and I want what I choose to be what You have chosen for me. I want my choices to line up with Your redemptive plan for my life. I do not want to mess this up or delay my purpose or progress ever again. I am asking You for everything I need to walk out the life You have for me. Jesus, I need You.

Father, every time I have questioned You in an irreverent way, I repent. All the time I spent wrestling against You, I repent. Here at the End Of Me, Lord, let this be my final surrender. That I will never try it alone again, doing my own thing, my own way. Turning away from what You would have me do. Lord, I want to be fully surrendered to You. Any area where I am still clinging to worry or control, please reveal it to me so I can let it go. I want to be totally fixed on You (Isaiah 26:3). I am thankful for Your correction in my life, I welcome it. I am grateful for Your saving grace rescuing me out of the sinking sand I was in. You are preparing me for whatever it is You have for me. You alone are my hope. I give You all of me. To walk hand in hand with You in unbroken relationship. Have Your way. Your will be done. Every last bit of me must be surrendered to You so Here am I Lord, in Absolute Surrender. In Jesus name, Amen."

Five Take Aways

1. Surrender is the only way we can have a successful walk of following Jesus Christ.
2. Anything not surrendered is now open season for satan to have his way.
3. Surrender is total abandonment of myself to dive into total trust in Jesus.
4. Our lives are care-free, in surrender, because we know the God we have. Not because everything is perfect.

5. Worry (look up the many synonyms for worry) and trust are dia-
    metrically opposed. If we worry, we cannot trust Jesus.

Picture drawn by Chloe Horsfall & Kaylie Horsfall

1 Corinthians 15:36, "... What you sow is not made alive unless it dies."

John 12:24 ESV (parenthesis added), "Truly, Truly, I say to you, unless a grain of wheat (a seed) falls into the earth and dies, it remains alone; but if it dies, it bears much fruit."

Chapter 4

Die To Live

Die, Baptized, & New

I did it, I took the leap. I took the leap of faith, and I jumped. In that moment, suddenly, I realized what I had done as I was quickly falling. I had jumped off the highest summit. I felt a myriad of feelings as I dropped. I will admit I was scared; I did not know what to expect. I just knew I had to do it. I had to go. I could not stay where I was. And I heard Holy Spirit gently whisper to me, "You can do it, Sunshine, you can do it." So, I did it, I jumped! Down I go, go, go, go.... with a lifetime full of failures, regrets, and shame speeding by me as I was falling.

I was watching a movie of my past life on the way down. Seeing it all there in technicolor and on display. All the good, the bad, and the ugly. But somehow, I knew it would all be okay. That life as I knew it, there on the movie screen, would not stay the same. Oddly enough, I knew it would change from here on out. And as I quickly plummeted towards the ground, Jesus reached out His arms and caught me. Just in time.

Not only did He catch me, but I landed in the waters of baptism. With a huge splash washing over me, engulfing me, cleansing me. The water felt good to my soul, and I have never been so pure in my entire life. As I came up, I gasped for air, and I experienced a new birth. I came up out of that water NEW. A brand-new creation born from above. The old was gone (2 Corinthians 5:15-17), completely gone.

Sometimes I think we take for granted the "little" words. One day I am going to write a book on the not so little, "little" words. So, let's take a look at the definition of new. New; is something that has **never** existed before. Selah. Really think about what the Word of God is telling us. In this case there is someone that has never existed before. That someone being me. In this moment is a me that has NEVER existed before. All things are made NEW in Christ.

And just like that all my past that had flown by me on the movie screen called life, on my way down from the highest mountain top, was now gone. Forever gone. Every regret gone! Every failure gone! All sin and shame gone, all gone! Now...now I have entered the Promised Life.

However, to become this new creation and live this Promised Life, there must first be a death. The old gone so the new can come. We are to deny ourselves and stop living for ourselves. We cannot live a **new** life if we continue to live in all our **old** ways. We must understand we have been crucified with Christ being made dead to sin and our old ways (Romans 6:1-23, 2 Corinthians 4:10-11, 2 Corinthians 5:17, Galatians 2:20 (KJV), Galatians 5:24, 1 Peter 2:24, 1 Peter 4:1-2, Colossians 3:3-10, Romans 8:12-14). Just a few of the Scriptures to reference this.

This is what happened when I jumped. I made the definitive decision not to live for my-self any longer (which all of self is ruled by satan) and to consider my-self crucified with Christ. I chose from here on out to live in Jesus Christ alone. Holding nothing back for "me" as so many of us do. But I gave Him all of me.

To remind you, the death I speak of, and the Word of God speaks of is not a physical death of our physical body. It is also not the death of our soul (our mind, will, and emotions). The death spoken of is **dying to the self-life** to truly live (Romans 8:13). If we do not consider ourselves to be dead to sin (Romans 6:11 ESV) and all that is of the flesh (Galatians 5:24), we will not live and come into this new Promised Life that is only available by living IN Christ Jesus. 2 Corinthians 5:17, "Therefore, if anyone is in Christ, he is a new creation; old things have passed away; behold, all things have become new."

IF anyone is IN Christ, he is a new creation. Another not so little, "little" word is "in." If you look up the word "in," in the Greek you will find a statement saying, "to give self wholly to." To live as this new creation, it is a giving of oneself wholly to Him and then abiding (staying, dwelling) in Him all day long every day (please read John 15:1-8).

One day I was journaling this thought: "You know if you are in or not." You know if you are sincere, have given yourself to Him completely, and are living in Him. Yet I believe there are many who are deceived. They think they are living in Jesus with their facade, and they do not even realize they are so far out. This is a disheartening realization and has been a great motivation for this book.

For Example: Someone can read their Bible for an hour every day of the week and they can think they are "so in" because of it. However, if they do not look like Jesus and act like Jesus then they are really "so far out," and they do not even know it. **By this** we know we are IN Him. He who says he abides IN Him ought himself to walk just as He walked (1 John 2:6).

I long for people to know Him. To enter this life of fellowship with Him and really be IN Him. Living in this world just as Jesus did. Living dead to their flesh and sinful ways. After journaling this, I kid you not, the very next day I had received an email from a retail store and in the subject line it says this very thing, "You. Are. So. In!" "Lol, God, I Love You!" I am telling you He has a sense of humor. He is so funny!

Back to 2 Corinthians 5:17, there is also an "if" in this passage. And an "if" is a really BIG "little" word in the Bible. An "if" implies there is a condition. That means it is contingent on a decision we have to make. "If" always declares we have a choice. I am a new creation IF I have given myself wholly to Christ and I abide IN Him. If I am not living my life in Christ, then I will not have access to the new creation that is available.

We can believe in Jesus and yet not abide IN Him. Never becoming new and not bearing fruit (please read John 15:1-8). Because again, the sign of abiding in Christ is to walk just as He walked. We can believe in Jesus, go to Sunday service, read our Bibles, and still struggle with the same old habits, and same old sin nature day in and day out. Because we are not living (abiding) IN Him by giving ourselves **wholly** to Him. We are still very much alive to our flesh. I get it I was here too!

Sidenote: I am not trying to imply you are not saved here. If you are saved and still living in the flesh it is because you are carnal as Holy Spirit tells us in 1 Corinthians 3:1-3. You are still ruled and controlled by your flesh. You are a babe, still on milk, that is not growing up and living the crucified life. We are to grow up in the Lord just as we grow physically. From babies, to toddlers, to children, to mature sons and daughters.

While we are going over the meaning of some of these "little" words, I just want to point out something. I have realized a lot of times, we Christians, have the "right" words to say. We can say all the "right" things. We have the lyrics but not the melody (the life) to go with them. This is because we are not living our lives IN Him. Jesus is the music of our souls. He is the rhythm of our hearts. He is our heartbeat. I, **for a long time**, lived a miserable life saying the "right" things and even doing some of the "right" things. These things were not always "wrong," there was just no Life in them. There was no heartbeat because I was living them outside of Jesus. I was a believer who was not dead to self. I was not a new creation. I was still living the old life.

Quite frankly there are a whole lot of people out there who live this way because they have never believed themselves to be dead to sin. They have never died to their old ways of living. They have not lived crucified in the self-life, denying themselves. If you have "signed" up for the <u>body of Christ</u> and say you are a member of it, you have signed up to live dead to your self-life, old ways, attitudes, and sin. Do not consider this a "bad deal," it is the greatest thing that could ever happen to you in this life. **The Greatest!**

Please understand (in all your getting get understanding Proverbs 4:7), you cannot have a NEW life, if you are still living your OLD ways. Mark 2:22, you do not put new wine into old wineskins. He will not put a new life into your old ways of living. There must be the end of something (a death) before there can be a NEW beginning. Are you still doing things to satisfy and gratify your flesh? Why would you seek to satisfy what is supposed to be dead?

Andrew Murray says in *The Master's Indwelling*, "The reason Christians pray and pray without results for the Christ-life to come into them is that the self-life is not denied." The two cannot occupy the same space. Jesus tells us if we want to follow Him, we must **deny ourselves** and take up our cross (Luke 9:23). Looking up the Greek word for deny it means to deny utterly that is disown. Jesus told us, our self is to be utterly disowned to follow Him. This is not an option to follow Him, it is a must.

Matthew 10:38 Jesus says, "And he who **does not take his cross**, and **follow after Me**, <u>is not worthy of Me</u>." Wow! If we choose not to deny our flesh, if we choose not to be dead to selfishness, our own will, everything lustful, sinful, prideful, etc., AND follow Him, we are not worthy of Him! Think about this. What does it look like to follow Jesus? Jesus did not walk in one bit of selfishness or in His own will (John 5:19) or in ways that were lustful and sinful. And He tells us to FOLLOW HIM. Selah! These are not my words. They are Jesus' words.

He also says in Luke 14:33, "So likewise, whoever of you **does not forsake ALL that he has, cannot be my disciple**." We talked about what forsaking all looks like in Chapter 3, in the section "Surrender All: What It Means." These passages, just referenced from Scripture, are some tough words to swallow. **I get it!!** I was there too at one point. When I was facing this head on in my life. Now, it's time we get real with what Jesus is saying and stop trying to brush it aside as if He doesn't really mean what He says. Trying to justify His Words to fit our own wants, desires, and selfish lives. It does not work that way.

I mentioned the song "I surrender all" in the last chapter. Another song we will sing boisterously in church with all the others is, "I have decided to follow Jesus, I have decided to follow Jesus, I have decided to follow Jesus, no turning back, no turning back." Do we even know what this means?? To give up me and deny my-self (utterly disown) to follow Thee? Please Read 1 Peter 2:20-25.

We really do and absolutely turn our backs on self, and on self's motives, self's aims, self's will, all of the self-life! But this is the most glorious decision you can ever make! Self, which is controlled by satan, only leads to death. Self will steal from you, kill you, and destroy you! Jesus came to give you life more abundantly (John 10:10)! When I started living this life in Christ, is when I really came alive! Truly living life to its fullest. It is beautiful! It is glorious! No turning back, no turning back.

Unfortunately, most of us have bought into a shallow "me first" faith. Many Christians want to worship Christ the Messiah and King, but we do not want to look like Jesus the Man. We want His miracles, blessings, prosperity, and provisions but we do not want to partake in His sufferings like picking up the cross to deny our-self, as we are instructed to do by Jesus Himself. We want the benefits and gifts He has to offer but not the life He is calling us to. We accept Christ for our benefit, and we get mad when we do not get what we want. Consider your-self dead, crucified with Christ!

Romans 6:1-4, do you not know those baptized INTO Christ Jesus have been baptized INTO His death? And now we should walk in NEWness of Life. What a great tragedy we do to the meaning of baptism when we do not fully understand what we are supposed to be declaring by doing it. Die to self and be raised/resurrected in Christ to walk in newness of Life.

Dead to sin (read Romans chapter 6) and all of the self-life, this is what baptism is. But we make it more about giving our lives to Christ and an outward expression of our confession of faith rather than **living a dead-to-self, life.** What you are really saying, declaring, and expressing when you get baptized is, "I DIE." Please do not do this lightly. Know what you are committing to. It is your life given over to your Blessed Savior, and what an amazing life it is!

In our natural birth we were all born into corruption, through Adam, and we all need to be born again, from above, to bring us back into who God created us to be. His image. His reflection. We were first born selfish; we need to be born again as selfless and a servant to all (Mark 9:35). We do not need "self-help" remedies, we need self-dead.

Once we make the decision to consider ourselves dead to our self-life, it is Holy Spirit who has the power to make us into this new creation (which we go over in The Transformed Life chapter). Self cannot cast out self. Only Holy Spirit can evict your-self out and keep it out. Galatians 5:16 NKJV & ESV, I say then: walk in the Spirit, and you will not (not you might not, but you will NOT), fulfill (gratify) the lusts (desires) of the flesh.

Jesus died on the cross and bore all our filth so we could be this NEW creation IN Him. He has accomplished what was necessary to bring us back into unbroken, unhindered relationship and fellowship with our Father. Where God intended for us to always live. Holy (pure), blameless (sinless), and above reproach (without a single fault) in His sight (Colossians 1:19-24), IF (your choice) indeed you continue in the faith, grounded and steadfast. Jesus paid the price to bring us back to original condition = His image (Genesis 1:26).

Jesus died for you and for me. And this too is what we are called to do "...Follow Me" (Matthew 4:19), Jesus proclaims. We are to believe and receive the death of ourselves. That we have been crucified with Christ. So that we do not live for ourselves, but we live for Him (2 Corinthians 5:15). This dying to ourselves means we die to ALL that is in us that is not of God, for God, or from God, it all must go.

I encourage you to take the leap and jump off of that highest summit you have been teetering on. Going back and forth, back and forth, into the world and then into the Christian life. Living for yourself then living for Jesus. I sit here in tears as I write this. My heart cries for you to make this decision. I promise you it will be the best decision you have ever made. My life has been better than I could have ever imagined it to be. Not because everything goes perfectly but because I have given myself wholly to, He, who is perfect in every way.

Someone had shown me a Facebook post once. It was a skeleton sitting on a bench dressed in woman's clothes with a sign that said, "Waiting for a perfect man." As in she has been waiting that long for the perfect man to come along! I chuckled, but then my immediate thought was, "Jesus is waiting for you!" Give yourself to Him, the perfect Man in every way. Do it! Take the fall test! Take the plunge into the waters of baptism! Die to truly live!!!

A PRAYER TO PRAY:

"Jesus, today I make the decision to live as a dead man, who is dead to myself, and I choose to live in You alone. To where it is no longer I who live but You who lives in me. Thank You, all things are new according to Your Word, as I live in You and walk in Your Spirit. Everything not of You, for You, or from You be cut off and thrown into the fire. According to Your Word, the old me is crucified, dead, and buried. I abandon my old ways of thinking and the old ways of doing things. I come into the new life You have for me. I am a new creation, old things have passed away, all things are new. In Jesus name, Amen!"

MY PAST GONE & FORGIVENESS

Someone once said to me something along the lines of, I can't imagine how I would be if this (someone else's life) was my story. If this is what happened to me. The way things ended up for my life. I understood the compassion in what this person was saying. However, I quickly realized this is how most of us live our lives. Who we have become is according to the "hand that life dealt us," and everything we have been through, instead of who Christ is in us.

It doesn't matter what our story is if we are living dead to self. Our only answer always, is to be Christ-like. Not to live according to our own feelings of the flesh. Being self-absorbed, having self-pity, holding grudges, etc. But to live according to the feelings of Holy Spirit (We learn about this way of living in the chapter Detox My Heart).

Then my thought shifted to, "How am I "supposed" to act, or what "should" I be like because of my story and all that has happened to me?" The answer is exactly the same. I am to be like Christ. Not hurt, offended, holding a grudge, disappointed, discouraged, walking around with a chip on my shoulder, etc. (Did Jesus ever do any of this?) Then say these are all "justified" feelings I have because of what I "went through." When we are dead to self the only way, we are to be is Christ-like. We never have any excuse to not be. Ever. No matter how our life has turned out, Christ in us has never changed.

Hebrews 12:1-4, We are told to consider Christ Jesus who endured such hostility from sinners against Himself, lest we become discouraged. Yet we consider everything else but Christ Jesus! What Jesus has been through ought to motivate us more than what we have been through. We did not have to die for the sins of the world. No trial I go through is as difficult as what Jesus endured. We must take the focus off us and fix our gaze on Jesus! Let it be, wherever we go from here on out, it will be known from our Christ-like lives, behaviors, and conversations we are followers of Jesus Christ and not a product of our story.

When we enter this new Promised Life in Christ Jesus our past has been redeemed by Him. He is the only One who can re-write history. No matter what has happened or what we have done, we get a brand-new fresh slate. A new start. We get a "do over." I am holy, pure, blameless, and in my original created condition which God always intended for me, from here on out. What happened in the past does not exist anymore. There may be repercussions of my choices that have to play out, but it does not change the Truth that my new Life in Christ has begun. I am a new person henceforth.

When we believe, come to full surrender, and receive the crucified life Jesus accomplished on the cross, we can lay down everything in our past and let go of it for good. We can give every single memory of our past to Jesus. We can give Him every behavior that was put into place due to those memories and what may have happened in our past. We can repent, forgive, and give it all to Jesus. We do not have to stay here in these same old ruts and cycles. The healthiest thing to do is to go before the Lover of your soul and pour it all out to Him. Give Him everything!

Do not deny your past or what happened by trying to skirt around it. Face it with Him, feel it with Him, express it to Him. Do not rationalize your past away or make excuses for it. Stop burying it in the yard or ignoring it by sweeping it under the rug. Only for it to pop back up again whenever it rains, or the rug gets moved.

We are very good at not facing things, so we don't have to think about it.

We are proficient at taking detours around difficulties and finding "short-cuts" to not have to deal with everything. However, Jesus will deliver us **through** these difficulties, trying times, and events, not by going **around** them. But by facing it head on. Go through it WITH Him and receive your healing Jesus has paid the price for. Your complete healing. Not just partial healing but wholeness. He heals every part of us.

I have to say this here and now, there are lies, BIG LIES out there, that living dead to self is harder than staying the same. There is a lie that denying the flesh will hurt more than continuing to live the way you are living. A lie that says living for your-self and gratifying your flesh is the more fun and easy way to live.

Things are said like, "I don't want to go there or open that door, it will just bring up old stuff and I will hurt all over again." It may! It may open old wounds. But going through it with the Lord will bring you the healing you need. They will no longer be "old wounds" but **healed wounds** that do not hurt anymore and never will hurt again. Now, you never have to think about them again if you don't want to. But if you do it will not bother you, because they will not hurt!

We also will say, "I don't want to face that (sin, issue, addiction, brokenness, etc.) right now, that is another day's problem," because these things may seem unsurmountable and overwhelming. And "another day" never comes. Our own thoughts will deceive us. All the while we don't even realize the sin, the issue, the addiction, the brokenness in our life is killing us. Our soul is now on the slow fade to death. We need to face it today. Let's get this straight again, we want our flesh dead. We want to live dead to the self-life. We do not want our body or souls to die. We want our souls (our mind, will, and emotions) to be very much alive IN Christ and be led by Holy Spirit and not the flesh.

In His presence is the place where we can be real with Jesus. We do not have to hide what we are feeling, what we are thinking, how we may be hurting, or what we are struggling with. There is a healing that comes in this place like no other. When you can cry in His presence and just let Him hold you as a child, His dearly beloved child. He heals you so completely and perfectly here. In essence, Jesus says, "Bring this all to Me. Now let's watch it all die. So, I can resurrect you, brand new in Me. Now you can be conformed to My ways and My thoughts, and I can live through you."

Now we can truly forgive (this means to even forgive ourselves). When we have received His healing, we can let go. The past no longer exists. As if it never happened. This is how we remain free of offense. You may say impossible, but I tell you it is not. I have lived this kind of freedom in forgiveness. Where I no longer hurt. Jesus has completely healed every wound.

Now we can pick up our cross, and follow Him (Matthew 16:24), and forgive others even as God in Christ has forgiven us (Ephesians 4:32). How were we forgiven? Completely and totally. We were extended mercy when we were in our sin (Hebrews 8:12), and this is what we are to do for others, "even as."

In Matthew 18:23-35 (please read) this is where the servant who was forgiven all his debt then went out and demanded payment from his servant. This is one of those Scriptures I have read or heard about many times but one day when reading it I was brought to tears and to my knees in repentance. It hit me hard this day, the realization that I have been forgiven ALL my sin. Jesus paid the debt I owed and then I in return want to hold on to what someone else has "done to me?" All I can say is, I was wrecked!

We can forgive, **forget** it, move forward, and be free from it! It is all in the sea of forgetfulness (Isaiah 43:25 & Micah 7:19). I think I heard more gasps and a response that sounds something like this, "We are human, we can forgive but we will **never** forget. God can forget but we cannot." I used to believe this until I experienced for myself the Truth and power of His Word. In Isaiah 43:18-19, He tells us not to remember the former things nor consider (regard) the things of old. <u>Do not remember or even consider</u>! Why would He tell us to do this if it were not possible?

In Philippians 3:13 we are told, this one thing I do <u>forgetting those things which are behind</u>. In Ecclesiastes 5:20 ESV (AMP in parenthesis), "For <u>he will not much remember</u> the (troubled) days of his life because God keeps him occupied with joy in his heart." These scriptures are truly how we can keep no record of wrong. How do we keep record of something that has been erased from our memory?

People say we can forgive but never forget. My God says otherwise. So, I put it into practice. Let me tell you, His Word does not return void (Isaiah 55:11). What I do remember is so far healed <u>(with no side effects)</u> that it serves as a testimony to what God has done in my life. A testimony of His healing, goodness, and faithfulness to me. Where He has brought me from, and what He has brought me through. All to the glory of God, Praise Him! Yet there is so much of my past I do not remember, nor do I need to, and again Praise Him!

Jesus, by His blood, death, and resurrection, has destroyed the power of every negative effect the past has had on us. Jesus has broken the chains of every negative behavior that was put into place because of our past. We can receive Jesus' healing for every negative effect the memories have had on us. Receive His healing and be filled with the newness of Life in Christ Jesus. Receive everything it is you need from Him and be free! This is His healing, Love, and care for you.

When we choose to forgive and keep no record of wrongs, we can let go and forget the former things to walk in freedom. When satan tries to remind us, we choose to say NO! We do not rehearse the wrongs done we rejoice instead at God's amazing grace. We rejoice because as we are forgiven by God, we also forgive others and now these things are in the sea of forgetfulness. As if they never happened. The following are some Scriptures to turn to should you ever have difficulty with saying "No" to rehearsing the wrongs of the past. Please look them up in your Bible and read them in full. These are only in part:

1. 1 Corinthians 13:5, Love keeps no record of wrong.
2. 2 Corinthians 10:5, Take captive every thought to the obedience of Jesus Christ. Why think on anything less than Jesus??
3. Isaiah 26:3, He will keep in perfect peace the mind stayed on Him.
4. Isaiah 55:3-9, His thoughts and His ways are higher than your own.
5. 1 Peter 5:7, Cast the whole of your cares onto Him.
6. 1 John 4:4, Greater is He that is in you than he that is in the world.
7. Romans 8:28, He works all things for good to those who Love Him.
8. Genesis 50:20, What was intended for evil He turns for good.
9. Jeremiah 29:11, His thoughts towards you are peace to give you a good future and hope.

PRACTICAL APPLICATION:

There was a time when I struggled to forgive someone. I had a friend tell me to go to the lake and find some stones. Take a stone and say what I needed to forgive, and then throw the stone into the lake. I thought that was a great idea! So, I did it. If you can find a body of water where you will also be able to find some stones do so. In my example; I would take the stone and say, "I forgive this person for being so selfish." I threw the stone in the water as far as I could, watching it the whole time. Then I took the next stone, "I forgive this person for not loving me." I threw the stone as far as I could, watching it sink into the water. After I did this several times the Lord says to me, "Now are you going to go after them? Even if you did, will you ever find them? See? They are in the lake of forgetfulness." Wow! Selah! I continued to do this until there was nothing more I could think of. Then I fell to the ground and sobbed. As I walked back to my car, I could actually say the words, "I forgive you" and really mean it.

A Prayer to Pray:

"Father, I choose to forgive. I will not remember or even consider the things that have happened. I forget them and they do not exist anymore. Since they don't exist, I cannot replay them in my mind and rehearse them over and over. Instead, I choose to fix my eyes on the new thing You are doing in me and for me. I do perceive it. You are the only One who can rewrite history. Just as if it never happened. Thank You! In Jesus name, Amen."

Now we can truly walk away from our past and move into the future He has for us. The past no longer has a say in our lives. The past does not define who we are, ever! And now the past does not direct our future anymore. Again, we may have some consequences due to our past choices, but it does not negate the Truth that every day is a new day in Christ from here on out. You may be in prison, you may be going through a divorce, but yes even there, all things are NEW! Live it out! Be the Light in the darkness you may be currently going through. Neither divorce nor prison defines you or directs you, only Jesus does.

We no longer have to say, "If I could do it all over again." We have a new beginning in Christ. A new Life we can choose to walk in. If we repent, lay down our past, and give it to Jesus forever, we can walk in the newness of Life He has given us. No one else can do this for you. Giving you a 'do-over.' Rewriting your history. I no longer believe the lie that I am a product of what life has dealt me, or what I created myself by doing things my own way. My-self died, and my past along with it. <u>Anything that may arise from my past is now a part of a former life that no longer exists.</u> There is nothing about who I used to be (before Christ) that exists today. The most powerful testimony is a Life that doesn't look anything like it used to. Praise the Lord!

JOURNAL ENTRY:

You are the One who has been there with me through it all, to hold me. You stepped out of heaven to save me from my mess. I can see You now, in every moment of hurt and pain, you were there holding me. Giving me Your strength to carry on. Now I willingly climb up on that cross, to crucify my flesh. Kissing Your face. Cheek to cheek. Tears flowing and intermingling. I am crucified with You once and for all. I do not want to have anything to do with this flesh anymore. All I want is to follow You. **End of journal entry.**

LIVING AS THE WORLD

It wasn't until I was 42 in December of 2018, broken on my living room floor, that I made the decision to receive Christ's finished work on the cross. This being the death of my-self. I finally gave Him all of me. As I intentionally lived this out, I began to experience the freedom of this blessed Life of dying. It is not always easy, but it is worth it!

I believed in Jesus and was baptized when I was young, around 11 years of age, but I still very much lived as the world all growing up and into my adult years. I never fully received my freedom Jesus had paid the price for. When I was married and raising my boys I went to Sunday and Wednesday services. Because it was the "right" thing to do, to raise them in a "godly" home. I loved Jesus the best I knew how at the time. Paying Him homage by going to services on Sundays, reading my Bible every now and then, and putting in my prayer requests, but for the most part still living like the world.

Living like the world does not always have to mean you go out and party, drink, smoke, do drugs, steal, lie, cheat, etc. Living like the world also means being ruled by feelings and emotions of the flesh. Being ruled by misery, discouragement, fear, worry, anxiety, jealousy, offense, bitterness, anger, etc. Being ruled by insecurities (is a big one). Being ruled by our selfish desires and wants. It means being unstable in our own self-ways. Living for only fun, fun, fun, and gratifying our flesh.

Living like the world by filling our minds with their television shows. What Netflix or Hulu shows do we waste hours binge watching? And what worldly movies can we watch these days without any sexual scenes or innuendos? We also fill our ears with the lyrics to their music (mostly demonic and ungodly). We fill our eyes with their "fashionable" clothes (or lack thereof). Then we end up thinking we are "cool" or "in style" when we wear what we wear with our lack of modesty. Does what we watch bring glory to God? Does what we listen to honor Him? Is He pleased with what we wear? These things matter!

Living like the world by what we post on Facebook or Instagram. Are we trying to prove something? Show off something? Who are we trying to impress with what we post? Do our posts bring God glory? Do they honor Him? Is He pleased with them? Or are they all about us and bringing glory to ourselves? Who and what do we "follow," on social media? What do we "Tweet" on Twitter or "snap" on snap chat? Are we like the world? Or are we like Jesus?

Living like the world in the way we talk to people or treat people. Do we treat others poorly? Do we get frustrated or annoyed with them? Do we act as if they are "less than?" Or do we think more highly of others than ourselves? Do we Love as Christ has Loved us? Do we put others first and are we a servant to all? People should know the Love of Christ through our actions and how we talk to them.

Living like the world in how we spend our money. What do we place value on? This would be the condition of our heart, because where our treasure is (what we put value in) there is our heart also, (Matthew 6:21). What we treasure will determine how we spend our money. What do we think we "have" to have? Are we self-focused in our spending?

What we treasure will also take over our affections. This goes for any area of our lives not just monetarily. Where do we pour our money, emotions, time, and energy? Take an honest inventory of this now and it will give you a good idea on what you treasure in life. Is it Jesus Christ? Your own comfort? Or things of this world?

All these worldly things will lead to destruction if we are not lined up with God's Word and following His instruction. **Only** His ways will lead to Life. Wide is the road (the world's ways) leading to destruction. His way is the narrow path that leads to Life and only a few will find it, agree to it, or choose to go down it, (Matthew 7:13-14).

It was not until I chose to receive and live the crucified life that I began to grasp and understand the mysteries of Christ. I have journals upon journals of things God was showing me and things I was learning over the years, yet I had not fully grasped them or understood them. I had even been in the transformation process for years, albeit trying to change myself most of the time, and failing to do so.

When I made the final surrender and started coming before the Lord every morning and all throughout the day, emptying myself of all of me, so He could fill me with all of Him, this is when things changed. When I desired Him more than anything else or anyone else in the world, this is when I changed. I began to understand what life is all about.

As I denied my-self in surrender to Holy Spirit I started to live for the first time ever. I was not held hostage to my flesh any longer. I was not being taken captive by self, remaining under the rule of satan, anymore. As I was renewing my mind in the Word of God (Romans 12:2), and abiding in the Word, the Truth I knew made me free (John 8:31-32).

The Truth <u>you know</u> makes you free. There are many Christians who are still living in bondage because they do not know Truth. Jesus is the Way, the Truth, and the Life (John 14:6). Jesus is Truth. When you **know Jesus,** He makes you free. <u>We are where we are in this moment, either free or slave, from the Truth we know or the lies we believe.</u>

As I was living dead to my–self in surrender, Holy Spirit was transforming my soul. I was beginning to look and act more and more like Christ. As I look back at my journals over all the years, I see how much God was teaching me, but it would not become my reality until I lived dead to my-self. When self-died it could not have a say in things. When self is alive it gets in the way and breaks fellowship with Him. Self must die so it will not get in the way of Truth. Until self-dies it will distort everything! Self is so selfish.

Once we repent and surrender our lives to Jesus, we must make the choice to deny ourselves, as Jesus tells us to. We are to consider the old ways, the old man, dead. Otherwise, we just get dragged back into the same mess we were in before. Most of the Christian population, who say they are born again, have not received the crucified self-life. They have not died-to-self. It is evident in the way they live and where they put their value. They still live life very selfishly from their own self will, desires, and pursuits. They live in worry, doubt, fear, insecurities, sin, and every other way of the flesh.

Colossians 3:5-6 NLT (NKJV in parenthesis), "So put to death the sinful, earthly things lurking within you. Have nothing to do with sexual immorality (fornication), impurity, lust, and evil desires. Do not be greedy, for a greedy person is an idolater, worshipping the things of this world. Because of these sins, the anger of God is coming on all who disobey Him."

Are there things you are doing that you know do not line up with the will of God? Are you living in adultery or any sexual immorality? Are you pursuing a homosexual lifestyle? Are you chasing after your own selfish desires and the things of this world? Are you greedy, lustful, and coveting? Are you just plainly being disobedient to God?

"So put to death the sinful, earthly things lurking within you!"

BEING BORN AGAIN

Since I mentioned the subject of homosexuality, I am going to address it now. If you are struggling with homosexuality, transgenderism, or any kind of identity crisis, I want to come across very clear to you, and that is for you to know this; you are Loved! Even if you are steeped in sin, you are Loved and worth every bit of freedom Jesus paid the price for on the cross. You must know, you, as a person God has created, are so Loved, deeply Loved. And He has made you free from sin. You just need to believe this Truth and receive it in faith.

There are a couple of statements that are said about living in this sin today I will address. One is, "God made me this way." I will not sugar coat this. I will tell you plain and simple. No, He did not. He did not make you or create you as a homosexual (Leviticus 18:22 ESV & Romans 1:18-32 ESV). If He did, this would go directly against His Word and He is not a man that He should lie (Numbers 23:19). To those who struggle with gender identity, you are Loved! AND God is not confused. He created you as He designed for you to be. It is not up to you to choose what you think you should be.

The second statement is this, "I was born this way." The problem with that statement is we are ALL born into iniquity, we are all born into sin. Since Adam and Eve ate of the tree and sin entered the world, we are all born into a sinful and selfish world. "Being born this way," does not mean God created you this way. It is simply the effect of the fall of sin.

Until we are born again, who we are is never who God created us to be. We are all born into the sin nature, full of selfish desire. Then as we grow up, we are further formed by our society, our environments, other people's opinions, our circumstances, situations, the enemy...life. But never who God created us to be. Yes, even as a baby we can see the selfish tendencies from the effect of the self-life. Just take a pacifier away from a baby who is totally pacified, and they cry. Take a toy away from a toddler and they cry. Children fight with each other yelling, "No mine!" "No mine!" This is all a result of the self-life from the fall.

With that being said, if you want to make the statement, "I was born this way," this is the exact reason why we ALL need to be born again from above. When we are born again, of God, we **then** receive everything God created us to be from the beginning. Being made in His image. When we believe and receive that we are pure, holy, and blameless, we then are transformed into the very likeness of Christ.

We are not here for selfish reasons or to live life for our **fleshly attractions.** If you are struggling with homosexual thoughts or confusion on gender identity, please know that when you come to Jesus in **full** surrender and Holy Spirit transforms your life, you will be made into a NEW creation. Your attractions and desires will submit to the Lordship of Jesus Christ. There is no other way around it. They must submit to Him when you are surrendered to Him. When He is your desire, you become what you behold. Keep beholding Jesus. Never look away. "And the things of earth will grow strangely dim in the light of His glory and grace."

Anything in us that does not look like Jesus is to be denied and put to death. If we cannot see (where it is written in the Word of God) Jesus doing it, then we do not do it. **For Example:** Jesus never sat around with His disciples complaining about His Life. Jesus never put all His time and effort into worldly gain or making a name for Himself.

If we cannot see (where it is written in the Word of God) Jesus saying it, then we do not give ourselves permission to say it. **For Example:** "I hate you," "you are so stupid," "I just worry about you," and a million other things we say, that He would never say. However, Holy Spirit must do this work in us. Our part is to be surrendered to Him and give Him full access to transform us. To have His way in us.

We are to gain His perspective and see everything through His eyes. We are to follow Him. Christ is our example in all things in every way. We have no excuses for, "why we do what we do," or "why we are the way we are." We are crucified with Christ. Everything that was born in Adam must die and be born again of the Spirit. Then we follow Jesus. Because as He is, so are we in this world (1 John 4:17).

God does not want our old nature to survive!! He wants the old nature and its affections, attractions, lusts, complaining, miserable, angry, offended, resentful, doubtful, fearful, insecure, perverted, adulterous, addicted, greedy etc., self-life dead. Most of the time we are so alive to ourselves, and we do not even realize it.

Francis Frangipane says it this way in several statements I have either read or heard by him, "God does not want to make us better but deader."

"He saved me by killing the part of me that was vulnerable to the devil." "To crucify that part of my soul that was so easily exploited by the devil in the first place." This is all referring to living dead to any and all of the self-life that is in us. We are not here for behavior modification but to die completely to self and be made new. Die to Live!

LIFE IS ALL ABOUT JESUS & HIS BRIDE, NOT ABOUT THE SELF-LIFE

I woke up at 2:30AM on January 22nd of 2019, with Holy Spirit speaking this in my ear, "There is a veil of deception over the bride of Christ that needs to be removed." Selah! That is exactly what I did, after I quickly scrambled for a pen and paper to write it down. I paused and thought about the meaning of this. Then I wept.

When we look through a veil, we can still see through it. However, it is not a clear view. By looking through a veil we have a distorted view, a partial view. This is what a veil of deception does to us. It will cause us to not see clearly. Creating lies and distorting the Truth. The lies come ever so subtly in an effort to get us to follow them. By way of religion, religious traditions, false humility, and self-exaltation just to name a few ways the lies will infiltrate us. Holy Spirit was showing me, at large, the church (who is to be the bride of Christ and not a building we go to) has been deceived and following lies.

If self is dead, if we have an intimate relationship with Jesus, if our life is hidden with Christ Jesus in God (Colossians 2:20-3:4), if our life is FULLY surrendered to Holy Spirit, and if we follow Him, then we will not, we cannot be deceived. We will recognize the lies and we will not fall for them. My sheep hear My voice and another's they will not follow (John 10:4-5). "My sheep hear My voice." Knowing His voice comes by being in intimate relationship with Him. Like a baby in a mother's womb can hear the voice of the mother. In nearness and closeness, the child recognizes the voice of the Father.

This was the beginning of Him revealing to me His purpose for this book and what He wants to do through it. This book is meant for us, the church, which is to be Jesus' precious and beloved bride. This book is to help us get ready because He is coming back for a bride that is without spot or wrinkle or any such thing, holy and without blemish, to marry! In the Greek without blemish means blameless or without fault (Ephesians

5:27). We are in the time of preparation to meet our Bridegroom King! The Church has been sleeping and has been largely deceived about what this life is really about. But it is time to wake up and remove the veil of deception. We are to prepare, to become like Christ, and live in expectation for our wedding day!

Now some of you may say, "There is nothing we can do to 'get ready.' It is not by our works. Jesus has done it all." To this I say, "Yes and no." I agree it is not by our works and Jesus has already made us pure, holy, and blameless through His death and resurrection. We are His righteousness. However, we must receive this Truth. If we never receive it, we do not have it.

When we receive it, we then have a sanctification (being transformed by the renewing of our minds Romans 12:2) process we must go through. Revelation 19:7 (KJV) says, "... His wife hath made herself ready." When you look into what this means in the Greek it says that this refers to an internal fitness.

Our relationship with Jesus always requires our participation. Yes, "It is finished" and He has accomplished everything. However, our part in getting ready (having internal fitness) is by giving Him our yielded life. So Holy Spirit can transform us into His image. We are to live the crucified life and abide in Him in intimate relationship. We are to have oil in our lamps and not run out (Matthew 25:1-13). Also, it is our responsibility to receive what He has given us. These are our parts in getting ready.

He cannot do anything unless we give Him our absolute surrender. And this is where the church, as a whole, has "missed it." There are too many who are half-hearted part-timers. Who do not receive the Truth of His Word, are not fully surrendered, and are not living the dead-to-self life.

In Revelation 3:1-2 (ESV), Jesus says to the church, "...I know your works (acts, deeds, labor). You have the reputation of being alive, but you are dead. Wake up, and strengthen what remains and is about to die, <u>for I have not found your works (acts, deeds, labor) complete</u> in the sight of My God."

I know I have been talking a lot about dying so a reminder, we are to die to the self-life and be alive to Christ in us. We do not want to be dead physically, or on the inside (our soul), or dead to Christ. Here Jesus is telling the Church they think they are alive (in Him), they think they are so in, but they are so far out that really, they are dead (in Him). It is time for us to come alive church! Wake up and strengthen what remains. Get ready!

Part of the deception we have fallen for is we have been tricked into seeing a Gospel that ministers to us all the time, instead of making us ministers of Jesus Christ. That "me first" faith I mentioned earlier. **For Example:** We get saved to get to heaven, but we do not live as Christ in this world. We largely have accepted Christ to benefit us instead of transforming us, becoming One with Him.

And if we are not benefitted, we get discouraged because things did not work out the way **we** had planned. Then we get mad at God for it. I would dare to say the greatest death-to-self we need to die to is thinking this life is our own. We are so used to making the Gospel all about us, selfishly about us, and not about the bride of Christ and us becoming like Him. Living in union with Him. Being One with Him.

When the entirety of the Bible is about Jesus, why He came and died for us, and giving Him all the glory He deserves. We bring Him the glory we do not glory in ourselves. We glory in ourselves all too much these days. No **flesh** (self) glories before the Lord (1 Corinthians 1:26-31). Stop thinking about your-self at all.

Sidenote: As a culture, we love ourselves way too much. In saying that, I want to clear up something. When He tells us to Love our neighbor as ourselves, it has zero to do with my-self (my selfish self, my sinful self, my flesh) and everything to do with <u>who Christ is in me</u>. I can Love myself because <u>it is not I</u> who lives but Christ lives in me (Galatians 2:20). I Love who I am because of Him. I Love who He is in me. Who He has made me to be. This is not a selfish love for my-self at all. Most people love themselves selfishly, and it is the wrong kind of love and very damaging to themselves and others around them. The same is true for those who do not know how to love themselves in the right way. They are hard on themselves, don't like themselves, etc. When you cannot see who you are in Christ, then you cannot Love yourself in a healthy way. This is also damaging.

We are not to "use" Christianity as a tool to get what we want or just a way to get to heaven. This is not a come and go as we please kind of life. We are either all in or we are all out. You may not want to hear this but there is no straddling the fence. There is no lukewarm. There is no "maybe." There is no blending. There is no mixture. There is no gray. I say this again, **there is no gray area.**

It is very much white or black (1 Corinthians 10:21-22), right or wrong (James 4:17), Life or death (Deuteronomy 30:15), faith or sin (Romans 14:23), Truth or lie (1 John 2:21), yes or no (Matthew 5:37), hot or cold (Revelation 3:15-16), Spirit or flesh (Galatians 5:16-26). Are we following Christ or are we following satan? Are we dying to the flesh or are we following the lusts of the flesh? Are we surrendered to Christ or are we surrendered to ourselves?

We enter this Life by believing on the name of Jesus and we will be saved (Acts 16:31). Believe in the Greek means to put trust in and to commit to. To believe is to receive Jesus Christ and become obedient to what He says in His Word. To put to death all self-interest and self-reliance, and to trust Him completely. It is our complete surrender, commitment, and dependency upon Him in all things. It is not just acknowledging the facts and realities of Truth because the demons <u>also believe</u> and tremble (James 2:19).

As you can see to believe is the first step of faith, but it does not end there. Jesus welcomes everybody into the family, but it is not just repentance, a prayer, and that's it. While going on with your life, your plans, and your ways. <u>It is repentance, a prayer, and then a standard is put into your life called, "Follow Me</u>." Our actions, our ways, our life, must accordingly follow our confession of faith in Jesus Christ.

The life of faith looks like the cross. It looks like crucifixion. Galatians 5:24, "And those who are Christ's have crucified the flesh with its passions & desires." When we say we believe on Jesus we are committed to Him. If we are committed to Him, we will then do as He says in His Word. We will not be making excuses to live our own way or to do our own thing. We will not be ignoring the convictions of Holy Spirit when we are living in sin. We follow Christ and the ways of Christ.

Christianity is also not buffet style dining where you can pick and choose what you would like to partake of. Taking the things you want and leaving out the things you do not. "I will take the blessings and prosperity but leave out the suffering and picking up my cross to follow Him." There also is no menu in living a life of faith. Where you can tell the server, "I will take lettuce (the miracles) but leave off the tomato (I don't want to deny myself today). I will take cheese (I will attend services) but leave off the onions (the obedience)." This is not the way Christ lived. And yet somehow this is how we have ended up living all our lives.

How did we settle for such mediocrity in the church and call it the "norm," making life all about us? Only casually seeking Him. Making the Word of God all about what we can get from Him instead of finding out who He is and knowing Him. Making our services all about us saying, "Bless me, bless me, bless me." Instead of ministering to King Jesus.

Andrew Murray from *The Master's Indwelling*, "And until the church of Christ goes down into the grave of humility and confession and until it comes to lay itself in the very dust before God, to wait upon God to do something new, something wonderful, something supernatural and lifting it up, it will remain feeble in all its efforts to overcome the world. Within the church, what lukewarmness, what worldliness, what disobedience, what sin. How can we ever fight this battle or meet these difficulties? The answer is Christ. He must come and live in the individual members. But we cannot expect this except as we die with him. We must go down deeper into the grave of Jesus. We must cultivate the sense of weakness, dependence, and nothingness until our souls walk before God every day in a deep and holy trembling. God keep us from being anything in our own power."

A Prayer to Pray:

"Lord, forgive me of any self-glorifying attitudes I have had and all selfishness. I repent. I seek You and want to know You because You are everything I need. Lord, please uproot out of me every bit of selfishness and utterly obliterate it!" I die to my self-will, nail it to the cross! I kill my will. Forgive me Lord where I have made this life about my-self. Life truly begins and ends at the cross. You are teaching me selflessness. This life is not about what I can get. It is about what I can give. Actually, what You can give through me. Teach me how to give You all my pursuit, attention, devotion, heart, Love, adoration, praise, and worship. Teach me how to minister unto You and what it is You prefer and Love. Teach me how to give You all of me as Your betrothed, as Your bride, Jesus. That I would live forever in union with You, my Bridegroom King. In Jesus name, Amen."

Love Not Your Own Life

Another Scripture I have always heard quoted is Revelation 12:11, we overcome by the blood of the Lamb and by the word of our testimony! Sounds great, right?! And we all yell, "YEAH!!!" However, never did I hear anyone say the rest of that verse... "for they loved not their lives even unto death" (ESV). Woah, woah, woah, you mean I might have to die? I cannot love my life so much as to want to save it? Or what about to "save face?" Can I save my reputation? Or what about my "rights?" Or will we Love not our own lives even if it means death?

Following Jesus Christ may mean we lose our own lives. Following Him may mean we lose relationships, our own agendas, our own plans, material things and yet we still choose to follow Jesus. We overcome by the blood of the Lamb, by the word of our testimony, AND loving not our own lives even unto death.

I want to address what I mentioned of our "reputation" or "our rights" with Scripture. Philippians 2:5-8 ESV & NKJV, "Have this mind in you which was also in Christ Jesus, who, being in the form of God, did not count equality with God a thing to be grasped, (or equality with God was not a thing to cling to for His advantage) but made Himself of no reputation (emptied Himself) by taking the form of a servant being born in the likeness of men. And being found in human form, He humbled Himself by becoming obedient to the point of death, even death on a cross."

Jesus gave up EVERY rightful right He had. His rightful throne. His rightful crown. His rightful place next to the Father in heaven. He had no rights that He laid claim to. And He made Himself of no reputation. He was emptied of Himself. And He says to us, "Follow Me." So, we have the right to deny ourselves. Being emptied of ourselves and to follow Him.

We are not to love our own lives. We are not our own (1 Corinthians 6:19). We are not to count our lives dear to us (Acts 20:24 & Philippians 3:7-8). If we love our own lives satan has much advantage over us. he has much to hold over our heads and to conquer us by. If we love our loved ones more than Jesus, the same holds true, the enemy has much to destroy us with. What we have, what God has blessed us with, the most precious things in our lives, and even our own lives, cannot possess us or control us. My crucifixion with Christ has SEVERED all ties to this life.

When those things do not possess us or control us, and when we do not cling to our own life, when we do not fear death, there is really nothing satan can do to us. Being in this place overcomes any weapon the enemy tries to come at us with. When we believe Philippians 1:21, to live is Christ and to die is gain, how can satan have any advantage over us? Or how can any threat against us be effective? How can you kill a dead man (one who is dead to the self-life)? You cannot. One cannot kill what is already dead.

People can get gripped with fear of dying. I have good news, to live free from your-self is to live free from fear. When you are selfless you are fearless. Because you have nothing to lose, and you have everything to gain (again Philippians 1:21). Fear comes because you think for your-self. The biggest bondage in your life is you thinking for you. And your biggest betrayer will be your-self, and will be what kills you, if you do not kill it first. Mark 8:35, For whoever desires to save his life (or tries to keep it or tries to hang on to it) will lose it.

If we are alive to ourselves, we are prisoners of the flesh, the self-life, to satan. Whether it be pleasures, control, attitudes, issues, insecurities, and sin, our enemy is self. From this place of self-satisfaction and gratification we have been conditioned to make decisions. The human nature gravitates towards what is easy, comfortable, and pleasurable. Avoiding anything difficult or painful at all costs. Therefore, satan deceives us to believe satisfying the flesh is so pleasurable. If people view living in the flesh, sin, and self, as pleasurable, instead of knowing it is the sure way to death (of our soul or physical death) this is what they will chase after. We need to know the Truth that makes us free!!

This is a great deception and trap of satan if he can keep us pacified here then we will not move from this place. We will not seek the things of God. We will remain content in our self-centered lives. John 6:63, It is the Spirit who gives Life; the flesh profits nothing. The flesh profits nothing! This means zero return on investment! Why do we continually invest our time and money into the flesh? Investing most of our lives in our flesh to get nothing in return except brief momentary pleasure that fades. It does not last otherwise we would never need another "fix" to pacify the craving. Romans 8:6 To be carnally (of the flesh) minded is death but to be spiritually (of Holy Spirit) minded is **life** and **peace**. To be carnally minded is really the more painful way to live. To be spiritually minded is where we will find all the pleasures of this Life in Christ.

We need to know this; anything apart from God leads to death. So, let's set this straight now. Galatians 6:8, when you live to satisfy your flesh, yourself life, you will die (in your soul or physically). NLT says, those who live only to satisfy their own sinful nature will reap decay and death = PAIN. This is the way that is difficult that satan keeps so seductively hidden. But those that live to please the Spirit will reap everlasting life from the Spirit = PLEASURE.

Everyone, please see and understand it is more pleasurable to live a life with peace than to decay and die. Do not listen to the lies of the deceiver!!! Remember Jesus came to give us Life and life more abundantly (John 10:10). More abundantly in the Greek means beyond, superabundant (in quantity), or superior (in quality), and excessive, just to name a few. Can there be anything more pleasurable than this? No!

How can one die to themselves knowing they are going to do what their flesh wants anyway? One cannot. We cannot be duplicitous. We must be single eyed. Choosing Jesus over all else. It is not I who lives, it is Christ who lives in me and through me. When it is I who lives, Jesus cannot live through me.

Do you want to die to your flesh to really live? Or live to your flesh to really die? You cannot choose your flesh and Jesus at the same time. It is one or the other. Which one will you choose? It is a choice. Your choice.

Where the Spirit of the Lord is there is freedom (2 Corinthians 3:17). If the Spirit of the Lord is NOT there, there is NOT freedom. People want to think if they are living any way they want to live then they are free. You are not free. You are a slave to your flesh reaping death! The Spirit and the flesh are diametrically opposed, you cannot serve both (Galatians 5:17). The more you are in the way, the less He has control. Those controlled by the flesh cannot please God (Romans 8:8)

He is our only real pleasure and therefore everything that is sent from Him we can have pleasure in. This is full enjoyment of God in all that He is and all that He has given us. Anything apart from Him is meaningless. We absolutely can experience full enjoyment of the things He has given. He has given us marriage, children, grandchildren, friends (relationships of all kinds), occupations, ministries, hobbies, talents, giftings, laughter, etc. Enjoyment conditioned by the reverence of God is essential for living this Life of complete satisfaction in Him. So, keep in mind He is the only One who can truly satiate us (satisfy us and fill us to overflowing). Everything else is a gift and only temporary.

To become completely selfless and to the place where we love not our own lives, we are going to have to go through some things. He is going to have to purge us, prune us, and refine us. Unfortunately, we like to avoid these words, topics, and ideas because we don't want to be uncomfortable, and we do not like pain. We don't want to go through the ridding, the cutting, or the fire. Let me remind you, what Jesus went through; betrayal, rejection, taken for granted, mocked, spit upon, slapped in the face, His beard ripped out, beaten and scourged beyond recognition, had a crown of thorns forced into his head and was nailed on a cross. How uncomfortable is all of that? What are we willing to give and suffer for Him? Consider Christ (Hebrews 12:3-4)!

However, we complain, get discouraged, frustrated, annoyed, and back away from what little we do have to face in this life of following Christ. Jesus never complained or defended Himself. He carried His cross for the joy set before Him (that joy set before Him was us, His inheritance, His bride). He Loved us despite what we did, how we reacted to Him, or how we treated Him. Despite prostituting ourselves out to our flesh. Every time we choose the world over Him, we commit adultery.

Our objective in this life of surrender is not more status He can give me, or a better life He can make for me, but to be like Jesus. He is our example to follow. When affliction is walked through rightly it develops character and humility. What we become **far outweighs** what we may have had to face by going through the process!

We are not to look to ourselves, by feeling sorry for ourselves, in the difficult times. We look to Christ. Consider Christ and what He endured. By doing this we will overcome any difficulty we face. How did the disciples go through everything they went through and even glory in tribulations (Romans 5:1-5)? They did not consider themselves. They loved not their own life. The Love of God was shed abroad in their hearts (Romans 5:5 KJV). How did they go through everything and still be content in whatever condition they were in (Philippians 4:11-13)? Some words associated with content are; peaceful, happiness, satisfaction, acceptance, not wanting more, having enough, and sufficient. Selah. Because they knew they could do all things through Christ who gave them strength.

It is not our circumstance that will discourage us, it is our perspective in the midst. We will get discouraged when we are focused on self (my troubles, my tribulation, what has happened to me, my pain, my hurts, my fleshly feelings are always self-focused). Thinking in a manner that creates offense, defense, disappointment, discouragement is always about our-self. It's hard to hear Him, when our own thoughts and feelings are screaming SO LOUDLY in our heads. You may not want to hear it, but it is Truth.

Our thought life determines our contentment. Not our circumstances, our spouse, our children, friends, job, ministry, money, etc. But our thought life. Where are we going to fix our thoughts (Philippians 4:8-9)? When we put our focus and thoughts on Jesus there is no way we can remain discouraged, we just can't. He is too beautiful for that.

No matter what we are going through in life nothing changes who Christ is. Nothing changes who He is in us, what Christ did for us, or why He did it. Nothing changes His purpose for us. Nothing changes the fact that we are His bride. So, if you are discouraged it is your perspective that is allowing it. Somebody could go through the exact same thing with a different view and come out completely different. Singed versus unsinged. Discouraged versus content. Do not be formed by anything, anyone, or any circumstance. Only be formed by Jesus. Having His perspective, thoughts, and motives.

One last thing I would like to touch on about loving not your own life, and that is speaking Truth in Love. This is one thing that will make people free. John 8:31-32, "...If you abide in My Word, you are My disciples indeed. And you shall know the Truth, and the Truth shall make you free." If I cannot speak the Truth in Love (Ephesians 4:15) to someone, because I do not want them to be upset with me, I care too much about myself! I care more about what might happen with our relationship, what they might think of me, how they might react, if they will get angry with me, etc. than the person being made free by the Truth being spoken. Galatians 4:16, "Have I therefore become your enemy because I tell you the Truth?"

A Prayer to Pray:

"Lord, help me to not care about me at all and to care more about the other person. Holy Spirit give me holy boldness to do this, to speak Truth in Love. Transform my heart to Love others more than myself. I do not want to think twice about speaking Truth that will make them free. Even if it is just a seed planted. That seed has the potential to grow into a tree! I want to be so dead to myself, I do not even consider my-self, only the other person's well-being and freedom. Even if it hurts them for a moment or they are angry with me for a lifetime. Lord, help me to love not my own life! In Jesus name, Amen."

Overcoming Sin

Georgian Banov, "If you can't be free from sin until you die then Jesus isn't your Savior, death is."

Yes, it is time to tackle this subject. As always, I am writing from experience. What I have not mentioned yet is that God had me, for 3 years (2019-2021), living the Life of this book before He had me sit down to write it in 2022. What He was saying to me is, "I want you to become this book. Not just something you know about. Not just another great idea or theory someone is talking about. But you will write about what you have personally experienced and become."

So, as I tackle this subject of sin, I want to be clear, I am not saying I have attained to sinlessness. I am not perfect, yet (I am smiling, but it is true, "yet"). As I agree with Philippians 3:7-21, I press on toward the goal of the upward call of God in Christ Jesus. I also know I do not struggle with sin how I used to. I do not think about it the way I used to. I don't really think about it at all.

It is not just a theory that I do not have to sin, but it is the Word of God. 1 John 3:6, whoever abides in Him does not sin. Does it get any clearer than that?! When we know the Lord in an intimate relationship we do not want to sin. I Love the Lord immensely and I do not want to sin against Him in any way, ever. And IF I should stumble, IF, not when I do, but IF I should (1 John 2:1) I have an advocate, Jesus Christ.

I also want to address 1 John 1:8-10, because I know most of you are thinking about this Scripture already, "If you say you have no sin you are deceived." If we say we have no sin. If we say we have never sinned (past tense verse 10), then we have no need for what Jesus did on the cross for the forgiveness of sins. By doing this we are calling God a liar and we are deceived.

Yes, we have all sinned (past tense; meaning before we lived our lives IN Christ) and fallen short of the glory of God (Romans 3:23). But now if we are living our lives **IN** Christ we do not have to sin. Christ living in me (Galatians 2:20) doesn't even have the desire to sin and Christ in me lives ONLY unto God (Romans 6:10). John then goes on to say in 1 John 2:1, I write this to you **so you will not sin.**

What was man created to be? The likeness and image of God on the earth (Genesis 1:26-28). We were created to be like God, in his perfect righteousness and holiness. Jesus has brought us back to that. Be ye holy as I am holy (1 Peter 1:15-16). He has put His Kingdom inside of us (Luke 17:20-21) and with the Kingdom, we have Jesus Christ Himself possessing us.

Peter gives us a list of qualities to grow in that ensures us we will NEVER stumble (2 Peter 1:5-11). He also gives us a list of steps to follow Christ by (1 Peter 2:21-25), who committed no sin. He is our example that we should follow His steps!! It is amazing how this is written all throughout the Word of God and yet we do not take Him at His Word. We do not believe what He says is true. It is extremely sad to me we have allowed religion to bewitch us as Paul would say to the Galatians. And religious traditions and beliefs to form us instead of Jesus Christ Himself.

Appendix B in the back of the book is 2 pages worth of Scriptures you can look up that reference anything to do with sin or the flesh.

Jesus Christ being 100% God and 100% Man demonstrated for us how a fully human person should walk in relationship with God in the power of Holy Spirit, not according to flesh. Again, Jesus says, "Follow Me" so we must be able to do it too, or He would never have told us to. He did not say "Follow Me, except for when it comes to sin. You will always be a sinner so don't worry about following me in that area. Carry on."

As He is in this world so are we, having confidence being perfected with Love (1 John 4:17). We do not have to struggle and strive to do good if Christ is living in us. Jesus showed us in the wilderness there is a way to overcome when we are led by the Spirit of God. When we walk IN the Spirit, we **will not** fulfill the lusts of the flesh (Galatians 5:16). WILL NOT. How do we miss this stuff? Because it hasn't been our experience. However, it hasn't been our experience because we only receive what we believe. And most Christians do not believe this and they remain a slave to sin.

The original sin was and continues to be self. Self is the root of all pride and every sin. Everything got perverted through sin. The human choice to be ones' own god. Making our own decisions. Trying to control our own lives. Not to be accountable to anyone, not even God who gave us our very life. Try to think of a sin that does not revolve around your-self... exactly, you can't!!

We get good at minimizing sin as if "it's no big deal." We will make excuses for sin like, "I can't help it, God made me this way." Do not blame anything in you, that is of self, flesh, or sin, that may be in your "personality," on God making you that way. I can guarantee you He did not put that in you. It was formed by many other factors, many other things, but not God.

Or we say, "That's just the way I am." You need to be born again! If it does not look like Jesus, then God did not put it there. And you should not be ok with it staying there! Too many of us use, "oh that's just my personality" as a copout and excuse to be the way we are. I will say in their defense they do not realize it most of the time. They legitimately think it is true. Well now you know it is not true (smile).

One of the casualties of sin is our acceptance of it. Holy Spirit will bring conviction in areas where sin and self need to die. Where He will want to change the way you are. But if you continually ignore the conviction of Holy Spirit in your life, you will gradually get used to it. The scary thing is, there will come a point in time when you do not recognize the conviction anymore. This way of living has become "normal" to you. And because you do not recognize it, you will think you are doing "right" by God, or you are "good" with God. Instead of realizing you are sinning against Him.

When Truth is spoken it will bring conviction. Every time we reject seeds of Truth, we reject Holy Spirit's conviction. We are rejecting God. So instead of receiving the correction that is needed, which always comes with the conviction, we move on to the next "pleasurable" thing. The cycle of brokenness, not submitting to God, and doing our own thing continues. Thinking we are not the problem.

Beware of ignoring the conviction of Holy Spirit. satan does not mind if we are attending Bible studies or even praising Jesus with our songs. he likes it when we read the Word of God and do nothing with it (when we do not become it). he is so proud when we know we are being convicted, and we do nothing about it. Instead, we are <u>casual</u> about it and <u>complacent</u> with it. Therefore, we are <u>compromised</u>. These are just a few words that come to mind that are toys on the devil's playground: casual, complacent, and compromise. Where we play around all too often.

This is why we need to be surrendered to Holy Spirit fully, wholly, undoubtedly, completely, not holding anything back from Him. It is when we do something about the conviction satan hates it. he hates for us to finally know who we are in Christ and to allow the Word of God to transform our lives. When we become the Word. he hates God's Word, and he hates for the Kingdom of God to be made manifest in us.

Isaiah 1:1-6, is just a glimpse to what sin does to us. My whole head is sick, and my heart becomes faint. My entire body is beaten and bruised. Wounds have not been closed or healed, they become infected. When I live in sin it means I have lost my source of strength so now I have become weak (Psalm 31:10). Sin wages war against me (1 Peter 2:11).

In a nutshell sin destroys life (Romans 6:16, Romans 7:5, Romans 7:11). Sin does not just affect the one area of your life (where you are sinning), as some may think. Thinking they can "get away with it." It will infect **all** areas of your life. Sin tarnishes relationship. Sin destroys everything around us if we keep choosing to live in it. Sin is like an infection left untreated and a cancer to the body, it will eat you alive.

Once we have sinned and have not come to true repentance, we have given satan a foothold in our lives, he has access to every area of us. Once we have sinned (without repentance) it softens us to do it again and before we know it satan has paved an access road in and out of our thoughts and our actions. It is much more painful when the enemy has invaded the territory that should have been fully submitted to God in the first place. The longer we remain in sin, the more we will become numb and dead inside. When we are living in sin it is ugly.

When we are living without Jesus, our perspective changes, our attitude changes, our thinking, our action, our words, everything changes. Not for the good but for the worse. Things become dark and distant and negative. Stop tolerating and getting entangled in what comes between you and God. "Let me get this straight, you are leaving God for that?" "You are choosing that temptation over Him?" Whatever stands between you and the Son/sun only creates darkness. If you are living in sin, it stands between you and God, and great will be the darkness. Do not be deceived in thinking that sin is better than God! More fun than God! More freedom than God! Lies! All Lies!

No sin or any bit of self is worth holding on to so hard that I cannot be with the Lover of my soul. I will not live in sin because I must be with Him. I cannot live apart from Him. Just as a body cannot survive without a heart. Also, if I am living in sin, I cannot hear Him clearly. His voice is the only voice I want to hear. His voice is the only voice I need to hear. His voice is the only voice to follow. I cannot live in sin because I must hear Him clearly. He is the only One who knows the Way. He is the only One who has all the answers. I must hear Him.

We cannot have an undivided relationship with Jesus while sin is in our life (1 John 3:4-10). Compromise Christianity is demonic. When you sin and you know what you are doing is wrong and you do it anyway, then call it His "grace" that forgives you, that would be demonic (1 John 3:4-10). Don't get me wrong, God still Loves you and He is full of mercy and grace. The reality is you do not Love God. John 14:15, "If you Love Me, keep My commandments," (obey Me).

Any "grace" that does not lead to a complete transformation of life is demonic in nature. The good news is we can have this life of 1 John 3:4-10 (please read). Because as we grow in Love with Jesus, we do not want to commit adultery or sin against Him. Just as we should not intentionally sin against our spouse. We want to have an undivided relationship with Jesus, and we can have it.

I learned the hard way that I cannot continually live in sin and think I can have a relationship with Him at the same time. It just does not work that way. That is not what we do when we are in a Loving relationship with someone (continually sin against them and think it is ok to do so). If we are enraptured in the Love of Jesus, there will not be a thought to entertain sin. Sin will be a repulsion to us. Much like if you detest and are repulsed by eating liver. When something is detestable to you, you will **never** partake of it.

God's grace enables us to say "No" to sin and live a holy and pure life. Not give us an excuse to stay in sin. Grace does not excuse our sin. Grace is the power of the presence of God that enables us to walk out what Truth calls us to; pure, holy, blameless, and righteous. Grace in the Greek means: "The divine influence upon the heart and its reflection in the life." Selah! I am to live full of grace by the power of Holy Spirit in me. Only He can do this in me.

Now let's read all of Romans 6 about being dead to sin. This is the Word of God, not my words. You are to believe it to be true because God says it is so. We are to consider ourselves utterly dead to sin. We have the death and the life of Christ working within us. But most Christians do not know this and, therefore, do not experience this freedom. We must say it even before we understand it, "In Christ, I am indeed dead to sin." Romans 6:11 is a directive, not just a suggestion. You, also, consider your-self dead to sin and alive to God in Christ Jesus.

If we are sin conscious, we will sin, and be a slave to sin. If we believe ourselves to be dead to sin, we will be dead to sin. A man's acts are always in accordance with who he thinks he is (Proverbs 23:7). How he sees himself to be, is who he will be. Do you think you are a sinner? Or a saint (Ephesians 1:18)? I know you **were** a sinner (past tense). We all **have sinned** (past tense). We **were** all sinners that had to be saved by His grace. But are you still a sinner with Christ living in you? Because 1 John 3:5 says, "in Him there is no sin."

We can only receive what we believe. If you believe you are a sinner, you will receive sin into your life. If you believe you are in Him (Ephesians 2:6) and that in Him there is no sin, then you will not sin. Yes, we may stumble at times, but we do not make a practice of living in continual, habitual sin. We cannot live the life of freedom unless we are fully aware of being dead to sin **in Christ Jesus.**

The more we are aware of Jesus, the more we behold His face, the more we are in His presence in our secret place, the more we grow in Love with Him, the more we want to honor Him, the more we do not want to have anything to do with the flesh (self and sin), the more we want to please Him, the more we want what He desires, the more the chains of sin and bondage fall off of us in adoration of Him. Praise God! And behold Him.

Now let's read Romans chapter 7. Another part of Scripture we will use as an excuse to always be a sinner and not live free. Chapter 7 is what the law and religion does, it makes things so complicated and confusing! What I want to do, I do not do and what I don't want to do, that I do (Romans 7:14-20). It makes you double minded, unstable in all your ways. Paul is explaining this is the exact life <u>we will live</u> **in the flesh** <u>if we do not die to self</u> (7:4 & 7:6).

All of chapter 7 he presents his case of why we must die to the flesh. This is what living in the flesh/sin does to us. It causes us to be as a wave tossed to and fro. He even says 2 times it is not him who is doing it but sin that dwells in him! This is why we must reckon ourselves dead to sin (Romans 6:11)! Romans 7:24-25, O wretched man that I am (in the flesh)! <u>Who will deliver me from this body of death? I thank God – through Jesus Christ our Lord</u>! There it is settled!! Jesus has delivered us from this life of sin! Thank You God!!! Now that that's over.

I also want to point out one more thing. Paul was a follower of Jesus Christ, just as we are followers of Jesus Christ. All growing in our life of becoming One with Jesus. Why are we making Paul the standard to live by? Jesus' life lived is our standard.

We are to stop dealing with sin and stand in the victory Jesus **already won** for us. Believe we are free, and we will live free. Free indeed! We can refuse sin in our life by reckoning ourselves dead to sin. 2 Timothy 2:19 ESV, "But God's firm foundation stands, bearing this seal: 'The Lord knows those who are His,' and, 'Let everyone who names the name of the Lord depart from iniquity.'" We need to depart from sin or... we can permit it in our lives.

When I fear (in Hebrew, reverence, morally to revere) the Lord, I will depart from evil (Prov 3:7, Prov 16:6). The definition of revere from *Oxford Languages* is to "Feel deep respect or admiration for."

A PRAYER TO PRAY:

"Because You, Lord, are worthy and You are holy, I am in awe of You. I deeply, deeply respect You and admire You. So, I will honor You in all I do, and be holy as You are holy. Because I hold You in such high regard, I will not sin against You. This is what Your Word tells me, and Your Word does not return void. In Jesus name, Amen."

OBEDIENCE

Why do we think if we do not follow the Word of God everything will be fine? If we omit the flour from the cake, does it turn out? If we leave out the chocolate chips from the chocolate chip cookies, are they still chocolate chip cookies? When we omit the Word of God and deviate from it (from His recipe) life does not turn out right. We are operating on our own when we are outside of obedience. When we are living according to our own will, our life will not look how it is supposed to look, be how it is supposed to be, or taste how it is supposed to taste (Psalm 34:4-10).

Then when the weapons that are formed against us come (Isaiah 54:17) which the weapons will be formed against us, they will prosper because we are operating according to our flesh and not in obedience to the Lord. If He tells us to do something, we do it. If He tells us not to do something, we do not do it. Anywhere outside of obedience is a dangerous place to be.

When He tells us not to do something in His Word, it is never just a rule to follow, it is always for our protection. I know sometimes deep within us we always want to know "why." "Why can't I do this or that, Lord?" It should never matter as to why or why not. We are to trust Him and what He says is true. Knowing it is always for our good and protection. It is His Love for us. In return we obey Him out of our Love for Him (John 14:15). We obey Him because we Love Him not because of a law that was put in place. When He tells us not to do something, then we do not do it.

What good is it to read the Bible and not do what it says? It is no good. It will not work that way. We are to be effectual doers of the Word (James 1:21-25). It would be like you not knowing how to fix the brakes on your car. So, you read an instruction manual on how to fix your brakes. Then you go and do the complete opposite because you think you might still know better than the manual. Are your brakes going to be fixed? No! This illustration even sounds ridiculous as I write it, but this is what we do! His Word is our manual on how to live life, we are to follow it, and do not deviate. Or else we crash and burn because what we thought would fix the brakes didn't work.

Please read Matthew 7:24-27. Notice He says that whosoever hears His Word and does it (obeys it), he will be like a wise man who built his house on the rock. And when the storms come, (because the storms will come) his house will not fall. But the one who hears His Word and does not do it, he is like the foolish man, who built his house on the sand. And when the storms come, his house fell and great was the fall of it.

AW Tozer, "The tragedy is our eternal welfare depends upon our hearing and we have trained our ears not to hear." We either have trained our ears not to hear Him or we hear Him, and we simply do not do what He is telling us.

His Love is unconditional, yet His promises are conditional. Based on our obedience and our choices. IF we follow His instructions. We see all throughout the Bible what is called if/then statements such as 2 Chronicles 7:14 (please read). We cannot continue to live a reckless lifestyle and think we will be covered under His blessing. If things are going well for you in that lifestyle it is just a matter of time before it falls apart, and great will be its fall.

Being a just God He cannot bless an unrepentant or disobedient heart. At that point you are trying to hold your life together on your own. You are deceived if you think it is God blessing you. Time will take its course because there is only so long you can hold it together on your own. If it is not under the blessing and will of God, it will fail. Acts 5:38-39, "...IF this plan or this work is of men, (then) it will come to nothing; but IF it is of God, (then) you cannot overthrow it – lest you even be found to fight against God."

Excerpt from the book: *Lessons From a Sheep Dog* written by Phillip Keller (parenthesis and emphasis added): "When I am under satan's rule (living for the flesh in disobedience to God) I am mishandled. My talent's twisted and subverted for destructive ends. My vitality being wasted in chasing after wrong things. My worthwhile work expended on empty pursuits. By staying here, I myself am forging the shackles of steel that bind me." Wow! Selah!

In other words, my success depends on my obedience to God. This is written all throughout time and history in the Bible. For the Israelites, every battle was won when they were obeying the Lord and His presence was with them. Do not underestimate the power of obedience. Do not underestimate the blessing of obedience.

I would like to discuss again the battles we face. Because a lot of you may be feeling and thinking you have "lost" a lot of battles. The problem is we get stuck when the victory may not always look like what we expect it to look like. We cannot always explain why things happen the way they do. Only God knows why. What we can be sure of is; God works EVERYTHING together for good to those who Love Him and are called according to His purpose (Romans 8:28). Also, we can be sure He will NEVER leave us or forsake us! As I can hear Him say right now, Psalm 31:24, "Take heart my child, be of good courage!" (Read all of Psalm 31 for that matter.) No matter what the outcome of any circumstance is, with God, you win! If you cannot see the victory in it ask the Lord to show you and He will.

Chasing after wrong things (as Phillip Keller put it) is a waste of time and energy. If it is not for Christ and His Kingdom, then it is a waste of time and energy. When you expose yourself to wrong things you will end up heavy, sad, hopeless, oppressed, and powerless. Stuck in worthless pursuits. James 3:14-16 says, <u>in all envy and selfish ambition demons are at</u> <u>work</u>. Ephesians 2:2 says, <u>in any disobedience demons are at work</u>. Proverbs 1:29-31 says, eat the fruit of rebellion and it will be nasty.

Proverbs 16:7 (ESV), "When a man's ways please the Lord, He makes even his enemies to be at peace with him." When you are in the will of God, He is committed to taking care of you. In obedience to Him there is refuge, and the battle is won. When you are outside of God's will you are on your own...destitute. Out there in the world without any help. Yikes! You may be thinking, "Well I have people (my friends, my family) here to help me." I am going to make a bold but true statement. Any help outside of God is useless. Only in obedience to Him is where we thrive and quite frankly survive.

We do not know how detrimental the choices we make can be until we end up in the middle of the storm we created because of a wrong choice we made. Either a choice from flat out disobedience or a choice we made by not acknowledging Him in all our ways (Proverbs 3:5-8). The way that seems right to a man ends in destruction (Proverbs 14:12-16). It is not worth it to go it on our own without His guidance!

God gave me a good visual of this one day. I was sitting at a park on a spring day with the snow melting away. There was a couple walking a dog coming towards me. The dog ran ahead of them and straight into a mud puddle. It laid down in it and started rolling around and then dragged itself through the mud puddle. When it got up it was a complete muddy mess. The couple was less than impressed and I couldn't help but chuckle.

Then God immediately spoke to me and said, "This is what happens when you run ahead of Me." Wow! We will do things that make a mess. A lot of times we are not even thinking about seeking God in **all** our decisions. We just do things of our own accord maybe even out of habit. We may think it is fun at the time and nothing wrong with it. But when we realize we have run ahead of God, and we stop and look around we will see we are a complete muddy mess. Because we did not seek Him in **all** our ways.

"Lord, I acknowledge You, for I know I cannot possibly know what to do without You! I can do nothing without You!"

Something else the Lord had shared with me one time is, "When you are disobedient to Me there are consequences that come from that disobedience." Much like when Moses struck the rock, when he was told to speak to it, he then was not able to enter the Promise Land. The Lord then went on to comfort me, "My sweet daughter, I forgive you and you cannot dwell on your past mistakes. Stop beating yourself up for the mistakes you made. This does not mean you, my precious, beloved, daughter are a failure. This means I still provide even in your mistakes. This means I still work all things together for your good because you Love Me and are called according to My purpose."

Think about being a Loving parent. You only want what is best for your child. The guidelines you lay out for them are for their protection. Not to hurt them. Not to keep something from them. Not to "ruin their fun" or to "ruin their life." Yet, if they do not follow the guidelines, there are consequences and there is discipline. The exact same is true of God, even more so of God. He has guidelines for us to follow for our very best life. The guidelines God has given us are what is most beneficial for us.

If there is a "no you may not" in this moment, it is only for a better future. Some things are delayed or withheld because there is an appropriate time, and you are simply not in that season yet... "yet!" He does not "take away our fun." He enhances our fun. He does not "ruin our lives." He protects us as a Loving parent would within His guidelines. All of this is done to give us the best life we could possibly have. Better than you can even imagine (Ephesians 3:20).

John 10:27-28, My sheep hear my voice, <u>and I know them</u>, and <u>they follow me</u>: And I give them eternal life, and they shall never perish; neither shall anyone snatch them out of My hand.

PURPOSE OF DYING

"It means to have no life but His life, to have no will but His will, to have no interests but His interests, to share His riches, to enter into His joys, to partake of His sorrows, to manifest His life, to have the same mind as He had, to think, and feel, and act, and walk as He did. Oh, who could have dreamed that such a destiny could have been ours!" Hannah Whitall Smith from the book, *The Christian's Secret of a Happy Life*. Every time I read this it makes me smile!

When we live the crucified life, being dead to self, it **solves every problem**. Another bold statement I know! But really it does. Just think about it! Since satan is the ruler over self, once you live as being dead to self, he has no control over you anymore! When you are not thinking for you anymore, he has no hold on your life. You were never made for you. Selfishness (self) is the root of all sin and the biggest problem in the world. Take away selfishness and you leave no room for arguments, strife, discouragement, offense, hurt, frustration, annoyances, etc., none of it!! Self-confidence, self-esteem, self-consciousness (all insecurities), get annihilated when you realize you were made for God and His glory, and it is not about your-self at all. Talk about being free! Amen! Hallelujah!

Dying is the answer to everything. One morning in my quiet time I was In John 17. It is where Jesus prays for our unity. That we will be one as He and the Father are One. I asked Him to show each one of us what we must do to live in this unity with each other. Immediately one word came to me, "Die." When we are, each one of us, dead to ourselves we only esteem others better than ourselves. When we are dead to ourselves, we are not thinking about ourselves at all. When we are dead, we have no "rights." Jesus laid down every right He had to come to earth and made Himself of no reputation (Philippians 2:5-8). As Christ followers we are to do the same. "Have this exact same mind and attitude in you," (using several translations). How much more unified would we be if every Christ follower would live the crucified life? Outstanding!

If one is not living as dead to themselves then you do not know what they will be like from one day to the next. Even worse, from one moment to the next. They will be like any worldly person and people are fickle. They are moved by the day. Bad day? Then they are doing bad or "not so good today." Good day? Then they are good! And it can turn at a flip of a coin, just let something happen and it changes everything. Sad to say this was me at one point in time, (YUCK!). It was a sad way to live especially for those around me! It is only in the one who is living dead to self that you will see consistency of peace and joy, no matter the day, no matter the circumstance. Consistency in their attitude and outlook. They are not shaken or moved.

I heard on Christian radio one time this phrase, "taming the flesh." At first it sounded good (what a cool concept I thought to myself). Then I looked to the Bible. Nowhere does it tell us to "tame the flesh" but to crucify it. I will crucify my flesh with the affections and lust that it has (Galatians 5:24). I will mortify the old life as I know it (Colossians 3:5 KJV). Not to moderate it by finding a balance. Not try to control it. Not manage it. Not temper it. Do not tame the flesh. Crucify it!

We must live as a dead man to truly live and the sooner we do it the better off our lives will be. Because us getting in the way is what messes everything up in the first place. Us getting in the way is what causes problems. We are our own worst enemy. Free me from me!!!! Christ died so I could live. I die so Christ can live through me.

1 Corinthians 15:36, "Foolish one, what you sow is not made alive unless it dies." The very purpose of death is to bring forth Life. 1 Corinthians 15:42-49 says, everything of the natural must die, be sown into the ground, and be raised up as spiritual. **From death life begins.** John 12:23-26 says, unless a seed be buried and die it abides alone but if it die it brings forth much fruit. Jesus was speaking of His own death here however it applies to us all, since we are commanded of Jesus to, "deny yourselves and Follow Me." We will not bear much fruit unless we die and be buried into the fertile soil of deep surrender and humility. God will create a garden of beauty from this dirt.

Think about an actual seed and harvest. The seed is buried in the ground, it is in its dead state. As it drinks in deep of the water and the sun it grows. It grows roots that go deeper yet into the soil and eventually it springs up out of the ground. It continues to grow until it bears much fruit. A tree's roots grow deep, deep, deep while growing up, up, up (tall) at the same time. As are we to grow deep into the Lord while growing up in the things of the Lord as well.

Luke 20:18 says, You can be broken, or you will be crushed. Broken in the Greek is to "dash together; shatter." But it is derived from a primary preposition meaning, "union with; making one complete." We either fall upon the Rock (Jesus) to be broken and brought in union with Him being made complete, or it will fall on us and grind us into powder. I heard Eric Gilmour say how the Lord had said this to him, "Will you allow me to break you so that you do not work anymore?" Selah! Hebrews 4:10 says, "For he who has entered His rest, has himself also ceased from his works as God did from His."

A PRAYER TO PRAY:

"Lord, break this self-will in me! The part that will only follow You to a certain point but not go all the way! Where I say, "Here's the line" and I go no further. Break me so I can be One with You! To be broken before You is wonderful. On the other side of broken is beautiful. Where You come in, You see me, You know me, You search my heart, and make me more like You. Yes, death can be painful. But You bring forth NEW Life from the dead places. I am happy to say I am broken because I know it is no longer me who is working (doing things my way). My way only leads to mediocrity, complacency, compromise, and death. Thank You, Lord. In Jesus name, Amen."

Only God can take ashes (the dust of our brokenness, the ashes of our mourning), and make them beautiful. The key is He gives beauty for ashes (Isaiah 61:3). We are trying so strongly to avoid suffering of any kind and hold our lives together, so it won't fall apart and what we get is counterfeit. Much like a counterfeit painting. It isn't worth much! If we allow ourselves to be broken before the Lord, if we allow our facade to crumble and give Him all our ashes, His Word promises us He will make us beautiful. I urge you to be broken instead of getting crushed.

I touched base on something I have not yet talked about, and it is the pain that can come with death. Yes, we are giving up what never belonged to us in the first place. However, we have made it our own for so long that for most of us this will be a painful process of cutting it away (the pruning God will do). There will be growing pains. There will be suffering. There will be a blazing hot refining fire. I would be remiss if I did not tell you, this death to self will not be the easiest thing to go through. But I can promise you it is worth it! And it will get easier the more you receive the Truth that makes you free. The more dead to self you become the better it gets. Look to Jesus! Consider Him!

Practical Application:

All right! Are we sick and tired of hearing about ourselves yet?! Good! Let's die!

The goal is not a "better me" but rather the goal is none of me. It is not less of me and more of Him but rather none of me and all of Him. He becomes my strength in the dying areas of my life. It is He who lives in me. Dallas Willard once said, "Crucifixion is the great door of liberation." It is freedom from everything that holds me back. Freedom from everything that holds me down. Freedom from me. Let the former things lie in the grave, for they are dead, and I am alive unto Christ. The freer I am the more I look like Christ.

In sincerity we must be yielded to Holy Spirit. Otherwise, we can say things and then never position ourselves to receive them. **For Example:** we can say, "I want to change, I do not want to live angry anymore," all day long and then never actually yield ourselves to Holy Spirit to do the work in us to rid us of anger. We yield fruit (results) to the degree we are yielded to Holy Spirit. This is why we must surrender all.

Self can never cast out self. I cannot do this. I cannot make myself change. I may change for a little while, but it is not any real lasting change. I quit smoking for 3 years and went back to it. When Holy Spirit annihilated it from my life there is zero desire to go back to it. I can do absolutely nothing without Holy Spirit. I do not have anything to "offer." I am absolutely nothing without Holy Spirit. When we come before God sincere and in perfect humility, we will then experience our utter nothingness while God becomes our everything. I am utterly nothing without Him. When we place ourselves here in humble surrender, Holy Spirit will surely do the work in us. The work we have committed to Him.

Until we get to the place of total dependency on the Lord, we will without a doubt slip into hypocrisy and idolatry every single time. The more dependent on Christ we become the more we mature. The more we mature the more we realize we need Him. The more we need Him the more we grow into the Lord and the bigger He gets to us. The more the Spirit of the Lord grows in our life the smaller we become...the flesh dies. Hebrews 4:10, the one that has entered into the Lord's rest, he has also ceased from his own works = total dependence on the Lord.

1. Flesh is crucified in sincere **surrender** and **obedience**: Not my will but Yours be done. Being obedient to death of your-self. You are to give to Him (putting off) life as you know it and receive (putting on) your new life in Christ (Colossians 3:8-10) and then follow Him. Being completely yielded to the leading of Holy Spirit. The flesh can have zero say.

2. Flesh is crucified in **humility** and **total dependency**: Sink deep into your own nothingness. Sinking down into your grave in humility. Take yourself completely out of the picture until you only see Jesus. Consider Christ. Only He can be your all in all. You can do no thing without Him.

3. Flesh is crucified in **presence**: Relationship and intimacy with Jesus in the secret place will grow you more than you can imagine. Where the Spirit of the Lord is there is freedom (2 Corinthians 3:17). Soak in His presence and be filled with Holy Spirit. Drink in deep from the well of Living Water. Be revived, get refreshed, and never thirst again!

4. Flesh is crucified in **adoration**: By beholding Jesus. You become what you behold (2 Corinthians 3:18). Set your gaze upon the One who is altogether Lovely. Adore Him. Fix your eyes on Him. Worship Him. Praise Him. Love Him. May He be your One desire.

5. Flesh is crucified in **Truth** (the Word of God): Where living for self becomes non-optional because of what you see and know. The Truth you know WILL make you free (John 8:32). Pray the Word over the areas you struggle with. Communicate with God in the

Word. Know who He is through His Word. Receive the freedom that is already yours!

For years, my struggle with dying to self was that I would read my Bible and I knew I was to become what I was reading. I would surrender it. But then I would try in my own power to stop being worried (for example). However, it would always creep back in. There were a few things I was not considering when this was happening.

1. I would surrender it and eventually it would come back. A lot of times I would take it back without even realizing it. So now I am carrying it around with me again. This is because I was not dead to this part of my flesh. If we are not dead in a particular area it will always come back because there is still a life source for it to come back to. It is not dead.

2. I was trying to die to self in my own power. There is only so far self-determination will take us. And self-determination will never completely rid us from us. Even if we are speaking Scripture over that area. Because sometimes that can be religious ritual. (Such as the Pharisees. They knew the Scriptures. Scriptures were wrapped around their foreheads!) Holy Spirit is the only One who can rid us of us forever!

3. There were Truths I simply did not believe or know or understand. We must believe it to receive it. We must believe when Jesus died on the cross, He accomplished everything for us. We are already free from it all. There is nothing left for Him to do. We are the ones who must step into Truth and receive the freedom that is ours. It is only a matter of time before our faith will become fruit. Between believing (salvation) and receiving (freedom) we need to become disciples of Christ and come to know Truth that makes us free (John 8:31-32). We do not quit believing just because we do not receive the fruit of our freedom on our timetable. Which leads me to #4.

4. I was very impatient. I wanted the fruit of my-self being dead, NOW! However, we are not to speed the process. **Every day our faith grows patience.** Patience is perfecting a work in us that makes us <u>perfect</u>, and <u>complete, lacking nothing</u> (James 1:3-4). Selah!

This may sound a lot like the things you struggle with. Keep in mind when we fail and we do not know what to do, we tend to "just try harder" or to "just do it right this time" those are dead ends. We are to practice the remaining in Him and abiding in Him (John 15:4). And the applications given above will no doubt be useful. It is not in our own power for us to do anything. Dallas Willard once said, "This is not a sin management course." This is so very true. We are dead to sin not managing it (Romans 6:2).

Results: What It Looks Like

Journal Entry:

Holy Spirit You know how desperately I want to receive the fruit, the real manifestation of this life of freedom. To not think about myself ever, in any circumstance or situation. I am so over thinking it's about my-self when it is all about You. I look forward to the day that before I know it, my responses are as Your responses, my reactions are as Your reactions. The first thing I think about is the other person and Your Love for that person. I do not think of me at all. Remove any trigger that triggers me to respond or react selfishly and replace it with Your Love and humility. This is the first day of the rest of my life!! **End of journal entry.**

Now the section I have been looking forward to writing this whole time!! What this beautiful life of walking in the crucified life looks like! It looks like bringing heaven to earth (Matthew 6:9-10). Your Kingdom come Your will be done on earth as it is in heaven! If His will is being done on earth as it is in heaven, wouldn't earth look like heaven then? His will gets done on earth through us. We are to become One with Christ.

The church at large lives far beneath what Jesus died for. Jesus has made us free in every possible way. He has given us everything we need to walk in that freedom, and we continue to live in the illusion of bondage. The prison door is open, but we are sitting in our prison cells saying it isn't true! Just walk out! The only reason why we do not walk in freedom is because we are believing lies. Lies we have been taught or lies we believe from our own experiences.

We can only receive what we believe. Whom the Son sets free is free indeed and where the Spirit of Lord is there is freedom (John 8:31-36 & 2 Corinthians 3:17)! Do you believe His Word to be true? Or do you believe the lie of bondage and religion? What we believe will only be transformed by the renewing of our mind! When we stop believing wrong thoughts, this is freedom. It is time we start taking Jesus at His Word! Not mine but His!

We listen to sermons, we read books, or attend seminars on 5 steps for this, or 3 ways to do that, etc. My question is what is this teaching us and who is doing the work? You are! And you will get tired. Do you want to be the best parent ever? Do you want to have the best marriage in the world? It takes but one step. There is only one way, (drum roll please) ....

1. DIE

Literally everything is solved in the crucified life. In this one step we learn how to serve and put others first. We learn how to Love as Christ. We grow in the fruits of Holy Spirit (Galatians 5:22-23) which are Love, Joy, Peace, Patience, Gentleness, Goodness, Faith, Humility, and Temperance (discipline & restraint). We are a NEW creation! Believe it! Receive it!

Results of a crucified man: (and The Transformed Life covered in the next chapter). Just a reminder we look to Jesus for our example **in all things** because we are to walk JUST AS He walked (1 John 2:6). If you cannot find it in Jesus, then you should not find it in yourself.

1. Humility: When you think of others better than yourself. When you are ignored for your good deeds and others are awarded and you do not feel slighted, but you celebrate with them. When you see others succeed and you are not critical, thinking it should be you, because your needs are great. When you do not boast of your accomplishments or look for acknowledgement, affirmation, or applause. When you do not need or crave the "at a boy." When you do not desire to have the attention.

2. Complete Dependence on the Lord: When you are entirely obedient to Him with **all** your life. When you do not rely on anyone else but the Lord. Knowing He is your provision. He is your protection. He is your supply. He is everything you need and more.

3. Rest: There is no place of rest like the grave. When you cease from doing your own works. The grave is the place where the mighty resurrection power of God will be manifested. From here on out you are living Life in Christ and He in you...United Bliss!

4. Freedom: There is freedom that comes from dying. Where the Spirit of the Lord is there is freedom (2 Corinthians 3:17). Freedom happens in His presence. You are free from sin (Romans 6:7), chains, bondage, addictions, insecurities, anxieties. When you are

completely free you are completely delivered. When you are not addicted to anything except Jesus, you are free Indeed! Free from you. Free from others. Free from everything.

5. Incorruptible: Your new Life in Christ will last forever (1 Peter 1:23-25 & 1 Corinthians 15:42-50). You have now entered eternal life. The flesh (the body) is temporary, but you will live forever.

6. Divine Nature: You are a part of His Diving Nature (not human nature anymore, 2 Peter 1:3-4). You take on the nature and characteristics of Jesus Christ now.

7. You will have no buttons to push: If self is annihilated then every button is obliterated except for the Love button. If a button gets pushed only Love will come out of you. You can maintain cheerfulness while others are grumpy and you are still Loving, kind, and attentive to them.

8. You have no nerves to get on: If self is annihilated people or situations cannot get on your nerves anymore. When you don't snap at someone for slurping their coffee, smacking their lips, for acting "dumb," or hit them in their sleep for snoring, or any other thing that would get on your nerves before. It simply cannot happen anymore if you are dead to self.

9. You have no bothers to bother: If self is annihilated then you cannot get bothered by things. When you remain calm despite interruptions to your day, your agenda, your plan. When you are unruffled with less than desirable accommodations. Whatever it is that would have bothered you before cannot bother you now.

10. You have no lines to cross: If self is annihilated there is no talk like, "if you do that again," "just one more time." Love keeps no records of wrong and does not seek its own. You cannot "get sick of it" anymore and say, "That's it I'm done!"

11. You have died to every bit of offense, frustration, irritation, and annoyances: If self is annihilated then you do not think of yourself if someone is late, cuts you off in traffic, or treats you harshly and unfairly. You can still respond in Love, having meekness, and maintaining peace. Can you imagine living free from each of these things?! You do not have to be annoyed or inconvenienced at all when self is dead.

12. You do not have to defend your-self: Because there is no self to defend. When your best intentions are misinterpreted, you know

that Christ alone is your defender. When someone takes you the wrong way, you do not have to defend or "explain" yourself.

13. You do not grumble, mumble, or complain (Philippians 2:14-15): You take on the form of a servant and you do not think, "I am better than this," (1 Peter 2:19-25). You will suffer for doing good and not grow weary (Galatians 6:9). Do we see Jesus grumbling or complaining about carrying His cross? Then neither do we.

14. All triggers have been annihilated: triggers that caused you to respond or react harshly, selfishly, or inappropriately, have been replaced with Love and humility. Triggers that would cause you to run to your addiction have been destroyed when self is dead.

15. It is not about what is "wrong" with someone else: You see the best in people. You see who God created them to be. You do not blame other people for your problems. When you do not think for yourself, there is no fussing or arguing. I am not saying you agree with everything, but you know how to take it to the Lord in prayer. You discuss things in wisdom with the words of the Lord not your own. You do not say things like, "What's wrong with you!?" Or "What is your problem?!"

16. You can never be disappointed: How can you be dead to your-self and feel sorry for your-self at the same time? You cannot. If you are feeling sorry for your-self or disappointed it is because you are thinking of your-self and for your-self. You cannot look to Jesus and be disappointed. "Turn your eyes upon Jesus, look full in His wonderful face and the things of earth will grow strangely dim in the light of His glory and grace." It's true!

17. You can Love without expecting anything in return: When you Love freely without anyone owing you anything, not even an "I love you" back. Because you are so secure in the Love of Jesus you can Love others without any expectations from them. You are not left wanting when you are FULL of Him.

18. You will empty yourself of all of you: Empty, to me, means there is no room in your mind or heart for anything but God. There is a "no vacancy" sign up. There is no place in your mind or heart for worry, fear, frustrations, confusion, hate, anger, pain, hurt, brokenness, insecurities, anxieties, bitterness, resentment. There is only room at the Inn for Jesus.

19. There is no permission to be discouraged: Discouragement comes from considering your-self. So, consider Jesus who endured such

hostility from sinners (Hebrews 12:1-4). How can you feel sorry for your-self and be dead to your-self at the same time? How can you look at what Jesus endured and feel discouraged for your-self and what you're going through? If we have the mind of Christ (1 Corinthians 2:16) and He, for the JOY set before Him, endured the cross then so do we. Count it all joy (James 1:2-8), when we must endure anything for Jesus Christ our Bridegroom King. This does not mean we just "lay down and take it." It means we stand in faith and Truth, and we do not grumble and complain while going through it. We rejoice in our sufferings because it produces valuable things in us (Romans 5:1-5 ESV).

20. You become 1 Corinthians 13 Love: How does one Love like this?? DIE. When self is dead and out of the way you are not looking to receive anything that serves your-self. You are now looking at how you can serve and Love others. You cannot think of your-self at all. You must surrender your thoughts to Him so you can think like Him. Get the focus off you and you can Love like 1 Corinthians 13 Love.

21. There is no deception: Being dead to self makes being deceived impossible. When the flesh is dead you can see clearly. You can hear clearly. Your-self is not in the way making muddy waters. Deception is impossible because you have a healthy single eye (Luke 11:34-36).

22. You have nothing to "figure" out: You follow Jesus. Your life is in His hands. He will make sure you are on the right path if you are obedient to Him and following Him. He will do all the figuring for you, so you do not have to.

23. You lose your "rights" and reputation: When you pick up your cross you lay down your rights and make yourself of no reputation. You are not trying to make a name for yourself. You are not trying to build your own kingdom. Your only "right" is to live as Christ. You lose your right to even think for yourself. You have the mind of Christ and He is the head of the body.

24. When you give up everything, when you live the crucified life... ***God gives you everything...All of Him!!***

There are absolutely no limitations to the resurrected Christ. Therefore, there are no limitations to Christ in me. With God all things are possible. And all means all.

Wherever we go, it will be known from our Christ-like lives and conversations that we are followers of the Lord Jesus Christ. And are not of the world, even as He is not of the world.

JOURNAL ENTRY:

How did I fall for the lies of satan in 2014? I was not fully surrendered and living the crucified life! Anytime we choose flesh over Holy Spirit we lose. Who rules the flesh? satan. And for the next 4 ½ years of my life I was in the biggest spiritual battle of my life. Holy Spirit drawing me near and satan dragging me under. Because I was double minded (wanting to live by the Spirit yet giving way to the flesh), I was as a wave tossed to and fro. satan was trying to steal my identity, kill my purpose, and destroy my life. I do not want to have anything to do with the flesh anymore. Lord, I do not ever want to be where You are not ever again!!! You are always with me, <u>but You were not in every decision I made</u>. I NEED You to be in every decision I make. All I want is to follow You. The amazing thing is what the enemy tried to do in almost 5 years, could not compare (or even come close) to what Holy Spirit has done in my life in 5 short months and I know it will only continue to grow. **End of journal entry.**

A PRAYER TO PRAY:

"Lord, I want to honor You with my life. Your will be done. I put myself into Your Loving hands. You are my great physician. I believe You have healed me and have made me whole (heart, mind, and body). I receive this from You, thank You. Now by faith and by receiving this Truth, I will stop reverting to old ways. Holy Spirit empty me of all of me. Even all my past, the things that no longer exist! I trust You and I trust what You are doing. You know where You are leading me. I will not be focused on things of this world. When my thoughts and eyes go there, Holy Spirit, please focus my attention on things above and what matters for eternity instead. I do not want to get caught up in worldly pleasures. I want to grow fruit of the Spirit and understand the great gain of godly contentment! I want to know the complete satisfaction of Christ alone inside of me. I deny my-self, I take up my cross, and I follow You. My flesh is crucified. I am seated with You, Jesus, in the heavenlies and Holy Spirit fills this temple (my body). It is no longer I who lives but Christ who lives in me. Jesus, I want everyone to see You in me and not me at all! I Die to Live! In Jesus name, Amen."

The Take Away

Hannah Whitall Smith from *The Christian's Secret of a Happy Life* (emphasis added): "The lesson the Lord is trying to teach us all the time is the lesson of self-effacement. He commands us to look away from self and all self's experiences, to crucify self and to count it dead, to cease to be interested in self, and to know nothing and to be interested in nothing but God. **The reason for this is that God has destined us for a higher life than the self-life.** Just as He has destined the caterpillar to become the butterfly, and therefore has appointed the caterpillar life to die, in order that the butterfly life may take its place, so He has appointed our self-life to die in order that the divine life may become ours instead. The caterpillar effaces itself in its grub form, that it may evolve or develop into its butterfly form. It dies that it may live. And just so must we." "The caterpillar cannot in the nature of things become the butterfly in any other way than by dying to the one life in order to live in the other. And neither can we."

Picture drawn by Braydon Horsfall

Romans 12:2, "Do not be conformed to this world, but be transformed (Metamorphosis) by the renewing of your mind, that you may prove what is that good and acceptable and perfect will of God."

CHAPTER 5

The Transformed Life

WHY TRANSFORMATION?

WHEN GOD (BEING Spirit) made us in His own image after His likeness (Genesis 1:26-28), He deposited everything He is, into our spirit. In that moment we were made in His image and likeness. We already have everything He is inside of us, within our spirit-man. However, as we learned in the last chapter ever since Adam and Eve chose to eat of the forbidden fruit, it ushered in the fall of man (read all of Genesis 3). We now are all born into a sinful world with a soul (our mind, will, and emotion) that is ridden with self and needs to be renewed. Therefore, we must die to self and be born again (John 3:1-8).

When we are born again from above, we are resurrected and are fully alive in the new Life that is only available in Christ Jesus (please read 2 Corinthians 5:14-21). 2 Corinthians 5:15, "and He died for all, that those who live should live no longer for themselves, but for Him who died for them and rose again." Therefore, if anyone is in Christ, he is a new creation; <u>old things have passed away</u> (not are passing away but have passed away, past tense) behold all things have become new (2 Corinthians 5:17). We must believe this to receive it. Jesus says in John 11:40, Did I not say to you <u>if you would believe</u> (to have faith, to trust) <u>you would see</u> the glory of God?

We make the decision to believe, "Yes, the old things are dead and gone and the new is here." However, our soul is going to need to catch up with our spirit through transformation. Transformation happens by the Word of God through the renewing of our mind (Romans 12:1-2). The word mind in Greek, is to include our thoughts, feelings, will, and understanding. Each one of these are to be **renewed** (to be made new) in the Word of God bringing them into agreement with our spirit which is already made in God's image. Through this transformation our soul is now being made in the likeness and image of God.

Our spirit, by way of Holy Spirit, is to become the sole source and power **to who we are** in our souls. Our flesh (which is ruled by satan) will fight and try to keep this transformation from happening. Our flesh and our spirit battle for this ground of the soul (Galatians 5:16-18). The spirit and the flesh are diametrically opposed to one another. Because of this opposition there will be tension in the transformation process, so do not be alarmed. But as Galatians tells us we are to be led of the Spirit and walk in the Spirit then **we will not** fulfill the lust and desires of the flesh. When we do not feed the flesh, the flesh will die.

Once again, God has already created us in His image. It is not something we have to work for. It is not something we have to strive to become. God has declared the end from the beginning (Isaiah 46:8-11 ESV). God finished us before He ever started us. We now, through transformation, step into His finished work and plan for our lives that He prepared for us beforehand to walk in (Ephesians 2:10). It is already done. It is finished.

However, just because it is set in order by God, does not mean it will become our encounter or our reality because God does not force His will on us. We have choices to make with our own free will. We can very well make decisions outside of Him that will land us in the "middle of nowhere." On a path He never intended us to be on. How we reach our destination is by going through transformation, in absolute surrender and obedience to Holy Spirit. As soon as we step outside of being yielded to Him, we step outside of destiny. Choose this day life or death, blessing or cursing; choose life (Deuteronomy 30:19-21)!

The will of God is made complete in our lives not only when we come out of the old life, but also when we enter the new life. We come out of Egypt, bondage, captivity, and prison, by living dead to the self-life. And we step into the Promised Land, our Promised Life in Christ Jesus, by being transformed to look like Him. These two go hand-in-hand, they are not to be separated. Until we do them both, come out and go in, we are only wandering around in the wilderness just as the Israelites did. It is a continual yielding of our lives for His finished work to work its way through us. This working can only be done by our beautiful and wonderful Holy Spirit through our surrendered lives.

The key is, we must remain in faith through the transformation process. Just because we may not "feel" free does not mean we are not free. Just because we do not see evidence of freedom, does not mean we are not free. **Faith is the <u>evidence</u> of things not seen** (Hebrews 11:1). When Jesus died everything was finished for us on the cross. In that moment Jesus set us free. And whom the Son sets free is free indeed. We **have been** set free from sin, again past tense (Romans 6:18 & 22).

Now through faith we bring the unseen (what is already a reality in God's Kingdom) into the seen (our realm here on earth). Illustration... One end of the spectrum is "it is finished" and our faith to believe it is so. Then the line going to the other end of the spectrum is the waiting period. But we are not just idly waiting we are renewing our mind in the waiting. We are being tested and tried in the waiting. Our faith is growing in the waiting. At the other end of the spectrum is the manifestation of our faith/the fruit/the reality of being free/seeing the fullness of the promise.

THE GREATEST OF THESE IS LOVE

<u>The greatest thing</u> God wants to do in our lives is to transform us, in our entirety, into His likeness which is Love (1 John 4:16-17). Not to give us the greatest spouse, children, or family. Not to build us the greatest ministry. Not to make us the greatest athlete, musician, or author. Not to create for us great businesses so we can own a dynasty and be millionaires. I am not saying He will not do those things, but those things are not His greatest priority in our lives. His greatest priority for us is to transform our souls into His very likeness, and He is Love (1John 4:8). He wants to teach us how to Love **just as** He has Loved us (John 13:34-35). We are not only to Love others, but we are to be Love. Living, breathing, walking, Love.

We get so wrapped up in everything else in life, our families, our jobs, our hobbies, our own interests, or even our ministries, we forget the main thing and that is to be like Christ in this world. When we choose to surrender to Him to be transformed, Holy Spirit will transform us into Love, and we will then be Love just as Christ is Love. We will lay down our lives for one another. We will serve one another. We will think of others first. We will sacrifice and pour our lives out for others.

However, <u>we cannot in any way, Love like Christ in our flesh.</u> Being dead to self must happen to even know true Love. Being dead to self must happen to know how to Love. Self-love, the only love the world knows, is a no go and a dead end. It is not genuine Love at all. It is a love that is false, fake, inadequate, and full of self. We can only Love as Christ when it is no longer us who lives but Christ living in us (Galatians 2:20).

We cannot become Love unless self is dead. Otherwise, self continues to take back over, and then we only have selfish love again. As we grow and transform into the deepest level of Love, we live crucified to the self-life. So, Christ is the only One living in us and through us. His Love becomes our Love, and His Life becomes our Life. Self is to no longer live in any part of us.

When our souls are transformed into the image of Christ, we will walk out a Love walk to a world and a church that is hurting and dying. And by doing so, we will draw others to Him. Our world needs the Love of Christ. Our brothers and sisters need the Love of Christ. As we live the crucified life and give Him our heart in undivided devotion to be transformed, He teaches us how to Love perfectly. Luke 6:40, ".... Everyone who is perfectly trained will be like his teacher."_

We should want nothing, other than to look like Jesus, Love like Jesus, and live like Jesus. The power of Holy Spirit will do this in us. Being in His presence and passionately pursuing intimacy with Him changes everything within us. As I delight in the Lord I am changed, my heart is transformed. By being in His presence we become His Light in this world. In this place of intimacy with Him we will undoubtedly be transformed. We become what we behold. We become who we hang around (associate with). Instead of "guilty by association," we are transformed by association.

It is absolutely nothing we can do to change ourselves. It is by being yielded to Him where we do nothing but surrender and He does everything else. He even gives us the ability to be obedient in walking it out. When we give Him our lives as a living sacrifice (Romans 12:1), It is no longer I who lives!!

I like how Francis Frangipane puts it, (parenthesis & emphasis added). "Fulfilling God's external plan for us is secondary to what **we become** to Him in the process (Christ-like ones). The sooner we attain virtue and character which stays pure under testing, the sooner we move toward fulfillment of God's promises." "God is patiently watching and measuring our reactions (responses) to difficulties." "<u>The outcome of our trials is that</u>

the real Jesus emerges in our spirits and is expressed through our lives." "If you arm yourself with the purpose of Christ, to reveal His Love in the midst of your suffering, to reveal His forgiveness in the midst of your offenses, if you arm yourself with this, then that which was meant to destroy you becomes that which perfects you and reveals Jesus."

THE BEST LIFE EVER

If you had the opportunity to live the best Life you could ever live, your Life here on this side of eternity, would you take it? Truly, absolutely, and undoubtedly the best Life ever. I am sure the answer is emphatically, "Yes!" I mean, who wouldn't want this? Who would say "no" to such an opportunity to live this kind of Life? Doesn't it sound too good to be true? The best Life ever... come-on, really?

Now the hard question. Would you do **whatever** you had to do (anything God asks you or tells you to do), to experience this incredible life? This is where we get tripped up. We will hem and haw, "Hmmm let me think about it," "I don't know about that," "Well, maybe.... tell me what I have to do first." It reminds me of Matthew 19:16-30 (please read). Where the rich man is asking Jesus what he had to do to have eternal life. Jesus told him to go and sell all he had and give the money to the poor and follow Him. When the man heard this, he went away sad because he was very rich and could not do what Jesus was asking him to do.

I encourage you to go to the Word of God and look up each verse on suffering or picking up your cross or dying to the flesh or denying yourself, in the New Testament. This will help you to realize, and for it to sink into your soul, that to follow Christ we must die to ourselves. And death can hurt, it can be painful, there will be suffering (Romans 8:17, 1 Peter 6-7, 1 Peter 4:1-2, James 1:2-4) and it can be hard. By now I am sure you are thinking I have put this part in the wrong section no doubt...weren't we supposed to be talking about "the best Life ever" and not the worst?

Here we go, the good news to this is, facing whatever pain and suffering dying may cause, the transformation that happens, will far, far, far, far, far (a million times far) outweigh staying the same. Romans 8:18 (KJV) says, "For I reckon that the sufferings of this present time are not worthy to be compared with the glory which shall be revealed in us." This is the Truth to cling to as we are being transformed into His same image from glory to glory (2 Corinthians 3:18). We want to be saved from suffering, but He saves us through suffering by transforming us in the process. Until the way of Christ is what we instinctively choose every time. He teaches us how to be Christ-like in all things and at all times.

We are not to hear this and say, "Ok, now I am going to go and <u>do</u> this." No, you are not. You are going to <u>become</u> this by the power of Holy Spirit. Through your surrender to Him. In relationship, fellowship, and communion with God. By being in His presence, which is intimacy with Him. You are not who you are because of what you <u>do</u>. You are who you are because of who you have <u>become</u> through the power of Holy Spirit. Only Holy Spirit can do this, as you surrender all of yourself to Him and live crucified to your-self.

We are either choosing to live the surrendered Life to Jesus or we are choosing to live our own life. When we live the surrendered Life, we choose to become like Him. Therein we are transformed into His likeness and are obedient to His ways. Therein we are filled with His Love, peace, joy, gentleness, humility, goodness, etc. Therein we will find the Life of beauty, rest, and real contentment. Therein we will have the very best life we could live here on earth, truly fulfilled, and satisfied. I am telling you now, when we do exactly as Jesus tells us to do, **it is the absolute best Life to live always!**

When we live life our own way, we are choosing our own path. Therein we will follow our own selfish ways and desires. Therein we will have a life that will continue to leave us empty. Therein it **always** leaves us searching for more (the next best thing). Therein we are full of toxic feelings of the flesh such as anxiety, jealousy, comparison, discontentment, frustration, anger, worry, etc. Therein we end up with a very less than and mediocre life. Therein we are living a life that leads to destruction. Do not be left wanting for more when you can have Jesus! Do not be desperately looking for something else to fulfill you. In humility come before Him and lay your life down into His hands and live your best life ever!

The Battle That Wages

"It is very important that Christians should not be ignorant of the devices of the enemy; for he stands ready to oppose every onward step of the soul's progress," Hannah Whitall Smith.

When we say "yes" to all the Lord has for us, when we fully surrender ourselves and say to God, "Whatever You say, have Your way," when we enter the Life of living crucified to self and being transformed into His likeness, the enemy will fight us. I believe with all my heart all hell breaks loose because he knows if he doesn't stop us, we will hit a point of no return. Once we get to this point it is over for him in our lives. he will have no more say to us. he will have no more rule over us. him, having his way with us is done and over with forever. We will not go back there, where we were held captive by him, ever again.

So, he will try to pull out of his arsenal, a full-on attack to try to stop us from advancing in God's will for our lives. Once we have our mind set on what God wants and we move forward in it, satan will fight us every step of the way to try to get us to quit. If he can turn people against us, he will. If he can use people to persecute us or to cause us trouble, he will. If he can use people to hurt us or abandon us, he will. If he can use our past against us, he will. If he can use current circumstances against us, he will. He will use and do whatever he can to get us to quit.

When these challenges come, we will either continue to move forward in God's plan for our life (no matter how difficult it may be) or we will succumb to the difficulties and stop, to take the "easy" road instead. Which it will never be an easy road to follow satan. It may be for the moment, but it will not remain that way! satan knows he must take his chances now to get us off track, or he will lose us forever!

One way he will fight us (most people may not realize) is through our flesh. People may not realize it because they think it is "normal." But flesh is never normal. It needs to be crucified. When we feel our flesh kicking and screaming about something we can be assured it is satan doing his work to keep us very much alive instead of crucified. When the flesh is kicking and screaming it is fighting against what God wants of us.

For Example: One time God had asked me to send someone an email asking them to forgive me for not being Christ-like to them in our relationship. Now, this person I was to send this email to had hurt me badly over several years. Even the thought of having to do this hurt and it felt so wrong (to my flesh). So, my first knee jerk reaction was, "Surely this is NOT the Lord asking me to do this. Nope. Not the Lord!"

As you can guess, it surely was the Lord. I can tell you, my flesh immediately rose up wanting to fight. As it was kicking and screaming saying, "No, no way am I going to do this." Everything within my flesh did not want to send this email. Yet, Holy Spirit won this battle and helped me through writing it and sending it, even while my flesh was saying, "I can't believe I have to do this."

However, this was a lesson of obedience for me. Obedience with humility and Love. We know we are broken before the Lord in humility when we stop the fight against Him, stop the wrestling match. When all we can do is cling to Him for dear life while He asks us to do some incredibly difficult things. I had to come low in humility and Love to ask this person for forgiveness. Ultimately, what the Lord did through this whole event was reveal to me how I was still in unforgiveness myself (which led to my throwing stones talked about in the last chapter).

Everything He asked me to do was for my own freedom. And I would have missed it or at the very least taken the long road to freedom and healing if I would not have listened to Him and obeyed Him. How long would I have walked in unforgiveness without even knowing it? If I would not have been humble and do what He had asked me to do? You know sometimes it is easy to say we have forgiven somebody when in reality we are still holding on to things deep within our heart. God was graciously revealing this Truth to me.

No matter how hard it may be to hear something He has said to us, whether it be what He wants us to do or doesn't want us to do (when we want to do it), we may not like it at the time at all, but it is always His best for us. And in that moment, we must choose, His best or our worst. Because even "our best" is still the worst option possible. And in the process, we will become what we choose.

The battle can be intense at times and sadly most people quit before they receive the fruit of freedom. They give in to the kicking and screaming of their flesh. Or they give in and take the detour on satan's "easy" road before they can get to the point of no return. Therefore, they remain broken and the same. satan uses the trials to break us and cause us to give up. If we are focused on ourselves, **we will** get tired and quit. However, <u>God works in the trials to free us from ourselves</u>. He shows us how to look like Christ through them.

If we keep His perspective, we will remain steadfast, strong, and persevere to the end. We must have the right perspective and stand firm in the freedom that is already ours. So many people quit too soon, and they do not see or receive the beauty of the heavenly places of healing and wholeness in Christ Jesus...it is a shame. They miss out on truly KNOWING Him in His fullness of who He is.

Jesus said to John, "Come up here and I will show you" (Revelation 4:1). The problem is, we are trying to bring Jesus down here to "our level." We are trying to show Him what is going on, "See what is happening to me Jesus?!" "See what I have to put up with?" This is a bad idea and a no go! When we can see from His perspective "up here" we have a better clearer view.

Keep the story of my example in mind. I could have stayed in my perspective, "No way! I was hurt by that person. Why would I do that? Not doing it!" And I would have remained broken. Instead, I chose to rise up and by faith do what He was telling me to do. Even though I could not see from His perspective at the time. I could not see why He was having me do it. I did it anyway. Then in time I could see the full picture and see from His perspective and receive the healing and freedom He had for me through my obedience to Him.

As you learn to live the crucified life and renew your mind with the Word of God there will be a battle waging against you. The demons of hell will fight you to keep you in the places satan wants you. Where he has had you all your life, in prison. Enslaved to your self-life. But know this, Philippians 4:13, You can do all things through Christ who strengthens you. And because of Him, you have the victory (John 16:33) so stand firm (Ephesians 6:11)! satan is under your feet and has no power over you, NONE (Luke 10:19)! he only has power if you give it to him.

If you remain in relationship with your Father, stay in humble surrender, renew your mind in Truth, speak the Word of God with the authority of Jesus that He has given you (Luke 10:19), be led by Holy Spirit, and remain in faith, **you will** (not you might, but you will) walk in the fruit of your freedom. You will see the results of what Jesus has already accomplished, in your life. Where the Spirit of the Lord is there is freedom (2 Corinthians 3:17)!

You will recognize freedom as you see you are no longer in:

1. The chains of living according to the feelings of the flesh (anger, jealousy, worry, fear, frustration, bitterness, offensiveness, resentment, anxiety, sadness, depression etc.).
2. The chains of addictions.
3. The chains of living in past hurts, failures, regret, and shame.
4. The chains of insecurities.
5. The chains of living for yourself. Some people think if they live

doing whatever they feel like doing, it means they are free. When you are living for your-self, you are not free, you are a slave to you.

These are just to name a few areas where satan likes to try to keep us imprisoned for most of our lives. Creating learned wrong behaviors and **wrong beliefs** in us all along the way. Some of the roots of these things have been growing in us since childhood. We have been rooted and grounded in these wrong ways and thoughts for a long time. This means the roots have grown very, very deep in us. Only the Lord can uproot these things (these weeds) out of our lives. It will take Truth, His Love, and Time, so be Patient. We must remain surrendered to Holy Spirit to allow Him to change us thoroughly.

Francis Frangipane: "The more we are transformed into His image the less vulnerable we are to the evils of this world." "The transformation of our souls positions us outside of the devil's reach. It raises us up spiritually to seat us in the heavenly places." Selah!

Ephesians 1:21-22 tells us Christ is seated in the heavenlies at God's right hand. Far above ALL principality, power, might, dominion, and every name that is named. ALL things have been put under His feet. Ephesians 2:1 & 5 tells us God has made us alive together with Christ and raised us up together with Him. God made us to sit together in the heavenlies in Christ Jesus. So, in Christ, we are seated far above ALL principality, power, might, dominion, and every name that is named. ALL things are under our feet. Let us learn to live like it! This is the Truth of God's Word. This should be, it must be, our reality we see and live in!

It Is Worth It

In this life we tend to live from one exciting thing to the next. Once the one is over (the nice vacation, the thrill-seeking adventure, the holiday, the honeymoon, etc.) we may have a sense of dread as we return to our every-day lives. Taking on the "Oh no, it's back to life, back to reality," mentality. The boredom, the sadness, or the discontentment of every-day life sets in. Making one to plan the next "big" thing they can look forward to. If not immediately, it does not take long for the planning to begin.

The only way to be sincerely content is in Jesus. Living in His very real presence and joy every day. Sadly, most people do not experience this satisfaction. How many of us are living a life that is truly fulfilled and satisfied with contentment and joy? Yet this should be the normal everyday life of a Christian. I have lived all kinds of different ways. And they all have failed to live up to what they portrayed to me they would be. satan insinuated to me by living the following ways it would bring me to freedom, fulfillment, and happiness. satan is the great deceiver. he is the father of lies.

1. I have lived in total rebellion to God. Doing everything wrong but having "fun." I did whatever it was I wanted to do. The good, the bad, and the ugly. However, this way of living only leads to death (James 1:14-15) ...failed.

2. I then did what I thought was "right" or "good." I went to church and said my prayers, but still had one foot in the world and I was absorbed with self. Proverbs 14:12, "There is a way that seems right to a man, but its end is the way of death." That is pretty explanatory...failed.

3. I then tried to do what God would have me do. I was trying to surrender. I was trying to be obedient. I was trying to be transformed. However, I was trying to do it all in my own power. John 5:30, "I can do nothing on my own." ...failed.

Oh sure, some of these ways were "fun" at first. Happiness was present in the beginning and at various times throughout. However, as Proverbs so clearly states they always, eventually, led me to self-destruct. Ultimately all of this is what led to the death of my soul in the first chapter. I was anything but free. I was enslaved to my-self and far from experiencing the constant joy of the Lord.

Which His constant joy is truly powerful to have. There was a period where the enemy was working overtime to really try to steal my joy. I had to fight the good fight of faith (1 Timothy 6:12) to keep my joy. Sometimes I had to fight through the numbness and through tears. But I Love how Jesus says in John 16:22, "...and your joy no one will take from you." What a promise we have to receive and hold on to! Even when it doesn't "feel" like it's true.

Also, when I was living those different ways, I was far from experiencing the peace that surpasses all understanding (Philippians 4:6-7). Peace in any storm, which I now experience daily. Living those kinds of ways put me on the worst roller coaster you can think of. Living up and down, up and down, all around, and around some more. You know the roller coaster or any fair ride where you get off from it and it makes you immediately want to hurl. There is no peace in living in any of those ways at all.

I had gone round and round those vicious circles too many times to count. Talk about someone who had to learn the hard way! But what I found was, there is no life worth living doing it my own way or trying to do things in my own power. These ways were all living apart from Jesus. They were pointless, meaningless, and fruitless. There is definitely no life worth living apart from Him! Actually, there is **no Life** apart from Him at all (John 15:1-8).

In the beginning stages of going through transformation it was hard and grueling (for me it was). I had tears flow that seemed they would never end. I would scream out in agony when another realization would hit me in the face of things in me that needed to go. Needing to die! Things I had always lived with thinking they were "normal." Things that had been so "normal" to me they were rooted deep within me. When these things are rooted so deeply, it can hurt when they get pulled out and cut off. Because by now they have become a part of my-self.

Things such as getting frustrated, annoyed, irritated, being disappointed, and having discouragement which I learned all stemmed from pride. None of those things are rooted in humility. They are all rooted in self. We get frustrated because we are thinking for our-self. We are irritated because we are thinking for our-self and the same is so for each one of those feelings and attitudes. However, there is no way possible we can stay disappointed, frustrated, annoyed etc., when we truly look at Jesus. When we fix our gaze on Him. I tried, it does not work. When I realized these things needed to go because they were far from "normal" and **far from looking like Jesus**, it was painful. Even the thought of it was painful. There was so much in me that needed to change it felt impossible... overwhelming.

It was not an extremely fun and exciting journey for me to get here, to this way of living, living in absolute surrender to Jesus Christ. It has become that way now. But at the beginning of the ultimate death to self, we'll just say, it was not all sunshine and roses. Now, I can say it is fun, exciting, beautiful, peaceful, and carefree, having constant joy. It does not mean it is always easy (meaning it is not difficult to endure). But it is simple (meaning it is uncomplicated). It does not mean all of life's problems and sufferings go away. But we have the promise of Jesus with us in them, and that changes everything.

Living the crucified life to self and to all the sin we have been so easily entangled in (Hebrews 12:1) <u>can cause</u> excruciating pain. This mostly happens though when we are focused on ourselves throughout the process. Unfortunately, I struggled with this immensely during my journey. (Remember hard-headed and stubborn?) However, I want to share a "secret" with you, it is great news! It will change your transformational journey drastically.

The reality is it is not difficult at all when we see the prize we are gaining, which is beautiful Jesus! Rather than what we are "losing," which is yucky self. Guys, there is no comparison here, NONE! When we can turn a perceived negative into the ultimate positive, we will not dread it. We must keep our focus on our prize and not on ourselves! Fix our eyes on Him. Set our gaze on Him and do not budge. Behold His wonderful face and everything else disappears. He is our Bridegroom King. He is everything glorious and marvelous. He is altogether Lovely in every way. This is where we are to remain... in Him. We will grow more in Love with Him, and this will far outweigh anything we face.

"Jesus, what is so hard about Your Love and surrendering to it? What is so hard about Your grace and receiving it? What is so hard about having a relationship with You? What is so hard about having communion, fellowship, and intimacy with You? What is so hard about You, Holy Spirit, doing the work in me??"

Why does it have to be such a high price to give back attitudes, mentalities, and perspectives we were never created to live by or to have? Why is that such a high price? It is not, and it should not be! This is about perspective. My experience was a little different and I shared it in case this happens to some of you. I would not want you to be taken off guard. However, I highly encourage you to keep the afore mentioned at the forefront of your mind. It will go much easier when you keep your eyes fixed on Jesus. Locked in a steadfast gaze.

However, the emphasis and focus usually gets put on how difficult things will be or how difficult they are. Because we are focused on ourself. Plain and simple. When we focus on our-self it is difficult, but it does not have to be. When we keep our focus on ourselves, we allow the flesh to fight back instead of keeping it nailed to the cross. When we surrender to Jesus and look to Him, we will find that His yoke is easy, His burden is light, and we learn from Him (Matthew 11:28-30). We will see it in Him and know it can be ours. Transformation does not have to be a hard process.

What makes it so hard is the flesh kicking and screaming. The flesh not wanting to let go of our old ways of doing things, our old habits, our old ways of thinking, our old perspective, etc. This is why we must consider the old dead! It is imperative to make the intentional decision to consider the old dead (Colossians 3:1-17 & Romans 6). When we consider the flesh dead it does not, it cannot, have a voice in the matter. Dead things have no ability to speak. They have no voice.

I know it will be different for each person. My story will not be your story. And one of the reasons why it was so difficult for me was because of the stubbornness and hard headedness that was inside of me (WOW is all I can say). I had an extremely hard time coming into complete submission to Jesus because of my own stubborn will. I thought I knew best. I wanted what I wanted, and it caused me a lot of pain and heartache. When transformation came, I was hit with a lot of hard realities of things in me that needed to go. So, it was pretty intense for me.

If what you go through and experience in living the crucified life and going through transformation is hard and grueling, please know to hang in there! It will get better. It does get less difficult in time. The more self is out of the way the less it will affect you (because you are dead and not thinking for your-self). The more self that is annihilated, the easier it gets!!!!!

It becomes the best life we could ever live on this side of eternity. I can promise you it is worth it. Is everything perfect? No! However, on this journey as we grow remember, we are growing more Christ-like. We will respond to things differently. We learn how to handle things differently. We see through the eyes of Jesus now. We have His perspective. We are like Him, and this makes all the difference in the world. This life is so worth it! It is worth going through anything you have to go through to receive the Life lived through Jesus Christ. To receive complete healing, wholeness, and the fruit of freedom, it is worth it!

LOOKING LIKE JESUS: WHAT IT MEANS

As we follow His ways we are to look more and more like Jesus Christ. We are to be transformed into His likeness by the power of Holy Spirit through our surrender to Him. Here I will give you only a few examples through Scripture of what this means for us and what it looks like in our lives. Because this could be a whole book in itself. So, here we go:

1. John 1:2 "He was in the beginning with God." Jesus was with God.

This means He set aside His crown and left His throne to come to this sin-filled place called earth to save us. He came to save His bride. Selah. Not only was He our perfect sacrifice on the cross, but He was also the ultimate example of sacrifice to us by leaving His rightful place with God in heaven. **To look & be like Jesus means we are to sacrifice**. But here's the kicker. Our sacrifice is not carrying the weight of the entire world's sin on our shoulders. Our sacrifice is not dying the most cruel and horrific death known to man. Our sacrifice in no way compares to what Jesus endured. Our sacrifice of suffering may last a little while, but it **always** ends up with something even better. We sacrifice the trash of this world and even what is considered good, and God always gives us His great. Is this really sacrifice?

2. John 1:14-17, "And the Word became flesh.... full of grace and Truth." Jesus is the Word. **To look & be like Jesus we are to become the Word**. Not just read it. Not just study it. Not just quote it. But to become it. We do not really know something until we become it. This is to be our only way of life. Living out the Word of God. **Being full of grace and Truth!!**

3. John 10:30 Jesus said, "I and My Father are One." **To look & be like Jesus we are to be One with the Father** (John 17:21). United to Him in every way. Our every move and every word as being one with Him. Our Father will be identified through our actions and what we speak. How we act and the things we say shows who we belong to. Also, our speech and actions will show how well we know our Father. Are we ONE with Him?

4. John 14:8-11, Jesus was God revealed in the flesh. **To look & be like Jesus we are to reveal God**. Therefore, be imitators of God as dear children (Ephesians 4:29-5:4). When God is revealed through us then we can release God here on the earth. His will becomes our will. Then we can say, "Your Kingdom come Your will be done on earth (in me) as it is in heaven" (Matthew 6:10). This is done in and through us! The King lives in us therefore, we are His Kingdom here on earth. We will bring heaven to earth as we reveal God and walk this out. It starts in me and continues in you as we make disciples.

5. John 5:19 Jesus said, '... The Son can do nothing of Himself, but what He sees the Father do; for whatever He does, the Son also

does in like manner." **To look & be like Jesus we are to have complete dependence on our Father**. Doing everything we see our Father do. We can do **nothing** of ourselves!! Everything we do should be of Him, from Him, and for Him. It is no longer I who lives (Galatians 2:20).

6. John 5:30 Jesus said, "...I do not seek My own will but the will of the Father who sent me." **To look & be like Jesus we do not seek our own will at all**. It is not about what we want but what God wants. It is not about our own plans but God's plans. His will is to be our will. And what we obey and do.

7. John 4:34 Jesus said, "My food is to do the will of Him who sent Me, and to finish His work." **To look & be like Jesus we are to do the will of our Father and to finish His work**. More than physical food, we are to feed from doing His will and finish what He has for us to accomplish in our lives. As our bodies hunger for food may our soul's hunger to do God's will <u>and complete it</u>. I do not want to come to the end of my days not finishing what He has for me to do.

8. John 5:41 Jesus says, "I do not receive honor from men." If you look up honor in the Greek, it means also "glory & praise." **To look & be like Jesus we do not accept honor, glory, or praise from other people**. We are to seek the honor that comes from only God, verse 44. What people say or think about us should not move us. Only what God has to say and think about us moves us.

9. John 17:4 Jesus said, "I have glorified You on the earth. I have finished the work which You have given Me to do." **To look & be like Jesus we are to glorify God only, in all we do**. We must not glory in ourselves saying, "Look what I can do!" It is not about what we have done or what we can do. It is about what Christ has done and will do in us and through us. He has done it, not us. Glory be to God alone.

A Lot of people think if we only do exactly as Jesus did, we are then conformed into the likeness of Christ. If we pray for the sick, give to the poor, perform miracles, signs, and wonders, we are then Christ-like. Or if we read our Bible, do our devotionals, and attend our Sunday services, then we are surely Christ-like.

Being transformed into His likeness is not only doing as He did but it is also being who He is. We are to be like Him in His character and nature. Our heart, our attitude, our nature, and our character should be the same as that of Jesus. We are to reflect His image in **all** we do, **all** we say, and in **all** of who we are. When you look in a mirror, are you looking like Jesus? Do you see His reflection looking back? We should. This is why it is important to be sure our attitude, speech, and conduct reflect that of Jesus Christ.

2 Corinthians 3:18, "And we, who with unveiled faces **all reflect the Lord's glory** are being **transformed into His image** <u>with ever increasing glory</u>, which comes from the Lord, who is the Spirit." There has been a veil of deception over the bride of Christ that needs to be removed. The deadliest thing we can do is unconsciously live a lie. The great deception is thinking we can believe in Jesus and still do whatever it is we want to do. Live however we want to live. Be whoever we want to be. It may not even be that extreme. We may do some of the things Jesus did but not everything. With the excuses of, "Isn't 'everything' a bit extreme?" "I will never be perfect you know." We may live and conform to some of Jesus' ways but there are things we are still holding back from Him, and we will not change. We give the excuses, "That's just me!" "It's who I am." These excuses will not work any longer! We are to be transformed to become One with Christ.

BEING A CHRIST FOLLOWER

After my first divorce had begun in 2011, I realized I had been "playing" church. I went to Sunday services because that was what, I, as a Christian was supposed to do. Especially with children, I wanted them to learn about Jesus. Don't get me wrong, I would hear some good sermons! Then walk out the door and say, "Wow that was really good!" But did I allow it to change my life? To transform me? Did I allow Holy Spirit access to work it in me?

Francis Chan made a comment I had heard one time, "Be careful when you can hear the Word of God and do nothing. Because it quickly becomes a habit. And that is a scary, scary habit to have in your life." In the book, *The Master's Indwelling*, Andrew Murray calls these "carnal Christians." He says, "The majority of people in our congregations are carnal. We give them spiritual teaching, and they admire it, understand it, and rejoice in such ministry. Yet their lives are not practically affected." (Please read 1 Corinthians 3:1-3 & Ezekiel 33:30-33.)

There is very little growth in their spirituality. They struggle with the same things, day in and day out, for years. They continue to struggle because spiritual food cannot enter a heart that is already full of self (carnality). Self is the problem and always has been. If we empty the heart of ourselves, I mean emptied of ALL of us, we can then be filled with all of Him.

This emptying is done in our alone time with the Lord. Go before Him and give Him all. Everything you struggle with. Everything you need to die to. Everything that is on your mind. Everything you desire. You tell Jesus, "I empty me of all of me here at Your feet so You can fill me with all of You. There is no vacancy in me for anything else that is not of You, for You, or from You. Keep me. Fill me. Do Your work in me. Transform me!" It is a simple exchange. We give Him all of us, and He gives us all of Himself. He will never hold Himself back!

Be assured being a Christian in name is not the same as being the nature of Christ or a Christ follower. I know what it was like to call myself a Christian but was I a Christ follower? No, I was not. And I have learned there is a big difference.

A Christian will go through their routine and check off their boxes. They go through their religious motions. Believe in Jesus, check. Went to a service this week (or these days, watched it online), check. Read my 5-minute devotional this morning, check. Said my daily prayer, check. Helped a fellow human being out, check. I say I love Jesus, check.

On the other hand, a Christ follower will pursue Jesus with all they are, and with all they have. They will anchor themselves into a personal and intimate relationship with Him. They will actually Love Jesus, truly Love Him. Not just **need** Him to make everything "okay" or "right" in their lives. They will not use Him for benefits and blessings. They will want to look like Him and commit to a life of change. To transform into His Love. They will be completely dependent on Him. They will hunger and thirst for righteousness. They will seek Him with their whole heart because they cannot get enough of Him, and they cannot live without Him. They are not just hearers of the Word of God, but they are doers of His Word (James 1:22-25). They actually have become His Word i.e., transformation!

In Loving Jesus, they will follow His commands (John 14:15), this is called obedience. A Christ follower will obey the Word of God! Not just the parts they want to or the parts that fit into their lifestyle. Not just the parts that are easy or convenient. But a Christ follower will obey ALL of God's Word. Yes, even the parts that can be hard and not fun. Like living the crucified life. Forgiving those who have painfully hurt you. Loving your enemy. Doing good to those who hate you. Blessing those who persecute you and praying for those who spitefully use you (Luke 6:27-36)! However, obeying these hard parts, will be by far, the most beneficial for you and for your freedom from self.

This is a lifestyle we must choose to live. Repentance is a lifestyle. Surrender is a lifestyle. Transformation is a lifestyle. Communion (Intimate Relationship) with Him is a lifestyle. Obedience is a lifestyle. These are all lifestyles and not one-time events.

It is not a double life we can live, by living like the world on Friday and then gathering with the church on Sunday. We cannot love the things of this world and God (1 John 2:15-17 & James 4:4-8). We cannot bow to the lusts of our flesh and bow to Jesus. We cannot live for ourselves and live for Jesus. Choose you this day (Joshua 24:14-15). Whom will you serve? The world or Jesus? Your-self or Jesus?

Please understand me, I am not saying that calling yourself a Christian is wrong. What I am saying is if you are calling yourself a Christian then make sure you are following Christ. That you are a Christ-like one. Our daily walk and conversation ought to be very marked by Him and pleasing to Him. We must come out from the world and be separate. Our character and purpose are to look very different from the world's. Romans 8:14, "For as many as are **led** by the Spirit of God, they are the sons of God." As a son (and daughter) of God, we should have our lives surrendered to Him, being led by Holy Spirit. We should be denying ourselves daily. Being transformed by Holy Spirit into the image of Jesus Christ.

This means we will represent Him accurately to others as Love. We are to be kind, tenderhearted and forgiving. We return good for evil. We think of others better than ourselves (we are humble). We will not seek our own. We are a servant to all. We will abstain from the appearance of evil. We are to be holy as He is holy. It means we absolutely live crucified to our flesh, our self-life. As a son (and daughter) of God, all we do is done for the glory of God. This lifestyle, of being a Christ follower, can only be lived through a transformed Life.

If you are not being transformed, then you are only a Christian checking off your boxes. Doing your own thing and living like the world. Living according to your own flesh. Living according to your own wants, desires, and selfishness. If we as Christians live this way, it distorts who Jesus is to a world that is lost and hurting. They see no reason to have Jesus. They have no need of Him if we, Christians, are living just as they are. It also distorts Jesus to our fellow believers, and we then become a stumbling block to them. If we are not reflecting Jesus in any area of our life, we need transformation.

Practical Application:

Do not be conformed to this world but be transformed by the renewing of our mind (Romans 12:2). We are not to live like everyone else in this world. We are not to follow the same pattern of the world. We are to be set apart, living differently as they do. Transformation is not an option. It is not a hobby or a part time job. It is not a "Well let me think about it." If we are a Christian, transformation is our life, and it requires every bit of us.

The definition of transformation by *Oxford Languages* is: "a thorough or dramatic change in <u>form</u> or <u>appearance</u>." *Dictionary.com* adds the change in <u>nature</u> and <u>character</u> as well. However, I want you to catch the words "**thorough**" and "**change**." Change begins by doing things differently.

I cannot emphasize this enough and at the risk of sounding like a broken record, this "doing" things differently is done by our surrender to Holy Spirit and our obedience to Him. Keep in mind transformation mostly happens in the secret place, inside our cocoon, with Holy Spirit doing the work. We do not work at it at all! We cannot change us only He can. The following is a brief outline of the thorough change (transformation) Holy Spirit will bring, by the renewing of our minds:

1. He changes the way we <u>think</u>, which
2. changes what we <u>believe</u>, which
3. changes how we <u>feel</u>, which
4. changes what we <u>speak</u>, which
5. changes the way we <u>act</u>.

Which changes the way we live our entire lives. Talk about a thorough change!

Now let's go into more detail:

1. **Change the way we think (repent):** To think differently is repentance. Repentance is always the first step in transformation. It is the first thing John the Baptist proclaimed (Matthew 3:1-2). It is the first thing Jesus said when He started His ministry (Matthew 4:17). Romans 12:2 tells us how to think differently, by the renew-

ing of our mind. We are to be transformed by the renewing of our mind in the Word of God. Which means we will begin to think according to the Truth of God's Word because we have the mind of Christ (1 Corinthians 2:16). When we look up the Greek meaning for mind, we see it says this, "Divine or human in thought, feeling, or will and understanding." Since we have the mind of Christ, we are not referring to a human mind here, but we have His divine mind. We have Christ's thoughts, feelings, will, and understanding. Selah. We are to bring <u>every thought</u> into captivity to the obedience of Christ (2 Corinthians 10:4-6). By doing this, it will line ourselves up according to Jesus in every area of our lives. We are to take control of our mind (by deciding where to put it) otherwise it will be a runaway train (and that is dangerous). We are to put our thoughts, feelings, will, and understanding into the obedience of Christ or they will be put into the obedience of the flesh, which is controlled by satan. We are to no longer live in the effectiveness of our own, fleshly, mind but the mind of Jesus.

2. **Change what we believe:** As we are being renewed in our mind, Holy Spirit is penetrating our heart with His Word as well. In this process Truth goes from being only head knowledge to becoming heart knowledge. We not only know Truth with our mind, but we experience Truth in our heart. When we experience Truth in our heart, we will begin to believe according to the Truth we now know. We are aligned with Truth instead of lies. And the Truth we know will make us free (John 8:32). But if we believe wrong, we will choose wrong. **For Example:** If I believe I am worthless, I will choose to live up to what I believe I am worth. If I believe I am priceless and worth dying for then I will make choices based on being priceless and worth dying for. I will not be given away or sold short ever again by thinking I am anything less than what Jesus paid the price for. If I believe I am a sinner, I will continue to sin. But if I believe I am holy as He is holy (1 Peter 1:15-16) then I will choose holiness.

3. **Change how we feel:** What we believe (whether Truth or lie) is our perspective (how we see things), and how we see things is how we feel. So, what we believe determines how we feel. **For Example:** If I believe and see myself as worthless, I will feel worthless. If I believe and see myself as priceless, I will feel priceless. I want to use

some other examples here as well. If I believe (or perceive) I have been wronged by someone then I am going to feel hurt by that person. But if my eye is good, my whole body will be full of light (Matthew 6:22). This means I will have Christ's perspective. So now let's take that exact situation and see it through the eyes of Christ. If someone has "wronged" me then I am not hurt by them (because I am not thinking of my-self), but I hurt for them. Because if they have acted outside of the character of Christ then they do not know who they are. And it is a miserable place to be, to not know who you are in Christ. Another example: If I believe someone offended me, then I will feel offended. But when I see through the eyes of Christ, I will take no offense (because I am not thinking of my-self). Therefore I will not be offended, nor will I feel offended. We will only have Love for the other person. This only can be done when self is crucified, and we are not thinking for ourselves. When we see from Christ's perspective, single eyed, healthy eyed, we will be full of light. Our feelings will then be aligned with Holy Spirit in Truth and not with our flesh in lies. Always look to see everything through the eyes of Jesus and not by the feelings of the flesh, which is to be dead.

4. **Change how we speak:** Once we believe and see through the eyes of Truth we will feel differently about things and because we feel differently, this causes us to speak differently. Out of the abundance of our heart (Greek: our thoughts or feelings; mind) our mouth speaks (Matthew 12:34). What comes out of our mouth comes from the overflow of our thoughts and feelings. Here, it is important to understand that life and death are in the power of the tongue (Proverbs 18:21, 10:11, & 12:18). We will speak Truth and life into things, circumstances, and people or we will speak curses and death into them. satan will try to steal the Word of God from us, because he knows God's Word is where the power lies. It is the Sword of Holy Spirit after all (Ephesians 6:17). If he can keep us speaking curses over our lives, he keeps us bound. **For Example:** "I have no money." "I am so sick." "I am worn out and tired of this, I can't do it anymore." "I can't live without you." If he can keep us speaking curses over others it can keep them bound. **For Example:** "You are worthless." "You will never amount to anything." "You will never get it, will you?!" "You are so stupid." The list can

go on of all the death and curses we will speak over ourselves and others. We are to find Truth in the Word of God to speak Life into every person and situation. It is so simple when our feelings are lined up with Holy Spirit and not our flesh, to speak Truth and not curses, Life and not death. God has entrusted us with His Word, His will, His ways. Only Holy Spirit can do this transformation in us and through us by our surrender to Him. Then we will speak Life according to our obedience to Him.

5. **Change the way we act:** A good man out of the good treasures of his heart brings forth good things (Matthew 12:35). A good tree bears good fruit (Matthew 7:15-20). This whole string of events started by renewing our mind. It all starts with a thought, one thought. Thoughts will determine what we believe, how we feel, what we say, and how we act. Thoughts decide the choices we make, good or bad, right or wrong. By having a renewed mind this will change the way we live our lives. It will change the way we act. Change means we must do things differently than before. We should be noticeably transformed. The Word of God is more than something to be thought about or believed it is something to become, to be lived! Only Holy Spirit can do this in us and through us by our surrender to Him and then we will live out our lives in obedience to Him.

If thoughts do all of this, I can see why Holy Spirit tells us to be transformed by the renewing of our mind. Surrounding our thought-life must be the Word of God. Our thought life cannot be careless. Fruitless thoughts will pass through, but they should not be viewed as harmless. God tells us to take captive every thought to the obedience of Christ. Why would we think on anything less than Jesus? We cannot allow thoughts to wander around and go all over the place. Also, our minds are not playgrounds for everyone to romp around and play in. Nor are they public gardens for others to plant their own ideas in. satan is trying to get a foothold wherever and however he can. Even if it is through what other people say. We are to take captive every thought and set our thought-life aside for God's purposes alone.

Reasons Why We Will Not Go Through Transformation

The gospel preached today is muddy waters. The fact is, we typically only want to hear and do what makes us "feel good." What will support the lifestyles we are living in. What will boost our egos and self-confidence. What will make us comfortable. What will be easy and what will make us "happy." We want to hear these things spoken to us from the pulpit and by no means should you contradict us about the way we think, what we are doing, or the way we are living our lives. Sadly today, there are a lot of people behind pulpits accommodating that mentality. They are motivational speakers and entertainers more than they are Shepherds.

Another way of putting it is the gospel preached today is stagnant waters. We want to hear what we want to hear so we do not have to change our lifestyles. So, we can remain right here where we are "happy" and stagnant. When water is stagnant it means it is not moving. It is still. Water that is still and remains stagnant will start to stink, it begins to grow bacteria that causes diseases, and if you drink it, it will kill you.

What we really want is to experience the "feel goods" of these messages and in life because we do not want to suffer, nor do we want to change. As a Culture, we mostly look at change from a negative perspective. We do not like change or even the connotation of the word. We do not welcome it. And it typically sets us in a place of unease. We do not want the hard things. We do not want to disrupt our comfortable lives. We do not want the inconvenient things change (transformation) will bring. We do not want our lifestyles to change. "Just leave well enough alone," is what we will say.

Let's face it, in this self-centered world who really wants to pick up their cross daily, die to their selfish ways, and follow Him in complete obedience every day? That sounds hard and like such a drag. So here we are. Because we would rather take the "easy" road. The way that is more "comfortable" and "fun." To remain in our "happy" bubble. Which are all lies and illusions of satan, by the way, he is deceiving you. We end up living enslaved to our flesh, rather than being free.

There is nothing easy about living for satan who controls your flesh, your self-life. There is nothing comfortable about living in bondage to him. There is nothing, not a thing, fun about that roller coaster ride. When we continue to live in the flesh it will leave us hurt, broken, empty, tired, bitter, angry, offended, and so much more.

Sadly, most of us would rather keep dealing with anxiety, worry, stress, frustration, insecurities, fear, addictions, etc. instead of dying to the self-life and walking away from it **completely**. We say we believe in Jesus, but do we pick up our cross daily and follow Him to receive true freedom from it all?

We end up believing lies that prevent us from changing all the time. Any reason for not wanting change will always come from lies, fear, and the fact we do not want anything that may mean we have to suffer. These all are intertwined with each other and are all tools of satan to keep us from being free. **They are all rooted in selfishness** and thinking for self.

Here are some examples of these negative perspectives and lies that keep us from freedom:

1. We think of change as being uncomfortable: We do not like the idea we might have to do something outside of our comfortable, "normal," routine. For example, if we do not like talking to people and that has become our normal routine, then we will not like it when we have to talk to people. We also think of change as being uncomfortable because we know we will have to change what we do and how we live in our now comfortable lives. For example, we may have to give up our weekend drinking and partying. We may have to change the way we celebrate holidays and special events. We may exhibit a "token" change by attending Sunday service or giving up a particular sin. But ultimately, we want to retain owner-ship of everything else and how we live our lives. We are not will-ing to leave (die to) the lives we are now living. Our own desires, lifestyles, or certain sinful habits are too precious to us. We may have to end relationships we do not want to end. We may have to leave a job we do not want to leave. We may have to move from our home of 20 years. The list is endless of what "uncomfortable" things we may have to do.

2. We think we do not need to change: The mentality we carry is, "I am good just the way I am. I do not need to change. I like me." A lot of times we do not see anything wrong with what we do or who we are. We call it "normal." We will also say, "This is how God made me." The truth is most of our behaviors are what we came into a fallen world with. Think about it, no one had to teach a baby to cry when you take its pacifier away. No one had to teach a toddler to cry and say, "No, mine!" when a toy is taken away. Also, most of the

behaviors we have were formed in us through life and not God. So no, this is no excuse to not change. When, in fact, that was not the way God made you at all. We are made in His image. And as He is, so are we in this world (1 John 4:17). If we cannot find that behavior in Jesus, why do we give ourselves permission to be that way? Just when we think we do not need transformation, that is when we need it the most. When we embrace the life of transformation, everything about us will change for the better.

3. <u>When we truly believe we are not the problem, they are</u>: Behavior is a habitual thing and change can feel wrong. Do we really think we do not need to grow up? This is ultimately what change/transformation is. It is growth. Growing up into the likeness of Jesus. Transformation is internal and external. What we do influences all aspects of life. Our faith in Jesus Christ should change our behavior and how we treat people. What we say and do (especially to those who have not died to self) affects them more than we can imagine. Our focus is never to be on someone else being the "problem." But on our own transformation. Asking ourselves, "How can I change?" "How can I be more like Christ?" And not pointing the finger to someone else.

4. <u>We think, "This is just how life is"</u>: We will get hurt, frustrated, annoyed, irritated, and take offense, and we say, "These things just happen it is part of life," and "There is nothing we can do about it." These then become our automatic reactions. Because we think it is "normal" and "This is just how life is." However, I have learned it is far from "normal." As I learn more about living the crucified life, I find that it is simply not true. I do not have to succumb to living life that way, according to my flesh and self-centered feelings. I do not have to get frustrated. I do not have to get annoyed. We do not have to live in bondage to this way of thinking or feeling any longer. This is not just how life is. We can live free from all of this through transformation.

5. <u>We think change is elusive</u>: We say things like, "**It is too hard,**" so we quit. Or "**It hurts too much,**" so we avoid the suffering. We end up avoiding the pain of change at all costs. And I do mean at all costs. Some of us will destroy our families and/or ourselves because we think it is impossible to change. Or we simply do not want to go through the process of change (especially if it involves

pain and suffering). Or we think it is unnecessary (again, we are good the way we are). We live broken lives as a result. Maybe we become more aware of the addictions we need to stop doing and we think there is no way we can ever stop doing this now... impossible! God never asks us to do anything we can do on our own. Knowing that the power of Holy Spirit at work in us can accomplish everything to make us free and transformed. "According to His working, which works in me mightily" (Colossians 1:29). Where we think it is impossible to give up these addictions that have been so engrained in us for years. They have been our "crutches," our "go to's," our way of living. He is saying, "Holy Spirit in you can do this!" "By the power that works in you" (Ephesians 3:20). It is possible. He asks us to live a life which we can never live and do a work we can never do. 2 Corinthians 3:5, "Not that we are sufficient of ourselves to think anything of ourselves; but our sufficiency is of God." So, in essence, <u>He does give us more than we can handle</u>. Because we are not meant to handle it. <u>He will not give us more than He can handle</u>. **And He can handle all things**. God's will cannot be carried out without God's strength. We are to be in full reliance on Him. We are not to carry our burdens (our cares). We are to cast them onto Him.

6. <u>We enjoy our sin and selfish ways</u>: Maybe it is we enjoy our addictions and do not want to quit. Maybe we do not want to change because we do not want to give up the sin, we are living in. We do not want to stop doing certain things we may like. We might not want to have to change the lifestyle we have grown accustomed to living or come to enjoy. We may have accumulated much wealth by sinful ways. We may be living with someone we are not married to. Changing these things now will change our lifestyle. However, selfish ways, self-satisfaction, or self-pleasure typically win out and we continue to live in sin. We are deceived if we believe sin is a better life, or the better way, or it is more fun. Living in sin is never the better life, the better way, or more fun. Sin will destroy us. We may think we are happy doing it. We may think we are having fun doing it. But we are not to be deceived. satan only wants to steal, kill, and destroy us by keeping us enslaved and in an illusion of better, happy, and fun. Sin is not an evil thing to desire. Sin is an evil desire that will destroy us. Sin is not only an action we

can do, but also an entity that wants to control us. 1 Corinthians 6:12 says, "All things are lawful for me, but all things are not helpful. All things are lawful for me, but I will not be brought under the power of any." Transformation means dying to that addiction and the sin we are so easily entangled in (Hebrews 12:1-2). We must surrender it to Holy Spirit to eradicate it from our lives. When we consistently engage in a personal and intimate relationship with Jesus we begin to, in no way, ever want to sin against Him. The desire to want to engage in sin or in that addiction is eradicated from us completely.

7. <u>We are afraid</u> of getting hurt, afraid of trusting Him, and flat out afraid of change: The question that will go through most of our minds is "If I surrender my all to this transformation, what will God <u>make me do</u>?" "I just know I am going to have to do something I don't want to do!!" I went through this fear. I thought God would make me stay single for the rest of my life and that was the last thing I wanted. So, I forged my own path in a relationship that was never meant for me, and then asked God to bless it. And let me tell you, it was not worth it. Doing what I wanted was not worth it! To not be in God's will is NEVER worth it! satan will keep us gripped with fear to not go through transformation and to keep us from doing God's will in our lives. We also are afraid of giving anybody else control of our lives. It may sound silly to some and to others this may be your life right now, but we fear having to trust God with every bit of our lives. We fear we will get hurt. We fear He won't come through for us. We fear it will not be what we want. It is a sick and twisted thing the enemy does by lying to us to try and make us believe we can better control our lives. Therefore, we only trust ourselves with them. When the truth is our life in our own hands only leads to destruction (Proverbs 14:12).

8. <u>We believe we are justified for living the way we are living</u>: Are you offended? Are you resentful? Are you neglectful? Are you hurtful? Are you closed off? Or whatever else, it may be that you are. Are you "justified" for living any of these ways? You may think "Yes, I am justified." You may be thinking things like, "I was hurt by this person, and it will not happen again." Or "If you knew what happened to me you would understand why I am the way I am." Or "I never had a good example to follow." Or "They said this, this, and

this to me and that's just not right!" But I am here to tell you, if Jesus gave up every "right" He had in surrender to His Father, then as a Christ follower, this is exactly what we are to do. We have no "rights" or "excuses" to be "this way." Do not believe the lie thinking you are justified for any sinful way you are acting. We are to make ourselves of no reputation as Jesus did (Philippians 2:7). We must let go of any toxic intentions of our heart. Such as treating someone poorly because we were never treated right. Wanting to make someone pay for what they have done. Giving someone the cold shoulder until they apologize. We must give up any and all forms of manipulation. We also have to let go of the destructive attitudes we hold onto, all in the name of "justification." There is a lot of forgiveness we will have to give that we may not want to give. There are a lot of things we will have to let go of as we keep no record of being wronged (1 Corinthians 13:5 NLT). Letting go of the hurts may seem unimaginable. However, I want to tell you, letting go of all these things will be the most freeing thing you will ever do. **To be transformed into the likeness of Christ, is the freest we will ever be.** Jeremy Taylor says, "Men are apt to prefer a prosperous error to an afflicted Truth." A good example of a prosperous error is thinking we are "justified" for living the way we live or feeling the way we feel. Therefore, we are good with the way we are acting, "We have good reason, and every right to be this way." But it's just not true! The "afflicted" Truth is we need to forgive, let go, and be like Jesus to that person. We are to be Love. Let me say, the only reason why you will feel afflicted by this Truth is because your flesh is still alive.

9. Another lie we tend to believe is that this will be a boring way to live: We believe we will have no fun in our new Life in Christ. Because we are largely a people all about pleasure and "I just want to have fun," we tend to keep to our old ways of living. The Truth is, yes, you will have to change the way you live your life. However, this transformation will be the most stable life you have ever lived. You will never experience more peace and true joy. It is far from boring. It is wonderful, and yes, it is fun and exciting. It is all those things and more. Without having to feel regret the next day. Without wondering what you may have done the night before. Without waking up with another hangover, feeling awful. You will never be

freer in your entire life. You will no longer live on a roller coaster of fleshly emotion or tiptoe on eggshells of uncertainty. You will be on a Holy Spirit roller coaster of activity and emotion which is far from boring.

The Truth is change will disrupt your life! Allowing Holy Spirit to transform you will disrupt your life in every **best way** possible. Yes, there will be extremely difficult days. Yes, there will be tests that try you that feel like they will never end as you deny your-self, and all fleshly desires. Yes, you will have trials you just wished, "would get over with already." As you transform, every day might not be an exceptionally great day. Especially in the beginning, when you are learning the new ways of Life in Christ. There are birthing pains of what Holy Spirit is birthing in you. There are growing pains of what Holy Spirit is growing in you.

However eventually in the process of things, every day will become an exceptional day. The beauty that comes on the other side of these tri-als, fires, and testing's is incredible. As you grow and transform you will have a greater portion of peace and joy through it all. Your Love for people will grow. You will handle "difficulties" with patience and ease. Yes, I said ease. You may say, "Impossible!" Yet I tell you it is true. In transformation, Holy Spirit is growing in you, His fruits. The greatest deception would be to think this kind of change would be dreadful, not attainable, or boring. It will be the best thing to ever happen to you and satan's objective is to keep you from this life of freedom as much as he can. Period.

The fact is this life is not about us and what we want. It is to be lived completely for Jesus. Not just some areas but ALL (Colossians 3:23). And **whatever** you do, do it heartily, as unto the Lord. I have also finally realized it does not matter what God wants me to do, I will do it. And He is a good, good, Father who only wants the absolute best for me. So, I trust Him.

OUR INWARD REST

Our behavior and character are transformed by the renewing of our mind and there is another fundamental Truth. Our behavior and character de-pend on our inward rest in Jesus. Jesus says, "Come to Me, all you who la-bor (feel fatigue, work hard) and are heavy laden (loaded up), and I will give You rest (refreshment)" (Matthew 11:28-30). "For My yoke is easy (bet-ter, good, gracious, kind) and My burden (task or service) is light (easy &

less).” Come to Me all who are fatigued and loaded up and I will give you refreshment. For My yoke is good and my task is easy. This is an inward rest that will transform our lives when we take time to sit here with Him in this place. Instead of being frantic, stressed out, and aggravated.

Yet, how many Christians do you know who live here? Hannah Whitall Smith says this (parenthesis and emphasis added), “No soul can ever reach its highest fulfillment except through His working. The only thing that can hinder this work is our own failure to work in harmony with His plans for us. The Scriptures outline for us a life <u>abiding in rest</u> and <u>continual victory</u> which is far beyond the ordinary life of the Christian experience. Allowing Jesus to carry our burdens and managing all of our life (casting the whole of our cares). Instead of trying to do it ourselves, trusting ourselves to Him, absolutely and continually. Here is where we are to rest.”

Holy Spirit tells us in Ephesians 2:5-6, We are made alive together with Christ and He has raised us up together, and He made us to <u>sit</u> together in the heavenly places <u>in</u> Christ Jesus. When we see ourselves seated in Christ, our walk will take its character from our seated position in our union with Christ. Transformation derives from resting in Him in His presence. If we for a minute lose our rest in Him, we will surely get tripped up and stumble and try to start doing it on our own again. But if we dwell in Christ and Christ in us, our position there with Him in the heavenlies will empower us to walk worthy of Him here on the earth (Ephesians 4:1-6).

The beauty God possesses in His nature and character, He imparts to us in intimacy. God's beauty we receive while in His presence is transforming. It shifts our emotion, and He takes away from us the dross, sludge, and drudgery of this world. Ask yourself this, “Have I taken time to linger and rest in the presence of God?” This is where all lasting transformation will begin. Surrendering ourselves to Him. Being obedient to His Word. And knowing Him as the Lover of our soul. As we dwell in His presence.

You have a choice to make. Will you choose to stay the same and settle for a shallow, hollow, mediocre, miserable, or “less than” life? Any kind of life outside of Christ will lead to these options. If not, immediately eventually it will. Or will you choose to surrender to Holy Spirit? Read the Word of God and obey Him? Have an intimate relationship with Jesus, resting in Him, and allowing Holy Spirit to transform you? This is the only path to true freedom and to live a life of constant healing, wholeness, peace, Love, joy, kindness, forgiveness, etc., no matter what storms may come. By trusting in the only One who will NEVER change. I know what Paul speaks of now when he says, "...for I have learned, in whatever state I am, to be content" (Philippians 4:11).

We will never find everything it is we need in this world. We will never find everything it is we need in other relationships, our spouse, or our children. We will never find everything it is we need in ourselves. We will never even come close. We will only find everything it is we need in Jesus Christ! But my God shall supply ALL your need according to His riches in glory BY Christ Jesus (Philippians 4:19). I took the long, hard, and painful road to get here to this understanding of full surrender, dying to self, and being transformed. My prayer is to help you, so you do not have to take that same road.

THE PROCESS OF TRANSFORMATION

I will warn you the process of transformation takes time. It is a lifetime commitment. So be patient with yourself and with God, and do not ever quit. Because you may want to at times. I know this very well. There were days where I would run to my prayer closet with my suitcase in hand. I would cry to God, "That's it! I'm done! I quit!" It was one day my Abba Daddy, ever so gently pointed out to me (through a very close friend) that I had my bags packed and I was telling Him I was running away from home. But in reality, I was running straight into His Ever-Loving arms there in my prayer closet with suitcase in hand.

Without a Loving relationship with your Father, how will your life ever be transformed? By you trying to change you? You trying to change you will never work. Discipline is good and it is a fruit of the Spirit (temperance), but self trying to discipline self will never work. Self trying to cast out self will never work. Real change comes from the grace of God. Only Holy Spirit can do this kind of work in us, but He needs a yielded vessel in order to do it.

I realize now, most of the time I was doing it on my own. I was seeking God, I was searching His Word, and then going out trying to put it into action. Never fully grasping "Christ in me." It is not by power or might but by My Spirit, says the Lord (Zechariah 4:6). He is the only One who can do the work to transform me. And I truly can do nothing without Jesus. May this be our prayer, "Lord, I rest in You. Come and do the work in me. Move everything around that You need to move and remove everything that needs to go."

Be prepared, transformation is not a quick fix. It is a daily dedication to Him. It is a daily yielding ourselves to Him. Positioning ourselves for change. Be sincere, take your convictions, and shut the door behind you to be alone with Him. Here, allow Him to do a work in you. It is one thing to be convicted of something, it is another to allow Him to work that thing out of you by being alone with Him. Surrendered to Him. Talk with Him about it. Take His Word and in prayer start agreeing with what you were created for.

A Prayer to Pray:

"Thank You Lord, for bringing this to my attention (for conviction). Thank You for forgiving me. I know this is not what You created me for. You have created me for a greater purpose than this. I yield to You so You can work this out of me. I choose to die to this. I give it to You. I do not want it. Thank You for transforming me. Thank You for taking what is wrong in me and making it right. I do not want to be anything that people cannot recognize as You, Jesus. How I respond to what would be considered disappointments and even the unexpected things. How I respond to unkindness. I am not here for others to serve me or make me happy. The whole reason I am alive is to Love and Love is not self-seeking, and it keeps no record of wrongs. You have obliterated selfishness in my life and have removed it far from me. Thank You Holy Spirit for forming Christ in me. Make me like You in every way. In Jesus name, Amen."

Every day is a process and at times a very intense process at that. This is not a split-second miracle cure, but it is a miracle cure of unimaginable proportions if you continue in it. When you finally surrender your all to Jesus and say, "I can't do it on my own anymore," or "I can't just give you breadcrumbs anymore," or "I am tired of being a prisoner to my own feelings," transformation begins. And you will continue to transform into the likeness of Jesus, "Being confident of this, that He who began a good work in you will carry it onto completion until the day of Jesus Christ" (Philippians 1:6).

Surrender yourself to the power of Holy Spirit in you, to change everything about you that needs to be changed. Everything that needs to go must go and everything that needs to grow must grow! Yes, it may be hard at times, yes it may be scary, but perfect Love casts out fear (1 John 4:18). Change is for our good. Change is to make us whole and complete in Him.

Change is to make us more like Christ in this world who so desperately needs Him. We are to count it all joy, to lose our own life, so we can find true Life in Jesus Christ. For only He is our Way our Truth and our Life (John 14:6).

Nail yourself to the cross once and for all and commit to being transformed. You will be better off for it. Do this and trust Him to do the good work in you. "Holy Spirit, continue to do what only You can do; transform me more and more every day, moment by moment. I live for You and You alone."

Practical Application:

Go into your secret place and,

1. Ask Holy Spirit to show you everything that is in you that needs to go. Holy Spirit is the Light of the Lord that shines in us and exposes things. It is His mercy that He points these things out in us (Psalm 90:8 & Psalm 51:6). All of Psalm 51 is a good prayer to start with!
2. As He shows you, make a list. Ask Him where to start. Write down scriptures that pertain to that area. Speak them over yourself. For example, if you are struggling with anger. Repeat James 1:20 (NLT), "Human anger does not produce the righteousness that God desires."
3. Then pray over it. "Holy Spirit, I surrender this to You. I choose to die to the anger that is within me, and I thank You for filling me with the righteousness that God desires. Thank You for working anger out of me and filling me with Your peace, Love, and joy. Help me to recognize when the anger comes so I can surrender it to You immediately. Help me to respond in Love instead. Let it be known that I desire to choose You over all else. Thank You for the good work You are doing in me."

Sometimes things can change in an instant, or rather quickly, or it may take time. Trust me, I have done this enough to know change does come, eventually. One day you will realize what used to make you angry, has no hold on you now. You no longer get angry. Submit yourself to the process of allowing Holy Spirit to grow you, it is worth it, beyond any earthly treasure it is worth it. We do not have the power to change ourselves. It is only in our submission to the power of Holy Spirit that He can change us. Our one job is to surrender. There is nothing we have to do to "prove" ourselves to Him. Stop striving to prove yourself. Stop trying to do the work. Believe Holy Spirit is doing everything in His power to remove everything that needs to be removed. Rest in His transforming Love and enjoy being His.

Do not speed the process with the mentality of, "Hurry up, transform me already." "Why is it taking so long?" "I want it now!" There are many lessons we are learning during this time, but we just want it to be done and over and rush through it. Sometimes the biggest lesson we learn is our complete need for Him. If we were just "over it" we would not recognize our complete need for Him every moment of every day, as we do during this seemingly long and drawn-out process. It teaches us the consistency of relying on Him and being with Him every moment. So, when the trial is over, we remain in Him and not drift away because we think "we got this" now.

Another lesson He is teaching us in the process is patience. James 1:2-4, "My brethren, count it all joy when you fall into various trials, knowing that the testing of your faith produces patience. But let patience have its perfect work, that you may be perfect and complete, lacking nothing." When we face delays, without self in the picture, we will know God uses these delays to produce patience, deepen our trust in Him, and strengthen our faith. When self is gone, we are not focused on the delay or how the enemy may be trying to use it, or what the enemy is "doing to us." We are focused on what God is doing in us! The self in us will gravitate towards what can God do for me, instead of what God is doing in me. How is He changing me through this? What is He producing in me? Do you want to be perfect and complete and not lack anything? Then pray for patience. And in this process, when we just want to see results, understand He is growing in us patience for these very reasons. So, rejoice!

He also, in this time, is preparing us in advance for what lies ahead. He knows what is coming. What we are not yet prepared for. **For Example:** I wanted something to be done and over with so bad. I kept wanting to speed the process, yet the Lord kept me in His care and waiting on Him (thankfully). One day He gave me the revelation of what it means to be seated in Christ (Ephesians 2:5). I had a vision of me literally sitting on His lap with Him moving everywhere I needed to go. It was as if He was my fuel station I was permanently attached to. Giving me everything I needed.

Allowing me to rest in Him. Knowing He was taking complete care of me. Once I received this vision, the very next day I received the information I was waiting for. He knew I needed the revelation, of the previous day, to get through what was coming this day. Sometimes we need time of preparation. His timing is perfect. Do not speed the process of freedom and transformation.

Do not hinder the process by holding on to anger, frustration, unforgiveness, offenses, resentment, etc. Do not hinder the process by trying to bury it (ignore it) or trying to cover it up (mask it). We hinder our healing and being made whole when we do any of these things. We cannot hold on to this stuff and be made whole at the same time. We must let go of the one to receive the other. We cannot move forward when we are still stuck in our past. Do not be like Lot's wife and turn back (Luke 17:32-33) only to be frozen in time.

There was something the Lord showed me one day when I was so hurt and broken. I was being quick to speak the Word of God over my life, just wanting the emotional pain to go away. I was quick to cover it up by using Scripture, not realizing I was only masking over it. Do not get caught up in hiding behind Truth when you haven't received the healing you need. I was also quick to minimize it and try to bury it with excuses like, "This would have never happened if I was obedient in the first place." Which was true. But what I needed to do was face the hurt and the pain. To mourn the loss of hopes, dreams, future, connection, and the loss of anything else that was tearing me apart.

Once I could let this go in honest reflection with the Lord, face the pain of it all, and not try to bury it deep inside, only then could I receive the healing He had for me, move forward, and not look back. Once we have done this with Him, and if hurts and brokenness keep coming back up and hitting us in the face, now we speak the Scriptures over it and stand on His Word. Not in hiding but in confidence. Because now this is the enemy attacking us. he wants us to rehearse our past over and over and over so we will always remember it and remain broken. But once we have truly poured it out before the Lord and received His healing, let it all go, and cast our cares upon Him, now we can forget the former things and take every thought captive. My friend says it this way, "Rejoice! Do Not Rehearse!" So, when the rehearsing tries to come, rejoice in the Lord instead! And do not hinder the process of freedom and transformation by rehearsing the past.

Reasons Why We Do Not Fear

All the while between wanting to speed the process and the possibility of hindering the process, is the fear of the unknown. We have a hard time not knowing what the end result looks like. What the end result will be and what it will mean for us. Trust. We are to trust Him in the process and trust Him with the outcome. Trust He is taking care of us perfectly the whole way through no matter how much it may hurt or when anxiety tries to rise from the unknown. We are to trust in His Loving care and know He has the best plan for our lives. Trust the One who Loves us the most, Jesus. Trust Him all the way through it. The whole time we are in it.

Fear of the unknown is stronger when we are going through something difficult. But the fact is every day is an unknown. We get quite comfortable in the everyday routine of life. Thinking we know what is coming next and that it is "just another day." We know the routine, but we do not know when an assault, an attack, or a testing of our faith, may come. At all times we must put our faith and trust in what we do know:

1. Jesus has already defeated the enemy: The enemy is powerless in our lives. The only power he has is what we give to him. We do not need to fight a devil who has already been defeated over 2,000 years ago. Do not waste our time or energy. Trust in the Lord and simply **stand** in the victory we already have (Ephesians 6:10-20)!

2. We are seated with Christ in the heavenlies: He is in us, and we are in Him. We are hidden (concealed, kept secret) with Christ IN God (Colossians 3:3). Selah. He is our refuge. The enemy should in no way be able to get to us!!! So do not allow him to. Take our **seated** place IN CHRIST

3. We are sitting above all that is going on: So, get Jesus' perspective on the situation. "Come up here and see." We are to have His mind in all things. See with His eyes. Have His understanding. He will keep us in perfect peace (the Hebrew is shalom = safe, well, happy, healthy, rest, prosper, favor, friendly, good, and whole) whose mind is stayed (lean upon or take hold of, set, stand, sustain) on Him, because we trust (confident, sure, bold, secure) in Him (Isaiah 26:3-4). Take time to ponder this.

4. Therefore, we have already overcome: no matter what it looks like in the natural realm. When we walk, we walk by faith not by what we see (2 Corinthians 5:7). He is our victory.

5. <u>Now we can actually **rest** in Him</u>: in the midst of the storm because He is holding us steady. He is our anchor. We need not fear. He is our stronghold. He is our refuge.

6. <u>We cast the whole of our cares onto Him</u>: We need not worry for anything.

7. <u>We are to trust Him in the process</u>: We trust in His finished work and what He already accomplished on the cross.

Wow! Are you encouraged yet? I know I am!

A Prayer to Pray:

"Father I completely surrender to You. Everything I have and all that I am, I leave to You, in Your hands to do Your work. Holy Spirit I need Your power to change me! Transform me into the person You created me to be. Help me to live in forgiveness, kindness, Love, humility, and respect. I desire to live Your way in all things. Whatever You want Lord, show me, and I will do it! Teach me to be Your Love, Light, and Life to every situation and to bring Truth in all things. I rely on You, Holy Spirit, to transform me. Matthew 11:28-30, I lay all my burdens at Your feet Jesus, all my cares, concerns, and circumstances. I give them all to You, Jesus, take them. All I want is You. You are my Life, my breath, my food, my drink, You are everything to me!! I die to my-self and surrender to You Father. I will learn from You and find rest for my soul as I live The Transformed Life!"

Five Take Aways

1. God has already deposited in our spirit His image. Created in His likeness. It is our souls (our mind, will & emotions) that need to be transformed.

2. To look like Jesus is our greatest priority and goal in life. The majority of this will happen in our secret place and in intimacy with Him. We become what we fix our gaze on, what we desire, and delight in.

3. Looking like Jesus is not just doing what He did but becoming who He is. To take on His nature and character as well (Luke 6:40). Only Holy Spirit can do this in us.

4. When we are led by Holy Spirit, doing exactly what Jesus tells us to do, it will always be our best life ever!!

5. As the metamorphosis of the butterfly: When we die to self (our grub form/the flesh) and enter into our cocoon (our secret place with Holy Spirit) to be transformed, we will come out as a butterfly (looking like Jesus). Living the life, we were created to live. Bringing heaven to earth.

Picture from the internet.

Isaiah 53:3, "He is despised and rejected by men, a man of sorrows and acquainted with grief. And we hid as it were, our faces from Him; He was despised, and we did not esteem Him."

CHAPTER 6

The Truth About Rejection

I FEEL SO dead inside. The pain cuts deep. I prophecy over every part of me, to every inch within my heart, come alive! I have been given a heart of flesh that will Love fully. I have been given Life to live abundantly. I have exceedingly great joy. I will breathe. I will live. I will Love with gladness. I am **fully accepted** and Loved by You, Jesus. I do not **need** anything from anyone else. <u>Therefore, I will not fear rejection</u>. No one can reject me when I have been accepted by You, my Bridegroom King. I will not be afraid to Love more than I have ever Loved before. I do not have a spirit of fear but of power, Love, and a sound mind. I will Love more boldly and courageously than I ever have. Lord, You, take me from glory to glory and from faith to faith. Break off fear, the fear of being hurt.

Holy Spirit tear down every barrier I have placed around my heart to protect it. Which in turn is only preventing me from receiving Your Love fully. I have placed these barriers in fear. Fear of being hurt again. Fear of being rejected again. Help me to understand that because You have accepted me, no one can reject me. Also, because my flesh is dead no one has the power to hurt me. I ask that Your Love penetrate every lie I have believed and break down every wall I have built to protect myself. I realize I do not know how to Love without You. Please teach me. Teach me to Love without expecting anything in return, without conditions. I want to receive Your Love freely so I can Love freely. I want to receive Your Love fully so I can Love fully. I want to receive Your Love unhindered so I can Love unhindered. **End of journal entry.**

Feeling Rejected?

We tend to receive our identity from other people. We seek to get attention from them. We strive to get approval from them. We want to be validated, appreciated, accepted, and respected by them. When this does not happen, we get hurt or possibly even angry about it.

Oh, we will pretend this isn't true. We will say we know we find our identity and all these other things in Jesus, until... we do not get the job promotion, we are neglected, or we are mistreated by others (especially those closest to us). When we notice they begin to distance themselves from us. When we begin to feel how they act unusual toward us. How they view us differently. How they love us or not. If they accept us or not. If they approve of us or not. If they agree with us or not. If they ignore us. If they leave us...

This is an area both women and yes even men struggle with. We will look to people of the opposite sex to make us feel good about ourselves, searching for compliments. We will look to role models, parents, friends, mentors, pastors, leaders, boss', even our jobs and professions to receive validation, approval, and status. This is how we know how good we are, how attractive we are, if we are regarded, respected, and how well we are doing in life. And if we do not receive what we are so desperately looking for, then we are distraught, angry, or sad. Or it could even be we are so used to not receiving anything, so we feel indifferent to it. It is like a numbing gel on our heart.

There are those who live in a place of feeling rejected and it has cut you to your core. In some, you have been rejected so much it has beat you down and has left you almost paralyzed in life feeling completely numb inside. It could be rejection from a spouse, a child, your mom, dad, or any other family member. Is it from a friend? In the workplace? In the church? Do you feel like you have been overlooked (that you are not seen), disregarded (shoved to the side), or not chosen (as if you are back in elementary school and you are the last kid picked for the team)? Rejection of any kind? I understand, I have been there as well. I understand how it can steal your identity, your worth, and your life if you allow it to.

I started out with an excerpt from my journal to let you know, I do not take this chapter lightly. I struggled in the area of rejection for a **long time**. There was a period of time where I had deep, deep wounds from the feeling of being rejected. I mean festering, infectious wounds. They were ugly. God had to take me through many lessons and some visions to bring me to a place of understanding Truth. Understanding my value and my worth IN HIM and TO HIM. I will share what I am led to share. My prayer being it will help any of you who struggle with knowing the depth to which you are accepted, recognized, approved of, valued, and Loved in the Beloved, Jesus Christ. He gave His life for you; you must be worth THAT MUCH to Him. And if that much **to Him** (the One who matters most), then why do we put so much weight on other people?!

I will preface the rest of this chapter with the fact that this was about a year long journey for me, to comprehend the Truths that will be revealed here. I do not like giving time frames, because it may take someone else less time or more time. Nevertheless, there are some words I had to continue to contend with along the way and they are steadfast, perseverance, and resolve. To know if I kept pressing through and clinging to Jesus in the valleys and the darkest of nights, one day, I would be FREE from the lies that tried to destroy me. Freedom is when you are free from you and the "needs" of others.

THE LESSON OF THE DOGS

I was in a really low and lonely spot in life. By this point I had felt rejected and disregarded for many years now. On one particular day Holy Spirit took me into a vision:

I saw two dogs in a house. The owner of the two dogs had just walked in the door. Both dogs ran up to him wanting to receive their share of attention. The owner bent over and started petting, rubbing, and scratching one dog while the other one jumped around waiting for its turn. The owner kept lavishing all his love and attention on the one dog and after many attempts to get the owner's attention the other one finally realized it was not going to get it. So, the dog hung its head and sulkily walked over to its bed in the corner of the room and laid down. Immediately I knew the picture of the sad, sulky dog was me.

I went to bed that night and I woke up at my usual time early in the morning. I went to the place in my living room where I would have my quiet time with Jesus. I had praise and worship music on, and I was just sitting with Him, thinking about His Love for me. When He took me back to the dog laying sadly on its bed, which was a very accurate portrayal of me at the time.

Then suddenly, Jesus' presence became like a cloud over me (over that dog on the bed), covering me, comforting me. I could feel Him lavishing all His Love over me. It felt like a hot summer's rain falling, drenching my parched soul as He poured all His attention on me. I sat there soaking it all in, "More Lord, more." He filled me with His Love and when I was overflowing, He whispered in my ear, "Which one has it better?" I immediately perked up and all I could do was cry and then laugh. I knew I had it better, as I answered Him with excitement, "I do Jesus, I do, I DO!!!"

Receiving the Love and affection of Jesus was way better than receiving all the "love" and attention from another person. From a broken person, for that matter, who does not really know how to Love. The other dog receiving everything that broken person had to offer, compared to receiving everything I need and more from Jesus, is no comparison. Not even close! From Jesus we receive completeness, wholeness, healing, perfect Love. We receive satiation (Jeremiah 31:25) which is an abundant satisfaction (an overflow) of things eternal that will never fade, fail, fall, go away, grow apart, break, or decay. Jesus satiating us with His fullness, presence, Love, peace, joy, strength, perspective, purpose, and plan.

Something we NEED to understand is, <u>we CANNOT be rejected when we are accepted by God.</u> Ephesians 1:6, ".... God made us accepted in the Beloved." The Beloved is Jesus, who is our Bridegroom King. That is exactly what Holy Spirit was showing me in the vision with the two dogs. When I am in a place of fully receiving His Love for me, then I am not in a place to notice the one who may not be paying any attention to me at all. All my focus is on Jesus, the One who matters most.

When I completely turn my face to Jesus Christ, and I, with open arms **receive** all His attention and affection, I am not aware of anything or anyone else around me. When I realize in my heart I am accepted by Jesus Christ, how can I ever let the feeling of rejection steal from me again? Stealing my peace and joy by stealing my identity or worth. If I keep, in the forefront of my mind, God's Love and His approval of me then how can

I ever let feeling rejected by someone else ruin my day? No one can have that kind of power over me unless I give it to them.

Our worth, our value, our identity, our acceptance, our approval, only comes from Jesus and His view of us. "And You, Jesus, said I was worth dying for." Christ crucified is the Truth about us. Our identity and worth come from Him ALONE. Stop and truly think about it. Jesus left heaven to rescue His bride, to purchase us back with His own Life. He said we were worth it or else He would have never died for us. Jesus has paid the highest price for us. Do not de-value the price Jesus paid by saying we are not worth it, and that we are not worthy of Him. Did He die for nothing? No! We are of highest value to Him and of utmost importance. We are His bride.

Nobody else matters, they have no say in this matter (of our worth, value, and identity)! Nothing can be added or subtracted from our value by someone else accepting us or rejecting us when we know who we are in Christ and that we are His. There is a quote from Lysa TerKeurst that caught my attention, "Live from a deep assurance that I am fully loved, then I will not be begging for scraps of love from anyone else." Wow! There is a difference when we receive something real from someone who is filled with Christ (real and true Love) and when we receive scraps from people who are not filled with Christ who are ultimately still broken. They try to love but it is the world's way of loving. There is a Grand Canyon of a difference. It's like receiving the finest, choice cut of steak versus a piece of a hot dog. Just kidding, it's so much bigger than that.

When we do not need to be Loved by other people, this allows us to be free to Love them unconditionally. Because we do not need their love to validate us or make us feel better. When we are fully, deeply, and extremely Loved by Christ, we can then be Love with no strings attached. When we are full of His Love and His presence then we can go Love people without resentment or bitterness. It is pure Love; it is real Love. Love that takes **no account** of a suffered wrong (please read 1 Corinthians 13:1-13).

Side note: We are so used to hearing this part of Scripture that we do not take a good long look at it anymore. We may expect others to Love us this way and never understand we are to become this. We are to BE 1 Corinthians 13 Love. Not expecting it of others.

When we are full of His blessed assurance, we will not look for reassurance from anyone else. We will not need their compliments to make us feel noticed or to make us feel good about ourselves. We will not need acceptance to make us feel approved of. We will not need respect from others to make us feel important. Because we know Jesus approves of us, that is all that matters. Keep in mind, anything anyone else can give us can also be taken away (we go further into explaining this a little later). No one can take from us what Jesus has given us. No one can add to or take away from that!

satan, on the other hand, wants to bait, hook, and sink us by having us take rejection personally. he wants us to rehearse feeling rejected and what has been "done to us," over and over and over until it becomes an infectious disease in our soul. He builds rehearsal stages and programming studios in the minds of people all the time, "Take 84.... Action!" So that we re-live it over and over. We never let it go, and it becomes bigger and bigger in our minds. Until it becomes the biggest fish we ever caught!!!

We are not to rehearse the wrongs that have been done to us. Because Love keeps no record of wrongs (1 Corinthians 13:5 NLT). We are to let it go, forgive, and trust it into God's Ever-Loving and capable hands. Do not trade something that is truly valuable (the Love of Christ) for something of lesser worth (the feeling of rejection). It is a perspective shift. When we see through Truth everything changes.

One of the Truths I needed to know and understand is that I am NOT here for people to love me. I am not here to receive anything from anybody. I am here to give. I am here to be Love. I am here to serve others. I am here for the Lord's purpose and plan. Not for me to get what I want. Nobody owes me anything. This took a long time for it to sink in and I continue to grow in it daily.

EXPOSING THE FEELING OF REJECTION

The feeling of being rejected is a lie from the enemy. We fall for that lie, and **we allow ourselves** to be hurt, offended, discouraged, or disappointed by rejection. I am not discounting that rejection happens. I know people will reject us. And now I sound like I am contradicting myself since earlier I said you CANNOT be rejected when you are accepted by God. By this I mean when we are rejected by man, we do not have to let it have any power over us because we are accepted by God. So even though we are rejected by man, we cannot be rejected because God has infinitely more say than any human.

1 Peter 2:4 NKJV, (Jesus) "rejected indeed of men, **but chosen of God,**

and precious." If Jesus was rejected, we will be rejected too. John 15:20, a servant is not greater than his master. And here is the beautiful part, let this get grounded and rooted into your soul. Even though you will be rejected, YOU are chosen of God and PRECIOUS to Him! **Just as** God Loves Jesus, He Loves you (John 17:23).

The lie you have to be <u>affected</u> by other people's rejection and **feel** hurt, offended, discouraged, disappointed, distraught, etc., is just that, **a lie**. Remember you are chosen by God and precious to Him, who is the King of the Universe, your Creator, your Savior, and Bridegroom King. Let that bring a smile to your face and hold your head up when someone tries to hurt you through their rejection (either knowingly or unknowingly). When you know Whose you are, that you are God's chosen, you will never cower to the feelings of rejection again. He matters infinitely more than anyone else in this world.

Also, the lie you have to <u>accept</u> other people's rejection... No, you do not! Stop accepting what somebody else (who does not know their own identity in Christ) has said to you or portrayed to you by their actions in how they have treated you. Stop putting it on as your coat, wearing it around, and letting it affect you. Do not believe someone who does not know who they are. If they knew who they were in Christ, and the Love of Christ was fully in them, they would have never said what they said. They would have never treated you the way they treated you. They would have never done what they did.

When someone does not treat you as Jesus would, it could just be a momentary relapse. Where they have momentarily forgotten who they are in Christ. Or it is from their own brokenness. Where the Love of Christ has not been allowed full access in their life. Truth has not penetrated their heart for them to do any differently yet. Or they have rejected Christ in this area of their life, and this is far more sad than my "feeling" of being mistreated or rejected. They are deceived and believing a lie.

This does not mean we are to treat them in any other way but in Love! We are to display compassion and forgiveness on them. Knowing they are living without the Truth of Jesus or maybe not even knowing the Love of Jesus for themselves. How empty they must feel to even treat someone that way. How they are scrambling to find fulfillment in whatever ways they can to fill the void in their own life and not even recognizing it.

Some people think they find satisfaction in saying mean things, being cold-hearted, or just flat out rude. They do not know what they do.

Even if they know what they are doing, they do not understand why. Have compassion on their broken soul. "Hurting people hurt people." Instead of allowing the enemy to make us feel hurt by them why aren't we hurt for them and the state they are in?

Why don't we understand if they are in a place where they do not even know Christ's Love, how can they ever give it? We are expecting something from someone they cannot give. People can only give away what they have, what they are full of. If someone is full of hurt, they will hurt you. If someone is full of emptiness all they can give you is empty promises. If someone is full of themselves, all they can give you is selfishness (themselves). If someone is full of sickness in their soul, all they can give you is their sickness. Only when someone is full of Jesus, can they give you Jesus and His Love.

JOURNAL ENTRY:

John 12:47-48, "And if anyone hears My words and does not believe, I do not judge him; for I did not come to judge the world but to save the world. He who rejects Me, and does not receive My words, has that which judges him..." This brought conviction to me. With Holy Spirit speaking to me, "Have compassion on this person's soul." Have compassion on them for they have a judge already. We are to Love, show mercy, have compassion, and not condemn and judge. I was so wretched, and You never gave up on me. So many choices I made that were flat out wicked. Thank You for not giving up on me. Thank You for Your constant pursuit of me. Thank You that You saved me out of every mistake I made in every season. **End of journal entry.**

So instead of me getting hurt by that person, I will hurt for that person and the place they must be in to be so selfish, unloving, and unkind.... they must be so hurt. And most of the time they do not even know it themselves. It is masked over so well. I will not be hurt by them; I will hurt for them and bless them by praying for them (Romans 12:14, Luke 6:28).

When you know Whose you are, that you are God's chosen, you will never walk away carrying someone's rejection on your shoulders again. I mean **KNOW**. Truly know. In your heart know. Experientially know you are chosen by the Creator of the Universe, and you are His precious treasure. Then you can freely and unconditionally Love the ones who try to hurt you. If you continue to get upset and are affected by rejection, finding it hard to Love them, then the "knowing" is not in the depth of your being yet. Do not let this discourage you! Keep yielding this to Holy Spirit and He will help you grow up into Christ in all Truth.

If Jesus is truly my everything, it should not matter what other people do or do not do "to me." Author Raymond D. Trice in his book *Hidden in the Process of Time* says these profound yet true statements. "As soon as God becomes real to us, people pale in comparison." "Nothing that other saints do or say can ever upset the one who is built on God." Selah! No, really pause and think about those two statements. Powerful!

Reflecting on the lesson of the two dogs, this is how the dog who gets zero attention or love from its owner can fully Love its owner in return without receiving anything from him. This is how a wife can remain connected to a husband who consistently ignores her, or vice versa. This is how an employer can continue working for a boss who disregards them or takes advantage of them. We must drink of the Living Water (John 4:13-14). Draw from the true well of Life, Jesus Christ, and we will never thirst again or run dry!!! Praise the Lord. This all has to do with a perspective shift. We must see in the Light of Truth.

If you are not received by people and you are rejected, shake the dust off your feet and move on (Matthew 10:14 & Acts 13:49-52). Do not let that become a weight on you. Do not be held back by someone else's lack. Lack of seeing Truth, of understanding, and of receiving you. Do not let their lack affect your identity let alone determine your identity. Lay aside every weight that would slow you down or hold you back and run with endurance the race that is set before you, looking unto Jesus the Author and Finisher of your faith (Hebrews 12:1-2). You are full in Him, lacking nothing.

EXPOSING EXPECTATIONS

Another part of the lie of rejection is we feel they "did this to us." "So and so, did this to me, I can't believe they would do that!" Let me ask you, was it your expectation of them that led you there to feel rejected or let down? I only ask so bluntly because I have done this very thing. Let me explain. I used to expect much from people. Whether it be what they did for me or how they treated me. And when I didn't get what I wanted, or what **I had expected,** I felt rejected, disregarded, vulnerable, etc. (Interesting fact, this would happen in my relationship with God as well. If He did not do something for me, I felt rejected by Him. This is a sick tool of the enemy.) Then

I would go into self-defense mode and throw up my wall to protect myself. This self-protection looks differently for everyone. This is why "I" has to die!

A Prayer to Pray:

"Lord, remove the deep roots that have grown in me of self-defense and self-preservation. That when hurts try to creep in, I do not retaliate, defend myself, or throw up walls to "preserve" myself. That I will instead, run to You to be my defender and protector. Help me to see when I am closing up my heart. So, instead I can run to You and You can keep it open. So, I can Love the way You Love. In Jesus name, Amen"

Let me ask again, what kind of expectation are you placing on people? When you give someone a gift, do you expect anything in return? Even if it is only a "thank you," you are still expecting something. Then you feel let down when you do not get anything from them not even a "thank you." When you say, "I love you" to someone do you expect them to say it back? And what if they don't? Where does that leave you? Hurt? Confused? Let down? Our hearts will grow bitter over time if we keep expecting things from people and we do not receive it from them.

If you have been expecting from people to be only what God can be, or do what only God can do, then you will be hurting until you stop expecting from them. Because let's just face it, they do not always live up to these expectations and then we feel disappointed, discouraged, and rejected when it happens or does not happen. You cannot expect someone to give you everything you want. Not even some of what you want. Get filled from the right source (Psalm 146:3-10).

We put identities on people such as being a husband, a wife, a parent, a child, a pastor, etc. Then we expect them to act a certain way. We want or expect people to do things they were never created to do like make us feel beautiful, or wanted, or valuable, or worthy, or happy or fulfilled, or respected, or important, etc. Then we get disappointed, hurt, or frustrated when they do not live up to our expectations of making us feel good.

For Example: We say things like, "Well this is what husbands are "supposed" to do for their wives." "A wife is to be "this" for her husband." "You are my mother, and this is what a mother is." "This is what a father is supposed to be." "You better honor me." "I better get some respect around here." "I need you to love me and pay attention to me!" The list goes on of what we expect and demand from people. And when we expect these things (because this is what the Bible says after all) we end up getting hurt by the very ones we say we love. You know the 1 Corinthians 13 Love that does not seek its own or keeps no record of wrongs done.

Even though the Bible gives us clear guidelines and instructions on how we are to Love others in every situation and with every "title" we have been given, it does not mean we now expect this from other people. This must be conceived in people through a relationship of Love with Jesus Christ. And it must be birthed from Him through them. It cannot be mustered up on our own. Otherwise, it will fail. That is the world's way of doing it, and the world's way is severely distorted and broken. It is my responsibility to take the Word of God, to walk in it, and become it. Not to expect it of others towards me.

I do not want to give you permission to hurt me. I do not want you walking on eggshells to live up to my ideas of what or who you should be. That you must be a certain way for me to be ok, that is not ok. I must stop living only as good as "you do me." I must stop expecting people to fill needs only Jesus can fill. And now that you have let me down because you could not fill me, or be who I needed you to be, my life is a shell of an expression of "how you let me down." When Love is supposed to keep no record of wrongs suffered. <u>You are not the one who makes or breaks my day</u>. If I **need** you to love me for me to be ok then I will stay self-conscious, self-focused, and insecure. Then when do I become Love?

Most people still believe, "Those closest to you will hurt you the most." Let me ask you why would this be? Is it **because you have put demands and expectations on those closest to you?** And now you are depending on them? Let's get really honest here. Wouldn't that be why those closest to you can hurt you the most? Because if, "You don't owe me a thing" is really true then how can you "fail me" or "hurt me?" You are not here to serve me. I am here to serve you. We are here because we have the privilege to reveal Christ to everyone around us. So, why would we have all these expectations on other people to only be left hurt, disappointed, frustrated, and aggravated?

We have heard, "Those closest to you will hurt you the most," for most of our lives so this is what we expect. And we are setting ourselves up for heartbreak. Because on the day they don't seem to be as sensitive as they could be or as thoughtful as they used to be, we become insecure. Suddenly it doesn't seem like the people we are depending on are here for us anymore, and now we are shattered. We allow the way somebody treated us to be an excuse for not Loving them. We allow ourselves to stay guarded (set boundaries) so we will not get hurt. And the whole time Jesus is Lord. He Loves us. And our position in Him has not changed. Who He is in us has not changed!

I was here too, **I get it!** I lived too long here!! What we need is Truth to make us free (John 8:32). We have been inundated with the world's psychology and lies. We have grown accustomed to the world's programming. We so relate to our flesh (why it must die) more than we do to the Truth! We listen to what the enemy whispers in our ears and we think the lies are true. Then these little attitudes sneak in, these mindsets, these things we haven't allowed to be renewed in the Word of God. We just keep believing what we always have heard because it sounds good, it sounds "right," and this sure is how I feel. It's the way that seems right to a man, but its end is death (Proverbs 14:12).

We need to care enough and Love enough to speak Truth into people's lives (Truth in Love, Ephesians 4:14-15). Not to fear what they may think or how they may take it or even that they may really dislike us or even hate us for saying it. When we have the fear of the Lord it totally wipes out the fear of man. Jesus is our credential and we do not have to fear the qualifications or the rejections of people. The Truth is we are to receive Love from Jesus and then we are to be Love to others with the exact same Love. With unconditional Love. We are free to Love and give unconditionally when we become Love and we do not need love. We do not need someone else's love or validation to make us feel loved or validated. We are to Love others without expecting anything in return.

No one owes me a thing. When we can truly believe this, it takes the focus off us and puts the focus completely on God. All to bring Him glory. We do not expect anything from anyone. If we do, eventually they will let us down. Only expect from the Lord. He will never fail us. We can expect our Father to take care of every need of ours. People were not put into our life to fill our needs.

There is only One who we can expect from. His name is Jesus. And yet everyone searches for what they will never find in other people. Broken people at that. Then get disappointed when they cannot find it. Our expectation (my hope, the thing that I long for) is to come from God (Psalm 62:5). Even our desires are to be **from** Him (Psalm 37:4). We can EXPECT ample supply from God and more than we could ever ask or imagine (Ephesians 3:20).

We must look to our Provider of all things, Jesus. Expect to receive His Love so we can be Love to others. Expect to receive His Truth so we can be Truth to others. Expect to receive His goodness so we can be goodness to others. We are to become these things so that it becomes our lives lived. Instead of becoming resentful and bitter because we have not received these things from other people. And then we give those who mistreated us or rejected us, our hurt, pain, and brokenness instead of Jesus.

JOURNAL ENTRY:

Lord, we are expecting our spouse, children, family, or friends to fulfill us when only You can. We expect them to serve us when we are to serve them. We expect them to Love us when we are to Love them. If I am not Love, then what am I doing here? I close the door to all compromise. And I stop living at the expense of others! **End of journal entry.**

A PRAYER TO PRAY:

(Read Psalm 62 first), "Lord, take away all expectation I have that is not from You! When I expect from anyone else, remove it from me. From this point forward I wait silently on You for my expectation is from You. I trust in Your ample supply. In Jesus name, Amen."

JESUS OUR EXAMPLE

No one could have possibly been more rejected than Jesus. For the very people He came to save, they rejected Him at every turn (John 1:11). His own did not receive Him, and He never changed who He was or how He treated others. He remained Love. He gave everything and laid down His life so they would not be eternally separated from Him. He came to the world He created, but what He created, rejected Him. They didn't want Him. This happened to Jesus!

Isaiah 53:3, "He is despised and rejected by men, a Man of sorrows and acquainted with grief. And we hid, as it were, our faces from Him; He was despised, and we did not esteem Him."

In doing a study on this Scripture this is what I found:

1. "Jesus was despised." Thought to have been a vile person. Held with an utmost degree of contempt.
2. "Jesus rejected by men." Unworthy of the company of all men. He had no "respectable" men with Him of rank, stature, or authority. His close-knit group was made up of fishermen, women, tax collectors, and prostitutes. Men of "stature" refused to associate with Him.
3. "And we hid, as it were, our faces from Him." This is as one covering their face from a leper because they cannot bear the disgusting sight. Loathed to look at Him. A turning away from Him. (This brings tears to my eyes even writing this).
4. "We did not esteem Him." We did not appreciate His worth. We did not think Him dear. We disregarded Him. We put no value on Him. He was not worth noticing. He was not worthy of our affection or regard. We estimated Him as nothing.

I want us to really think about the above study and think if this was you, everything you would feel. If this was (or maybe it even is) the way you were (are) treated. Talk about having a reason to be offended. To "go off" on someone putting them in their place and giving them a piece of your mind. To give them the silent treatment or stop talking to them altogether, completely cutting them out of your life. A really good reason to have a chip on your shoulder and talk bad about them to all your friends while defending yourself. Definitely a good reason to have hurt feelings, be discouraged, disappointed, let down, and holding a grudge, taking it out on the person who hurt you, "making them pay for it."

Bring Jesus into any of those scenarios, and now it sounds foolish, right? Do we see Jesus ever acting any of those ways? Is that how Jesus Loves? No! If we do not see these things in Jesus, then why are we doing them? It ought to sound just as foolish for us to be doing this, because we are made in His image. Why can we take the things we say and do, the mentalities we live in, and the attitudes we have and justify them? But enter Jesus in there and it sounds silly and ridiculous? Because that is not who He is! But it doesn't sound silly when we are in there because we don't know who we are. It ought to sound just as silly and foolish for us.

Jesus is Love and He never changed. Man, and the way they treated Him, had no power to change who He was. He remained the same. So, the rejection didn't change a thing about Him and why He was here. How else could Jesus do this if He was not Love? How else could He come to the world THAT HE CREATED, and it not know Him, and come to HIS OWN and they not receive Him, and He stay the same? Because there is not one selfish bone in His body. He didn't come for Himself; He came for you. To redeem you. To save His bride. To walk out Truth. To be Love to a world that mistreated Him extremely unjustly, making this our model. He is our example!

What Can Never Be Taken Away

When people do nice things for us sure it is nice to receive it from them. When people say nice things about us sure it is good to hear. I do not want to discount nice gestures people do. Because it is nice! However, these things should not be what makes or breaks us. It should not be what makes or breaks our day. What other people do or do not do, say, or do not say, does not make us any more or less important. <u>Our importance is strictly held tight in the eyes and thoughts of Jesus Christ our Lord.</u>

When we receive anything anyone else can give us, it can also be taken away. **For Example:** Someone can give you peace of mind one minute and leave you in turmoil the next. They can give you a compliment and then tear you down in the same breath. They can say they love you and then abandon you. They can say you have the promotion and then give it to someone else. They can say they are leaving you an inheritance and then leave you with nothing.

If we rely on other people to give us peace, joy, assurance, acceptance, security, and yes even Love we will at some point be let down by them. These are all things we must receive from our relationship with the Lord, who will never fail us, forsake us, or leave us broken hearted.

No one can take from you what God has given to you. You are accepted in the Beloved. You are Loved in the Beloved. You are valued in the Beloved. You are worthy in the Beloved. You are secure in the Beloved. You are justified in the Beloved. You have purpose in the Beloved. You are chosen by God. When you know this deep within the core of who you are, you will not look for any of these things, from anyone else. We can refuse to be disappointed because Jesus Loves us and that is all that matters. No one can take His Love from us. We can refuse to be discouraged because Jesus is good. No one can take His goodness from us.

Anything anyone else can do to us, good or bad, does not change who we are in Christ and why we are here (the purpose of Christ in our lives). If someone does something good for me, it should not make me feel any more important than if they do nothing for me at all. Yet if we are honest with ourselves this is how we tend to feel. Christ determines our importance, our value, our worth, alone! And what He did for us can never be matched by anyone else.

So, if my spouse does not give me a gift for my birthday, does this change my value or determine what I am worth? No! Then we should not let it. We must surrender to Holy Spirit and say "no" to the urge to be let down, disappointed, and not feel loved. Die to self and you will not give them that cold shoulder for not getting you something. We must see by now, all these responses we have called "normal" are of the flesh!

If my boss does not give me the promotion, does this change my value or my worth? No! If I own a business and my employees do not show me respect does this change my value or my worth? No! Should any of these examples change who I am or how I treat people? No! We must learn to see through the eyes of Jesus Christ. I have said this multiple times in this chapter, and I will say it again, it is a change in our perspective that must happen! For His thoughts and His ways are higher than our own (Isaiah 55:8-9).

This goes to say what other people say about us, either good or bad, does not change who we are in Christ either. Someone can give me a very nice compliment and it will not inflate me and make me feel even better about myself because I know who I am in Christ already. Or someone can say something very mean to me and it will not deflate me and make me feel worse about myself because I know who I am in Christ. People cannot take from us or add to us what was never theirs to give. We do not get our worth or value from other people. No matter what anybody says it does not define who we are. Only what Jesus says about us defines who we are and again, Jesus says, we are worth dying for.

When we really take these Truths to heart, we will find, it will no longer be necessary to "set boundaries" to protect ourselves from each other. Because we do not have to be vulnerable to each other. We grew up learning this stuff from other people, the world, and psychology. So, when people say, "Oh, you crossed the line!" Let's just erase the lines so there are no lines to get crossed! We can either operate out of strongholds that have been constructed (and boundaries we have created through lies), or we can learn to operate from Holy Spirit alone. Are there any boundaries Jesus set for people, so He could protect Himself? I don't know of any...

PRACTICAL APPLICATION:

1. <u>Communion</u>: One thing Holy Spirit led me to do during this period when I was struggling with the feeling of rejection and knowing my worth was to take communion every day. To meditate on what the cross means to me. To visualize Jesus hanging on that cross in my place. Talk about a way to impact you forever, and it did. Get alone in your prayer closet, with your communion elements and just be there with Jesus at the cross as He dies for you. There were many times I would visualize myself clinging to Him, kissing His mangled and disfigured face (Isaiah 52:14), tears streaming down my cheeks in irresistible gratitude. Seeing myself being crucified with Him. As we are called to crucify our flesh. Jesus dying for me is now something I know I am worth!

"Jesus, I am Your promised one, Your treasure, a pearl of great price, the apple of Your eye, Your bride. How can this be, that You think this of me? But You do and You show me and tell me how worth it I am. I am worth Loving. I am worth dying for."

2. <u>Lament</u>: You can lament to God as David did. Pour out your heart to Him in truth and brutal honesty about how you may feel in that moment. However, also just as David did you always must end that time with building yourself up in the Lord. In Truth, in who He is and who you are in Him, praising Him, and giving Him thanks. When you do this, that feeling of hurt and rejection will fade away. The more times you do this and practice this and be intentional about it, the more this becomes your way of living, and it becomes who you are. Then you will not live according to hurt, disappointment, discouragement, offense, or rejection anymore. I know you may be shocked when I say this but in fact, you will in time, not have those feelings anymore at all because it is truly Christ who lives in you. You are dead. You must not allow yourself to run down that bunny trail of lies. Following your hurt feelings with the enemy leading the way.

3. <u>Presence & Prayer</u>: If you feel let down by someone or even hurt by them then you need to take all these things to the Lord. Sit with Him. Let Him Love on you. Draw very near to Him. Put all your attention and focus on Him. Change your perspective and where you have been putting your expectations. When you do you cannot possibly walk away from being in His Presence, receiving His Love, declaring His Truth, and remain hurt. He gives you complete healing and wholeness. You can count on His promises to be true.

4. <u>Truth & Surrender</u>: The myth believed is there may be a love that is greater than the Love of Jesus. People are so wrapped up in receiving the love of other people or loving themselves, they cannot even comprehend there is a Love that puts all others to shame. Nobody else's love could stand the test next to His Love. And yet everyone searches for what they will never find in people. Only in the one that is fully surrendered to Christ, will someone find that kind of Love. Because it is Christ in them. And what a beautiful thing when that happens!!

A Little Testimony

This all was something that did not just happen overnight for me. I had to remind myself of these truths over and over and over. You know... repetition. I had to be intentional to repeat it, speak it, boldly declare it, and pray for it. Because let's face it, I was going through my second divorce now. This was a time of great pain and brokenness. The enemy worked overtime at making me feel ultra-rejected, unwanted, and worthless. "You are just a throw away," he would say to me. "You are not enough, you were never good enough to keep." "You are such a failure." "You are not worth anything." These are the lies that pummeled me day after day, wave after wave.

As I cried out to God, "Truth be told, Lord, I do not want to be known as someone who has been divorced twice. With everything within me I DO NOT want this as part of my story at all!!!!!!! But here I am, and it is. With tears flooding down onto the floor, I lay this burden down and let it go into Your Ever-Loving and strong hands. I also let go of any pride that is attached to this feeling I have. The pride and concern of what others may think or say about me. Help me to know what You want to do with this story. I am giving it to You, for You to have Your way."

Immediately He spoke back to me and said, "This is not what defines you. Your past does not dictate who you are, and it does not dictate your future either. It is only I, who defines you. I will finish your story"

For the amount of pain I felt with 2 husbands leaving me. God was showing me how much I was infinitely worth. How valuable I really was. The enemy would have been so happy to destroy me with his lies. He would have enjoyed having "taken me out for the count" many times. But with every fiery arrow that flew at me, it would be quenched with my shield of faith. As I would wield my sword of the Spirit, which is the Word of God, sharper than any two-edged sword (Hebrews 4:12). Jesus is my impenetrable Fortress that surrounds me always, everywhere I go. You cannot keep me from Him, so what are you going to do to me now?

To know Jesus would never give me up. In those places where I had been given up on, He met me there and told me I was worth the fight all along. To win my whole heart and full surrender, I was worth it. He had more for me than this. No, I did not want two divorces to be a part of my story, but God is doing something much greater in me. He is creating a masterpiece. I will allow Him to define me and not the divorces. Yes, they are a part of my story, but they are not the end of my story. He has the final say. What I felt was so shameful, He would use for His glory (Isaiah 54:4-6 AMP).

I laid this all down through my tears. The feelings of shame, disgrace, the humiliation, the inadequacy, I laid it all down at the feet of Jesus. "Thank You Jesus, for Truth You speak to me in its stead. Thank You for Your healing oil over each of these wounds that You bind. Mourning will last for a night, but joy will come in the morning!"

A Prayer to Pray:

"I thank You Jesus, that You can handle everything. You can handle everything about me. You can handle EVERY part of me. You can handle EVERY detail!! There is nothing about me that scares You away. There is nothing about me that will make You run away. There is nothing about me that will turn You away from me. You Love me. You created me so You could Love me. I will rest here in Your Love for me. Your Love for me will never fade away. Your Love for me will never diminish. Your Love for me will never wear thin. There is no certain way I have to be for You to Love me. There is not a certain way I have to look for You to Love me. I do not have to do anything special for You to Love me. And this is how You have called us to Love. JUST AS. Just as You have Loved me, I am to Love others. John 15:12, "This is My commandment, that you Love one another, **as** I have Loved you."

"Lord, that rejection will never steal another minute of my life. That I give no place to feeling hurt, disappointed, or discouraged over what other people do or say. Keep me in Your perspective. Seeing through Your eyes. Knowing Your Love for me will never die. Yet in Your Love for me, You died. May I Love this way! I Love You Lord, In Jesus name, Amen."

FIVE TAKE AWAYS + TWO BONUS

1. Nobody owes me a thing. You are not the one who makes or breaks my day.
2. I did not wake up for you to love me. I woke up to be Love. We are to Love others without expecting anything in return.
3. People can only give you what they have.
4. Our importance is strictly held tight in the eyes and thoughts of Jesus Christ our Lord.
5. People cannot take from us or add to us what was never theirs to give or take.
6. Jesus was rejected more than any other and it never changed who He is. So, it should not change who we are and how we treat people.
7. When we have the fear of the Lord it totally wipes out the fear of man. We will never fear being rejected again.

Picture created by Gary Ambs

2 Corinthians 3:18, "But we all, with unveiled face, beholding as in a mirror the glory of the Lord, are being transformed into the same image from glory to glory, just as by the Spirit of the Lord."

CHAPTER 7

Godentity

THIS IS YOUR WORTH: THE LESSON OF THE BIRDS

I KNEW BECAUSE of what Jesus did on the cross that I was worth dying for, and I am not saying that lightly. Truth be told, this still had to get from my head to my heart. I lived a long time knowing it without knowing it. I knew in my head I was worth dying for, but I did not know in my heart. The enemy knew I struggled with this my whole life. Therefore, he always knew how to "get me where he wanted me." Making decisions from the mentality of "this is all I am worth." Now, during the second divorce, the enemy was working hard at trying to keep me down. Spewing his lies at me. So, the Lord had to teach me I was extremely valuable.

The Lord took drastic measures to get through to me. I was not a "throw away." I was not "worthless." I may have been rejected by men, but I was HIS valued treasure. Remember in chapters past how I mentioned I was stubborn, and hard-headed? Well, it is important to remember as I share this next section. And this is how the story goes...

I was on my way to my oldest son's college soccer game. Driving down the highway, in the distance, I see 2 birds on the side of the road. They appear to both be tugging on a piece of food while trying to fly upwards. I did not think anything of it, because as you know, a bird always flies out of the way just in the nick of time. And I have never hit a bird before. Well, these two birds did not make it... as my car hit them. I looked in my rearview mirror and I saw them land on the side of the highway.

Now, you must understand that I DO NOT like to kill anything (yes, I am one of those people). I'm not saying others cannot, it's just that I do not. I got a sinking pit in my stomach and asked God, "Oh God, You say that you watch over the sparrow. Did those birds know they were going to die today?" I can laugh at this now (saying that was silly) but at the time I was very distraught. I pulled off at a rest area and texted my cousin, "Well, I just killed 2 birds with 1 car."

I do not remember how much time had passed, but I am pretty sure it was within weeks, that I was driving my mom's car with her in the passenger seat. Going down the road and... yep you guessed it, I hit another bird! I could not even believe it! Once a fluke maybe, and that was 2 birds.... now 3?! "Ok, God what is going on here?"

By now, every time I am driving, and I see a bird on the side of the road, I am literally flinching and carefully swerving. Yelling at the birds, "Get out of my way, if you want to live!" I told my cousin about the second incident and that I seriously thought this was a sure sign the world was coming to an end because, "I am confident the birds have lost their minds!"

I am not sure how long after this incident, maybe another couple of weeks, I am riding with my cousin, this time as she is driving. There is a bird on the ground in the middle of the road and she hits it. She thought it was going to fly away but it didn't. She immediately looked at me and said, "Get out of my car!" We couldn't help but laugh! She then said to me something along the lines of, you really should be seeking God as to what this is all about! Which I had been asking Him to show me if there was something to all of this (other than the world going crazy).

But that was not the end of it. The last incident, I was driving behind a truck and saw the truck hit a bird right in front of me. I said to myself, out loud, "That did NOT just happen!" Each one of these took place within a couple month span. By now I was serious, **"Ok God, You have my attention, I am listening!!"** Remember "stubborn" and "hard-headed?"

I was reading in Matthew 6 and came to verse 26, "Look at the birds of the air, for they neither sow nor reap nor gather into barns; yet your heavenly Father feeds them. *Are you not of more **value** than they?*" The very next morning I was reading in Matthew 10 and in verses 29-31, "Are not two sparrows sold for a copper coin? *And not one of them falls to the ground apart* *from your Father's will. But the very hairs of your head are all numbered. Do not fear therefore, you are of more* **value** *than many sparrows."*

I immediately stopped reading and pondered these Scriptures. "Oh, my Lord, You have been trying to get through my thick skull how valuable I am." I was finally getting it! Letting it really sink into my heart. "I am worth more to You than even the birds of the air. I am of great value to You. I am worth dying for! Jesus, I really get it! I really do. May I please stop hitting birds now?"

Some of you may think this is silly nonsense. But I assure you I have not hit one bird since (or have I been with others hitting them or seeing them get hit). When I told another one of my friends about this series of events, her comment to me was, "Oh sure Dawn, 5 sacrificial birds for you to know how valuable you are." We couldn't help but laugh. That was funny! Yet true. One other friend told me how she was reading Matthew 12:12, "Of how much more value then, is a man than a sheep?" She said at least you didn't have to hit sheep, as we laughed. I am so thankful for that! "Thank You Lord!" It still stands, I do not like to kill anything. But God took drastic measures to teach me literally, a "valuable" lesson.

WE LIVE UP TO WHAT WE THINK WE ARE

Since childhood I had no idea what my value was and what I was really worth. This had been a lifelong lie the enemy had me entangled in. I had allowed (unknowingly at the time) different circumstances in my life and how I was treated to dictate what I was worth. And I lived up to those "standards" and all the dysfunction it brought with it. Not able to break free of the barrier the enemy had around me.

The enemy spoke to me:

1. "You are not good enough." Which brought about the need <u>for me to try</u> to be perfect. Which was only more failure. Then I was hard on myself for "not being good enough." And because I expected this of myself of course I expected it from others. You can imagine the ugly pit that got me in.
2. "You are not wanted. You are just a piece of trash that people throw away." Which brought about the desire for attention. Even the wrong kind of attention was tolerable. What a slimy pit that was.
3. "You are not worth it." Which brought about strongholds and ad-

dictions to cover up my pain. They were what I ran to, to cope and try to feel good about myself even if it was for only a moment. he is so ruthless in his attacks. he had reminders for me at every turn, of these lies.

Until **I heard** Jesus say, "You are so worth it." If we do not know what we are worth, who we are, and whose we are, then we will make decisions and live our lives according to the thought processes and lies of the enemy. Thereby living a life of deception because we are not living as God created us. A lie has no power that can compare to God. It is only when we believe the lie that makes it powerful. We can see what someone really believes by the way they live their lives and the things they say about themselves.

We live up to what we believe we are. We behave the way we see ourselves. What's in our heart determines what we see. We become what we behold. We will reflect what we see in the mirror. Are there any more ways I can say this?

For Example:

If you believe you are a sinner, you will continue to sin.
If you believe you are holy, you will be holy.
If you see yourself as unworthy, you will act unworthy.
If you see yourself as a royal priesthood, you will act as a royal priesthood.
If you feel you are nothing special (or feel like a piece of trash), you will see yourself as nothing special (or as a piece of trash) and live that way.
If you know you are God's special treasure, then you will see yourself as God's special treasure, and live that way.
If you see yourself as the image of Jesus, you will become just as Jesus, and act just as Jesus.

When we say, "I am just a sinner" or "I am not worth a nickel" or all the other things we say about ourselves, this is not the way of humility. We live up to what we say we are, and who we say we are. We need to be humble enough to believe what God says about us in His Word and speak Truth into our lives and not the lies. Christ in us makes us significantly more than "just a sinner" or "just a dude" or "just another regular girl" or "nothing special." He makes us magnificent, wonderful, amazing, anointed, gifted, holy, righteous, beautiful, and so much more.

We can have a right view of ourselves and know who we are in humility. It is not us but Christ in us. Therefore, I called this chapter "Godentity." It is not my "I"dentity, who "I" am, that matters. It is my Godentity, who God is in me, that matters. This is how we do not think more highly of ourselves than we ought (Romans 12:3). Because we know it is only Christ in us that makes us who we are. We can have confidence rooted in God and not in ourselves. We can have confidence that is rooted in humility and not narcissism.

I want to go through some Scriptures with you here:

Proverbs 23:7, "For as he thinks in his heart, so is he..." What we think about ourselves is what we will be.

Please read all of Matthew 12:33-37. I am pointing out verse 34, "...For out of the abundance of the heart (Greek meaning; thoughts or feelings) the mouth speaks." So again, what we think and how we feel will come out of our mouths. And our lives will go in the direction of what we say as we will see in #3 & #4.

Proverbs 18:21, "Death and life are in the power of the tongue..." We speak either death into our lives ("I'm so stupid"). Or we speak life into our lives ("I have the mind of Christ," 1 Corinthians 2:16). And in Matthew Jesus says we will be held accountable for every idle (Greek meaning; inactive, useless, barren) word spoken.

Please read all of James 3:1-12. Several things I want to point out in this section. He says that no man can tame the tongue. I want us to remember the Lord can. He is the only One who can tame it and guard it (Psalm 141:3). This part of Scripture In James, is painting for us the picture that our tongue will control the direction of our lives. As a rudder directs a ship in the direction the pilot desires, so does what we say direct our lives. It also is a fire such as a forest fire, set on fire by hell. It can destroy everything, and it defiles the whole body when it is not being led by Holy Spirit.

See how powerful what we speak is? I hope we can understand from these Scriptures how we need to be very mindful of what we think, feel, and speak. Words are important! What we say matters! What we say comes from the abundance of our hearts. And what is in our hearts comes from our thought life. We must be very mindful.

It is important to know the flesh is not Truth. This is why we must deny the flesh (live the crucified life where the flesh is DEAD)! What we feel in the flesh and what we think in the flesh is not Truth. satan rules over the flesh with lies which leads to death. Holy Spirit leads and guides our spirit in all Truth which leads to Life. John 6:63, "It is the Spirit who gives life; the flesh profits nothing. The words that I speak to you are spirit, and they are life."

We speak to our spirit (led by Holy Spirit) in Truth and the soul will follow. **For Example:** we say, "I am the righteousness of God IN Christ" (2 Corinthians 5:21). This will cause our soul to say, "You're right!" Then we follow what we say into Life. On the other hand, the opposite is true. We speak to the flesh (ruled by satan) the lie and the soul will follow. So, we say, "I will always be a sinner." The soul will say, "You're right!" Then we follow what we say to death. This is the battle for our soul.

Practical Application:

We are going to practice speaking Truth and Life into our lives. The more we speak this over ourselves the more it will become the abundance of our heart. We will receive it and it becomes the Truth we know that makes us free. Then we will walk in it and live it! Repeat each of the following. This is your Godentity (all found in Scripture, look any of them up in your Bible that is right next to you, wink wink):

I am saved. I am blessed with every spiritual blessing. I am the temple of God. I am holy. I am blameless. I am called. I am chosen. I am accepted. I am healed. I am whole. I am complete. I am restored. I am redeemed. I am forgiven. I am justified. I am anointed. I am glorified. I am filled with the power of Holy Spirit. I have authority over all the power of the enemy. I am crowned with glory and honor. I am royalty (a child of the King). I am an heir. I have an inheritance. I am sealed with the Holy Spirit of promise. I am a royal priesthood. I am Loved. I am new. I am the righteousness of God. I am pure. I am valuable. I am God's special treasure. I am a masterpiece. I am worth dying for. I am the apple of God's eye. I am the bride of Jesus. This is only some of what God has to say about us.

We think we are being humble when we say we are not "worth it," or we are not "worthy." But this is disregarding what Jesus did on the cross. Why would God sacrifice His Son for a people who were not worth it? Why would Jesus have given His life for us if we were not worth it? Wouldn't that be considered "a waste?"

The entirety of the Bible is about God being reconciled to His children and Jesus coming back for His bride. Truth is if we were not worthy to be saved, Loved, or forgiven, God would have never sent Jesus to pay the

HIGHEST PRICE for us. He did not come to condemn us but to save us (John 3:17).

We must understand Jesus died on the cross because our created value was lost at the fall of man. Then we will live up to this Truth. He died to bring us back into our created value. Jesus Christ in us is the real us. This is our Godentity:

For God so Loved the world that He gave His one and only Son (John 3:16), for the many sons and daughters. Jesus gave His life to purchase us back. To bring us back into the family of God. To reconcile us to our Father. He is coming back for a spotless bride without wrinkle. There will be a wedding day at the end of the age. His bride was worth His life (Romans 5:6-11).

A Prayer to Pray:

"Thank You Jesus, You came to reconcile me back as a child of God. Thank You Jesus, You came to restore me back to original condition; holy pure, and blameless. Thank You Jesus, You came to redeem me back to Your image and nature. Thank You, Jesus, You came to rescue me, so You can take me as Your bride. Thank You, Jesus, You came to give me back the keys to the Kingdom with power and dominion to subdue the earth. This could only be done by the sacrifice of Your body on the cross and Your blood purging me of all my sin. Thank You Jesus! I am eternally grateful!"

We Become What We Behold

2 Corinthians 3:18, "But we all, with unveiled face, beholding as in a mirror the glory of the Lord, are being transformed into the same image from glory to glory, just as, by the Spirit of the Lord."

We are to become! And this is what most people miss. We are so busy trying to do everything that we go in circles and drive ourselves crazy. We end up doing lots of "Jesus things" instead of becoming Him. When we become what we behold (Jesus) it is then so easy to do! When I become a servant, it is easy for me to serve. When I become Love, it is easy for me to Love. I am not "trying" to Love because I have to. I Love because I am Love!

Becoming the Word made flesh. This is what must happen, and we cannot do this on our own. Only Holy Spirit can do this in us. Through intimacy, communion, and relationship, in His presence. Everything depends upon Jesus occupying all our attention and affection.

This is what people are missing out on. Then they live miserable lives because they haven't given Jesus their attention. They haven't been with Him. Therefore, they do not see Him to become like Him to go out and do (being as Him). Instead, they try to do everything in their own power. And a lot of times they are doing these things to try to become something. They "do" to try to "be" somebody. Instead of simply beholding Jesus.

I become what I behold:

I am peace because I am beholding Jesus the Prince of Peace
I am joy because I am beholding Jesus the Source of all joy.
I am Love because I am beholding Jesus who is Love.
I am patient because I am beholding Jesus who is the Master of patience.
I am kind because I am beholding Jesus who is the Master of kindness.
I respond as Jesus would respond because I am beholding Jesus.
I see with the eyes of Christ because I am beholding Jesus.
I think with the thoughts of Christ because I am beholding Jesus.
I speak with the words of Christ because I am beholding Jesus.
I hear with the ears of Christ because I am beholding Jesus.
I behold the beauty of Jesus and His servanthood, so I will become His beauty to Love and serve others WELL.

Do Not Allow Your Experience to Identify You

There are times where we allow our experience or circumstances to define who or what we are. We also allow our experiences to define what is going on and who God is, instead of letting the Word of God do the explaining. I have several questions I want you to take time to answer being really honest with yourself.

1. Why do you let these things determine where you are?
2. Why do you let these things decide how you are?
3. Why do you let these things define who you are?
4. Why do you let these things break you?
5. Why do you let these things determine your view of God?
6. Why do you let these things decide who God is?
7. How have these things changed who Christ is in you?
8. How have these things changed what you are here for?

Time, circumstance, and our experience, have no ability to change Truth. We just let them. We are so consumed with what is happening "to us." We keep our focus on what is going on in the storm all around, instead of on Christ. We end up seeing things from our own perspective and think it is Christ's. But, in reality, we are so consumed with the happenings that we cannot see clearly. When we see from our own perspective we will get preoccupied with our own life. We cannot see past ourselves to see what God is doing in us and around us.

We allow our circumstance and what we are going through to define how we see God and who He is, instead of Christ defining who God is. Jesus Christ is God revealed. His life lived and Him crucified is who God is. Consider Christ and what He endured. We must remember we are here for God alone. We are not here for our own sake. We are here to become like Christ in every situation, to shine no matter what may come at us, just as Jesus did. We are to be the light in the darkness, not to get snuffed out by the darkness!

When we look at the way we respond in a crisis, or any adverse circumstance, most of the time we will see we are not bringing life into the situation. But we are costing life by the way we respond.

Here are more questions to ask yourself:

1. Are you consumed with yourself (or your family) over what is going on?
2. What are you beholding? The storm, the waves, the dry desert place, the wilderness, your money, your job, your "go through?" Or God as your perfect Father and Provider, the peace of Christ, the Love of Christ, Christ crucified and what He endured (Hebrews 12:1-4)?
3. Who are you beholding? Other people, your family, your spouse, your kids, or Jesus?
4. How are you beholding the situation? Is it your own perspective or Christ's perspective?
5. Is it costing you your identity? Is it making you look down on yourself, seeing yourself with a negative view?
6. Is it giving you your identity? Is it defining you in any way?

For Example: You have been praying and tithing for years and you still get laid off from your job. You do not understand why. You need the money to take care of your family. No one is hiring you. You have been going to interviews for weeks that turn into months. Everything has hit the fan, all is falling apart, and you are worried about paying the bills. You let this confuse you about who God is and about who you are as a child of His. You end up in a quandary because God is supposed to take care of you and come through for you, but He has "not!" The quandary causes you to question God's Love for you and question Him as a provider. You cannot see past yourself to see anything else God might be doing in all of this.

You are frustrated with not having what you have been praying for. But where is the frustration leaving you in your relationship with God? Has it created doubt? You may not doubt His power or His ability to do the thing you are asking Him for. But since you do not have it, you are left with doubting His Love for you. Because otherwise this thing would be a done deal, right?

With any form of doubt, does He give to those who doubt (James 1:2-8)? His Word says, with no doubting. Your focus must be kept on Jesus and not on the situation, circumstance, or struggle (the chaos all around). Then you will be able to keep your perspective intact, accurate, and always lined up with Jesus' perspective.

But because your eyes are on all the chaos; getting laid off, worried about paying the bills, struggling to take care of your family, these have all become your identity now. Because you never saw yourself as a child of God in the first place. You started to question it the 3rd or 4th time you asked Him for a job, and nothing came through. You have now become your circumstance instead of who He is in you. Which is supposed to be the light in the darkness.

The problem is when human reasoning and intellect start to become our "wisdom" when trials come, and God does not answer immediately. We can be tenacious in our faith for some time but let it go on for any length of time and we wear thin. We are not anchored in Him. We have tried to anchor ourselves in shifting sand; our jobs, our families, our money, and our emotional disposition. Then when the storms come, we are letting our experience define **everything** instead of who God is. Therefore, we begin to complain to God about everything He is not doing. We tell Him who He "really" is because we are looking with our eyes and thinking with our own mind instead of His. We do not realize we are letting everything else define who God is instead of God Himself.

This scenario goes for any difficulty we face. Anyone who is divorced, adopted, has been sexually or physically abused, lost a loved one, forced to resign from a job, been in prison, been wrongfully accused, or the one who has done something horrific. Anyone going through any difficult situation or season. Do not let these things define you or identify you by beholding them rather than Jesus. By lifting them up higher than Jesus. By putting more attention on them than Jesus. There must be something bigger than how you feel and what you are going through. Whatever gets magnified (as with a magnifying glass) gets bigger in perspective, in your mind, and in your focus... So, magnify the Lord!

When we do not know the "whys" of the storm or we do not know the "whys" of God's ways, we must know His heart. If we do not know the heart of God, we will always question His motives. We cannot afford to falter over the "whys." We must trust His heart and know His ways are perfect. His ways are nothing other than Love, always. If we do not know Our Father's heart, we will constantly misinterpret what we are going through. John Paul Jackson said, "When we understand the ways of God, we understand that the enemy plays right into God's hand." This is every time (Romans 8:28). Every single time.

Hope we have as an anchor for our souls (Hebrews 6:13-20). Let us anchor ourselves to Jesus. Knowing we are going to deeper places in Him. Deeper faith and trust in Him. Let His voice be our anchor. Let His presence be our anchor. Let His Love be our anchor (rooted and grounded in Love, Ephesians 3:17). His Love will carry us through anything we face. Anchor our hearts in Him (Proverbs 23:26). Anchor our thoughts on Him. Anchor our eyes to Him. If we are anchored in Him the storm cannot carry us away when it rages. Nor will we drift away from Him when it is calm. He is the only One who can keep us secure and steady.

This next quote is from Hannah Whitall Smith from the book, *The Christian's Secret of a Happy Life* (emphasis added). I want to remind you how I mentioned in a chapter earlier that 3 of her children had died by the time this book was published and 4 altogether. This was a woman who had been through some of the toughest storms of life and she remained a woman of great faith and had great Love for her Lord.

"It is grand to trust in the promises, but it is grander still to trust in the Promiser. The promises may be misunderstood or misapplied, and at the moment when we are leaning all our weight upon them, they may seem utterly to fail us. But no one ever trusted in the Promiser and was confounded. The God who is behind His promises and is infinitely greater than His promises, can never fail us in any emergency, and the soul that is stayed on Him cannot know anything but perfect peace." "There may not be a prayer answered or a promise fulfilled to our own consciousness, but what of that? Behind the prayers and behind the promises, there is God, and He is enough. And to such a soul the simple words, GOD IS, answer every question and solve every doubt."

When you have never been through the fire, you don't know that God is in the fire. You have just heard someone else's testimony (Shadrach, Meshach, and Abed-Nego in Daniel 3:19-30). But when you have met God in the fire, now you **know** God in the fire, and you are then ready for the next fire.

Do Not Allow Your Past to Identify You

Journal Entry 2/28/19:

I heard the Lord say, "You cannot take this into the future I have for you, if you want My best for your life, give it all up for Me." Lord, the truth is right now my hope is in You, but I am not expecting much. I know You will work all things together for my good. I just don't see anything great. I have hope of a future. But I cannot picture a great one. **End of journal entry.**

Then the Lord, over the next couple of months, continued to show me what was hindering me from moving forward. From moving into my future. We cannot walk forward when we are looking back. Eventually we will stumble and fall, just try it (I will try not to laugh). To be able to take hold of the future we must let go of the past.

1. I asked God how I was supposed to let go of my past and move forward when it stares me in the face every day? There are people I have let down and hurt with the decisions I have made. He impressed upon me very clearly, "That is between them and I. I will be the One to help them and heal them, when they come to me." He then showed me just as He is the only One who can meet me where I am at and give me what I need. He is the only One who can do that for them as well. He said to me, "Now let it go and move on."

2. He showed me I was believing the lie that He does not have great

things in store for me. I was struggling with not expecting much. Therefore, this was holding me back from moving forward. If I believe my future isn't that great, then I am just going to stay right here in the wilderness and set up camp. This was the mentality I had to overcome.

3. Also, the enemy comes to steal, kill, and destroy. he was trying to steal my identity by keeping my thoughts in the past. I was identifying myself with my past, "Well this is who I am now." For me it was, "All I am is someone who has been divorced twice. What an embarrassment. What a failure." Which, in turn, was trying to kill my purpose; the good works that God has before ordained for me to do (Ephesians 2:10). And destroy my hope of a great future (Jeremiah 29:11). Trying to keep me stuck in quicksand. satan, you might be sneaky, and you may be sly, but you are not greater than the One who is in me!

We must remember, our destiny is all God's idea in the first place, and He will see it through. We must remain surrendered to Him. We must perceive our destiny through His eyes. It is too great to imagine on our own. Let it sink down deep, into the depths of our soul; we are born for greatness in God. We are Christians to accomplish His purpose.

I recommend reading all of 1 Samuel 17 which is the account of David and Goliath. I almost never say I have a "favorite" Scripture because I could never choose just one. However, there are some that "get" me every time I read them. And 1 Samuel 17:45 is one of these. I get chills, excitement, tears, and awe all at the same time.

Verse 45 says this, "Then David said to the Philistine, 'You come to me with a sword, with a spear, and with a javelin. But I come to you in the name of the Lord of hosts, the God of the armies of Israel, whom you have defied.'" (Yep, here I go!)

It does not matter in what manner the enemy comes against us. It does not matter what weapons he forms against us and brings to the fight. Those weapons will not prosper (Isaiah 54:17). Jesus has defeated the enemy once and for all. We always have the victory now and forever more. We must know who we are in Jesus. We must know what we have in Jesus. "I come to you, satan, in the name of the Lord of hosts, the God of the armies of Israel, whom you have defied."

There is no denying what the enemy has done to try to steal, kill, and destroy in our lives. But the greater Truth is what has been done through Christ. EVERYTHING has been accomplished. The enemy IS defeated. This is where our focus needs to remain. Not in the rehearsal studio, rehearsing the wrong or the past repeatedly in our minds. But rejoicing over and over and over again at what the Lord has done and is doing. He continues to do a good work in us (Philippians 1:6). He is restoring the years that have been eaten away (Joel 2:25).

Why we are still hurting is not so much about what people have done to us. It's not even about what the enemy has done. Or what we have gone through. It's about where we are living from. We are living from the hurt, pain, brokenness, resentfulness, offense, etc. and we end up being controlled by any one of these or all of these. Without forgiveness and letting go we are allowing the past to dictate our future.

For Example: We "cut someone off (out of our lives)," because we are angry at them, or they hurt us very deeply. However, every day they are fashioning us. Because we cannot let it go, forgive, and forget. They are molding our life and we actually think we have cut them off and shut them out (we think we are protecting ourselves). Except the Truth is, this causes insecurity, and we will live from this place until we forgive and forget. We must let go of what has been done. Even if it is continually happening, we still must continually forgive. Stop waiting for others to change and pursue this place we are called to live; to be the Love of Christ. Receive the healing that is needed. Let it go and move forward. Remember, we cannot move forward while we are looking backwards. We cannot receive, with open hands, our future while we are holding on so tightly to the past. Do not be like Lot's wife and get frozen in time.

A Prayer to Pray:

"Father, I thank You that You have great plans for my future far beyond what I could even ask for or think because Your ways and Your thoughts are higher than mine!"

Speak Truth until we believe it. Until it becomes our reality. Then continue to speak it and never stop. Here are some Scriptures:

1. Isaiah 43:18-19, "Do not remember the former things, nor consider the things of old. **Behold**, I will do a new thing, now it shall spring

forth; Shall you not know it? I will even make a road in the wilderness and rivers in the desert."

2. Philippians 3:13, "...But one thing I do, forgetting those things which are behind and reaching forward to those things which are ahead,"

3. 1 Corinthians 3:22 "...or the world or life or death, or things present or things to come – all is yours." Read verses 18-23, but I want to point out here that He does not say things in the past are yours. Things in the past are not yours. Let them go! Forget the things that are behind, the moment they are past, leaving them with God.

4. Romans 8:38-39, "...nor things present nor things to come will be able to separate us from the Love of God..." Read verses 31-39, I want to point out here that again things past is not listed. I used to think this Scripture said, "I am persuaded <u>nothing</u> can separate us from the Love of God." But it does not say this. It specifically lists the things and then says <u>these</u> things listed will not be able to separate us. So it must be that the past can keep us from receiving the Love of God. It does not keep God from Loving us, but it keeps us from receiving Love. When we live in the past or identify with the past, we are cutting ourselves off from the Love of God and from our future.

A Prayer to Pray:

"Thank You Lord, that my past does not dictate who I am, You do. I am not defined by where I've been. You are removing all shame and I will walk confidently in humility. I do not care what people think. Because I know Whose I am. I am Yours, Jesus! In Your name, Amen."

There is only One who validates us, and His name is Jesus. We are children of the Creator of the Universe and we do not need anyone else's validation. We bear His signature = Holy Spirit. He is our seal of approval. We have right standing in the sight of God through the blood of Jesus, without any guilt or shame.

Jesus wants to separate us from the past. Not only to forgive, but to get us out of there. God says, "I am going to see you apart from everything you have ever done. It's as if you have never sinned. I am going to set you apart from everything anyone else has ever done. It's as if they never sinned." This is called being justified! When we do not believe all has been justified (as if it has never happened) or we do not receive justification as our identity, then we make it a theory and we miss the point and the power of it.

Journal Entry:

I do not want to be limited by my experiences!! I am not a failure, I am a joint heir with Christ. I am not an embarrassment, I am royalty. I am not a throw away, I am chosen. I am not broken, I am a masterpiece. I am not ashes, I am beautiful. I am not ashamed of what I went through, I have purpose. NO ONE can take what He has put inside of me. The important thing is, have we learned from our mistakes? Are we allowing Holy Spirit to teach us and correct us? Lead us and guide us? The best people we can get counsel from are those who have grown from their mistakes and have come out the other side as gold that has been purified in the fire. **End of journal entry.**

A Prayer to Pray:

"Father, I want all the regret of my past out of my mind and out of my heart because it is just taking up valuable real estate. Remove it from me once and for all and fill my heart and mind with You. May You be my obsession. You are what I am beholding. You are what I live for. Your healing is greater than the pain of my past. Your healing is greater than the pain of all my mistakes. Your healing is greater than the pain of the memories. You are greater in me than anything else. Free me from the past. Every failure redeemed. Help me to become as a child, continually awe struck at the wonder of who You are. Grow me in Love. Tear down the walls I have built around my heart. I will not return to what is familiar (my old life or my old ways). I will not cling to what I "know" because it is familiar. Those are lies from the enemy to keep me in bondage. Everything that needs to go must go. Everything that needs to grow must grow. In Jesus name, Amen."

Do Not Allow Insecurities to Identify You

Journal Entry:

I am struggling. I am so gripped with fear of seeing or running into a certain person it is almost paralyzing. This plays a factor in where I go, and I just want to hide away never to be seen. Lord, I do not want the fear of seeing this person to decide my life, to dictate what I do. As I am bawling here on the floor, I admit I do not even know what that looks like. Lord…I do not even know what that looks like. In my spirit was this immediate response… "FREEDOM, it looks like freedom!!!" I know I do not want this ruling my life at all. Jesus, I want this to be so far dead in me, so far gone, that it doesn't affect me ever again! Eradicate every bit of insecurity, fear, self-consciousness, and lie that is in me. That I am no longer bound to myself, the flesh. I am so tired of these things holding me back and taking me captive. I need Your perfect Love to cast out fear. Jesus pour Your Love over me. Let it be only You who moves me. That I am moved by Your Love. I will become what I am beholding. I set my sight on You. Come and comfort me, be my refuge and strength. **End of journal entry.**

Let me explain this scenario a little bit. I was so hurt by a certain person that I never wanted to see them again. I was embarrassed by what had happened and I just wanted to leave. You know, skip town, go to another state, another country, maybe even another planet? My stomach would literally get tied up in knots when going in the vicinity of where I might run into this person. But due to my job, at the time, it was unavoidable. The possibility of seeing this person was pretty good. So, fear and insecurity gripped me. I thought this was all because I was deeply hurt, and I just needed the Lord's healing.

It went on for about 6 months. The Lord was working with me on MANY other things during this time (Yeah, I was a full case load, smile, but true!). Such as the bird incident, forgiveness, and more. The Lord had been teaching me and growing me in many things and in many ways. Now was the moment of more Truth to be revealed in my life. What came next was completely unexpected.

One day I was driving, and I hear this question as clear as day, "Do you want to know why you are still hurting?" I knew it was Holy Spirit, so I said, "YES! Yes, please tell me. I don't want to feel this way any longer," (with all the hurt, insecurity, and fear swallowing me up). I heard back, "It is your pride." UGH! It felt like I was hit with a ton of bricks. A gentle ton of bricks, but a ton of bricks, nonetheless. This is the amazing thing about Holy Spirit, He can reveal Truth (even if it hurts) in the gentlest way. It hurts, at the same time He comforts you. It is like none other!

I pulled the car over to not get in an accident and I sat there and wept.

"How Lord? How can this be? This person is the one who hurt me!" As I heard in my spirit these words, "It is because your pride is hurt by what happened. Your pride is hurt by the situation and the circumstances. You are embarrassed and humiliated because of pride. I will rid you of all that pride and then you will be healed." My response, "Yes Holy Spirit rid me of ALL pride that leads to self-consciousness. Rid me of self! I am nothing. I am nothing. I am nothing **without You**. Here have Your way!"

All the insecurity, embarrassment, hurt, and fear I was having was all rooted in pride, YUCK! Pride makes us self-assertive and self-conscious. Think about it with any insecurity we have, why are we insecure? Because we are thinking of ourselves. This revelation was totally unexpected and felt like a gentle sucker punch to the gut. Yet...Yet this was the Truth that made me free. I would have never known otherwise if it were not for Holy Spirit showing me. God You are so, so, so good to me!

JOURNAL ENTRY:

Holy Spirit, thank You that You Love me so much You will not leave me broken. You will not leave me the same. You will not leave me drowning in pride. Thank You that You compassionately revealed it to me. Thank You that You tenderly showed me so I would be free from it! You showed me the subtleties of pride. When satan cannot come through the front door anymore he will try to sneak in the back door, the windows, the nooks, cracks, and crannies. **End of journal entry.**

All insecurities are rooted in pride. Thinking of ourselves and for ourselves. The following are only a few examples of these insecurities:

When we are insecure about the way we look...this is pride. People getting all kinds of surgeries to get rid of wrinkles, double chins, fat, etc. All kinds of surgeries to change the things they don't like. Nose jobs, cheek implants, lip injections, the list is endless of what people are doing to try to love the way they look. When we are rid of self, we will not look at ourselves the same way anymore. When we look in the mirror all we will be concerned with seeing is Jesus. True beauty is only found in Him!

When we are insecure about not getting other people's approval...this is pride. We need people to approve of us so we can feel important, feel good about ourselves, feel wanted, or feel we are good looking and beautiful. It is never up to anyone else to make us feel any of those things. We humbly receive all these things in Jesus alone. Never rely on anyone else to be what only Jesus can be.

When we are insecure of the way we performed...this is pride. Change the way we approach "messing up." Stop being more aware and focused on what we did wrong than what we did right. We get so hard on ourselves and condemning. Like, "I am such an idiot," "that was so stupid," "I need to do better so you can be 'proud' of me." Condemnation is not from the Lord. Be God focused. Focus on what Holy Spirit is doing in us and what He is doing right, rather than self-focused and "how far we have to go." We have this false need to prove ourselves. We want to even prove ourselves to God. We have a false idea that we need to be a certain way to be Loved. We must believe we are already accepted and Loved in Jesus Christ. There is nothing else we can do to "prove" ourselves or to be Loved. And we certainly do not have to do this for other people.

When we are insecure if people do not respect us, affirm us, give us validation, cheer us on, or give us accolades...this is pride. We have the false need to receive these things to give us motivation, to encourage us, or make us feel like we are worth something. We like to receive these things, so we know we have status, importance, or clout. And if we don't we then become insecure. Maybe even get insulted as we think... "Do they know who I am??!!" Again, we are to receive from the Lord. He is all we need to motivate us and encourage us. His acceptance and affirmation are all we need. By what He did on the cross, we know what we are worth.

A.W. Tozer "The meek man has long ago decided that the esteem of the world is not worth the effort."

When I am secure in Christ it eradicates every insecurity and all low esteem. I am not living to be noticed by you. I am alive because I have been seen by Christ. I do not need your attention so I can like myself. I like myself because Christ is in me and who I am. I am not moved, flattered, or puffed up by words of man. What moves me is man's obedience to the Lord. I am not here to please people (Galatians 1:10). I am to be mindful of the things of God and not the things of man (Matthew 16:23-26).

Stop eating from the tree of lies. Instead eat from the tree of Truth. Stop eating the forbidden fruit of divorce (or whatever your past may be), failure, rejection, regret, shame, comparison, pride, and insecurity. Instead eat the Bread of Life. Eat from the Word of God which tells us who are in Christ Jesus.

A Prayer to Pray:

"Lord, When I think on You alone, I know my importance. I know my worth. I know my beauty. Not as the world would say. Not compared to what the world would say makes me important or successful. Not compared to where the world would say I find my worth. Not compared to what the world would say is beautiful or attractive. THERE IS NO COMPARISON. Only what You say is True. Only what You see in me matters at all. Thank You Jesus, in Your name I pray, Amen."

Who Do You Say God Is?
Who Do You Say You Are IN HIM?

I am only going to give you some examples of the answers to these two questions (which are all found in Scripture). Otherwise, this list would be infinite. More importantly who do YOU say God is? Who do YOU say you are in Him? Can you fully agree with these lists? Because it is your view of Him and your view of yourself that will either move you forward or hold you back.

God You are:

Love, Peace, Joy, Patience, Kindness, Goodness, Merciful, full of Grace, Truth, My Perfect Father, My Stronghold, My Hope, My Rock, My Salvation, My Fortress, My Refuge, My Help, My Strength, My Portion, My Vindicator, My Provider, My Security, My Deliverer, My Redeemer, My Shield, My Guide, My Healer, My Mender, My Comforter, You are the Lifter of my head, You are my Protector, You watch over me. And this is just a smidgen of who You are.

"Lord, I honor You my King, Blessed Trinity, for You are holy, and worthy of all honor, glory, and praise. I respect Your righteousness, mercy, Loving kindness, forgiveness...all of who You are. Your whole nature is perfect and beautiful. Why would I ever worry? Why would I ever not trust You? Why would I ever doubt?"

"Who do you think you are?" Is the evil whisper I would hear in my ear, hurling his accusations at me. For a long time, my response was, "nothing good." In the section "We live up to what we think we are," we went over a long list of who we are. Now is a good chance to go over some more!

In Christ:

I am alive, I am brought near to my Father, I am raised up and seated in heavenly places, I am family, I am a partaker of the heavenly calling, I am fearfully and wonderfully made, a marvelous work, I am joint heirs with Christ, I am the head and not the tail, I am above and not beneath, I am Love, I am of a sound mind, I am a co-laborer with God. I am God's husbandry (under His care and cultivation), I am God's building and Christ is my Cornerstone, I am a tree of righteousness the planting of the Lord that He will be glorified, I am a crown of glory in the hand of the LORD, I am Hephzibah (the Lord delights in me, I am His delight), I am rejoiced over by the Lord (I am His joy). I ravish His heart with one glance of my eye. Selah!

We spend a lot of time trying to be **what we already are.** As you can see from what is listed above. This would be what we call "identity issues," or an "identity crisis." We, more times than not, find our identities in everyone else but God. Then when they fail us, we are broken. We, more times than not, find our identities in our circumstances instead of God. Then when the storms come for us, we are left broken.

We cannot expect stability if we have a broken Godentity. Our search for stability in anything other than Jesus will not hold us up. Godentity is not tied to circumstances, other people, or anything else for that matter. The more intimacy we have with Jesus, the more we behold Him, the more secure our Godentity will be. We become what we behold.

We will never find ourselves outside of Him!!! People who do not know who they are and go on these "self-discovery" trips. Let me save you time. You are only found in Jesus. Every temptation and thought coming from satan is always against the identity of who we are. he did it with Eve, he did it with Jesus, and continues to do it with all mankind. Every thought we think comes from the depth of our identity. Who do we know ourselves to be in the depths of our heart? Whether we know who we are in Christ (knowing our Godentity), or whether the enemy is trying to tell us "who we are." Who do you say you are? When being a child of God really hits your heart, you will never succumb to lies again. You will never look anywhere else again.

The mindset we embraced through the fall is deception. satan tries to get us to believe we are something we are not. However, Jesus knows the

Truth about us. This is why He could say on the cross, "Forgive them for they know not what they do." Because He knows who we are. The problem is we have not known. He saw past the sin and into who He created us to be. He saw the potential of the calling He placed in us.

THE NATURE AND CHARACTER OF JESUS CHRIST

We are to live fully understanding Christ in us. We are ONE. No separation, no divide. We are filled with ALL the fullness of God. It is no longer we who live, but Christ lives in us. If He is the One in us, He should be what comes out of us. If Love is in me, Love will come out of me. If hate is in me, hate will come out of me. If self is in me, self will come out of me. If Christ is in me, Christ will come out of me. Why are we Christians not looking like Christ in the way we walk and talk? Because we are filled with everything but Him.

Romans 8:29, "For whom He foreknew, He also predestined to be conformed to the image of His Son..." If He is in us and we are conformed to look like Him this means, we represent Him. We are to represent His character, nature, thoughts, feelings, and desires. We are to think and act according to how Christ would think and act under any circumstance. We want His heart, His nature, and His ways because this is our freedom. If it is not Him living in us, then it is ourselves living in us and living for ourselves is a prison and such a drag.

If we are to be conformed into His image, we should know what this looks like for us. Also, we must know this is the work of Holy Spirit to do in us, through our yieldedness. We cannot do this in ourselves. We cannot muster these things up on our own. And the Holy Spirit cannot do this in us, except He have a yielded, empty (dead to self), vessel. As we surrender and yield to Holy Spirit we will look like Christ; made in His image!

The nature/character of Christ is: Love, sacrifice, a servant, meek, gentle, kind, good, patient, having temperance, peace, joy, faithful, pure, forgiving, does not seek His own (self-less), keeps no record of wrong, not envious, not boastful, not proud (He is humble), not rude, not irritable (not provoked or annoyed), does not delight in sin (has no sin), rejoices in Truth, never gives up, never loses faith, always hopes, endures all things (always perseveres), never fails, obedient to death, does good to those who despitefully use Him (washed Judas' feet), a servant to all, puts others first, never complaining, never offended, never defending Himself, not condemning, calm in the midst of the storm (zero worry or anxiety), fearless, completely reliant on the Father (could do nothing of Himself), had zero selfish ambition, zero selfish thoughts, zero selfish feelings, the only praise He was after was the praise of His Father, full of grace and Truth, did not seek His own glory, Love was His only motivation. Selah!

Journal Entry:

Matthew 12:35, "A good man out of the good treasure of his heart brings forth good things." Matthew 6:21, "For where your treasure is, there your heart will be also." Jesus. You are the good treasure of my heart and only You can make me good. When I take time in Your presence, making You my absolute treasure, marinating in You, giving You my full attention, out of this time with You, You will cause me to **be** good which causes me to **do** good. I will not have to work at it or try harder because it is who I am. This is the transformation power of Holy Spirit in me. And from being in Your presence. Matthew 12:33, make the tree good (Jesus being the good treasure of my heart) and the fruit will be good (the fruit of Holy Spirit cultivated by being in His presence). Isaiah 61:3, I am a tree of righteousness the planting of the Lord that HE may be glorified. Ephesians 3:17, That Christ may dwell in my heart through faith; that I, being rooted and grounded in love... If the root is good, the tree is good, the fruit is good.

When **we realize** we have been made a good tree we cannot bear bad fruit, it is impossible. It is our Godentity. Just as an evil tree cannot bear good fruit, again it is impossible. Do we need to beg an apple tree to give us apples? Do we ever see an apple tree give us bananas? No! Trees yield fruit after their own kind. In the same way the person who is One with Christ will just as surely bring forth a Christ-like life.

Genesis 1:28, "...Be fruitful and multiply." If the enemy can lie to us about who God is, then he can keep us from coming into God's presence. If he can keep us from coming together with God in intimacy, he can keep us from reproducing. If the enemy can lie to us and keep us from seeing who we have become through Christ, he can keep our lives from being multiplied (making disciples). We desperately need to understand and KNOW who God is and who we are in Him!

Thank You Holy Spirit that You are strengthening me with might in my inner being (Ephesians 3:16) which is my mind, my will, and my emotions. You are bringing me in alignment with Your mind, Your will, and

Your emotions. You are rooting me and grounding me in the Love of Christ (Ephesians 3:17). You are the One transforming me into the same image of Christ from glory to glory. Thank You for changing me, for growing me, for making me fruitful. All I want is You to make Your habitation and dwelling place in me. So, I will carry Your presence and who You are to the world. Lord, keep me on track, if I am anywhere outside of who You are in me, let me be very aware. I am always grateful for Your correction in my life. Don't let me miss one drop of what You paid for. **End of journal entry.**

God Is Love

I want to go back to this "God gave His Son" statement I made in the section "We live up to what we think we are." Because this one statement hangs a lot of people up. This one line will keep people from knowing who God is. This one line will keep people from coming into a deep, personal, and intimate relationship with Him. I had a friend who got stuck on the fact that God sacrificed His Son. They could not get over it. And the question they had is, "How is this a "Loving" God? How could a "Loving God" do that to His Son?"

As a parent who has two boys, I would do anything for them. If we were together in a place and someone came in with a gun pointing it at them, you can bet every penny you have I would be jumping in front of that person with the gun saying, "No take my life instead, spare them, take me! I beg you, please take me!" Romans 8:32, "He that spared not His own Son, but delivered Him up for us all..." Selah! Really think about this and what this means. God GAVE His Son for us. It was a GREAT sacrifice for Him to do that. Just as it would be a great sacrifice if I had to do that with one of my sons. I cannot even write this without crying. And I ask myself the question... "Would I be able to do that??" There is nothing more sacrificial than what our Father did FOR US. Other than Jesus freely laying His Life down. And Jesus Christ is God in the flesh. "With so much gratitude, I could never express sufficiently, thank You Lord, thank You Lord, thank You for Your sacrifice!"

Journal Entry:

I am going through a difficult season where I miss my boys, Lord. One is off to college and the other is living with his dad full time because he doesn't want to live with me. "Abba, how do You do it? You Love us infinitely more.

And every day You watch Your children walk away from You, disregard You, ignore You, choose everything else but You. How do You do it?" He spoke softly to me, "Love. I show them Love. I Am nothing but Love." God's Love is not a dimension of Himself, it is His whole self. Everything about Him is Love. And this is what draws His children back to Him. His kindness leads us to repentance (Romans 2:4). I will be Love, Lord. Holy Spirit do this in me, I am Yours. **End of journal entry.**

God IS Love. The way to know this kind of Love and become it is through His Word and by being alone in His Presence. Allowing Holy Spirit to move in us and through us. We must drench ourselves in knowing the Love of our Father. True Love, unconditional Love, a Love like we have never known. A Love that never leaves us like others can and will. A Love that makes no demands and never accuses. A Love we never have to impress. A Love we never have to prove ourselves to. A Love we never have to perform for. Anything outside of this kind of love is of the flesh.

His Love is designed to transform us and get us out of a wrong identity. As He is, so am I, in this world (Please read 1 John 4:7-21). The goal is to become Love. When we become the Love of Christ, it is a selfless Love. Do we know what this looks like? Do we know what it is to be selfless? It looks like Jesus. We do not know Love until we are dead to self. It is no longer I who lives but Christ lives in me (Galatians 2:20) and through me, and Christ is Love. Love is what courses through my veins. I am to bleed His Love.

We are called to a life of Love and so many Christians do not even know the Truth of what Love is. We are so used to saying, "I love pizza, I love those shoes, I love that car, I love basketball, or I love to shop." However, Love is a person. Love is God. To increase the value of money you reduce its circulation. If we want to increase the value of Love let's reduce its circulation and stop saying, we love everything. We are to Love as Christ and He did not Love the world or the things in the world (1 John 2:15-17), but He did Love people.

We are to Love people for who they are called to be and created to be. Not who they have been or what they are being. This is just how Jesus Loves us. Does He ever change who He is or how He is because of us? Because of how we are acting or how we are treating Him? NO! Does He ever change His mind about us? Emphatically NO! Not ever. This is exactly how we are to Love others.

God never said to me, "I Love you. Now, come on, say it back, or else I will feel insecure, unsure, and confused." Sounds silly, right? Yet this is exactly what we do. We say it, then expect something in return. We get taught this stuff by life and people, but it is NOT God. When will we ever say, "I Love you," simply because we do? Instead of needing them to love us back so we can feel secure and maybe even like ourselves?

We Love because God first Loved us (1John 4:19). We cannot even Love until we have received the Love of God. If you have not received the Love of God, whatever it is you are feeling is lust or the broken world's way of loving. The world's "love" is selfish, manipulative, needy, toxic, sexually driven, sensually driven, and has all the wrong motives. Most of the 'love' people experience is of the flesh and is distorted love. Where we have to impress people, prove ourselves to people, or perform to their standards to receive their love. Which is nothing like God's Love. The world's "love" is demanding and unstable in all its ways. Once we receive the Love of God, we can know true Love and know how to truly Love others. We can then Love the Lord our God and Love our neighbor as ourselves (Mark 12:28-31).

But suppose that is exactly what you are doing? Loving your neighbor as yourself. Without having received the Love of God, you are giving your broken love instead. You are so hard on yourself, so you are hard on everyone around you (I was there). You cannot Love yourself, so you cannot Love them. You think poorly of yourself, so you think poorly of them. You are critical of yourself, so you are critical of them. Isn't it amazing how we do not even like ourselves and yet we want everybody else to like us? When you hate yourself, you are incapable of Loving others.

I will love people with the same measure, with the same outlook, with the same love I have for myself. And in an earlier chapter I talked about how we Love ourselves. It is not a narcissistic love for ourselves. It is Loving who Christ is in us. Love is not a method; it is our life. It is not a one-time confession; it is a life lived. Where I am willing to give everything I am because He gave everything He was for me. I cannot bring glory and honor to God if my actions are not motivated by a pure heart, a heart of Love.

For those who mourn the loss of a Love they shared with someone for a lifetime, I say this with all sincerity, please know there is a greater Love to be had. He knew you before you were born. He knit you together in your mother's womb. He is the only One who fully knows everything about you. He is the One who has Loved you from eternity. Only God can Love you like this. I pray you will come to know His Love and be swept away!!

JOURNAL ENTRY:

In this season You are deeply rooting me and grounding me in Love. I am Loved more deeply, more passionately, more intimately than any other person could ever Love me. You Love me to wholeness. You Love me to health. You give me Your Love and teach me how to Love in return. How will they know Your Love if I do not show it? No matter what people say about me. No matter what people do to me. I will be Love. Many will not understand, and it is ok. I will live by the Spirit and be free. My Love is not contingent on someone else's love for me. True Love does not need to be loved back. Love with no strings attached. No expectations. Love motivates, withholding it does not. **End of journal entry.**

WE CAN ONLY GIVE WHAT WE HAVE

A gift we receive. To re-gift it, we must receive the gift in the first place. Before we can give grace, we must receive grace. Before we can give kindness, we must receive kindness. Before we can give mercy, we must receive mercy. Before we can give Love, we must receive Love. We cannot give what we do not have. If we do not have the right perspective, we cannot give the right perspective. If we do not have the Truth, we cannot give the Truth. I do not want to give anyone my experience only and not Truth.

Bible Recap with Tara Leigh, "All my sacrifices to God and for God originated as gifts from God. Nothing I offer God; worship, or faith, or good works, or time, or money, none of it finds its origin in me." Selah! 1 Corinthians 4:7, "...And what do you have that you did not receive...?" I will add to this that everything I have to offer (anything good or of any value) to anyone else originated from God as well. None of it finds its origin in me. Talk about confident humility.

Anything good in me is because of Jesus. It is His goodness in me. In our surrender to Him, He puts who He is in us. Everything good about us and who we are is Jesus in us and this is astounding. Jesus is the only reason why I am who I am today. As I go deeper in Him (my roots go deep) He grows me up in Him. This is the circle of Life. The true circle of Life. I receive Jesus and all His goodness and in return I give Jesus and all His goodness to others. He will draw people to Himself through His presence displayed in my life. And the cycle revolves.

Oswald Chambers: "The saint who is intimate with Jesus will never leave impressions of himself, but only the impression that

Jesus is having unhindered way, because the last abyss of his nature has been satisfied by Jesus. The only impression left by such a life is the strong, calm sanity that our Lord gives to those who are intimate with Him."

Our life is the book others read. Our lives lived is to BE the witness of Christ. Who we are will determine what we do, what we say, and where we go. We must take the time to become and not just try to go and do. Becoming the witness of Christ will only come from the place of intimacy with Him.

The bottom line is we can be with Jesus (in our services, in our Bible studies, in our devotionals) and still not know Him. The evidence of knowing Him is when we become like Him. We will only represent Jesus in the way we know Him. If I don't see His heart as gentle, humble, kind, patient, and lowly, I will never re-present Him like this to others. I cannot reflect a light greater than what I have seen or experienced for myself. Prov 4:18, "The path of the just is as the shining light, that shineth more and more unto the perfect day." If you still struggle with this area of knowing Him and becoming like Him through intimacy, please go back through "Knowing the Lover of My Soul," Chapter 2.

Journal Entry:

I thank You that I do not have to impress anyone and yet I want to leave Your impression on everyone. What is Your impression? Love. I want to impress upon people Your Love. I want to give everyone Your Love. I want to be who You created me to be. I need You to make me the mother, daughter, sister, aunt, friend, etc. that You created me to be, to the best of Your ability in me.

Those places You created in me, that feel like they have died, please breathe life into them. Resurrect Love. My Love for life; taking in every moment in awe and wonder. My Love for people; passionately Loving them to freedom. My Love for laughter; the silliness You created in me, the quirky sense of humor You gave me. And not caring what people think. Just living life to the fullest. Come and heal every bit of brokenness. Come and shine Your light into all the darkness. That You can calm all the chaos in me, what a beautiful mystery. **End of journal entry.**

PERSPECTIVE SHIFT

Matthew 6:22-23 (KJV), "The light of the body is the eye: if therefore thine eye be single, (Greek meaning: as a particle of union) thy whole body shall be full of light. But if thine eye be evil, thy whole body shall be full of darkness…" How do we see things? How do we perceive things? Through a single eye that is fixed on Jesus, in union with the Light of the world? Or through everything else and everyone else around us? We must have a change in perspective = seeing Truth. Seeing as Christ sees - through Love.

So now let's revisit the difficult trials we go through with the right perspective. It is not really the situation or circumstance we are facing that discourages us; it's our perspective while we are going through the trial. **It's what we are looking at.** No matter what we are going through, nothing changes the purpose of God in our lives. Nothing changes why Christ is in us (to shine in the darkness). So, if we are discouraged it is our perspective during the trial that is allowing it. We must live beyond the flesh (which is to be crucified with Christ) and what we see in the natural.

I want to remind us again of Hebrews 12:1-4 (please read). Discouragement, frustration, offense, etc., all will end when our perspective and motive in life changes. All the stuff Jesus is NOT, is what we have been trained by and we call it "normal." But it is far from Christlikeness. So, if we didn't learn it from Him then where in the world did we learn it? (Exactly the world, we learned it from the world.)

Somebody could go through the exact same thing as you, with a different perspective and come out of it totally different. If you are hypersensitive, you are going to receive things with hypersensitivity and react in like manner. If you are irritable, you will be irritated by everything. If you are easily offended, you will take offense. If you are selfless the same situations will happen, and you will not be touched, irritable, or offended. The troubles haven't changed. So, what's changed? The place from which we live. Are we living for ourselves in our feelings and flesh, or we are living for Jesus Christ and His glory. There is a BIG difference.

We must make sure we have Christ's perspective in our life. That we love not our own lives unto death, and we seek first the Kingdom of God. We must fully understand we are not here for ourselves (our own life or our own agenda). We are not even here for our family. Our families, our jobs, and many things the Lord has given us **are gifts**, but not the reasons for our lives. We need to get a real clear understanding of this. Because most of us live our lives for these things all the time.

We are so motivated by these things. We find our identity through our job titles, how much money we have, our children, our spouse, and a number of other things. And if any one of them are in trouble or skating on thin ice, then we are in trouble and skating on thin ice. We associate our well-being with the circumstances in our lives and how everything and everyone is doing around us instead of with the Good News of the Gospel and our salvation (2 Corinthians 4:8-11).

I must remind myself; I am NOT here for me. I am here for God alone. To become like Christ and to shine no matter what may come my way. Just as Jesus did. I am a representative of Jesus Christ. I wake up every morning understanding nobody owes me a thing. Not even God. If He gave me nothing else in this life, I mean nothing, He saved my soul. He saved me from the pit of hell. He has given me Himself and relationship with Him and that is enough, no, that is more than enough!

But we all relate to each other with the things that happen in life because we are full of fleshly feelings. So, we sympathize with each other and call this compassion. Yes, we are to have compassion for people. Yes, we are to mourn with those who mourn but we are not to leave them there. We empower people to stay broken when we live there with them in their mess. So now they go all over the place wearing the dysfunction of their job, money, children, or spouse instead of wearing the fulfillment of Christ in their lives. What we go through is not the end of the world. It is the opportunity to shine. It is a yielding and surrendering to Him.

I must reiterate here; I KNOW we go through some REALLY difficult things in life. I am not saying we do not cry. I am not saying we do not mourn or grieve. I am saying we mourn and grieve with ones who have hope. We are to mourn and grieve with thanksgiving to the Lord (1 Thessalonians 5:16-18). We are here for a bigger purpose than how we feel. When we stay in the place of feeling sorry for ourselves, we get caught in the trap of making life all about us.

I remember hearing about a worship leader whose 2- or 3-year-old daughter died. She died in her sleep. What a tragedy! I did not know her, and I cried with her. I remember watching her, I cannot remember exactly how long after I feel like it was about a year later, and I was moved to tears. I mean sobbing. The way this woman worshipped the Lord was astonishing. The lyrics to the songs she was singing, inspiring! I kept thinking how she could have blamed God (or kept blaming God). She could have been so angry with Him (or stayed angry with God). Yet, she worshipped with all she had, and it was absolutely beautiful! A moment I will remember forever. It still makes me cry.

This next example used is a direct example from Dan Mohler and it is such a good one. I do not give this example lightly. I am not being cold hearted about it nor am I not able to understand it. However, what he says is True. So, I am exposing the deception we fall for when we think for ourselves. And revealing Truth in one of the most dangerous and slippery slopes a marriage can go down.

When there is adultery in a marriage, the one "cheated on" feels so betrayed, hurt, rejected, and ashamed. This becomes their story. They rarely ever recover from it, and "what happened to them." People come to them and sit there with them in their mess, having "compassion" on them but rarely ever point them to Truth. You are no less in covenant with God. You are of no lesser worth or value because of the decisions your spouse made. And if your spouse is living this way they must be really deceived. They must be in real trouble. They must be really lost.

How many of us weep for the one who is in the most trouble? The one who is really confused, and has lost their identity of who they are in Christ? When we play the victim/villain card nobody wins. Do you have the ability to weep for your spouse and not for yourself? The one cheated on is not the one who has the problem. Christ is still in them. Christ in them is the hope of glory and that has not changed. They still have purpose. What has been "done to" them should in no way define them. When Christ and His life lived is what defines them. Again, the one cheated on is not the one who has the problem.

The spouse who is doing the cheating is the one who is in trouble. They have lost their identity. They do these things because they are deceived and lost. They are going down a really dangerous road. They need help. How can Jesus live inside of us (who have been cheated on), and we will cry for ourselves all day long, and be so crushed and consumed with our "situation" and not once cry for our spouse who is in spiritual trouble and demise? When we are to deny ourselves, pick up our cross, and follow Jesus? Washing the very feet of the one who would betray Him. Yet we will be so angry with them, so hurt by them, not wanting to talk to them, and maybe even hate them for what they did.

As a friend of one who has been hurt, if all you are doing is relating to their pain and calling it compassion and you know you would be just as hurt as them if this happened to you, now you are sympathizing with them. You cannot even help them because you cannot point them to Truth. You do not have an answer because you would be what they are if you were in their shoes. You would feel the exact same way they are feeling. (This is the end of Dan Mohler's example). Yes, we are to mourn with those who mourn but we are not to leave them there. We must speak Truth in Love.

JOURNAL ENTRY:

Father, forgive me for only thinking about how things have made me feel or what they have done to me. Remove every bit of self from me. That when I am in situations from now on my first thoughts are of the other person and not me at all. To where I can react and respond in Love. Love for the person and understanding of where they are at. To always remember this life is always about bringing You glory. In Jesus name, Amen. **End of journal entry.**

Then we tend to gravitate towards people who have been through the same thing we have been through. We call these "support" groups. I get it, I was here. I wanted a small group of women whose husbands had left them. I can laugh about it now. But at the time I was serious. I desperately wanted to be around people who knew what I was feeling.

One day the Lord showed me that pain is pain. We do not have to experience exactly what someone else has experienced to weep with them, to know their pain. Because we all have experienced pain in one way or another. What is more important than knowing the exact pain someone is going through **is knowing the answer**! Pointing to the Way, the Truth, and the Life.

Yet here we are in our support groups, everyone being in the "same boat" ... stranded. We "get" each other. We understand what each other is going through, but we are still lost at sea. Unless we have someone in the group who is pointing us to the complete healing and restoration of Jesus Christ, we will still be stranded. Jesus, who is our only Lifesaver, is the Way. There is only One answer to any of our "go throughs." What works for one works for all. Jesus Christ is the answer for everything! He is the universal answer to anything or any place that any of us find ourselves.

I do not have to relate to your story. I just have to know the answer. The direction of Truth to point you in. Not to just wander in the wilderness with you and call this compassion. To be a broken record (smile)... I am not saying to not have compassion with people, we mourn with those who mourn. Then we speak Truth into their lives. We do not leave them there where it can turn to self-pity. We speak Light, Love, and Life into their circumstance.

Jesus is our only source of Life. We are not to discern with our natural eyes and ears! We are to be single-eyed, single minded. We become what we behold. Jesus becomes the manifestation of our life without us even "trying" when we behold Him and not the "go through." Because this is where we live from. We are what we see. We are to become the Word of God. So, when the trial comes, we have a response and not a reaction to it. We do not have options. There is one way to handle it and it is the Way. The Way of Christ.

However, some people are open to this, and some are not. Some are hungry for Truth, some are not. What is it about one's heart condition that they get offended or feel like they are being judged when we talk about these things? Where we are at determines what we believe. Once we form a belief in our heart, we will subconsciously hear through that belief. We receive things that are said according to our heart condition. And then we will see through the belief we formed.

For Example: If I speak Truth to you but your heart is full of offense then you will hear what I say and receive it through offense and not as Truth. Then you will be offended with me. The same goes for insecurities, hurts, our past etc. If your heart is full of insecurities, then you will hear what I say through your insecurity. Then you will feel judged by me instead of hearing the Truth for what it is. In both of these scenarios you will then see me as insensitive because you are seeing me through your offense and insecurity, and not Truth.

It is important to have Truth in our heart then we will walk in Truth. We can be encouraged and ministered to and even touched by the Spirit of God but if we do not walk in Truth and live in His presence, we will end up right back where we started (deceived, broken, addicted, etc.). What are two things that make us free in Scripture? Truth (John 8:32) and where the Spirit of the Lord is (1 Corinthians 3:17), His presence. We can have an amazing and powerful encounter with the Lord, so many people do, and then months or maybe even years later we are right back where we started.

This happens to people who are miraculously freed from addictions. They walk in this freedom for a while because they are still living off the "high" of the encounter and then they end up right back in it. Why? Because they are not stewarding Truth and Relationship with Holy Spirit.

The encounter can give us an amazing miracle. It can push us in the right direction. And it can wake us up and get our attention, but we still must walk it out every day! We must walk in the Truth we know every day and live abiding (constant, never ending, every moment) in Christ.

Without these two things (Truth and Presence) our perspective will change. Our attitude will change. Our actions will change. Our words will change. Our thinking will change. Everything changes and things become dark, distant, and negative. We see through our own life again and Jesus says, "Come up here with Me. It looks a lot different from up here."

A Prayer to Pray:

"Lord, continue to teach me how to view things, with Your perspective. How to see what You see in any given circumstance. How to think what You think. Please continue to put me in line with You = One with You. One with You in mind, perspective, emotion, and action.

I thank You Jesus, whatever I go through, whatever I face, You are here to heal me, and make me new, better than before! I have a stronger identity in You because of it. I have a deeper relationship with You because of it. I will follow Your Truth in all things and not allow deception to slay me ever again.

Jesus, I don't want to try to be anything without You. I am done trying that. The Truth is I am nothing without You. I want You to have all of me and I truly and humbly want You to be my everything. God, I don't want to be anything less than Your best!

I am Loved by You. I am chosen by You. I am destined by You. I am made to live and reign, bringing Your Kingdom to earth in all of life's circumstances. You have purpose for my life. I am Your will. I am so valuable to You that You gave everything You had to ransom me. You have made me right. I stand before You, Father, spotless, pure, clean, and beautiful in Your sight. Oh, how You Love me and desire me. Your eyes are always on me. You delight in me. You rejoice over me with songs of joy. You are ravished by my Love and with one glance of my eye. The light of Your face shines on my heart. You take such pleasure in me and I am a great treasure to You! This is my Godentity! No one or no circumstance can say any different! I receive all these in Jesus name, Amen."

The Five Take Aways + Bonus One

1. We need to be humble enough to believe what God says about us.
2. We can have confidence that is rooted in humility.
3. Jesus died to bring us back into our created value.
4. Time, circumstance, and our experience, have no ability to change Truth, we just let it.
5. We spend a lot of time trying to be what we already are.
6. We cannot expect stability if we have a broken Godentity.

Picture from the internet.

Ephesians 3:20, "Now to Him who is able to do exceedingly abundantly above all that we ask or think... "

Isaiah 55:8-9, "For My thoughts are not your thoughts, nor are your ways My ways, says the LORD. For as the heavens are higher than the earth, so are My ways higher than your ways, and My thoughts than your thoughts."

Chapter 8

The Great Exchange

M UCH LIKE A trade: I will give you "this" _____ if you give me "this" _____. Well, I know a bad trade when I see one, so I would think. However, Jesus says, "I will give you all that is Mine if you give me all of your junk." This is not even close to a "fair" trade, but He says, "Come on give it ALL to Me! Give me all that is broken. All that is hurting. Give Me all your fear, worry, anxiety, pride, burdens, cares. Why don't you just give Me all your life? Now take My Holy Spirit, My power, My authority, Love, peace, joy, humility. In fact, here everything I have is yours, have it all." Yet we want to cling to our disfunction...our junk.

It is like the picture of the teddy bear. We want to keep what is infinitely of lesser value instead of taking His best. Why is that? Why can we not let go? I have a few ideas for this:

1. We do not trust God with our lives.
2. We do not think He will give us what we want.
3. We think we can control our lives better.
4. Maybe we feel He has failed us before. Maybe we trusted Him for something, but He did not "come through" for us, so now we take our lives into our own hands.
5. We just flat out want to do our own thing. We want to live our own lives.

We think we know what we want but He wants to give us what is best. However, we believe what we want or what we are doing is what is really "the best" thing for us. So, we either argue with God about not wanting to give it up, or we flat out refuse to. I was here in this place where I had given up God's best for me because I thought I knew better. He knows exceedingly, abundantly more than we do. We need to let go completely and stop grasping so desperately to any part of what we think is better. It is not worth it! It can never be better.

Time to take inventory:

1. Is there anything truly valuable you are trading for something of lesser worth?
2. Are you making your own decisions that will rob you of the blessing God wants to give you?
3. Are you yielding to selfish choices and not God's ways?

When we are doing any of these things, we are sacrificing our purpose, our destiny, and our future for momentary selfish wants and pleasures. We limit ourselves by what we want, what we are doing, our own desires, and our own will. When God wants infinitely more for us.

Erwin McManus says this, "The choices that are made today will create the future we live in tomorrow." And then Michael Todd says, "Do not make a move that is in rebellion. You will turn a season of consecration into years of tribulation." These two statements are so true. I can attest to them with my own life. Trying to live our lives outside of the reason why we are here is a way bigger problem than what we are going through. We must walk in a higher Truth.

We can choose His best or our worst:

I choose Your desires for my life and NOT my own desires.
I choose Your will for my life and NOT my own will and what I think is right.
I choose Life and NOT death.
I choose the future You have for me and NOT my own agenda.
I choose Your new ways and NOT my old ways.
I choose to live out Truth and NOT live in deception.
I choose to let go and NOT hold onto anything but You.

I choose to look upon Your face and NOT look to the things of this world.

I choose You as my defender and NOT me or anyone else.

I choose You over all else and NOT any idolatrous thing.

I choose to share in the sufferings of Christ and NOT in my own suffering.

To share in the sufferings of Christ, I become more like Him (1 Peter 4:1-2). To suffer in my own suffering (because of selfishness) is meaningless and pointless. It is to suffer for suffering's sake. BLAH!

JOURNAL ENTRY:

You are the only One who knows me, all of me, the deepest parts of me. The longings of my heart. You know me better than anyone ever could or ever will. I receive everything I need from You. I do not find these things from within myself (my flesh), nor do I get these things from other people. Only from You, can You give me everything it is I need. Where it is perfect, complete, and whole. Never lacking and never broken. Philippians 4:19, You supply all my need according to Your riches in glory in Christ Jesus.

I need Your comfort.

I need Your healing.

I need Your peace.

I need Your joy.

I need Your kindness.

I need Your gentleness.

I need You to be the Lover of my soul.

I need Your patience.

I need Your goodness.

I need You to be my best friend.

I need You to hold me.

I need You to take my hand.

I need Your ear to listen to me.

I need Your counsel.

I need Your direction.

I need Your provision.

I need Your protection.

I need Your grace.

I need Your Words speaking to me – so I know Truth.

I need Your wisdom.

I need Your discernment.

I need Your ears so I can hear correctly.

I need Your eyes to see.

I need Your mouth – so I can speak with Your Words.

I need Your mercy.

I need Your compassion.

I need You to carry me.

I need Your plan.

I need Your purpose.

I need Your perspective.

I need Your presence.

I need Your strength.

I am such a "needy" person! Yet, all I need is You. No one could ever supply all my needs, but You. And You NEVER say, "Uh, really?? I have to do that for you? You are so needy! If I have to do that, then you can just forget it!" You never try to teach me how to be self-sufficient. In fact, You tell me I am not to be self-sufficient at all (John 15:5). You never get tired of me needing You. I cannot live without You. I depend on You. I rely on You. I cast the whole of my cares on You (1 Peter 5:7). Lord, I give all this need to You, and I trust You to take care of me.

You have made covenant with me. This means **all** You have is mine, and **all** I have is Yours. This is the Great Exchange. All I have to give You is broken, extremely broken. I give You this vessel that is full of nothing of value (as of now) to be emptied of all of me so I can be filled with all of You. I want none of me and all of You. I receive all You have for me.

Everything You pour into me is so I can be that to others. Pour into me Your mercy, so I can be merciful to others. Pour into me Your perspective, so I can carry Your perspective to others, etc. You take all my junk and in exchange give me You. So, I can be You to others. To be a servant to all. To be selfless. It is about what I can get to give it away (Romans 15:1-7). I cannot give if I am empty or dry. It is like a sponge. If it is immersed in water, it will come out of the water overflowing and able to pour water out. If it never gets immersed, it will remain dry and have nothing to give. I immerse myself in You. Fill me up so I can pour out to others. I cannot give if I am empty, and I certainly do not want to give people me! I drink deep of You. Fill me up! **End of journal entry.**

He will take away all our hurt, brokenness, bitterness, anxieties, frustrations, insecurities, etc. If we come to Him and lay it all down at His feet. If we allow Holy Spirit to transform us, we will experience freedom we have never known before. Jesus will heal our broken emotions. He will heal our broken life. He will comfort us and fill every longing. He is the only One who fully understands us, for He created us. He knows every part of us inside and out and therefore knows what we need. He will complete us and make us whole as only He can.

Hannah Whitall Smith from the book, *The Christian's Secret of a Happy Life.* "The care is His, the burdens are His, the responsibility belongs to Him, the protections rests upon Him, the planning, and providing, and controlling, and guiding, all are in His hands." "Therefore, those who are in His kingdom, are utterly delivered from any need to be anxious, or burdened, or perplexed, or troubled." "Surely no care or anxiety can ever enter here, if the heart but knows its kingdom and its King!"

The weight of the world is heavy His burden is light.

Practical Application:

Lord, remove everything from my life and from myself that can be shaken so the things that cannot be shaken only remain. Therefore, I receive a Kingdom which cannot be moved (Hebrews 12:22-29).

In the Great Exchange I Give to You Jesus these things that can be shaken. These things which are death. And I receive from You that which is Life in the Kingdom. The things that cannot be shaken or moved.

1. Isaiah 40:29-31, I give to You my weakness and I receive Your power.
2. Isaiah 40:29-31, I give to You my weariness and I receive Your strength.
3. Isaiah 43:18-19, I give to You the former things and I receive the new thing You are doing.
4. Isaiah 54:4-5, I give to You my fear, shame, disgrace, & reproach and I receive You, my Redeemer.
5. Isaiah 61:1, I give to You my broken heart and I receive Your healing.
6. Isaiah 61:1, I give to You my captivity and I receive Your freedom.

7. Isaiah, 61:1, I give to You my chains and I receive the prison doors that are open.
8. Isaiah 61:2, I give to You my mourning and I receive Your comfort.
9. Isaiah 61:3, I give to You my ashes and I receive Your beauty.
10. Isaiah 61:3, I give to You my mourning and I receive Your oil of joy.
11. Isaiah 61:3, I give to You my heaviness and I receive Your garment of praise.
12. Isaiah 61:7, I give to You my shame and I receive Your double honor (double portion) and everlasting joy.
13. Jeremiah 31:13, I give to You my sorrow & mourning and I receive Your comfort and joy.
14. Jeremiah 31:25, I give to You my weariness and I receive Your satiation (Your abundant satisfaction).
15. Jeremiah 31:25, I give to You my sorrow and I receive Your replenishment.
16. Psalm 30:11, I give to You my mourning and I receive Your dancing.
17. Psalm 30:11, I give to You my sackcloth and I receive Your gladness.
18. Psalm 34:5, I give to You my shame and I receive Your radiance (to sparkle).
19. Psalm 34:18, I give to You my broken heart and I receive Your nearness.
20. Psalm 34:18, I give to You my contrite (crushed) spirit and I receive Your saving (You rescue me).
21. Psalm 34:19, I give to You my afflictions and I receive Your deliverance.
22. Psalm 43:5, I give to You my cast down & disquieted soul and I receive the help of Your countenance (face, presence, person) and I will hope in You.
23. Psalm 46:1-2, I give to You my troubles & fear and I receive Your help, refuge, & strength.
24. Psalm 55:22, I give to You my burden and I receive Your sustainment (You will never permit me to be moved).
25. Psalm 147:3, I give to You my wounds and I receive Your binding up.
26. Matthew 8:16-17, I give to You my sickness/infirmities and I receive Your healing.
27. Matthew 11:28, I give to You my heavy burden and I receive Your rest.

28. John 14:27, I give to You my troubled heart & fear and I receive Your peace.
29. 2 Corinthians 5:21, I give to You my sin and I receive Your righteousness.
30. Philippians 4:6-7, I give to You my anxiety and I receive Your peace that guards my heart and mind.
31. Philippians 4:19, I give to You all my needs and I receive Your supply (according to Your riches in glory by Christ Jesus).
32. Colossians 3:1-17, I give to You the old man (fornication, uncleanness, lust, evil desire, greed (which is idolatry), anger, wrath, malice, blasphemy, filthy language, and lies) and I receive the new man (I put on tender mercies, kindness, humility, meekness, patience, forgiveness, forbearance with others, Love, the peace of God ruling my heart, thankfulness, the Word of Christ dwelling in me richly in all wisdom, and singing with grace in my heart to the Lord).
33. 1 John 4:18, I give to You my fear and I receive Your perfect Love.

Even though I may not <u>feel</u> anything now, I know this is Truth, and one day I will live in the fruit of this moment of **The Great Exchange!**

Journal Entry 3/5/19:

You saved me, You saved me, You saved me! You saved me on the cross. You saved me from myself so many times. Too many times to count. You saved me from the destruction of other people. You saved me from the mess I created. He will save you too if you let Him. If you run to Him. He does not force His freedom or His Love on anyone, but He offers it to everyone. Will you receive it? The choice is yours. **End of journal entry.**

Journal Entry 3/4/2022:

To know You is to know Your ways (Exodus 33:13). You speak to me, "One step at a time, trust Me, one step at a time." You have put in me everything needed to accomplish Your purpose. Meaning, You have put Your finished work in me. I am already free from every sin and every bondage. I am already healed. Isaiah 26:3-4, I have perfect peace, I have Shalom (Hebrew meaning: safety, wellness, happiness, welfare, health, prosperity, rest, favor, friendship, goodness, and wholeness). WOW! I will walk in the finished work You have already accomplished for me! **End of journal entry.**

A Prayer to Pray:

"Father, You spoke to the answer when You created me. You put in me exactly what was needed for this day and time I am in. You gave me the gifting needed and You gave me the ministry needed for such a time as this. You have made me to be one of steady strength. You are my inner strength that is immovable and unshakable. I will walk steady with You. With inner joy, peace, and Love, not having high highs or low lows, but I will be consistently content in You. I have shalom and I am full of Life. Through the Great Exchange, I have everything I need in You."

Five Take Aways

1. We think we know what we want, but He knows what is best.
2. Do not exchange your purpose and destiny for momentary wants or pleasure.
3. I want all of You and none of me.
4. In Covenant, **all** that He has is mine and **all** that I have is His.
5. The weight of the world is heavy, but His burden is light.

Picture created by Gary Ambs

Ezekiel 36:25-26, "Then I will sprinkle clean water on you, and you shall be clean; I will cleanse you from all your filthiness and from all your idols. I will give you a new heart and put a new spirit within you; I will take the heart of stone out of your flesh and give you a heart of flesh."

CHAPTER 9

Detox My Heart

JOURNAL ENTRY:

I CAME DOWN the road and You ran to me with arms wide open. You gave me a hug that felt like home. You went inside to prepare the celebration. Yet, I stayed outside circling the place. Walking around and around it instead of entering. I have been lingering outside instead of coming in to where You are. "Come inside," I hear You beckon me. "I am a mess, Lord." "Come as you are." I stopped walking around the house and headed toward the door. I made my way through the bustling winds and the chaos all around me. With dread of going inside, I pushed the door open with everything I had and slammed it shut behind me. As I looked around, I saw I was in my heart. I now understood why I was so reluctant to enter. My heart was indeed a mess.

I had been walking around and around storing up wounds instead of being rid of them. I didn't know how. All I knew was I didn't want to hurt anymore. I was so tired of hurting. I knew if I went inside, I would have to face these wounds and that would be painful. Not realizing the unforgiveness and self-pity I was living in was what was keeping the wounds alive. So, I stayed outside instead of entering in the home where You dwell

(Ephesians 3:17-19). I am here now Lord, inside Your home. Inside my heart with You. Watching it pulsate and beat weakly, nevertheless, it was still alive.

Now I notice I am lying on a surgery table where You are preparing to perform open heart surgery on me. To clean out Your home. To remove every bit of junk and debris that does not belong here. To mend it and heal it so I can know Love (Romans 5:5). The more I look around I see all the places where it has been hardened as hard as a rock. Where it has been frozen as cold as ice. Where the wounds are oozing with infection. Where the pain and hurt has caused it to bleed profusely. The places where it is walled up.

There's been construction going on in my heart...a wall being built, by me. I think it will protect me when it will not. It is not a good thing. God is showing me, it will hurt me more than it will save me from being hurt. Now I just need Him to show me how to live without it. How to live inside my own heart with Him; healed, whole, vibrant, and fully alive.

I will not continue to stay outside where it seems to be less painful. The unhealed places want me to continue out here but if left unhealed these places are what will continue to control me and dictate my future. To ignore the wounds is momentarily less painful but it will lead to only more destruction.

Lord, I am asking for every part of my wounded heart that I am so desperately trying to cover up and push away be revealed and exposed right now. The pain of what I am feeling is very real. I release it all into Your very Loving and capable hands. I choose to go down the road more beautiful. To go through the momentary pain to get to the other side where there is complete healing. I am here (available) for You to tend to my heart. To tend to my every need. To tend to my every longing and desire.

I give to You all the things I have been extremely hurt by... the offenses of my heart. I give to You all the areas I am weighed down... the burdens of my heart. I give to You all the places that have held me back or paralyzed me... the fears of my heart. I give to You all the annoyances and hostility within me... the anger of my heart. I surrender these things to You today in exchange for healing and FREEDOM. I let it all go to hold onto You, Lord. Knock down the wall I have erected on Your property. It does not belong here. **End of journal entry.**

A LITTLE TESTIMONY AND TRUTH REVEALED

Before we continue here is a reminder; <u>Self is the greatest destructive force in the world</u>. Living from a place that is all about your-self will destroy you. You will be the most miserable person if you stay here, and your life will be void.

I could not see past my pain and hurt so I started to live from the place of my pain. Living from this place made me very "needs" driven and there were insufficient funds in my account. Because of this deficit, I raised my expectations. My emotions were running wild and were simply not true. I was in "survival mode" therefore everything had false motivation behind it. I told myself, "I don't need them to do anything for me" (with an attitude by the way) yet I NEEDED them to do something, ANYTHING! I tried to surround myself with what seemed safe, but this only left me to wrestle with God over everything that was happening.

When I am wrestling **against** God, I am not running to the **very One** I need to receive the healing I so desperately need. So, I ran down a very slippery slope with the devil. I walled up, I closed up, I tried to protect myself. I had so much hurt that it would build up in me and then on occasion it would explode into fits of rage. My soul was dying inside. I was not who I was 3 years ago, that bright, shining, bubbly, carefree, Jesus girl. I was still not fully surrendered and dead to my-self, and now because of it, I was deceived, led astray, and in a deep, dark, slimy pit.

I was in this pit because the enemy had me sold on a lie and gripped with fear (as he does with many). Thinking if I continue to Love someone who is hurting me (which is ultimately putting them first) I will continue to be mistreated, miserable, not taken care of, walked all over, taken advantage of, and the list goes on of the lies we will buy. When the exact opposite is true. When we put others first, when we continue to Love, having the heart and mind of Christ (not selfish) we will be the most fulfilled we have ever been. This fulfillment only happens when we live outside of ourselves and live in Christ.

The enemy also says, if we continue to give endlessly to someone who shows us no care or concern, we will be disregarded, not loved back, become a doormat, and get rejected. Which this all may be true. However, these are all selfish thoughts. The enemy had me gripped with these distorted, messed up, and selfish ideas. So, I decided to "protect" myself and it destroyed me more than it preserved me (which I thought I was doing... how deceived I was).

I held myself back from Loving this person out of fear of being "taken advantage of." The lie was that I would give, and give, and give and the person would continue to think it is ok to treat me the way they do. They will think it is ok to treat me with disregard and insignificance. If I go on **as if** I am happy and all is good while still loving them, they will say, "She must be ok with it because she's good. She is still loving me."

Side note: Crazy thing is I heard on a Christian radio talk show a conversation that supported this way of thinking and then I felt "justified" for thinking this way. I didn't know how distorted this really was. This is a lie. It is a very selfish way of thinking. It only complicates things, and we end up making matters worse (James 3:13-18).

I was so selfish I was letting heartbreak stop me from Loving. This is completely opposite of Christ who hung on the cross for the very ones who were crucifying Him. "Father forgive them, for they know not what they do." He Loved the very ones who were beating Him and nailing Him to that tree. We have never faced anything like this. So, we can surely Love during our trials that cannot even compare to what He endured and still exemplified Love.

However, like I mentioned, I did not know this Truth at the time so in all my hurt I took matters into my own hands (following exactly what satan would have me do). Trying to control this person by what I did and what I didn't do. Some would not be as bold as to say it this way, but this is exactly what we are trying to do to people when that happens. It is called manipulation and it is a common tool in the enemy's toolbelt.

For Example: The thought is if I give them the cold shoulder or silent treatment then they will understand what they are doing is wrong and change what they are doing (manipulation). They might treat me better if I ignore them for a little while (manipulation). Or I am going to "teach them a lesson," by not showing them Love and then they will learn they cannot do this to me or be this way towards me (manipulation). We have reactions like these to defend ourselves or guard ourselves and we may feel justified in why we do what we do. We probably blame others for why we are the way we are (it's their fault).

Do you see how twisted and demonic this is? As if ignoring them and withholding Love from them is going to make them want to Love in return? Uh NO! This is wrong! We end up living miserable lives from this way of thinking. If we do not surrender these areas and die to our flesh, we will go about our life living it broken and unfulfilled. Not knowing how to truly Love and then think these ways are normal ways to react. "Because they are the one who needs to be thinking of me and how they are making me feel! Right?!"

As a Christ follower we need to train ourselves to surrender things as they happen and die to ourselves. May our first prayer always be "Holy Spirit, reveal Your Truth to me in this." Because the Truth is; it is kindness that leads to repentance (Romans 2:4). Maybe we understand that, but we don't know how to do it, show it, or give it when we are so hurt and broken (as was the case for me). We are to leave it in Holy Spirit's hands to bring conviction to them about the condition of their own heart. This is not our job. We are to know the condition of our own heart and camp here until our heart is His heart. Until we become Love.

I am to preface this next part with this; I understand there are some cases where there are extenuating circumstances. I am not in any way saying you are to stay in a situation if someone is physically abusing you. You may need to separate yourself from a person to work through things. Even in these situations we are called to be Love just as Jesus is Love. I am not saying it is easy. I am just saying what the Word of God tells us (1 Corinthians 13 Love). I have not seen in the Bible where it gives us any reason to not Love someone or where we are excused from being as Jesus to someone. Our ultimate goal is to become Love. Even to those who curse us, hate us, spitefully use us, and persecute us (Matthew 5:44-48 & Luke 6:28-36).

The ones I am talking to here are many of us who get upset if we are not treated the way we think we should be. If we are not being Loved or respected the way we want to be Loved or respected. Those of us who say we are emotionally abused when that is truly impossible. More gasps, I know, let me explain. When we know who we are in Christ and whose we are in Christ we cannot be emotionally abused. When I am **secure** in Him and rely on **zero** of the flesh (because it is dead), no one can have any effect on where I am emotionally. My emotional stability is in Christ alone always and forever. My emotional stability should not be based on what anyone else says or does or does not say or does not do.

I can say this so boldly because I fell victim to this lie of feeling like I was emotionally abused and then I learned Truth:

1. When we hold ourselves back from Loving, from giving, from serving, (from being Christ in us to others), we may think we are protecting ourselves when in reality we are holding ourselves hostage to ourselves.

We may think we are doing what is best for us when actually we are a prisoner to fear. Fear of being hurt, disappointed, disregarded, rejected, vulnerable, being a door mat, "getting walked all over," etc. We are bound up in those selfish thoughts and we are not free. We are not free to give. We are not free to Love. We are not free to serve. We certainly aren't under any protection this way; we are completely open and vulnerable. If we are so wrapped up in holding ourselves back, thinking of ourselves and for ourselves, we are not understanding giving ourselves away and following the example of Christ. Jesus who gave His life for us, never withheld Himself from us. If we are withholding ourselves from others, how can we follow in His steps who gave Himself willingly for us all? It was not that He put His trust in man nor did He put His heart into man's hands. It is that He committed Himself to Him who judges righteously (1 Peter 2:18-25). He put His trust and His heart in His Father's hands and by doing so He could serve and Love without reservation, without vulnerability. Without reviling back when He Himself was reviled. He trusted His Father who is perfect in every way with every part of Himself. How can we go wrong when we are in this place? We cannot. No matter if people treat us badly, we are unmoved because we are secure in our Father. And what we are giving them is Jesus. Not ourselves but Jesus; Peace, Love, Hope, Joy, Kindness, Gentleness, Compassion, Light, Life, etc.

2. If we fear being "taken advantage of" that is self. Did Jesus EVER think this way? "I better not be nice to them and show them Love anymore because they might think it is okay to hurt Me over, and over, and over again and that is just not right. I am NOT going to let them walk all over Me like I'm a rug to wipe their feet on! Like I am a nobody. I better make boundaries to stop them from crossing the line. I better protect Myself and hold Myself back from them." Can we picture Jesus saying any of these things or acting this way? No! Then why do we think it is okay for us to think this, say this, and do this to others? Why is getting "taken advantage of," "getting walked on," or "being a doormat," even in our vocabulary or thought process? We must get our minds out of the world's psychology; the world's way of doing things, and the world's way of thinking. You cannot take advantage of me because **I am called to serve you.** I Love you, and I give, and I give, and I give, be-

cause this is Christ's nature in me. You cannot use me or emotionally abuse me when my mind is in Christ and not on myself.

3. I was very frustrated with this person. I thought my frustration was them and how they were treating me and hurting me. However, truth is my frustration was hidden in my own selfishness. I was frustrated with not getting my way or what I wanted. With not being involved or being included. I felt rejected, disregarded, and not important enough to them. I was frustrated with not being Loved the way I wanted to be Loved or thought of the way I thought I should be thought of. I never realized this was all selfish. I thought I was just expecting what was "normal" to expect from someone you are married to. (We went over expectations in Chapter 6). I expected him to Love me in a way he did not know how to Love. I in turn made a bigger mess of things because of my human logic and reasoning. It is impossible to have no expectations from somebody or to say, "you don't owe me a thing" **when** we are so focused on ourselves and what we "need." This is selfishness. And Love does not seek its own.

4. The enemy had me sold on another lie that to be obedient and to Love this person who treated me with such disregard was too hard, too demanding, and pretty darn near impossible. I mean, "To Love as Christ has Loved me? COME ON! It is SO hard." Then the enemy used the fear of continually being hurt in return to stop me. So now obedience is not only too hard, and too demanding, but obedience also hurts me. ALL LIES. Well really, these are all absolutely true if we are living in our flesh (which is supposed to be dead by the way, smile). But we are to be living in Christ and Christ in us... One with Christ. Being just as Christ in this world... obedient even unto death of ourselves (1 John 4:17 & Philippians 2:5-8). The Truth is obedience is for our ultimate good and will bring us blessing. Therefore, do not fear being hurt. Do not let this stop us because in our obedience to the Father, He has us, and holds us, and defeats our enemies before our face (Deuteronomy 28:1-14).

A PRAYER TO PRAY:

"Holy Spirit, I cannot do this, only You can do this in me. Please forgive me for every time I have put myself before others. Where I have thought of myself more highly than others. Where I have allowed the lies of the enemy to control me instead of Your Love. Please remove every selfish thought and ambition from me. I do not want to be that person at all! Remove every ounce of pride, fear, and hurt. Please help me, Lord! I yield to You and Your ways. Heal all the broken places in me. I do not want anything in me that is not of You, for You, or from You! In Jesus name, Amen."

JOURNAL ENTRY:

A short time after I prayed this prayer, I had a friend send me a song "Everything" by Lifehouse. Herein lies my dilemma as I quote some lyrics from the song: "Your all I want, Your all I need, Your everything." The question hit me **hard** "is He really everything I want? Or do I find there are so many other things I want too? Is He really everything??" It is so easy for us to do lip service and say, "Oh Lord, You are all I want." So easy to say it, but is it truly my reality?

This takes a whole lot of death and dying to get to where there is nothing else I want in this world. It is deeper and more than we even know when He starts unpacking everything else it is that we want in this life. I must admit this day was a very painful day for me. Hard realities to face and anger was trying to rise up in me. So much self had to go. I felt like this was nearly an impossible task... very overwhelming.

My Prayer: Jesus, I need You! God, I admit I do not know what is going on here right now. I feel like I am going to literally crack under the pressure. I am running to You, the only thing I know to do. I feel the weight of the things You have freed me from trying to come on me. The pressure to give up and to fall back into old habits and old ways of doing things. The lies that come wave after wave right now, bring me to my knees before You in tears. I just want it to stop, and I know it will, eventually... Holy Spirit continue to strengthen me. I cannot do this without You. I am clinging to Your promise that **You will** bring beauty from these ashes.

Holy Spirit is working on removing every bit of selfishness from me. However, I never dreamed it would hurt so bad. I guess what hurts more than anything is I did not think I was a selfish person. But when you are hit with the reality that every bit of discouragement, disappointment, frustration, irritation, hurt, etc. all stems from a selfish root (because you are thinking of yourself and for yourself) it changes things.

This is the crossroads He has me at. The battle of my will at all costs. The complete death of self. Holy Spirit showed me a new level was coming because I was in so much struggle. The enemy ramping up his attacks and temptations for me to just throw the towel in, go back, and "do my own thing." Do it my way once again only to fail?! This is what the enemy wants.

Holy Spirit then showed me how it was much like labor pains. He is birthing something new in me, birthing something deeper in me. It may hurt for a moment but what comes out of this is beautiful. He is birthing in me deeper revelation. A complete death to self. A dying to all my will, all my wants, all my ways, all of me. Will I commit to myself, or will I commit to Him? Choose this day death or life. You choose, Sunshine... **End of journal entry.**

FEELINGS AND EMOTIONS

The definition of Emotion: a natural instinctive state of mind **deriving from** one's **circumstances, mood, or relationships with others.**

Feeling: an **emotional** state or reaction

Emotions and feelings if driven by the flesh are based on our circumstances, our moods, and on other people. They are completely needs driven and selfish. We can be up one minute and down the next depending on how our day is going or how other people are acting towards us. Others never know, in fact we ourselves don't even know, how we will be from one moment to the next. Because it all depends on how our life is going, how our day is going, and how others are treating us. If we live according to the feelings of the flesh, we are unstable in all our ways. The beautiful thing about dying to ourselves is when we die to self, we come alive in Christ. Instead of being led by the emotions of the flesh we are now led by the emotion of the Spirit of God.

Emotions and feelings when led by Holy Spirit are full of life, vibrant, exciting, rich, intense, powerful.... the most amazing emotional ride. I literally can laugh and cry in the same sentence. The Lord makes us very emotional! It is not that our feelings and emotions die when the flesh dies, oh no, this is where they truly come alive. They die to being controlled by the flesh (the old way of life) and live by being led by Holy Spirit (the new way of life). It is a new way of reacting, a new way of responding, because we are not feeling according to the flesh anymore. We are not feeling according to our own selfishness anymore. We are being led by Holy Spirit.

Proverbs 28:26, "He that trusts in his own heart is a fool..." *Strong's Concordance* says this for the Hebrew meaning of heart; "Used very widely for the feelings, the will, and even the intellect (mind)." Never trust in your own feelings and thoughts because then you will be led by your own feelings and thoughts. Being ruled by feelings and thoughts of the flesh; think of the worst fair ride ever... well the Scripture does tell us we are a fool: if we do this. It is a walk by faith not by our feelings and emotions.

However, we are so stuck in emotionalism that is of the flesh. It keeps us feeling sorry for ourselves and stuck in the place of what was done to us. Or what we never had. Or all the ways we are currently being mistreated and hurt. Our feelings (when of the flesh) are a gauge. They are not meant to be a guide. A gauge where Jesus can show us what we need to be delivered from.

Since 2011, I have had to fight the good fight of faith as I learned Truth about all the wrongly formed beliefs I had (about all of life and being a Christian), and the wrong behaviors I had. I had to learn to not be emotionally driven and reactive. I had to learn how to not live according to the feelings of my flesh. All my life I had lived with a bunch of feelings I did not like and did not want. Feelings of jealousy, anger, depression, insecurity, comparison, inadequacy, fear, condemnation, just to name a few. I never knew I did not have to live according to these feelings. I never knew how to overcome them. I thought they were just "a part of life," "it's called being "human." I thought they were "normal" to have and there was no escaping them. So, they festered inside of me.

Living according to these kinds of feelings is what destroys relationships, and they destroy us. The moment we start to live according to destructive feelings we are allowing satan rule over us. I learned I did not have to live as a slave to these toxic feelings any longer. As I surrendered to Holy Spirit, I could live the crucified life and be resurrected with the Word of God. I came into alignment with Truth and Love. Then the Truth and the Spirit of the Lord made me free. I found I can live in constant peace, joy, kindness, and Love. My feelings and emotions being guided by Holy Spirit in Truth, did not have to be ruled by my flesh and be led by satan to destruction. These are two very different lives.

More than anything, I do not live by feelings. I live by Truth. My emotions need to be channeled through Truth, through Holy Spirit. What if

I didn't feel happy? Is Jesus still Lord and does He still Love me? Yes! We must realize there is a place to see this and know this and be content in this no matter what. I do not live by my emotions. I live by every Word that proceeds out of the mouth of God. Feelings of the flesh are sinking sand and shift from moment to moment. Only the Word of God is stable. It never shifts or changes. We can never be securely anchored in quicksand, but we can be securely anchored in the Truth. Only then can we find stability beyond our feelings.

PRACTICAL APPLICATION:

Somebody does something to you and it makes you so mad. You feel let down, hurt, disappointed, disrespected, rejected, etc. Maybe you feel the anger rising and the blood rushing to your face. Immediately when you feel that, acknowledge it before the Lover of your soul. Tell Him "I feel so angry right now, I feel like I'm going to explode," talk to Him about it. Be honest and real with Him (He knows anyway). You don't have to talk to your 5 closest friends about it, go to the Lord first! Then choose to speak His Word over it, "but I know my anger does not bring about the righteous life that You desire (James 1:20). So, I choose to cast my cares (everything about this situation) on you for you care for me (1 Peter 5:7). Forgive me. Heal me. Transform me so I respond as You Jesus every time." Then let it go and choose to follow His Word in the matter. Continuing to give it to Him as many times as you keep picking it back up. According to Colossians we are to "put off" and "put on" (Colossians 3:1-17) and do it as many times as you need to.

Jeremiah 17:9-10 ESV & NLT in parenthesis, "The (human) heart is deceitful above all things, and desperately sick; who can understand it? 'I the Lord search the heart and test the mind, (examine secret motives) to give every man according to his ways, according to the fruit of his deeds.'"

The heart is the home of our feelings and thoughts as we already learned from earlier. This verse tells us our heart is deceitful which also means our feelings and thoughts are deceitful. In Hebrew deceitful means fraudulent, crooked, and polluted. So, the famous saying, "Just follow your heart," does that really sound like a good idea? Or this one, "What does your heart say?" The Word of God tells us the home of our feelings, our heart, is fraudulent, crooked, and polluted. We cannot live based off our feelings or emotions **under our own guidance**. This is the key. Under our guidance they will be misleading and false which will only lead to turmoil and destruction.

Surrendered to the Lover of our soul our feelings, our heart, will be guided in Truth and nurtured in Love. And brought into alignment with the Word of God. We must make the choice to say in every place, in every situation, "I do not care what I feel, I will stand on Your Word. Which is always the Truth of the matter." As we live the crucified life and Holy Spirit transforms us, in that process, there will come a time when the feeling and emotion of Holy Spirit will be our first response in any given circumstance. We will no longer respond according to the flesh. Amen!

The greatest difference between the emotions and feelings of the flesh and of Holy Spirit is the flesh is all about self and Holy Spirit is all about the sacrificial life. Laying down our lives for others. Never thinking about ourselves or for ourselves. If we live a highly intentional life, which is the sacrificial life, we do not have to give up joy, pleasure, or fulfillment. We find it. And we will live in joy, pleasure, and fulfillment. When life is not all about you and making yourself happy and doing what you want to do, you then come alive in Christ and fully live.

When we live according to the feelings of the flesh: (I have gone over some already, I will briefly list them again and then a couple of others.)

1. They keep us feeling sorry for ourselves. "What has been done to me." "What I never had." "How I am consistently mistreated or not respected." Just some examples of self-pity.
2. They destroy relationships and us.
3. They make us needs driven and then we are open to be let down, hurt, offended, and disappointed when someone does not fulfill what we "need" or want. We will also feel these ways if a situation doesn't turn out the way we expect.
4. We will have momentary pleasures, but this is all they are...momentary. We can have high highs, euphoric moments, but they are just that, moments. They do not last forever. In Christ you can have feelings that are consistent. Constant joy no matter what is happening around you. You can be emotionally steady in Christ.
5. We will never be satisfied. We will always want more. We will have lusts that cannot be quenched or fulfilled. We will always want the next best thing.
6. We will be self-protected and hold ourselves back from people, re-

lationships, and situations. Drawing lines and making boundaries.

7. We will have <u>defense mechanisms</u> like giving people the cold shoulder, silent treatment, or making crass or sarcastic comments.

Wouldn't it be wonderful to be free from all of this? I have good news, in Christ, we can be!

In the Spirit we are fully satisfied. He is the guard over us and our hearts. He leads us in every emotion and response. As our feelings and emotions are rooted and grounded in Christ (in Love) they only grow in capacity, in strength, in intensity (in profoundness), and yet they can be counted on to remain stable, secure, and trusted. What?! Think about that! To actually be able to trust your feelings and emotions? Wow! We cannot trust feelings of the flesh, but of Holy Spirit we can. To me that is powerful. It is total reliance on Holy Spirit and everything about Him is a sure foundation.

As you allow God to work in you, because you are in a real, personal, and intimate relationship with Him, the person you are becoming is eternal. Someone you can count on and not be concerned with how they will be from one moment to the next, from one day to the next, or one year to the next. A constant because you are becoming more like Christ, the Solid Rock. No more awful roller coasters, no highs, and lows. Just steadily trusting in Jesus to take you from one moment to the next. Which is a steady flow, steady stream, peace like a river that attendeth your way.

He has us lay our lives down so we do not live an unstable life for ourselves, but we live an intentional life for others. He has us think about others and not for ourselves. So, we will not give silent treatments, or anything else the flesh would naturally want to do when it is hurt or offended. We will not be hurt by people, but we will hurt for people. When we know the Love of Christ, we will be secure in Christ. We will then learn how to walk in the Love of Christ, and people no longer have the power to hurt us.

I have to say and must admit this kind of Love, these kinds of feelings, and emotions can cause us to feel vulnerable. We will feel exposed and naked at times. Especially when we first start living this way. However, vulnerability before the Lord is the most precious place we can live. Vulnerability with the Lord opens us up to Truth. It brings us closer to Him as we intentionally bring Him around us to make Him our guard. We are safe and protected with the Lord in our vulnerability with Him.

For those who have incredible empathy for people and can feel what other people are feeling. I understand the Scriptures say to mourn with those who mourn (Romans 12:15). This is Truth. The trouble comes when you are not dead to the feelings of your flesh (which are deceitful). So, now you are feeling what they feel, not only that but when you walk away you are now carrying it as your own. It becomes your burden, and it is heavy upon you. It weighs you down in your heart; in your thoughts, and in your feelings.

When you are free from the feelings of your flesh you can mourn with those who mourn and walk away without carrying it as your own burden (it is not yours to carry but the Lord's). We do not get some kind of hero badge for carrying other people's burdens ourselves. When we are to share in other's burdens, it does not mean for us to take them on ourselves. It means we help the person. We bear them by taking them to the Lord and leaving all our cares with Him (1 Peter 5:7).

When you are free from the feelings of your flesh you will be able to speak Life to them in a spirit of gentleness (Galatians 6:1) and pray with them in Truth. You can cry with them. But you will not leave them there in their despair. Because you are in line with Holy Spirit which is Light, Life, Love, and Truth. When your feelings are led by Holy Spirit, they will lead you into all Truth and not into emotional traps or lies.

People will reference Galatians 6:2 where it says we are to bear one another's burdens. If you look at the first verse, he is talking about restoring a brother who is in sin. This does not mean we are to bear that person's sin. We bear each other's burdens by speaking Truth in Love to people who are caught in sin. We bear each other's burdens by praying for each other. But as we learned in Chapter 3 (Absolute Surrender), we do not carry them ourselves. We cast the whole of our cares unto the Lord because He cares for us. We cast the burdens **to Him**. We do not walk away with them.

A Prayer to Pray:

"O Lover of my soul, You are the only One that can understand my heart. I give You my heart so You can lead my feelings and emotions in Truth. I don't want the feelings of my flesh any longer. They will only lead me to destruction. I crucify them, and I choose You. Every time the feelings of the flesh try to resurrect themselves and deceive me, I will seek You. I will run to You and talk with You and pour my heart out to You. I will find Truth in Your Word to utterly destroy the feelings of the flesh. I will live according to Your Word of Truth and not my feelings. Please expose all deception and every lie I have ever believed about my feelings and reveal Your Truth. In Jesus name, Amen."

WE CAN LIVE WITHOUT HURT, DISCOURAGEMENT, FRUSTRATION, ETC.

Jesus tells us in John 14:1, "Let not your hearts be troubled." Now again in the Greek as in the Hebrew the heart is the thoughts and feelings. In John 14:27 Jesus tells us, "Peace I leave with you, My peace I give to you... Let not your heart be troubled, neither let it be afraid." Troubled in the Greek is to stir or agitate. What is it you think you are feeling when you are discouraged, frustrated, disappointed, hurt, offended, etc.? You are stirred or agitated.

When we look deeper into the definition of this Greek word for troubled (tarasso) we find it says this: to cause one inward commotion, take away calmness of mind, to disturb, to make restless, to disquiet, to stir up, to strike one's spirit with fear and dread, to render anxious or distressed, to perplex the mind. Doesn't this sound like every single feeling we have ever had? And Jesus tells us to never, under any circumstances, give way for one single moment to any of this! "Let not your heart be troubled." Let not your thoughts and feelings be agitated or stirred.

Our initial response to people and situations is a good indicator of where we are at in living the crucified life. Is our flesh triggered to respond a certain way? Do we immediately get offended? Are we agitated, stirred, frustrated, hurt, discouraged, etc.?

We are so used to giving ourselves permission to be broken, hurt, and feeling all of those ways and we call it "normal." We say, "well it's going to happen," "that's life," "we are only human." Jesus was a man, and did He ever give way to selfish thoughts and feelings? We are also, partakers of the Diving Nature (2 Peter 1:4), just as Jesus. If we abide in Him, we are to walk just as He walked (1 John 2:6). Where do we get the idea we have any excuse to not walk as Jesus? I have a hard time understanding how we missed it all these years (me included)! We are to give ourselves no permission to be hurt or broken, thinking, and feeling of ourselves and for ourselves.

When our thoughts are in obedience to Christ we cannot continue making "justifications" as to why we are hurt or why we are offended. In obedience to Christ, we forgive and choose to Love those who may have "hurt" us. If we are dead, we will never hurt for ourselves. Love does not seek its own. Love keeps no record of wrong. We love not our own lives.

Where there is self-seeking there is confusion and every evil thing is there (James 3:16). Not just some evil things but EVERY evil thing is found in selfishness. I cannot stay in self-centeredness because it is a landing strip for unforgiveness, hurt, disappointment, offense, brokenness, frustration, despair, discouragement, etc. Thinking in a manner that creates these things is always about ourselves. We are to see everything through Truth and not the flesh. To respond, look, and Love like Jesus.

PRACTICAL APPLICATION:

How do I not get hurt? How do I not fear rejection or being "taken advantage of?" How do I not get discouraged? How do I not get offended? How do I keep no record of wrong?

1. Remove the "I" and Die! Then there is no longer a self-centered "I" to possess anything including hurt, rejection, discouragement, and offense. How can any of those things happen if self-centeredness is not at the core of your thoughts and feelings? Let God receiving all the glory be at the core of your thoughts and feelings, not your-self.

2. Get buried in the Love of God. The more God's Love dominates you the more you will not pay any attention to the "wrongs" "done to you." He Loves you and that's all that matters. And He causes you to become His Love.

3. Two ways you become free from self is by **Truth** and **Presence**. John 8:32, the Truth you know will make you free. 2 Corinthians 3:17, where the Spirit of the Lord is there is freedom. SELAH! Pour yourself into these two things.

4. Put off and put on according to Colossians 3:1-17. Go into prayer with this Scripture and receive the Great Exchange.

5. Do not believe discouragement is "normal." The Kingdom of heaven doesn't even know what that is. We are to seek FIRST the Kingdom of God and His righteousness (Matthew 6:33).

It is time for us to stop being so sensitive to these ways that seem so right to a man. It is language that sounds good but is deceptive and evil. "I am here only for You, Lord, and for Your glory." If we can always remember this, we will live the completely surrendered life, and no one can hurt us. All fear stripped away. Our identity secure. If and only if we are dead to "I."

When we are truly dead, we will never get hurt, disappointed, discouraged, or offended, because we are dead. We will be vulnerable to others and touchable if we have any bit of self in us. When we are dead, it's as the song of 1990 goes, "You can't touch this." (I've got most of you singing it now, don't I? Smile.) But it is true! We do not need people to treat us right for us to be ok. We will be untouchable when we are dead to self.

I have experienced that it is hard to talk with people about this because it can be intimidating. It challenges the world they live in. They know this is not their reality and what is being said confronts them. It makes them think twice about themselves. Because it challenges their own heart.

If they are insecure about where they are at then it causes some of these other things to happen that are not true:

1. They immediately think it is an impossible way to live.
2. They think it is absolutely not the way we are supposed to live because, "God gave us feelings, you know!" NOT of the flesh, He did not!! God has nothing to do with the flesh!
3. They may feel you are judging them.
4. They get insulted and they think you think you know more than they do.
5. They think you are thinking you are better than they are.
6. They just simply get offended by it. Instead of really hearing and being excited and encouraged by TRUTH, and to know this way of Life is possible!

Why do we resist the Truth? Yes, sometimes Truth can sting. It can cut our hearts (Acts 2:36-37 & 7:54). Yes, Truth can hurt! Yes, it may go against everything we have ever known or heard before. Deception is what satan uses to hold us hostage to keep us from living free. Because it is the Truth, we know, that makes us free (John 8:32). he keeps us living to our limited view. Captive to our own version of the truth and our own life experiences.

Why are we scared of the Truth? Instead of believing we do not have to be a slave to our flesh? Why would we rather live confined to a lie as a slave? My heart's desire is for this to change. For people to know they can be free! It is possible to live this Life of freedom in Christ!

It's not the amazing life of everything going "right." It is the amazing life of knowing Jesus intimately. Trusting Him with everything where there is no doubt. **Being made complete in His Love** where there is no fear (1 John 4:17-19), no frustration, no offense, or discouragement because as He is, so are we in this world. Why not do whatever it takes to get this freedom? Why not believe the Truth of every Scripture and be excited about even the possibility of it? Instead of being so negative and not wanting to hear it?

The Scriptures are quite clear we are to be just as Jesus in every way. In every response. In every season. In every difficulty. In every battle. Jesus said, "Follow Me." So that is what we are to do... obey Him.

If Jesus thought like a man, we would all be in big trouble! Did anything anyone ever say or do to Him, stop His ability to Love? We must put a stop to the excuses we have and the excuses we give. 1 John 2:6, He who says he abides in Him ought himself also to walk **just as**, He walked. When we walk in Love there is no cause for offense (1 John 2:10). Love is freedom and it keeps us in the right perspective. Whether other people are doing right or wrong, we don't lose sight of who they are. We are to see them through the eyes of Love. Isn't that how God saw us? God's Loving kindness brought me to repentance.

PRACTICAL APPLICATION:

If you find you are still getting offended or hurt or discouraged or frustrated about things just keep getting perfected in Love. Take the reality of where you are at in your life to your prayer closet. Be alone with Him in His presence. Go boldly before His throne of grace. Not all beat up with the stones you have been throwing in the air and letting them fall on you, condemning yourself. Guilt and shame only come to keep you out of His presence. Because in His presence and in His Word of Truth is where you are made free. So, go boldly before Him and pray:

A PRAYER TO PRAYER:

"Holy Spirit, things are still bothering me (talk to Him about whatever it is you are still struggling with). I need You to obliterate this from my life. I know this is not who You are in me. This is not who You created me to be. This is not the Love of Christ shining through me. So, I put off (whatever it is that needs to go) and I put on the clothes of righteousness you have given me. Holy Spirit grow Your fruit in me, that I may bear a 100-fold crop! I was not created to be hurt, angry, or offended. Truth is Jesus, You could have turned away from me because of my sin towards You. You could have been angry, hurt, and upset with me. Instead, You bore my sin on the cross and Loved me regardless. You showed me gentleness, kindness, and mercy. You gave me the example of who I am to be. I surrender any "right" I think I might have to be angry with others, hurt by others, or offended. I have no right to live in the flesh. I have no right to live self-centered. I have every right to look like You, and to act like You. To show others gentleness, kindness, and mercy. I cannot muster this up on my own, so do this in me, Lord! In Jesus name, Amen."

AW Tozer in the book, *Pursuit of God* (emphasis added), "**Root from my heart** all those things which I have cherished so long, and which have become a very part of my living **self. So that You may enter and dwell there without a rival**."

There is no place in my heart for the feelings of the flesh which are: worry, fear, anxiety, frustration, irritation, annoyance, confusion, hurt, resentment, bitterness, offense, lusts, addictions, guilt, shame, regret, burdens, cares, comparison, insecurity, envy, jealousy, greed, covetousness, discontentment, anger, hatred, grudges, judgements, unforgiveness, feeling let down by; unfulfilled desires, unmet expectations, disappointments, discouragement, and rejection.

When God has my **whole heart** there is no room for anything else but what is His. I am going to end this section with some Scriptures for us to meditate on and what the Scripture then means for us.

Isaiah 26:3-4, "You will keep him in perfect peace, whose mind is stayed on You, because he trusts in You. Trust in the LORD forever, for in YAH, the LORD, is everlasting strength."

Again "perfect peace" is shalom in Hebrew; safety, wellness, happy, friendly, healthy, prosperous, favor, rest, good, and whole. If our mind remains stayed on Him, we will have shalom. Therefore, we cannot have frustration, irritation, discouragement, etc. It is when our minds shift to thinking for ourselves and of ourselves, we will start to feel everything else of the flesh. Keep your mind stayed on Him because you TRUST HIM with everything!

Philippians 4:6-7 (please read through verse 8), "Be anxious for nothing, but in everything by prayer and supplication, with thanksgiving, let your requests be made known to God; and the peace of God, which surpasses all understanding, will guard your hearts and minds through Christ Jesus."

In the Greek when you look up "nothing" it says this: Not even one (man, woman, or thing). "Surpass:" held above, higher, superior, better excellency. "Understanding:" the intellect that is mind, human thought, feeling, or will.

When we go to God in prayer **with thanksgiving**. His peace which is superior to, which is of better excellency than our own thoughts, feelings, and will, His peace will guard our hearts and minds. We are to be anxious (be careful, have care, take thought) for NOT ONE PERSON OR THING. Because we cast ALL our cares on Him, who cares for us (1 Peter 5:6-7). Simply put: Humble yourself to not worry and trust Him!

1Thessalonians 5:16-18, "Rejoice always, pray without ceasing, in everything give thanks; for this is the will of God in Christ Jesus for you." Any situation I cannot rejoice in or give thanks in, I am losing the battle over my thoughts. Thankfulness keeps us from turning inward. It keeps our eyes on Jesus. There is ALWAYS something to be thankful for in Him. This is the will of God.

Francis Frangipane: "It does not matter what your circumstances are, the instant you begin to thank God, even though your situation has not changed, you begin to change." "This covenant of thanksgiving is the key which shuts and bolts the door to demonic oppression in a person's life."

Please read Ephesians 3:16-21. When we pray this prayer and ask Holy Spirit to strengthen us with might (power) in our inner beings, we are asking Him to strengthen us with His power in our minds, our wills, and our emotions (what is inside of us, our inner man). In doing this He will align us with His mind, His will, and His emotion. This is how we can be free from all annoyances, disappointments, anger, everything that is of the flesh. Because our inner man is being strengthened in Holy Spirit. Rooted and grounded in LOVE!

Please read Philippians 2:1-8. Let not one thing be done through selfish ambition (strife or contention) or conceit. In humility we are to esteem (consider) others better (superior, better excellency, held above) than ourselves. We are to have the exact same mind of Jesus Christ who even though He was in the form of God and equal to God, He made Himself of no reputation (He emptied Himself, made Himself of none effect). In other words, He became nothing in and of Himself. He was completely reliant on His Father. And He made Himself a servant who humbled Himself and was obedient unto death (for us this is being obedient unto the death of our flesh, the death of our self-life).

Then we will understand we have no rights, no entitlement, nothing is owed to us, we are to have no expectations on people when we are here to serve them, and we are to have zero pride. This life is not about me and what I can get for selfish reasons and selfish gain. It is about God receiving all the glory. Which leads me to one question for you... Can God gory in your selfishness?

JESUS' FEELINGS AND EMOTIONS:

In Him there is no darkness at all (1 John 1:5-7). Jesus does not have the feelings and emotions of the flesh. He is always the Light in everything, in every situation. Zero darkness in His thoughts, in His ways, in His will, and in His feelings... zero darkness in Him. And we are to walk JUST AS He walked (1John 2:6), if we say we abide in Him. There is a difference in abiding in Jesus day in and day out, all day long. And just visiting Him every now and then.

There was not one selfish motive in Jesus so when He felt, when His emotions moved Him, it was never about Himself. His heart and compassion were for others. It was never about His feelings getting hurt. He never had to counsel with His disciples to get over his feelings. He never had to tell them how they hurt His feelings because they didn't understand Him. And Jesus says, "Follow me!" If we did not learn these things from Him, then where did we learn it? The world's logic (world's psychology), other people (human reasoning), and our circumstances. The way that seems right to a man has taught us. We have been counseled by the world and these ways and ideas have all crept into the church!

We have pushed our selfish feelings and emotions on to Jesus. We will say, "Jesus got angry. He flipped tables for goodness sake!" Or "Jesus was sad, He cried you know." Jesus was "this" and Jesus was "that." When His feelings and emotions were never once about Himself. He had not one selfish bone in His body. I am tired of us trying to say that Jesus felt "how we feel." When 90% of the time everything we feel is from a place that's ALL about ourselves.

Jesus's feelings and emotions were never self-centered. Therefore, they never changed who He is (Love). They never changed His person, as they do ours. They could not take Him outside of His character and nature. And they certainly did not change His behavior (how He treated people or acted). We allow our feelings and emotions to change our behavior, thoughts, and actions towards people **all the time.** We must admit we are largely governed by our feelings and emotions, and this should not be.

This also goes for when people say He was disappointed or discouraged with His disciples when they did not understand Him, or they had little faith, or they would say things that were not from a place of Truth. Again, Jesus' feelings and emotions were never about Himself. So, it could not mean He was disappointed or discouraged. If He had those feelings, it was **for them** and where they were at. Never about Himself. Can we say that about us? When we get disappointed or discouraged with people? Again, I would say about 90% of the time it is about us and not them. Why we are disappointed and discouraged **with them** is because they failed us once again. It will remain this way until we live the crucified life. Jesus never did one thing or said one thing thinking about Himself. He did not have ulterior motives.

Jesus could never act outside of who He is, which is Love. We will read what He says to His disciples such as "O ye of little faith," and then <u>we will project how we would feel in that situation onto what He is saying</u>. Let me say this again because it is very important, **we project ourselves (our flesh) onto Jesus!** Jesus can be nothing but Love and selfless. We are not to project our feelings onto what Jesus said. We need to see Him for who He is (Love) and let that be the lens we see the Word of God through. His perspective. Not how we would feel in that situation.

A PRAYER TO PRAY:

(Please read Luke 6:39-42), "You say those who are perfectly trained will be like their teacher. I want this, Lord! Train me perfectly so I can look like You, so I can be like You. I do not want one ounce of anything in me that is not from You. Holy Spirit make me a true, holy, and pure representation of Jesus Christ to the world in everything and in all ways! Remove everything from me that needs to be removed so I can see clearly and help others to know Truth that will make them free! In Jesus name, Amen."

No Mixture

We were always meant to be separate from the world. Go back to the Garden of Eden where we were made in the image of the Trinity (Genesis 1:26-28). Where we were told to subdue (conquer, bring into bondage, keep under, bring into subjection) the earth having dominion (rule and reign) over it. We were never meant to be subject to it, but it was meant to be subject to us. We were never meant to be controlled and ruled by the flesh. We were made in the perfect image (representative, resemblance) of God.

Even when sin entered, we have been told not to be of the world but to be set apart from it. Having no mixture with it so we would not be contaminated by it. Not doing as they would do and not being as they would be (Leviticus 18:1-5 & John 17:16). This is why God always told the Israelites when they were entering the Promise Land to utterly destroy those that were there. Because He knew bad company ruins good morals (1 Corinthians 15:33 ESV) and if there were any mixture they would be deceived and led away from God's heart.

But time and time again the Israelites did not do as God had told them. And since the inhabitants of the land were not utterly destroyed the Israelites began to learn of their ways and do as they did (Psalm 106:34-39 ESV). We must remember all these other nations did not worship God. They were pagans who worshipped idols. They made human sacrifices (killing their own children) and did all kinds of evil things that were abominations to the Lord, disgusting things (Deuteronomy 12:31-32).

And here we are today as history repeats itself. We have not obeyed what God has told us to do by keeping ourselves separate from the world. This is where it saddens me to see just how much of the world has been mixed into the church today. We now have churches that support homosexuality and same sex marriages where it is clearly an abomination to the Lord (Leviticus 18:22, Romans 1:24-32, 1 Corinthians 6:9-11, & 1 Timothy 1:8-11). The church is doing as the world does and thinking as the world thinks, and we think it is okay! We have allowed so much mixture in us!

Do we think to Love someone we have to accept the sin they are living in? Wrong! We can Love those who are a slave to sin, but it does not mean we have to support their lifestyle. We can Love someone and not condone what they do. We are to speak the Truth in Love. Correcting those who are in opposition to the Truth (Ephesians 4:14-24 & 2 Timothy 2:20-26) to pull them out of the pit of deception they are in. And the Truth will make them free (John 8:31-32)!

Every kind of contamination in us is only meant to destroy us. We were never meant to be a part of this world, to be mixed in with it. So now is the time we set ourselves apart from it once and for all. Draw the line in the sand and do not cross it. Do not straddle the fence any longer, having one foot in the world and one foot in the church (James 4:4 ESV). No more lukewarm Christianity! No more grey areas! No more "maybes." It is a complete surrender to our King. Setting ourselves apart for Him alone.

Here are some Scriptures that reference us not being a part of this world. We are in it, but we are not of it. Come out from among them! John 15:18-19, 17:14-19, 18:36, Romans 12:2, 2 Corinthians 6:14-7:1, Philippians 3:17-21, Colossians 2:8, 3:1-3, James 1:27, 4:4-5, 1 John 2:15-17, 4:1-6, 5:18-21.

Detox/Pure/Purge/Prune/Refine = No Mixture

Ezekiel 36:24-27, "For I will take you from among the nations, gather you out of all countries, and bring you into your own land. Then I will sprinkle clean water on you, and you shall be clean; I will cleanse you from all your filthiness and from all your idols. I will give you a new heart and put a new spirit within you; I will take the heart of stone out of your flesh and give you a heart of flesh. I will put My Spirit within you and cause you to walk in My statutes, and you will keep My judgments and do them."

This chapter is called Detox my heart for this very reason. He tells us He will cleanse us from all our filthiness and give us a new heart. He will put His Spirit in us to cause us to walk in His ways. The definition of "detoxification" according to *Oxford Languages* is "The process of removing toxic substances or qualities." As we see in Ezekiel, the Lover of our souls wants to remove all the filthiness, toxic substances, and poisonous qualities that are in our hearts. The things that only hurt us. We were never meant to have these contaminations, impurities, or any other thing that would defile us and hinder us from being His image!

In Malachi 3:1-4, He says He will purify the sons of Levi in which the Levites were the priests. This section of Scripture is such a beautiful promise that God's Messenger will come and purify and purge so the priests can be righteous and **pleasant to the LORD once again**. In 1 Peter 2:9-10, He tells us we are a royal priesthood, a holy nation, His own special people. So, we too are the priests He has promised to purify and purge making us righteous and pleasant to the Lord.

Purify in Hebrew means to make bright, physically sound, clear, unadulterated, uncontaminated, morally innocent, and holy. Selah! Purge in Hebrew is to strain, extract, clarify and refine. The good news is Jesus is the Messenger who has already come and accomplished this for us (Hebrews 1:3, 9:14, & 1 John 1:7). We have been made pure. When we come to Him in absolute surrender, we will then begin to receive this purification He has made for us.

Jesus paid the price ("It is finished") to bring us back to the way He created us, in the very beginning! We are His image. We are His likeness. If we are still swimming in a cesspool of the flesh, all the filthiness, toxic feelings, thoughts, hurt, and brokenness, then allow Him to come in and remove all foreign matter and contamination from you. The mixture you have allowed in you, that is of the world and not from Him. All the pain, sin, lust, jealousy, insecurity, depression, frustration, idols, etc. That you can be free from it all, how beautiful is this???

We, at the same time, must renew our minds in the Word of God (Romans 12:2 & John 17:17-19). If we are not in the process of renewing our mind every day in Truth, then it is being contaminated by the world every day. It is being kept unclean, impure, and corrupted with self. Self gets offended, self feels judged, self has insecurities, self gets its feelings hurt. The heart condition is still full of self!

When we are renewing our minds, we are filling our hearts with the Word of God. When our hearts are **filled** with Truth this stops the negative qualities and substances from entering back in. There is no room, no vacancy, at the Inn for them. Only Holy Spirit can show you what is in your own heart that must go. Get alone with Him! Talk with Him! Sit with Him! Continue to make the Great Exchange with Him! You will be transformed! Its worthy to note also, that He says He will cleanse us from all our idols as well. Anything we have put before our First Love. He will cleanse us from everything and anything that holds us back from Him. Amen!

Proverbs 25:4 ESV, "Take away the dross from the silver, and the smith has material for a vessel." Dross in the Hebrew is refuse. The definition of refuse according to *Oxford Languages* is, "Matter thrown away or rejected as worthless, trash." A silversmith can only make something when all the impurities, dross, refuse, worthless, trash is removed. As with us. God will have a vessel that is fit for His use once all impurity (the self-life) is removed.

The definition of pure according to the *Greek Lexicon* is, free from corrupt desire, sin, and guilt. <u>Free from every mixture</u>. Blameless, innocent, and unstained. We were never meant to have a divided heart. God always meant for us to be pure with no mixture, no impurities, no dross, no chaff, no contamination... set apart, a holy vessel.

Matthew 5:8, Blessed are the **pure in heart**, for they **shall see God**. Again, heart here is the thoughts and feelings. When our thoughts and feelings are pure, when they are not contaminated and mixed with any other substance, when they are free of self, **then** we will see God! Selah.

Dying to self is what leads us to the heart of the Father. In the Old Testament altars existed for sacrifice/death. Today altars (in our sanctuaries) should exist for sacrifice/death; humility, brokenness, and repentance before the Lord. To give an "altar call" means to die. No one can see His face and live (Exodus 33:18-23). Only dead men can see His face. And the pure in heart will see God.

Oswald Chambers says (underline and emphasis mine), "When a man's heart is right with God the mysterious utterances of the Bible are spirit and life to him. <u>Spiritual truth is discernable only to a **pure heart,** not to a keen intellect</u>."

The pure in heart (no mixture) will see God and know what His Word says. Not the intellectual, not the theologians, not the analytical, not even the kind, compassionate, or empathetic ones, but those who are **pure** in thought and feeling. Those who are not contaminated with self.

Titus 1:15, To the pure all things are pure, but to those who are defiled (Greek meaning; sully, taint, contaminate) and unbelieving nothing is pure; but even their mind (thoughts, feelings, or will) and conscious (perception) are defiled.

He lists 2 kinds of people here where nothing is pure the 1) defiled and 2) unbelieving. If we are alive to ourselves (living the self-life) then we would be in the defiled group. We have mixture in us, and this means we are not pure. If we live according to self, we are tainted and contaminated and even our thoughts, feelings, will and perceptions are defiled. Wow! This is why self must be crucified with Christ. The flesh must die.

The next verse, Titus 1:16, <u>They profess</u> (covenant, acknowledge, promise) to know God, <u>but in works they deny</u> Him being abominable, disobedient, and disqualified for every good work. Selah!

Purify, purge, prune, and refining fire are all ways we are cleansed, they are all a part of purification. To take away what does not belong. To cause us to shine and to grow up bearing more fruit. Fire purifies, refines, sanctifies, and makes us holy. It causes all the dross to come to the surface so it can be separated and thrown away. Causing only the silver or gold to emerge. 1 Corinthians 3:9-15, fire burns away the worthless things; the wood, hay, and stubble so that what remains is the gold, silver, and precious stones. When I am put in the fire only that which is of Him can remain. Which would mean I come out of the fire pure.

The most effective way to surrender is to ask Him to send His fire over every part of our lives. Over our thoughts, our desires, our relationships, our plans, asking Him to burn away everything that is not of Him, for Him, or from Him. Burn away anything that could possibly get in the way of what He wants to do in our lives. Burning away any resentment, bitterness, offense, unforgiveness, fear, shame, insecurities, hopelessness, despair, etc. Even what we think is good. If it is not good, then burn it away! <u>And what is left is what is needed</u>.

A PRAYER TO PRAY:

"Father, by sight I see ashes by faith I see beauty. I choose faith. I worship You. I praise You. I thank You for every day You are transforming me more into who You created me to be from the very beginning. So, detox me, purge me, cleanse me from all impurities, from all the fleshly desires. Obliterate, annihilate, destroy every desire that is not of You, for You, or from You. I desire purity, holiness, righteous living. I desire to walk worthy of You alone and no one else. Jesus, breathe Life into my heart like I have never known before. I surrender to You, all of me.

Holy Spirit purify me with Your fire. Burn up the chaff of my life, the worthless things, the garbage, the trash. Burn away everything that is not in line with you. Everything that is not to be in my heart and mind. Replace in me a heart that is only for You! Burn away anything in me that is contrary to who You are. So, I can be Your Love to everyone around me and fulfill Your calling for my life. If it is not of You, for You, or from You then remove it. Have Your way and set me apart to burn for only You. Here I am, I am Yours. In Jesus name, Amen."

Detox My Motives

Another area needing to be detoxed is our motives. Being purified in the attitudes of our heart. Why do we say what we say and do what we do? The big attacking point of satan is our motivation in life. The enemy is tricky he knows what we want (he has seen our films) and he uses those desires, those wishes, against us in our own hearts and makes our motives a cesspool. As long as we are alive to ourselves we will always have motives that are not crystal clear. Because as we have learned self defiles us and is deceitful. It is the greatest destructive force in the world.

Practical Application:

We are not to judge according to appearance. Look beneath the surface so we can judge correctly with righteousness (John 7:12-24). Take a look at where your heart is at in performing an action. Since self is to be crucified, denied, gone, dead, and buried, (yes, I could go on... obliterated, annihilated, well you get the point) it is easy to ask some questions that are helpful in showing us where our hearts are at with certain things:

1. Do I want "this" (whatever this may be) because it will fulfill my flesh, or do I want this because it is God's will, and it will fulfill my purpose in His Kingdom?
2. When we ask God for something is it for selfish reasons?
3. Are we reading His Word to get something for ourselves? To see what He can do for us?
4. Am I willing to let "this" go if the Lord asks me to let it go? If the answer is "no" it has then become an idol.
5. If I want to say "something" to somebody; do I want to say something to get back at them? Do I want to say something to them because they hurt me? Or am I concerned for their benefit? Is my heart broken for them, and this being the reason I need to say something to them?
6. If I feel I am to correct someone; am I offended in any way? Am I correcting them to prove a point? To prove I am right? To make me feel better? Or is it because I Love the person and care for them? Am I correcting them because I am concerned about where they

are, what they are doing, or where it will take them? Not thinking of my-self at all.

If we are to bring correction to someone it must be done in Love and with the plank removed from our own eye first (Matthew 7:1-5). Not because we are disappointed in them or hurt by them. We correct them because we Love them and see what they are doing is detrimental to their walk with God and their relationships with others. We don't want to see them go down that road because we know where it leads... to destruction. It should never be because what they said offended me, or what they did hurt me. And "They ought to know better," so I am going to tell them just what they did and how I am disappointed in them. Because they NEED to know!

God revealed to me I had been motivated by selfishness at a certain point. I wanted someone to know "these things" they were doing so they would know how to Love me. So, they would know how to treat me better. I wanted them to stop hurting me. When my motivation should have been out of Love. When what I needed was Jesus to heal me, so I could have compassion on this person and have the deep desire for their healing. So, they could be whole and know what Love is for themselves and have their own brokenness healed. So, they could live in freedom. I should have been moved for that person and not moved by my flesh.

In **everything** we do there is an underlying motive. Are we motivated to do it in Love for others or in love for ourselves? Are we motivated to do it in Love or because of fear? Are we motivated to do it in Love or from a place of pain? We should never be motivated by emotion or fear. "Lord, purify our motives in everything!" The only motive that is good comes from a pure heart, His heart. If it is not coming from His heart, it is flesh, wicked, and evil. Only when flesh is dead can we have pure motives. When it is not about us at all. My Life is in Christ, and He should be glorified in everything I say and do.

How do we make sure our motives are crystal clear? By living the crucified life. By staying in relationship with Jesus. Always making our motive about looking like Christ. I died, it's not about me. Our motives can be purified when we ask the Lord to judge our hearts. And He will. He will show us the error of our ways, our thoughts, our heart, or anything that is out of line with Him. In this correction we simply repent, realign with Him, and He will lead us in the way everlasting (Psalm 139:23-24 KJV). The good news is when we become Love we do not have to think twice about our motives. It becomes easy to walk in Love because we are Love.

A Prayer to Pray:

"Father You are the only One who understands my heart and knows my motives. I am asking you to remove every impurity in me, any part of me with mixture (anxiety, worry, hopelessness, anger, depression, bitterness, jealousy, manipulation, etc.) which causes me to act and respond and maneuver in a way outside of You. Annihilate every bit of self! I thank You that You Love me too much to leave me the way I am. In Jesus name, Amen."

When our motives are not pure, we tend to pray for God to change other people rather than ourselves. Typically, it is about something to make our own lives better. "God, teach Him how to Love me." "God, show her when she nags me, she is just annoying me." "God, change "this" in him, change "that" in her," etc. etc. etc. These prayers happen all the time! When we try to get God to do something for us instead of becoming like Him, we will stay self-conscious. We remain very aware of how people treat us. We still need from one another. Which only makes us as good as what is happening around us and how we are treated. When we should be praying from a right heart – a pure heart. Not praying for someone to change but that the Lord will continue to transform us.

For Example: "Lord, in all I do, in all my prayers may I be motivated by Your Love alone! Holy Spirit, I thank You for taking all feeling of annoyance out of my life. That I do not get annoyed, irritated, or frustrated. Rid me of self, so no matter what happens, it does not bother me. Father, thank You for Loving me! I know Your Love is all I need. Because of Your Love for me, I can Love my spouse even when they do not Love me the way I would like them to. You will give me strength and everything it is I need to Love and respect them no matter how they treat me or act towards me. Make me like You. Transform me into Love. In Jesus name Amen."

However, Love is no longer a priority but an inconvenience in today's world, in our homes, and even in the church. And most of us don't even know what transformation is. When we are not looking through the lens of Love and transformation, ulterior motives come in, and we end up following the wrong things (our own feelings, our heart, our own thoughts).

When our motives are not pure even our thanksgiving to Him can be defiled. It may be rare, but it can happen. **For Example:** I am thanking God for my fortune, so I will not lose it. I am thanking Him for my health, so I won't get sick. I am thanking Him for healing my loved one, so they won't die. Thanking God for the things He has given us, so "He won't take them away." This is a wrong motive of the heart. We are giving Him thanks out of fear!!! And there is no fear in Love. How wrong motives can even slip into our thanksgiving. Yikes!

If Love is not the root then our motives are not pure. We end up wanting all the blessings of God, but we will never fully commit to Him and give Him our lives, to become like Him. And Jesus says, if you Love Me, you will obey Me, you will keep My Word, You will follow Me, and You will abide in Me. Anything less than this is manipulation and wrong motives for getting what we want and what He can do for us. And never becoming like Him.

For Example: Lord, I want Your Love, but I don't want to become Your Love. Lord, I want your forgiveness, but I don't want to become Your forgiveness. Lord, I want Your mercy, but I don't want to become Your mercy. Lord, I want everlasting life, without entering the True realm of Life (which is to die to live).

When our motives are not pure, we are more about being right than about righteousness. Trying to prove who is right and who is wrong in everything. Telling everyone what was "done" to me, "Can you believe it?!" We get out our list of "wrongs" which we shouldn't be keeping in the first place, and we try to get people to take our side. Where are we becoming like Christ in any of this?! Yes, this is the way we live.

The way we treat a brother is the way we treat Jesus. Acts 9:4, Jesus said to Saul, "Saul, Saul why are you persecuting Me?" Saul was persecuting the Christians and not Jesus directly. But Jesus shows us that what we do to another is what we are doing to Him. The same is so in the Scripture of Matthew 25:35-40, "Inasmuch as you did it to one of the least of these My brethren, you did it to Me." The way I Love people is a part of my worship to Him. The way I don't Love people is a part of my disrespect to Him.

It is fun to live with yourself when you like yourself. Because you know you do not have any false motivation in you. Knowing you do not have to manipulate to get your way. Knowing you have a pure heart, and you go to bed at night not being angry, frustrated, and disappointed. Knowing you agree with and look like Jesus. To live in Christ never gets boring. Living for self was a miserable way to live.

We are created to be passionate and full of life. We are created to have joy and peace. We are created to be alive. We are created to not take account of a suffered wrong. We are created to walk in a Love that never fails. If God did not change His mind towards us, why do we live so changeable towards everyone else?

A Prayer to Pray:

"Holy Spirit, destroy, completely obliterate every thought pattern that does not line up with Truth. Your Word is Truth. Make my motivations crystal clear and pure. Work in me to desire what pleases You. You give me the power to do what pleases You. Tear down every wall of deception that stands around me. I thank You, You are building me up on the foundation of Jesus Christ. Building me upon Truth. Building me up in Love, true Love, Your Love. Building me up on Your strength, so that no wind, wave, or storm will knock me down. You show me every trial You have brought me through. Showing me that You alone have been forever faithful to me. Continue to draw me close to You because I have drawn near to You. In Jesus name, Amen."

Being the Expression of Christ:

Excerpt by Hannah Whitall Smith from the book *The Christian's Secret of a Happy Life*, "Let us take home to ourselves in solemn consideration these words of the Holy Ghost, "He that saith he abideth in Him, ought himself so to walk, even as He walked." "Unless we are thus walking, we cannot possibly be abiding in Him, no matter how much we may feel as if we were. If you are really one with Christ you will be sweet to those who are cross to you; you will bear everything and make no complaints; when you are reviled you will not revile again; you will consent to be trampled on, as Christ was, and feel nothing but love in return; you will seek the honor of others rather than your own; you will take the lowest place, and be the servant of all, as Christ was; you will literally and truly love your enemies and do good to them that despitefully use you; you will, in short, live a Christ-like life, and manifest outwardly as well as feel inwardly a Christ-like spirit, and will walk among men as He walked among them. This, dear friends, is what it is to be one with Christ. And if all this is not your life according to your measure, then you are not one with Him, no matter how ecstatic or exalted your feelings may be."

Some of you may be insulted right about now. Or maybe just feeling uneasy or unsure. Or maybe even mad or indignant. So here are some

Scriptures to go along with what she is saying: 1 John 4:17, 1 John 2:6, Luke 9:23, John 8:28-29, John 5:18-19, John 5:30, John 6:38, Luke 6:46-49. This is Oneness. I have realized only people who abide (dwell) in Him daily, hourly, minute by minute can Love just as He Loves. It is impossible otherwise.

Another Excerpt from Hannah Whitall Smith: "Unless we are one with Christ as to character and life and action, we cannot be one with Him in any other way, for there is no other way. We must be "partakers of His nature" or we cannot be partakers of His life, for His life and His nature are one. But emotional souls do not always recognize this. They feel so near Christ and so united to Him, that they think it must be real; and overlooking the absolute necessity of Christlikeness of character and walk, they are building their hopes and their confidence on their delightful emotions and exalted feelings, and think they must be one with Him, or they could not have such rich and holy experiences." Selah!

When we don't ever think about ourselves, we then look like Christ. Heaven on earth is His character and nature IN US. He is how we respond, how we Love, how we act, how we think etc. There is no self in heaven, NONE. "Your Kingdom come, Your will be done, on earth just as it is in heaven," is more than power and miracles. It is our lives transformed. Christ poured out His life for others. As must we. Christ did not do things to satisfy Himself, He did things to glorify His Father. As must we. Christ was sacrificial. As must we be. All our lives amount to nothing if they do not produce these results. **This is the entire purpose of our lives.** We cannot come up with any circumstance that will excuse us to stop living as Christ.

We do not have permission to fall apart. Jesus sat at the table with His betrayer. Jesus washed the feet of His betrayer. Jesus received a kiss from His betrayer. And we do not want to be in the same room as someone who has hurt us or offended us? What an example when one can display that kind of Love, such as Jesus, and never make it about Himself. Only Holy Spirit can help us go through inner turmoil with someone and not let it affect the relationships around us.

We must understand when we gave our lives to Christ, we gave our lives for His glory. We are not our own anymore. Whose image is on the coin? Caesar's. Give to Caesar what is Caesar's. Whose image were you created in? God's. Give to God what is God's. You do not belong to you. Our anthem must ring as this, "If I cannot find it in Jesus, then I do not want it in me! Detox my heart, Lord!"

Five Take Aways + Bonus One

1. The greatest difference between the emotions and feelings of the flesh and of Holy Spirit is the flesh is all about self and Holy Spirit is all about the sacrificial life.

2. When God has my **whole heart** there is no room for anything else but what is His. Therefore, there is no room, no vacancy, at the Inn for any discouragement, frustration, hurt, disappointment, offense, etc.

3. My emotional stability is in Christ alone. I will not let circumstances, situations, or people determine my emotional health.

4. We were always meant to be separate from the world. Having no mixture with it so we would not be contaminated by it. Meaning we do not do as they do, and we are not being as they would be. If there is any mixture, we will be deceived and led away from God's heart.

5. The most effective way to surrender is to ask Holy Spirit to send His fire over every part of our lives. Over our thoughts, our desires, our relationships, our plans, asking Him to burn away everything that is not of Him, for Him, or from Him. And what is left is what is needed.

6. God will have a vessel that is fit for His use once all impurity (the self-life) is removed.

Picture drawn by Tiffany Isham Davis

1 Corinthians 6:15 & 17, "Do you not know that your bodies are members of Christ...?" "But he who is joined to the Lord is one spirit with Him."

CHAPTER 10

Life Redefined

A S YOU READ this chapter, I would like you to keep in mind **one thing**; our entire purpose in life is to be One with Jesus Christ. Through this one thing everything else in life will flow. When we are One with Him then it is no longer I who lives but Christ who lives in me. And we go into all the world and live His Life. We are His Love. We shine His Light. Then we can show others the Way, the Truth, and the Life (Jesus), making disciples. To be One with Jesus is why we were created. This is our only purpose. This is our destiny. This is Life Redefined.

Watchman Nee says, 'By the time the average Christian gets his temperature up to normal, everyone thinks he has a fever." What a true statement! In other words, by the time we start living the way God always intended for us to live (to be One with Jesus Christ; to look like Him, to act like Him, to do as He did), everyone thinks we are "fanatics." They tell us we are taking things a little too seriously. They say, "You're being a bit extreme, or a little too radical about this, don't ya think?" To this I would answer with an emphatic YES! As we should be!

This Chapter is called Life Redefined because we, as Christians, have been living the "Christian life" the wrong way for far too long. We have been living way beneath what God intended for us to live. Making life all about ourselves instead of Him. Incorporating the world's "logic" into everything. Instead of us being as Christ in this world (1 John 4:17), we have let the world dictate how we are in the church.

In this chapter we are going to cover a variety of areas where we maybe need some redefining. The title is "Life Redefined" because the way we are to live is completely different than the way we have been living. Instead of living for ourselves and loving the world, we are to live for Jesus and Love Him. **It is the way God always created us to live.** This life is "redefined" to us because we have gotten so far off track. Yet, it is the way we were always supposed to live.

What Are We Here For?

I already mentioned we are here to be One with Christ. If we are One with Him then we do what He does, and act how He acts, and say what He says, and He said, "... I do nothing of Myself; but as My Father taught Me, I speak these things." "... for I always do the things that please Him" (John 8:28-29 please read in their entirety). Also, in John 5:30, "I can of Myself do nothing... I do not seek My own will but the will of the Father who sent Me." We can of ourselves do nothing. We are here for Him. Pretty plain and simple.

Ecclesiastes 12:13 (ESV), "... <u>Fear God</u> and <u>keep His commandments,</u> for <u>this is the whole duty of man</u>." Fear in the Hebrew means to morally revere and reverence. The definition of reverence according to *Oxford Languages* is "A deep respect for someone or something." Other words that are used elsewhere are to honor and be in awe of.

Everything in this life will flow from two things we are to do. Which, by the way, are the exact two things Jesus did:

1. <u>Fear God:</u> in reverent awe and wonder. We are to have a deep honor and respect for Him. In doing this it will cause us to flee from sin (Proverbs 16:6, Proverbs 8:13, Proverbs 3:7, 2 Corinthians 7:1). When we fear the Lord, we will not want to have anything to do with sin out of reverence for Him. Charles Bridges says, "But what is this fear of the Lord? It is that affectionate reverence, by which the child of God bends himself humbly and carefully to his Father's law." In other words, this fear leads us to obey Him in all we do. This fear brings us to complete dependence upon Him. The word he uses here, "affectionate" is a key word. As we will see later it is from this affection, this Love, that causes us to be obedient to Him.

2. <u>Keep His commandments: = Obey Him in all we do</u>. In Matthew

22:37-39, Jesus tells us what our two greatest commandments are. First, we are to **Love the Lord our God** with ALL our heart (thoughts and feelings). With ALL our soul (breath, life, mind, heart). With ALL our mind (deep thought, understanding, imagination). In Mark 12:30 He adds with ALL our strength (might, ability, power). Then we are to **Love others as ourselves.**

Deuteronomy 5:29 says, "Oh that they had such a heart in them that they would fear Me and always keep all My commandments, that it might be well with them and with their children forever!"

Our whole duty in life is to fear God (which will cause us to flee sin) and to obey Him. We are to pour ALL our lives into Loving God and Loving others as ourselves. We talked in an earlier chapter how this is not a selfish love, but it is a Love of who Christ is in us kind of Love.

However, we can never know how to Love until we first know His Love and receive His Love for ourselves. We can only know how to Love Him because He first Loved us (1 John 4:19). This means we must know His Love for us. How do we get to know His Love? In our secret place. In intimacy with Him. Through His Word. In prayer and in the Great Exchange (Chapter 8). We invest our time in being with Him and we will come to know (experience personally) His Love. We talked about this in Chapter 2 (Knowing the Lover of My Soul). It may be good to go back through this chapter if you need to.

Also, we must receive His Love because we cannot give something we do not have. We cannot give God Love or anyone else Love if we have not received it for ourselves. We can know (with our minds) that He Loves us all day long, it is only when we believe His Love for us and receive it for ourselves that it will change things. This, as well, comes from a place of intimate relationship with Him. We were made by Him and for Him. Our highest priority in life is to have intimacy with Him. Receiving His Love and pouring all our lives into Loving Him. When we do this, we will be transformed into His Love. In the secret place is where we are formed into Christ likeness. And He is Love.

Then we are to Love others as ourselves (Matthew 22:39). John 13:34-35, "A new commandment I give to you, that you Love one another; **AS** I have Loved you, that you also Love one another. **By this** all will know that you are My disciples, **IF** you have Love for one another."

We are to Love just as He has Loved us. How has He Loved us? With everything! How are we to Love others? JUST AS, with everything! He did not withhold anything of Himself from us. He also did not say, "Love everyone except those who have hurt you. You do not have to Love them AS I have Loved you. Just watch yourself with them." The only reason why we think we have to hold ourselves back from others is because we are in a place of hurt or offense. We do it to try to protect ourselves. It is a self-defense mechanism. If it were not possible to Love everyone as Christ has Loved us, He would never have told us to do so.

THE IMPORTANCE OF OUR OBEDIENCE TO HIM

My obedience to Him is directly related to my Love for Him. John 14:15, "If you Love Me, keep my commandments." 1John 2:5, "But whoever keeps His Word, truly the Love of God is perfected in Him. By this we know that we are in Him." John 14:21, "He who has My commandments and keeps them, it is he who Loves Me. And he that Loves Me will be Loved by My Father, and I will Love him and will manifest (to exhibit in person, or disclose by words, appear, declare plainly, inform, show, manifest openly) Myself to him." By our obedience to Jesus, it proves our Love for Him. In our Love for Jesus, He will make Himself manifest to us! Selah! This is exciting news!

How do we know if we are Loving Jesus? How do we know if we have a personal relationship with Him? By our obedience to Him. Right now, I could ask everyone "Do you Love Jesus?" Undoubtedly all the Christians will say enthusiastically, "Yes I Love Jesus!" Are you sure? Are you obeying Him? Do you do as His Word says? If you do not obey Him, I am sorry, you do not Love Him. No matter how much you think you are Loving Him or feel like you do.

These are not my words but Jesus' words. "If you Love Me, keep My commandments." Are we Loving Him with ALL our heart, soul, mind, and strength? Are we Loving others? Are we keeping no record of wrongs? Are we patient and kind? Are we putting others first thinking more highly of them than ourselves? Are we Loving our enemies? Are we denying our flesh putting to death the sinful things? In short are we becoming the very Love of Jesus Christ?

His Word never changes. He does not bend the Word for you, for me, or anyone else. So, if you do not Love Jesus, because you are not obeying His Word, then you will never know what Love truly is. If there is no Love between you and God (your obedience), then there can never be Love between you and anyone else. Because only He IS Love.

By our obedience to Him is how we know we are Loving others as well. 1 John 5:2, "By this we know that we Love the children of God, when we Love God and keep His commandments." You do not know true Love, you will never know Love until you begin to obey Him. Until that day you are in the world's definition of "love." It will never be God's Love until you surrender your life to His ways.

He tells us in 1 John 5:3, "For this is the Love of God, that we keep His commandments. And His commandments are not burdensome." As a result of our Love for Him we will obey Him, and His commands are not burdensome. If they are burdensome, it is the flesh. The flesh is what will fight obedience. It will kick and scream and make obedience feel like a burden. Flesh must be crucified. Then obedience becomes like breathing. It is your life.

Out of our Love for Christ, and in our surrender to Him, Holy Spirit compels us to obey His commands and to desire His will (Philippians 2:13). While we may struggle at times and though we may stumble, Holy Spirit is here to comfort us, guide us, teach us, and correct us. He is here to grow us up into Christ in ALL things (Ephesians 4:15).

Jude 24 (KJV), "Now unto Him that is able to keep you from falling and present you faultless before the presence of His glory with exceeding joy." How is He able to keep us from falling? In verse 21 He says, "Keep yourselves in the Love of God." If we keep ourselves in His Love, He will keep us from falling. How do we keep ourselves in His Love? John 15:10, "If you keep My commandments, you will abide in My Love, just as I have kept My Father's commandments and abide in His Love." If I keep His commands (if I obey Him), I will then remain in His Love, and thereby I will not fall into sin and deception. He keeps me from falling when I am obedient to Him. And I am obedient to Him when I Love Him.

When the word "if" is used it always means there is a choice we must make. We have the choice to obey His commands **so that** we will remain in His Love. Or we choose to not obey Him, and we will not remain in His Love. Now this doesn't mean He does not Love us. What it means is there is no possible way we can walk in His Love and have an intimate connection with Him if we choose to disobey Him. He does not leave us, but we have left Him in our disobedience.

Can we see how everything is centered around Love? How important it is for us to know His Love? To receive His Love? To become His Love? So, we can be His Love?

Journal Entry:

Lord, I feel we have taken Your Love for granted. We brush it off to the side as if it is not that big of a deal as we say, "yea, yea, yea, I know the Lord Loves me...moving on. What's next?" We want the next greatest thing to discover. The next greatest thing we can learn about. We want the next big revelation You have to give us. As if there could be anything greater than Your Love!!!! **End of journal entry.**

Some more Scriptures I want to touch on about obedience:

Romans 8:1, "There is therefore now no condemnation to those who are in Christ Jesus..." I am sure this sounds very familiar to most of you. Do you know what the rest of the verse says? "... who do not walk according to the flesh, but according to the Spirit." This means to those who are walking in obedience.

Romans 8:28, "And we know that all things work together for good..." (do not stop there). "...To those who Love God, to those who are called according to His purpose." Notice it does not say to those God Loves. Because He is Love. But it is to those who Love God. And we have already learned, we Love God with our obedience.

1 Sam 15:22-23 (shortened), Does the Lord delight in burnt offerings and sacrifices as in obeying the voice of the Lord? <u>Behold to obey is better than sacrifice</u>. For rebellion is as the sin of witchcraft and stubbornness is as iniquity and idolatry.

A Prayer to Pray:

"Jesus, reveal to me the significance of Your Love again. Forgive me if I have taken Your Love for granted, if I have made other things more important. Holy Spirit grow me in Love so I can Love You with the same Love You have for me. I want to make Loving You the #1 dream of my heart. That I would make Loving You my #1 desire. That I would make Loving You my #1 priority in life. Loving You is the greatest thing I am to do in life. It is my first and greatest commandment. It is greater than the family you have given me. It is greater than the job or businesses You have given me. It is greater than the ministry You have given me. My reward does not change when I set my heart on Loving You. Because You are my reward. I Love you Jesus.

And I prove my Love for You, with my obedience. So, I will obey You. In Jesus name Amen."

Our Purpose in Life

John 17:4, "I have glorified You on the earth. I have finished the work which You have given Me to do."

We have gotten so used to thinking we are all here for different reasons. We each have our own purpose for being here. However, as we saw in the second section, we all have the exact same "duty" of our lives. To fear the Lord and to obey Him. We already learned to Love Him is to obey Him. And to fear Him is to depart from evil.

Contrary to popular belief we all have the same things God has purposed for us to do. We are all here for the same reason. We are all told to fear Him and to obey Him. We are all told to, "Follow Me." We are all told to deny ourselves. We are all told to go and make disciples of all nations. We are all told to pray; "Our Father in heaven, hallowed be Your name. Your Kingdom come, Your will be done on earth as it is in heaven" (Matthew 6:9-10). We are all supposed to do His will. We are all supposed to be His Kingdom here on earth just as it is in heaven.

In a nutshell, we are all here to be One with Christ. To be His Love. We are all here to shine as the image of Christ (Love) in this world. It is not for some of us but for all of us to walk just as Jesus walked. By doing this we bring glory to God, our Father.

Where we differ is God's giftings, ministries, and plans for our lives. We are different parts of the same body. God gives each of us our own area of influence to fulfill the same greater purpose. Think about the actual body. Each part has its specific function (plan, gifting, ministry) to accomplish the one greater purpose to keep the body, as a whole, in good health. The heart does what it needs to do. The liver does what it needs to do and so on. Each part needs the other parts to work properly for the body to be at full capacity. Each part has the same purpose in life (keep the body healthy) just different functions to accomplish it.

The Lord has the plan, gifting, and ministry for each one of our lives in order to fulfill our greater purpose. Our purpose is to be One with Christ. Then we are to become one with the rest of the body of Christ (John 17:20-26). With Jesus being our Head. Please read 1 Corinthians all of chapters 12 & 13, and Ephesians 4:11-16.

If you decide to make something, there is a purpose for this thing you have made. That thing does not have <u>the plan</u> (what it is to do, who it is for, where it is to be, etc.) to fulfill the purpose for which it was created, but you, the creator of it, does. And so, it goes with our Creator. He has the design and plan for each one of us. We do not know what His plan is for our lives outside of our **absolute surrender** to Him. John 8:28-29, "... I do nothing of Myself; but as My Father taught Me..." We cannot possibly know what to do without Him, without His Word teaching us and showing us. Without the Creator giving us our directions (instruction manual).

Until we give our lives to Jesus completely, we are only wandering around aimlessly thinking we know what we are here for. We think we know what we are doing and where we are going. And satan is so good at keeping us here in the land of distraction. he keeps us preoccupied with meaningless pursuits and selfish endeavors. Therefore, we end up making life all about us instead of about Jesus. satan's whole intent is if he can get us stuck in our self-life, then we will not become as Christ and then we will not be able to finish the work (our purpose) God has given for us to do which is to be One with Him. To be His Love.

When we do not recognize our purpose in life, we then make life all about us. We make life all about what we want. We make it about our spouse, our children, our business, our jobs, "our greater good," our own world, and even our troubles and what we are going through or what we have been through.

If I were to ask you, "<u>What is the greatest thing in your life right now</u>?" What takes up the most of your <u>time</u>, the most of your <u>attention</u>, the most of your <u>thoughts</u> and <u>care</u>, the most of your <u>resources</u>? What would you say? Your marriage? Your children? Your job? Your business? Your accumulation of money? Your "good" name? Your ministry? What satisfies you? The hobbies you get so engrossed in? The passions you have? Your own pleasures and desires? Are you consumed with the tribulation and trials you are going through? <u>What are you living for</u>?!

Some of these things are not all wrong or bad, IN MODERATION. However, we can make an addiction out of any person, place, or thing. An addiction is simply an idol we have put in place of God. Some of the things we do we find greater comfort in, than we do in God and that becomes an idol. The list could go on of what we place great importance on.

If any of the things listed above is true, then we have missed the point of life. We have not recognized His purpose and our whole duty in life. We have personal desires that long for something outside of God. <u>God's first and foremost goal for us is Himself</u>. **The greatest thing in this world is God!** The greatest thing in our life should be God. He is who we should be living for. Until this can be our answer we are wandering around in the wilderness, lost, and confused.

How many times do we go about living our lives "business as usual?" Without asking Holy Spirit what we are to do. What are the steps we are to take? Acknowledging Him in all our ways? Asking Him for His plan for us? We can never have a plan better than God's. However, we are taking things into our own hands and just barreling through life to get things done.

Then again, we may seek Him in our ways. Yet never <u>fully stop</u> to listen to Him and <u>wait on Him</u>. To wait for His direction. Instead, we keep trucking on ahead doing <u>what we think is best</u>. Because "It's gotta get done, somebody has to do it, and I don't have time to "waste" (to wait)!!" We are such a go, go, go society. We never have time to stop and listen. Tooooo Stoooop and Listeeeeen (imagine me saying it in a slow sloth's voice). In other words, SLOW DOWN!

All the while we are missing out on His order of things. We are missing out on His plan for us and His best for us. Because we do not have time to wait, and we are not surrendered to His ways. We cruise right along into compromise by doing things our own way.

We think we are really getting somewhere fast with our "good" decisions and promptness at getting things done (I'm throwing out a "thumbs up" and a "wink" here). While really, we are stuck in compromise which is a mud bog. One day we will realize we are spinning our wheels, making a mess, and getting nowhere fast. Because we didn't "have time" to wait on the Lord and do things His way! According to His plan for our life.

God has had the book of our lives from beginning to end since before the world was even created. All we have to do is step into His story for our life. It is already written. All we have to do is obey Him. Then trust Him. And rest in Him. It's amazing what God can do when we step out of the way. The story only gets messy when we try to "help God out" with it. As if we know better.

Our "best" is not enough. It will never be enough. We will work ourselves into the ground, into a frenzy, into stress, into frustration, into the hospital, and more. We can try, and try, and try, and fail. Only Christ in us can do anything. John 15:5, "...for without Me you can do nothing." He doesn't say we can do some things without Him, but we can do no thing without Him.

In *The Master's Indwelling*, Andrew Murray says, "The Lord longs to live my life for me. He comes inside of us, and He does the thing through us, as us." This is what is meant by, "it is no longer I who lives but Christ lives in me" (Galatians 2:20). This requires us surrendering **all** to Him and allowing Him access to **every** part of our lives. This is rest!! Hebrews 4:10 ESV says, whoever has entered God's rest has also rested from his (own) works as God did from His.

Christ in you moves and has His being. The mind of Christ makes the decisions for you. Holy Spirit leads and guides you in all things. He alone can fulfill your ministry and your calling. But this cannot happen unless you seek Him in ALL things and live a life of absolute surrender. So many people are just living life and "doing their best." It is His best that causes you to have peace and rest and to succeed and flourish and truly live. When you live in purpose your tank will be full, but God will never fill your tank to drive down roads you were never created to travel. Been there, done that. Now I'm writing the book. (smile)

We must awaken and see we are wasting our time doing anything less than what we were created for. We will never be content doing anything other than what our ministry is, to fulfill our purpose. This is the whole reason we are here. We do not have the right to change the assignment He has for us. Just as the heart can never do what the liver was created to do. Only when we are doing what we were created for will we find satisfaction, fulfillment, and contentment. We are a part of what Christ is doing on the earth. This gives a significance to our life nothing else or no one else can give. This is humbling, that what we do is of great significance in His Kingdom.

Acts 20:22-24, "And see, now I go bound in the spirit to Jerusalem, not knowing the things that will happen to me there, except that the Holy Spirit testifies in every city, saying that chains and tribulations await me. <u>But none of these things move me; nor do I count my life dear to myself, so that I may finish my race with joy, and the ministry which I have received from the Lord Jesus, to testify to the gospel of the grace of God.</u>"

Journal Entry:

<u>My life is valuable only for the purpose of fulfilling the ministry You have</u>

given me. Wow, sobering and humbling as it should be, yet very exciting!!! Life is so much bigger than me and the circumstances I am in. It is ALL about You, Lord. Always has been, always will be. We are not here for our selfish lives. Not one iota!! For us to get this understanding in the depth of our souls. Because we have made it all about us for far too long. I am not here for my agenda, what I deem is my purpose, what I think I should do with my life, what job or business I think I should have, or the goals I have set to accomplish for myself. Jesus, only Jesus!!! I was created for You, Your purpose, and Your pleasure. So, whatever each day brings it is to be lived for You alone and in You alone. My life does not belong to me. **My life is valuable only for the purpose of fulfilling the ministry You have given me.** And in this statement alone, do I find my value. And do I see how valuable You think I am!! **End of journal entry.**

What Is Eternal

CS Lewis: "It would seem that our Lord finds our desires not too strong, but too weak. We are half-hearted creatures, fooling about with drink and sex and ambition when infinite joy is offered us, like an ignorant child who wants to go on making mud pies in a slum because he cannot imagine what is meant by the offer of a holiday at the sea. We are far too easily pleased."

"Live like you were dying." When we see this statement, we ask ourselves these questions; "What do I want to do before I die?" "How would I live each day if I knew I had 3 months to live?" "If I could do whatever I wanted, what would those things be?" If your "to do's" or your "bucket list" is more worldly and fleshly minded, then why do you treasure these things more than what is eternal? Because you desire something more than God. The fact is every day that passes, we are closer to the end of our life as we know it here and now. What truly matters in this life is what will last for eternity and most of us miss it.

What are our days filled with? Where do our conversations lead? Where is our heart? What do we love most in this world? Everything in this world is fading. We are created for eternal things. We are created for the Lord. We are to live lives pleasing to Him. Going about His work for us to do which has everything to do with eternal gain and NOT temporal.

We are to have conversations of eternal worth. Nothing is as intriguing or as interesting or as exciting or as important as Jesus. People will occupy conversations with what they are interested in or passionate about. Do your animals, your businesses, your degrees, your hobbies, your own interests have eternal value? And they may... The things we do in our everyday life and what we talk about ought to show our eternal values. We say we Love Jesus, yet what we value most comes through in our conversations and lives lived.

If I am filled with passion for Jesus. Filled with passionate Love for Jesus. Filled with passionate intimacy with Jesus. Jesus is what will come out of me. I am like a sponge soaking in the Love of Jesus and when I get squeezed the Love of Jesus is what will flow out of me. My thoughts will not be consumed with anything else (no worthless thing). I will be consumed with His purpose for my life. I will not desire the lusts of the flesh or any worldly thing. I am a sponge; I cannot afford to get dried up and fall apart.

In intimacy and prayer is where we encounter the presence of God, where He changes our desires. Delight yourself in the LORD, and He will give you the desires of your heart (Psalm 37:4). This means he gives us the desires. He puts in our hearts His desires. Not that He gives us whatever our own selfish and fleshly desires are. Our focus is to remain on our delight in Him and our desires will begin to parallel His and we will never go unfulfilled. To delight in the Lord is true treasure.

He gives me all things for a season. Nothing is eternal except my spirit and my relationship with Him. Even If I have a relationship with someone who is a Christian, that relationship will be different in eternity. I am not saying this is a bad thing. I have full assurance of faith that our relationships in eternity are even greater and more fulfilling than what we can ever experience here and now. Obvious reasons I can say this is because there will be no tears, no death, no sorrow, no pain (Revelation 21:4). But just for an example to use; there will be no husband-and-wife relationships in eternity (Matthew 22:23-33). The only marriage there will be is the one between Jesus and His bride. So, **everything** He gives me is all on loan for a season of time to steward. I own nothing. It is all His.

Psalm 27:4, "**One thing** have I desired of the LORD, that will I seek after; that I will dwell in the house of the LORD all the days of my life, to behold the beauty of the LORD, and to inquire in His temple." **Singleness** of heart is uncompromising desire for God and to please Him in ALL things.

Journal Entry:

I do not want to be short sighted. I want Your vision of what I do here will <u>last into eternity</u>. I do not want to spend my time on things that are temporary. I want to invest my time in what is eternal. Everything I see with my eyes is perishing. Putting time into relationships can be of eternal value. It can also be very "worldly," I choose. Keep in the forefront of my mind this life I live is all about You and the eternal things. Lord, please divert my mind always back to eternal thinking: Love God, Love myself in Your image, Love others, be humble, and serve. What things will I do to impact eternity? What will last for eternity? Do not have my heart tied to worldly things!

Father, as I write this, I need You to move my mind/thoughts/heart to what is eternal and not of this world. That Your Love for me far outweighs any and every pleasure the world tries to offer. To know Your Love where nothing else matters. I need to die to myself so deeply so all I want is all You want. Where I just want You and nothing else. I want You to satisfy my soul. **End of journal entry.**

Jeremy Taylor: "Behold Him with the eye of faith and let my desires actually fix on Him, as the Object of my worship, and the Reason of my hope, and the Fountain of my blessing."

A Prayer to Pray:

"Father, I do not want to get sucked into worthless endeavors, selfish ambition, or meaningless hobbies and pursuits that do nothing for Your Kingdom. I want to pursue Your purpose. I want to be single-minded in doing Your will. Please help me to not get distracted with bunny trails or get entangled in the traps the enemy has set for me. Temporary things do not matter to me. I want to be the person You created me to be and to do the things You have prepared for me to do even before I was born. I want to be committed to You, obedient to You, and not waste my life on things that will not bring You glory. Help me to stay focused on You, Your Word, Your Truth, and Your promises, so I will not get distracted. I am sanctified, set apart, for Your cause and no one else's. Not even my own. In Jesus name, Amen."

The Church "Redefined"

We, at large, have been mistaken on what church is. We may know what it is, but we misuse the word all the time. <u>First</u>, we the body of Christ, are the church (Ephesians 1:22). The building we go to, or the place we gather is not the church. Acts 14:27, "Now when they had come and gathered the church together..." We are not going to church. We are going to the gathering of the church.

<u>Second</u>, when we gather the church together, we at large, have made it all about ourselves and being ministered to. We make it about going "to get what I need" and "to see what I can get out of it." **For Example:** Is the music going to move me and touch me today? What good word or blessing will I receive from the message today?

We are trying to find the way how this will benefit us instead of making it a way to minister to and bless the Lord. Please read Ezekiel 44:10-16. This is the difference between ministering to the people and ministering to the Lord.

The priests who went far from the Lord when Israel went astray were appointed as a minister in the sanctuary. They were to slay the offerings and sacrifices for the people and then stand before the people and **minister to them.** They were not allowed to go near God or enter the holy place because of their iniquity. However, the priests (the sons of Zadok), who kept charge of the Lord's sanctuary when the children of Israel went astray, they were the ones who were appointed to be near to the Lord, to stand before Him, and **minister to the Lord.**

We were always meant to minister unto the Lord in our gatherings. When we gather, we are to <u>come near to Him</u>. We are to <u>minister to Him</u>. We are to <u>stand before Him</u>. We are to <u>worship Him</u>. We are to <u>offer ourselves (a living sacrifice) unto Him</u> (Romans 12:1). We are to <u>enter His sanctuary</u>. We are to <u>come near to His table</u>. We are to <u>keep His charge</u>.

And in today's gatherings we have made it all about getting our own needs met, getting our cups filled, and being entertained, instead of worship to the Lord.

<u>Third</u>, Hebrews 10:24-25 (KJV) tells us not to forsake the gathering together, to exhort (to call near, invite, invoke, beseech, call for, comfort, intreat, pray) one another. To stir up one another unto Love and to good works. We are gathering to spur each other on. Not for us to be ministered to, receive a blessing, or be entertained. We minister (in Hebrew: to attend as a menial or worshipper, to contribute to, serve, wait on) unto the Lord

and encourage one another. We have One we are to worship and to please in our gatherings. We have One we are to be putting **ALL** our attention on.

Everything about our service should be to minster unto Him. If we allow Him to, He will show us what He wants to say to the church in our sermons. It's not about what we think they need to hear or what we want to preach about. If we allow Him to, He will show us what He wants to do in our services. It's not about what we think we should do. If we allow Him to, He will move us in the music as to what is pleasing to Him. He will lead us to what He wants to hear and what touches His heart. It's not about what we think the people want to hear, what they are moved by, or what touches our heart.

In our gatherings are we on His timetable or our time limits? Are we pursuing His agenda or our schedules? Are we seeking His order of things or are we stuck on what we want to accomplish? Are we waiting on Him to lead us or are we taking it into our own hands? When is the last time we came together and just waited on Him to move? We are so rigid in our schedules we leave no room for Holy Spirit to have His way.

When is the last time we just sat with Him, together, in His presence to see what He wants to do? But nothing is as more uncomfortable than sitting in a room full of people in silence is there? God will not conform to our comfortability. Now is the time for these things to change in our gatherings. We need to determine we will not have the fear of man, or the fear of religion stop us from pursuing what God is doing in us and around us. We do not need to care about anyone's opinion of our gatherings. We have an audience of One to please

Oswald Chambers says, "The remarkable thing about God is that when you fear God, you fear nothing else, whereas if you do not fear God, you fear everything else." Selah!!

We are to seek His face and be in intimacy with Him. Waiting on Him to have His way. Then everything else will flow through us and out of us and HE will give the church what they need, how He so chooses. Whether it be directly from Himself or through one another. But make no mistake it will be His Words, His agenda, and His way, not ours.

Psalm 127:1, "Unless the LORD builds the house, they labor in vain who build it…" If God is in it do not worry or fear. When He is in it, He assumes the care and responsibility of it all. Lay aside all self-effort and enter His rest (Psalm 127:2). In Acts 2:42-47, the Lord added to their numbers daily. Not the programs. Not the great sermons. Not the eloquent pastor. Not the entertainment of what we call praise and worship today. Not the cool youth pastor. But THE LORD.

Our services are not to be about "what I can get" from them. They are not about going to get our "booster shot" so we can be uplifted. Instead of us lifting God up. They are not for us to go and get our itches scratched either. We say things like, "Well the music was off today, I didn't really like that song, that was too loud, why did she have to screech like that, I didn't like the message, it was too long, it was too boring, it was too hot or too cold in the sanctuary, etc. The entire time we are so focused on everything we prefer (so focused on self). We have made it all about us and what we need, what we want, and what we desire that we are not ministering to the Lord at all and what God prefers. EXCEPT the sons of Zadok! We will minister to the Lord.

How many of our church services are geared towards man? Many of our gatherings today have been fabricated to entertain people. With our light shows and stunning performances. Either by our worship teams or our motivational speaking pastors. It was never supposed to be about "How do we get people here?" Trying to draw them in with all the "hype" of the amazing pastor, the "rocking" music, and "awesome" programs and events we put on. Then we have to continue to do these things to keep them coming. Because it is a "cool" place to be. So now we have to stay "cool." Once you create an appetite you have to feed it. Do not go to the gathering of the church looking for a show to be entertained with.

Tommy Tenney from the book *The God Chasers*, writes about how God had said to him, "Son, the services that you consider your favorite services and those I favor are not the same services." SELAH! Tommy Tenney continues to say, "We go away week after week self-gratified, with our itches scratched and our narrow personal needs met. When will we hear God's still small voice saying, 'would somebody just love Me'?" Brings tears to my eyes.

This is our first and great commandment; to Love the Lord our God with all our heart, soul, mind, and strength. Instead of putting our focus on Loving Him, we get so mesmerized by everything going on around us. Our focus is everywhere else but Loving Him. Then we get caught up in wanting to see His acts, His giftings, and His anointings that we do not look at Him. We do not minister to Him, but we want what He can offer us. The greatest blessing does not come from God's hand. It comes from His face, in intimate relationship. We can allow nothing else to enter this place that impedes our desire to Love God.

Do We Want Jesus (His manifest presence) in Our Gatherings? The following are some questions to ask ourselves:

1. Does He smell the sweet fragrance of our worship (the entire service) and find it to be in Spirit and in Truth? Or is it a stench of the flesh in His nostrils?
2. Does our worship (the entire service) minister to His heart? Or does He just find entertainment for the people?
3. Does He find pleasure in our worship? Or are they just empty words?
4. Is He pleased?
5. Is He blessed?
6. Is our worship to Him with a heart of repentance? Or are we just in it for ourselves?
7. Are His feet anointed with our tears and adoration?
8. Can He find His rest here?
9. Does He find comfort here?
10. Is His presence here? Or is the sanctuary only filled with the presence of people?
11. Can He say, "Oh that was good, I enjoyed that!"
12. Does He get His fill?

The Church in Unity

Please read John 17:20-26. In John 17:21-22, Jesus prays for us to be one just as He and the Father are One. He mentions this twice for us to be one. When we are one it is not possible to act as if we are two (or millions). When we are one, we are in unison not separation. Are our relationships looking united just like Jesus and the Father's relationship?? If they are not, then why not?

There is a lot of diversity we have amongst ourselves. Diversity is a good thing. What makes us to have unity is when we each wake up and know why we are here. When we each understand we are here to be One with Christ and one with each other. We are to be the Love of Christ and we are to shine. We become one in unity when we each Love like Jesus and look like Jesus. Are we looking like Jesus? Are we doing our part (God's ministry, gifting, and plan He has given us) in our greater purpose?

Unity can only come when we are dead to self. When everyone Loves just as Jesus Loves. When everyone is transforming into the character and nature of Jesus. When we are not thinking of ourselves or for ourselves but only thinking for the Kingdom of God. Walking out heaven here on earth. This is when we will become One just as Jesus and the Father are One.

In heaven there are angels around His throne singing holy, holy, holy in one accord. For us to have this kind of worship on earth, we must know who He is. To know Him in intimacy. We must have the fear of the Lord. To have awe and wonder of Him. To have deep respect and honor for Him. The angels are all in unity because they are not concerned about themselves, and they are not looking out for themselves. There is no thought of themselves whatsoever. Their only focus is on the Blessed Trinity, Father, Son, and Holy Spirit.

Prayer "Redefined"

Are we praying "me" centered prayers (selfish prayers)? Are we praying fear driven prayers? Or are we praying Spirit filled prayers? Faith works (is active, efficient, effectual, operative, powerful) by (channeled through) Love (Galatians 5:6), not because I have a need. Faith works when I **know** God's Love for me. How do I know God's Love for me? When I am in intimate relationship with Him. Faith does not work because we need Him to move in our circumstance. Because we are so worried and concerned about it. We end up praying to God and rebuking the devil, but our fear (and selfish motives) are the reasons he is there. We bind God's hands when we do not pray from faith and Love and we are praying from selfishness, fear, wrong motives, hurts, offenses, unforgiveness, etc.

That last paragraph I do not write lightly. When these Truths were brought to my attention it was like a friendly sucker punch to my gut. This was not something I could fully grasp in one sitting. I had to digest it and really allow Holy Spirit to reveal the Truth of it in my life. And He did. I am asking you to do the same. It may have hit you hard. The Truth may have hurt you. It may have even hit you the "wrong way." But I assure you Truth pierces our hearts. It is not always easy to swallow. But it is what makes us free (John 8:32).

A quote from the book, *The Hidden Life of Prayer*, written by David

McIntyre: "A man may pray much and instead of drawing near to God and enjoying sweet communion with Christ, he may draw nigh just to prayer. His thoughts may be more upon his praying than upon his God to whom he prays, and he may live more upon his knees than upon his Christ." Selah!

We pray because we are in relationship with the Lord! Not just to get something from Him. We pray because we are in Love with God and in Covenant with Him. <u>Our heart bursts with faith because **we know who He is**</u>. We know His nature. We know His character. We know His will (Ephesians 5:15-17). It's easy to believe in this place because we know who He is.

We have become so weak in our prayer lives because we do not grow in intimacy with the Lord. <u>We do not know Him</u>. We are Christian in name only and we can check off our boxes but when trial or tragedy come, we run to God in fear. Hoping He can do something. Hoping He can come through for us. Then we pray prayers because we are driven by a need. We pray from fear, anxiety, confusion, desperation, etc. Which are all satan's territory. We do not completely trust the Lord with our prayers because we do not **know Him**. We cannot trust someone we do not know. If we pray and trust the Lord in faith, do we have ANY reason to hold on to "concern?" When we know Him, truly know Him, we will trust Him. Completely letting go. Because we KNOW He is good.

When we think there is something God cannot handle it is fear based. We are only still concerned because we fear we will not get what we are asking for. We fear not getting what we want, the way we want it, and when we want it. It comes from pride. Thinking of ourselves and for ourselves. Even when we are praying for others, if we still hold on to concern over them, where is our trust in the Lord? Where is our faith?

Why would we ever think there is something God cannot handle?! Pride shows up through worry (1 Peter 5:5-7). Pride says to Jesus, "You do not care as much as I do," or "I can step in and handle this better than what You are doing." Therefore, "I will worry and stay concerned about this thing I have asked You to take care of until You show me You've got it," or "I will just handle it myself." Now of course we would **never** say these things out loud. But this is essentially what we are saying when we hold on to worry, concern, fear, anxiety, etc. We cannot trust Him and worry at the same time.

PRACTICAL APPLICATION:

If you are not to where you have this kind of faith and trust in the Lord, do not beat yourself up. Condemnation is NEVER from the Lord. Whenever we recognize an area where we need to grow in, we simply give it to Him in the Great Exchange. Asking Holy Spirit to do the work that needs to be done in us. "I give You this fear and I receive Your perfect Love. Bathe me in Your Love Lord where fear is not an option."

A PRAYER TO PRAY:

"Holy Spirit I recognize I still am afraid when I pray certain prayers. I am concerned it will not turn out how I want it to. I am struggling to trust You with it. Burn all of this out of me! Grow me in faith. Grow me in **knowing** my Father, who is my Provider and the Lover of my soul. Grow me in trusting You. Grow me in Love. As I know You and Your Love for me, as I Love You, as we are in relationship, I will lose any ability to doubt You. Thank You for our relationship. Thank You that I can recognize this for what it is and run to You to burn it out of me. The more You burn inside of me the more You burn everything else out of me and off me. Be a blaze inside of me! Thank You Holy Spirit, I Love You! In Jesus name, Amen."

When we humble ourselves under the mighty hand of God, we will cast all our cares upon Him knowing He cares for us (1 Peter 5:6-7). We pray from the connection of presence, adoration, affection, worship, and trust. We will not pray from worry, complaining, selfishness, or fear. Which ways of prayer gives God honor? Which ways move Him? Our fear, selfishness, complaining, etc. (that comes from satan) certainly do not move Him. Will He help us in that place? Yes! But He does not sit there and say, "Oh she is really concerned about that, I am just going to take care of it right now." He looks to our faith which is channeled through Love not our need. When we understand this, it will drastically change our prayer life!

Praying from a place of fear is an oxymoron. If there is fear, it is from the enemy. And if the enemy knows there is fear, it is giving him much ammunition. We can all be believers praying for a thing and not seeing the thing change. We know what the Bible says so we are all praying trying to contend for it. But faith works through LOVE (in relationship with the Father). And there is NO FEAR in LOVE. Just because we are praying because we have a need does not mean we are in faith. Praying and faith are not the same thing.

I was not given a spirit of fear (meaning timidity; but the word comes from: dread, by implication **faithless**) but of power (miraculous power, strength), Love, and a sound mind (discipline, correction, teach to be sober, self-controlled) (2Timothy 1:5-12). I will pray from there (power, Love, and a sound mind) and not fear (faithless). Because Your perfect Love, Jesus, casts out fear and anyone who fears has not been made perfect (complete) in Your Love (1 John 4:15-19). Amen!

We resist (stand against) the devil by being steadfast (stiff, solid, stable, strong, sure) in the faith (1 Peter 5:9-11). We are to ask in faith, not wavering (James 1:2-8). One who wavers will not receive anything. Because a double minded man (two spirited man = flesh/fear and Spirit/faith) is unstable in all his ways. When we ask **in faith** with no doubt, we are to know what we ask for, according to His will, and in His name, it is done for us (Matthew 18:19-20, 21:21-22, Mark 11:20-26, John 14:13-14, 15:1-8, 15:16, 16:23-24, 1 John 3:21-23, 5:14-15).

You cannot pray in faith, and nothing happen. The moment Jesus spoke to the fig tree it was dead (but seen the next day). Every time I pray something happens. It may not be seen immediately but my faith brings the unseen to the seen. It brings that which is already accomplished in the spiritual realm to the physical realm. Faith is the **evidence** (proof) of things not seen (Hebrews 11:1).

There is a place to pray from the place Jesus walked being rooted and grounded in Love. Understanding who we are in the Father. No identity crisis, no insecurity, no fear, no worry. Do you think Jesus had any of those things? And whoever says they abide in Him ought himself to walk JUST AS He walked (1 John 2:6). If we have ever prayed and then have become frustrated, discouraged, doubtful (second guessing), etc. right there we have already crossed the line. It's not about frustrated or any of the feelings of the flesh. it's about authority in the name of Jesus.

For Example: We pray for someone's healing, and it does not immediately happen. Most of us right there would get frustrated or discouraged at that. Or we get confused and start questioning God. The healing could come tomorrow if we have the faith for it. But if we are discouraged at the onset, we are already defeated. Remember the fig tree?

Mark 11:23-24 (ESV), "**Truly**, I say to you, **whoever** says to this mountain, 'be taken up and thrown into the sea,' and **does not doubt** (withdraw from, oppose, hesitate, stagger, waver) in his heart (thoughts and feelings) **but believes** (has faith) that what he says will come to pass, it will be done for him. Therefore, I tell you, **whatever** you ask in prayer, **believe that you have received it** (past tense, already done), and **it will be yours.**" A life of faith is a mouth of life. It is important to not speak curses, doubt, or fear into our prayers.

Interesting Sidenote: In Young's Literal Translation (YLT) Jesus says, "Have **faith of** God." Selah! Also, it is worthy to note here in Galatians 2:20 (KJV) it says, "… and the life which I now live in the flesh (the body) I live by the **faith of** the Son of God." (Just something to think about, smile.)

So, meanwhile, while I am waiting for the manifestation of my prayers, I wait (in Hebrew; to expect, look for) upon the Lord (Isaiah 40:31). Not wait upon the thing I am waiting for. But I wait upon the Lord, and I will not grow weary. I will remain steadfast and immovable always abounding in the work of the Lord (1 Corinthians 15:55-58).

The Truth of the matter is we are praying to God for things we already have. We are praying for victories that have already been won for us. We just need to have faith and believe it, so we can receive it. The sooner we can grab ahold of this Truth and stop fighting the devil the sooner we will walk in freedom. We are allowing the devil in our house and in the situations (when we have anxiety, fear, and worry). We honor the devil and give it attention with these feelings we have. Our focus and attention are to be on Jesus and know He has already defeated the devil. "It is finished." Everything accomplished. We take Mark 11:22-26, and we stand in faith. We stand firm on His Word.

Jesus destroyed the works of the devil (1 John 3:8). Jesus said in John 12:31, "**Now** is the judgement of this world; **now** the ruler of this world will be cast out (to eject, drive out, send away)." This happened at the death and resurrection of Jesus Christ. Jesus has restored our dominion in the earth. Back to original creation (Genesis 1:26). It is not satan's to rule any longer, he has been cast out. We have allowed him to continue to rule, but we must stand our ground, and take it back. Our victory has been won through Christ.

We are to put on our whole armor <u>and stand</u> against the devil (Ephesians 6:11-20):

1. To trust in the Lord with our belt of Truth wrapped around us. The Truth we know makes us free (John 8:32) and Truth transforms us (Romans 12:2).
2. We have Jesus, our breastplate of righteousness, to guard our heart.

3. We have our shield of **faith** to quench **every** fiery dart of the devil.
4. And if a missile comes flying at our head full of wrong thoughts, we will immediately take them captive to the obedience of Jesus Christ (2 Corinthians 10:3-5). Knowing our helmet of salvation will sustain us while we are being transformed by the renewing of our mind.
5. We wield our Sword of the Spirit. Which is the Word of God. Which is our weapon.
6. We walk in our shoes of the Gospel of peace.
7. We pray always in the Spirit.

We have our full armor to stand against the devil (not fight him but stand against him). When the term "wrestle" is used in this Scripture it is to vibrate or to shake. In other words, it is our struggle. Our struggle is not against flesh and blood but against the rulers of darkness. It is a struggle not a fight. Our only fight is the good fight **of faith** (1 Timothy 6:12). (Bear with me, keep reading.)

We are to fight by standing in faith. We are to stand in the victory that is already ours until it is made manifest (brought into the open). We are to remain seated in the heavenly places in Christ Jesus (Ephesians 2:4-6). There is no such thing as a "big devil" because he has been defeated over 2,000 years ago. We do not fight satan or his demons. We are to walk **just as** Jesus walked (1 John 2:6 & 1 John 4:17) and Jesus never fought the devil. He spoke to them, and they trembled and did as He commanded. Remember our Sword? It is the Word of God. We are to speak. Jesus did not even allow them to speak (Luke 4:31-37 & Luke 4:40-41).

When Jesus walked the earth, the demons were terrified of Him (Mark 5:1-20)! He would walk up to them, and they were more aware of who He was than the Pharisees were. The Pharisees have Scriptures wrapped around their foreheads, yet they did not even recognize the Son of God when He was standing right next to them. In each of the Scriptures we see where the demons address who He is, Luke 4:34, "Holy One of God." Luke 4:41, "You are the Christ, the Son of God." Mark 5:7, "Jesus, Son of the Most High God." We have demons more aware of Jesus' presence than the church. And at His command they flee. Jesus never had a problem with the devils, they did exactly as He said every time. No fighting. Where did we get this idea that we have to fight satan? (Still with me? Smile)

There is a level of authority God is calling us to and it is called seated and stand. We are in Christ. Christ is in us. He has given us ALL authority (Luke 10:19). Our only fight is the fight of faith. Faith is what we believe. What we believe comes from our thoughts, our mind. Which is also synonymous with our feelings. We talked about this in Chapter 5 (The Transformed Life). Our battle is the battle to align our mind and feelings with the mind and feelings of Christ. Fight the condition of my own thinking and my feelings by renewing my mind in Truth and Trusting in His Word. Trusting what He tells me in His Word is true!

We keep asking Him to move the mountains in our lives and He has. He has already moved through His Son Jesus Christ. He made the one move to win it all! But we keep resurrecting things by our fear, doubt, worry, anxiety, etc. Now it is time for us to move.

He has given US all power and authority over the enemy (Luke 10:19). We are asking Him to move when He already has moved and He is sitting there asking us, "Now what are **you** going to do about it?!"

This is some of what the Word says to do about it:

1. We <u>Submit to God</u> (which is resisting the devil) and he will flee (James 4:7).
2. We resist the devil by <u>being steadfast in our faith</u> (1 Peter 5:8-9).
3. <u>Draw near to God</u> and He will draw near to us (James 4:8).
4. <u>Seek first the Kingdom of God and His righteousness</u> and all these things will be added. **<u>Therefore, do not worry</u>** about tomorrow (Matthew 6:33-24).
5. <u>Cast the whole of our cares onto Him</u> because He cares for us (1 Peter 5:7).

And if we do not have what we pray for it is because we are asking amiss for selfish reasons (James 4:1-10), or we have doubt (James 1:6-7). Everything of the flesh is annihilated when we submit and surrender to God. When we seek His face, we will find Him. When we draw near to Him in relationship, we will know Him. When we know Him, we will not ask amiss. We will not ask for things selfishly. When we know Him, we will not doubt Him.

Sidenote: Sometimes we do not even realize how selfish we are. We touched on it in Detox My Heart how we can have wrong motives. If we are praying for someone for them to change to make our lives better. That is selfish. We can have hidden selfish motives and not realize it. As the flesh dies and transformation happens we will be able to spot these easily and eventually we will only pray from Love.

I have said this before I will say it again. **Everything flows from relationship with God**. Our self-life is annihilated when we draw near to Jesus, period. Fear is annihilated when we are perfected in His Love. Because we know Him, we are afraid of nothing. Because we fear nothing, we can remain steadfast in our faith which is what resists the devil.

Why do you think satan tries everything in his power to keep us from seeking God's face? From being alone with Him? Trying to keep us in condemnation and guilt to keep us from drawing near to Him??? Because it totally wipes him out of our lives once we know God intimately. The more we draw near to God the more everything else fades away. And satan loses his grip on us.

What happens in the secret place He rewards in the open (Matthew 6:6), with a life transformed. You end up in a situation where before your flesh used to be in an uproar and now you respond in the Spirit because you have been with Him. Now you are not trying to apply last week's sermon to your life (like a robot), the Word has become flesh and dwells in you.

A Prayer to Prayer:

"Thank You Jesus that You came and destroyed the works of the enemy and gave me back dominion over the earth. Now I need to take my rightful place and bring heaven to earth. I will stand firm with my whole armor and hold the ground You purchased back for me. Holy Spirit burn what isn't You even in my prayer life. Burn away the fear, doubt, worry, selfishness, wrong motives, or intent. When I pray, I will seek Your face and pray what You would have me pray. Your Word says I am to pray always in the Spirit (Ephesians 6:18), so that is what I will do. As always, continue to teach me, and grow me up into You in all things. In Jesus name, Amen."

Notes from Dan Mohler

This next section is almost word for word notes I have taken from Dan Mohler. Most of the notes are from "HCSKL 2011 (Harvest Chapel School of Kingdom Living), Day 17 and Day 30. It is a 52-day class I have been watching on YouTube or listening to on Spotify for the last 4 years (Praise the Lord)! As I mentioned in the acknowledgments of this book, Dan has helped me to understand Truth (which has made me free). I have grown in my understanding of what it means to be as Christ in this world. Holy Spirit used him to help me see how deep my selfishness went. As I started to apply his teachings (which is all the Word of God) is when my life drastically started to be transformed.

So here we go! Notes from Dan:

There is no place that tells a Christian it is okay to complain. In fact, we are told in the Bible the account of the Israelites was specifically told to us so we would learn from their mistakes and not be like them (1 Corinthians 10:1-11). They died in the wilderness complaining. Why are we not to complain? Because our life is not our own. It is never about how it is going or how we feel. It is about what we believe and who He is in us.

Why do we give ourselves permission to complain or "have moments?" Why do we justify it and say, "we are only human?" We are partakers of His divine nature (2 Peter 1:2-4). We were created in His image (Genesis 1:26). Just as He is, so are we in this world (1 John 4:17). It is not I who lives but Christ in me (Galatians 2:20). Where does any of that give us permission to not look like Jesus in every way?

"God could have saved my loved one."

My own excerpt here: I have said it before I will say it again, He doesn't owe us a thing, not even an explanation. If He never did one more thing for us in our lives, not one, He saved us and brought us back into unbroken relationship with Himself, and that is more than enough.

Back to Dan: "God could have saved my loved one." This way of thinking brings issues. Especially when you start missing your husband and you forget what you are a part of. You forget why you are in this thing. And suddenly you are just another person with a reason to be personally hurt. You forget it's a demon war against the Kingdom of God. Now suddenly, you're missing your husband asking, "Why didn't God deliver him?" "Why didn't God save him?" "Why didn't God heal him?" Then you get offended at God, and mad at Him.

Do you know what it means when it says deny yourself? When you agree with that you can't think those questions, when you really understand. Even if you feel that way you rebound because of Truth. Because the feeling is real. The missing him is real. Who knows the lonely and empty chair and empty bed is real? So, even more reason to dial in and stay focused on who you are and what you are a part of. Or you will never run this race. This is where faith comes in. Loving not your own life unto death (Revelation 12:11).

The accusation that comes day and night is you love your own life. And satan says, "I'll prove it. I will hit your life hard enough and you will be crushed. I will hit you hard enough and you will backslide. I will hit you hard enough and you will be mad at God. You are an American Christian, and you are in the Gospel for your own sake. I will prove you love yourself; I will prove it."

Then wham, wham, wham, wham. He is coming against the people of God to prove we are not who we say we are. If I do not understand I am in a demonic war against the Kingdom of God and the Kingdom is in me, I will think all the "whamming" is directed towards me. It feels like it is against me, but it is to stop the advancement of the Kingdom of God that is in me.

If I knew bad things were going to happen (rape, murder, arms cut off, loved ones killed, etc.) if I accepted Christ as my Savior, would I still make that decision? We have heard a different Gospel than other countries. We have to admit we have heard the Gospel in a way that we receive Christ to benefit our own safety. To benefit our own lives. Instead of receiving Him for the cause of the Kingdom no matter what the cost. That is why He says deny yourself and pick up your cross. Think of the intense language there. It just becomes "lingo" to us. It becomes "christianese" if we are not careful.

If I can know what it means to pick up my cross and follow Him, and go through every injustice and every unfairness, especially the stuff where I have Scriptural promises for my life, yet it is not my reality, I better have faith. This is where faith is needed to just stand. Where faith says, "I know God is good, I am in this for a cause, and I have no permission to be less than integral. I have no permission to be less than Love and who Christ is in me in the midst of all of this and to shine." This will go a lot further than worrying, wondering, and questioning. Because that subverts faith in the process. That is rationally substantiated through human wisdom. "If God Loves me then why is everything falling apart?" That only reveals I have a perspective this Gospel is to serve me. Where I am setting myself up for just another blow.

What is the proper response when the "whamming" comes? "Father, it seems like there is chaos all around me. Thank You that You are bigger than it all. You Love me. You have always Loved me. There is provision. Somehow You will make a way. I don't even see a way out of this, but that is why You are God. That is why You are the Way Maker and I just appreciate Your Love for me. I appreciate that You are going to reveal Your glory and shine Christ through my life. Because that is why I am on the earth. I admit this thing is trying to pull me and tug me at times. But I have got my eyes on You and who I am in You."

All of a sudden there is faith. And you are releasing faith over areas in your life. But it's not because you are falling apart and if God doesn't move, you're going to give up on Him. The "Where is God, I thought He Loved me" mentality should totally be stripped from our lives.

We do not find the Love of God in the circumstances of life. We do not decide His Love for us on whether we are healed or not, whether we are in prison and beaten or not, whether we have a child that died or not. We find the absolute fact that God Loves us through Christ crucified alone. Otherwise, we could never be rooted and grounded in Love if the Love of God is subject to change through the circumstances of our lives.

What happens in life does not change what the Word of God says. The Truth of who He is in you. The worship He deserves. The closer you stay in relationship with Him, the clearer you will see and live. If you are living for perfect circumstances, that is a myth.

If you have lost a child, some people think another person cannot speak into that because they have not lost a child themselves and the only person they would listen to is one who has lost a child. But unfortunately, if you only listen to one who has lost a child, they may feel just like you do. So, I do not have to had lost a child to at least be able to convey Truth in the matter. Because a Christian has a bigger view. The person's view who lost the child is very temporal, very natural, "I have lost." Physical loss is so real.

I asked the Lord, "How does one get past it?" He said one word, "Thankfulness." And isn't this the most opposite thing we think in that time? We were never called to covet the gifts of God at the cost of who God is. Life is a blessing. Life is a privilege. You can see the fall of man when we receive the grace and gifts of life to bring forth a child and then trauma comes, and we don't have any vision past today. We have been swallowed up in the natural then.

Every time that stuff hits you in the face and it is real. The response is thankfulness, "Father, I thank You the most I could lose in this life is the temporal time I could have had with Billy. But because of the blood of Jesus, You have given me the right to bring an eternal soul into this earth and my boy is alive forever in You because of You. And as much as my heart misses him and I just want to squeeze that boy, I thank You that You have held him through Your blood. And I am going to run hard to reach the finish line and we will all be together forever in You. So, thanks for the strength to run this race to keep my eyes focused and not be weary hearted or broken hearted because there is a bigger picture than missing Billy. You are Lord and I thank You for the gift of life."

Whether it is triumph or tragedy it is all the same. Every day is the same. Nothing has changed because Jesus is still Lord. We have to live beyond the flesh and not think in the natural.

There are ways that reveal if you are living for yourself or getting the wrong view. satan tries to find vulnerability. he roams around like a roaring lion seeking WHOM he may devour. That means he is looking for vulnerability. That everyone he sees, he just can't devour. He's looking for whom he can devour. Who has a different perspective. Sometimes we separate faith and reality and what should happen is faith should cover that reality.

There must be something bigger than how you feel and what you are going through. It's a higher perspective. So, if you lose Billy you have to have a faith to substantiate your life even in the midst of the real physical pain and loss of his empty chair. Feeling sorry for yourself is the track satan usually tries to get you to take.

Think not of yourself. You are before God for a bigger cause than how you feel. Feeling sorry for yourself is the biggest trap of your life. It is so all about you. We are surrounded by all the testimonies of these lives who are examples to us who loved not their own lives (Please read Hebrews 11:32-40).

The 3 Jewish boys (Daniel 3:19-30) no matter what, would not change their view of God. satan is so used to us changing our view of God when the heat gets hotter. Every time the devil touches us, he takes a risk of perfecting us and that we will have a greater revelation of God. But he believes we won't, he's banking on us not being who we say we are and folding.

Faith works through God's Love for me, it has nothing to do with me having a need and the Bible having a promise. "Brother you need to get stronger, you wouldn't be going through all of this if you had some faith." No, it's their faith (the 3 Jewish boys) that took them through the fire. We misunderstand faith. Faith is not perfect circumstances. That is a lie from hell, it is deception. Faith has to do with a perfect heart in the midst of trials.

In the world you will have tribulation but in Me you have peace so be of good cheer, I have overcome the world (John 16:33). "You are in Me now, and you live for a whole different reason now. You think a whole different way now. You look through a whole different eye now. And trouble doesn't look the same even though trouble is the same." So, what is the victory? The change of platform from which I live. I used to live for me and now I live for His glory. I used to live for me but now I live for His sake.

We are Christians to accomplish His purpose. It's not about the shots to the jaw, it's about what we are in this thing for. The shots to the jaw if they are not rightly discerned, you invite a whole lot more shots to the jaw. It's like an unprotected fire.

Faith doesn't stop things from happening. Faith causes you to go through them unscathed. And sometimes their faith actually cost them their life. If you start thinking for yourself, you'll take a step back. If you start feeling sorry for yourself, you will take a step back. You lose sight of this thing you are in, a war against the Kingdom and the Kingdom is in you, you will take a step back.

Luke 12:32 "Do not fear, little flock, for it is your Father's good pleasure **to give you** the Kingdom." And we are to go preach saying the Kingdom of God is here! Fear not the Kingdom is here. What do we do all the time in crisis? Fear and then pray. And we prove we do not understand. And we cry out to a God "out there" somewhere and He has implanted Himself in us to move **through us**. Christ **in us** the hope of glory (Colossians 1:27). **Out of our belly** flows rivers of living water (John 7:38 KJV). Every promise of God is Yes and Amen to the glory of God **through us** (2 Corinthians 1:20). Who ministers the Kingdom? The glory of God **through us**. Ephesians 3:20-21, "Now to Him who is able to do exceedingly, abundantly, above all that we ask or think, according to the power that works **in us,** to Him be glory in the church by Christ Jesus to all generations forever and ever, Amen." It is all through the Bible.

So, if Jesus says to a withered hand, "stretch forth your hand." Does the hand stretch forth? Yes. Why? **Because He sees bigger than the withered hand.** We look at the withered hand and it's a visual and we say "Hand stretch forth." And then we are going "Is it working? Is it going to stretch? Is it happening? It doesn't look like it's happening. It looks the same. Oh my God what am I going to do now?" And our minds are constantly spinning. Especially with visuals. Jesus is the revelation, and He lives **in us**.

So, we are growing and increasing. So, it is not a matter of right or wrong or if God is displeased or pleased. It's a matter of authority. The reason I am sharing this is because it's been deceiving us. Because we think our sentiments, our emotions, and our "prayers," are what indicates faith. Faith is settling on the will of God and seeing who He is in the face of every situation. Faith is different than the fact that we prayed. It's not speaking to the mountain that makes it move, its believing. We are speaking at a lot of mountains that are just sitting there.

We know the Word. We have been well taught. So, when we see the mountain, we know WHAT to say. The reason why this school is so fixed on becoming Love and receiving God's Love and walking in His Love is because **faith works through Love and if we get a clear identity we will walk in greater revelation.** If we see who we are we won't try so hard. We will realize it's already finished (and we will step into it) and we will see who we are in the place of where it's needed. We will recognize who we are when authority is necessary.

When we walk in a room and it is filled with tears and maybe even unbelief, you can end up letting what they don't see determine what you do see and your so overwhelmed that becomes your reality. But when we can keep our eyes fixed on Him and not get caught up in all the human emotion, feeling, and empathy, we can walk in authority. But who knows the whole time they are in that place, they are all praying? They have posters and scriptures up all over the place and music playing. We're "trying really hard." And none of that is the answer.

End of Dan's notes.

Hope/Expectation/Outcomes

Richard Wurmbrand who endured 14 years of imprisonment and was tortured, wrote in the book, *Tortured for Christ*, "They tortured by all means. They beat until they broke bones. They used red hot irons, they used knives, they used everything." He went on to say, "Hate the evil systems, but love your persecutors. Love their souls and try to win them for Christ." I will end with one last quote of his, "They thought they could contain me, but the heart is free, it can fly." Selah!

You don't have to have a bad day. If you read this statement before reading about Richard Wurmbrand, would you have believed it? Can you imagine being in Richard's shoes? However, as Richard said, "**The heart is free, it can fly.**" The circumstances could be ridiculous against you, all hell could be breaking loose, but you do not have to lose perspective. It is a yielding and surrendering to Christ. When we look to ourselves is when we lose perspective and then we will most certainly have a bad day.

During times of trials, tribulation, and suffering often we will put our hope in the outcome of something. What we think should happen or how we think God is going to work. In His Sovereignty, we do not know how our Father is going to move or work in our circumstances. Isaiah 55:9, "For as the heavens are higher than the earth, so are My ways higher than your ways, and My thoughts than your thoughts." If I am fully surrendered and submitted to God, I will not "need to know" how He is going to move in something. I will trust Him and His direction in my life. In obedience with faith, I will follow Him and wait on Him. And I WILL see His power move and His glory fall.

If our hope is placed in Him our hope will NEVER fail. Because He will never fail us, we have faith to trust in Him. Hope does not set dates or try to dictate to God when and how. Hope is based on God's promise that He is good. Hope trusts God for all the details. We are to place our hope in God alone and not on intended outcomes.

Putting our own expectations on God of how we think He should work or move in our circumstances will bring disappointment if or when it does not happen the way we expect. Then it opens the door for our trust in Him to waiver. A downward spiral can happen with doubt setting in. We will even begin to question His Love for us. We must not allow the enemy a foothold with any of his lies and deception. To doubt God's Love for us is to doubt who He is because God is Love.

We must take our focus off our emotions and place them solely on the Love of God and His Person. As we live the surrendered life, we will find all we want in our life is what He wants for us anyways. Along our journey our ways will line up with His ways. He will work ALL things together for our good. Because of our Love for Him and because we are called according to His purpose. Do not lose hope in Him, ever. He is doing something far greater in us than we could ever think or imagine! All for His glory.

Regarding the "why" questions we tend to ask, we need to be very cautious. I believe we can talk to God about anything. I believe we can ask Him any question we have. Where we will get tripped up is if we demand Him to answer us. Or if when He answers us it is not what we want to hear. If we ask the "why" questions we need to come to Him in a posture of humility before His throne of grace. 1) Not demanding we must have the answer. Because He will not always give us the answer. 2) Ready to hear what He has to say if He does answer us.

Quite frankly if we do not take on this posture of humility and are not prepared either for His "No" answer or His "Dreaded" answer, the enemy will use this as a snare for us to fall. We will get upset with no response or we can get upset with the response we are given and either way we will get mad at God if we are not humbled and prepared. There is nothing satan would like more than for us to blame God for "allowing" this to happen and then not telling us why or maybe even showing us it was our own doing that got us here. We know Jesus paid the ultimate price for our sins but there are still consequences for our sins if we continue to live in them.

These issues and questions will keep us stumbling and tripped up for a long time if we do not address it with Jesus in humility and say, "Lord, I am prepared if You do not answer me, and I am prepared for anything it is You have to show me or say to me." He will tell us what we need to know, and He will do it in His timing.

There are two things I do know always; God IS Love and God IS good, period. Only He knows His plan for me. Only He knows what I need; to grow in character, to grow in trusting Him, to grow in faith, to grow in my relationship with Him. Only He knows what I need for this journey of transformation I am on to become just as Christ in this world (1 John 4:17).

Just because God may not always work things out the way we would want Him to. He always works things out for what is best for us. He always works things out according to the plan He has for us. We cannot afford to believe the lies of the enemy any longer!

A PRAYER TO PRAY:

"This temple does not share occupancy with anything else. Only You, Holy Spirit. Jesus, my life is Yours completely! I Love You more than anything in this world. I long to live my life for only You. I long for purity and holiness. I am holy as You are holy. No one can ever hurt me, offend me, or reject me, because I know I am accepted in You. I am chosen by You. You, who matters infinitely more than anyone in this world. Holy Spirit, when I read the Word of God, please make me into what I read. I want every part of my flesh gone, every bit of it. I want to live a life of continual repentance. Correct me and transform me. Train me and teach me. May I live Life ("Redefined") the way You always intended. Where Jesus and I are One!"

JOURNAL ENTRY:

I had a visual of this one day. You know how at a wedding ceremony they have two different colored sands to represent each person? Then they put them into one container to represent the two becoming one? Well, I thought about it and realized you can still tell who is who. You can tell the blue sand from the red sand. You can still tell them apart. They are mixed but they are not "one." Then God showed me it's much more like two glasses of water poured into one pitcher. You cannot tell one from the other. And so it is to be, with Jesus and us.

Where the Two Become One.

We Are Irrevocably Yours!

THE FIVE TAKE AWAYS + BONUS ONE

1. Our entire purpose in life is to be One with Jesus Christ.
2. The greatest thing in our life should be God. He is who we should be living for. Until this can be our answer we are wandering around in the wilderness, lost, and confused.
3. My obedience to Him is directly related to my Love for Him.
4. God gives each of us our own area of influence, to fulfill the same greater purpose. We are different parts in one body.
5. The things we do in our everyday life and what we talk about ought to show our eternal values.
6. We become One in unity when we each Love like Jesus and look like Jesus. Are you looking like Jesus?

Faith: Hebrews 11

11:1, Faith brings the unseen into the seen.

11:2, By faith the people of old earned a good reputation.

11:3, By faith <u>we understand</u> the universe was created by the Word of God.

11:4, Faith moved Abel to offer a more excellent sacrifice.

11:5, By faith Enoch was taken up to heaven so that he should not see death.

11:6, By faith we please God and believe that He exists.

11:7, Faith opened Noah's heart to <u>receive revelation and warning</u>. With godly fear he obeyed and became an heir of righteousness that comes by faith.

11:8, Faith motivated Abraham to <u>obey God's call</u>.

11:9, By faith Abraham went to live in the land of promise as a foreigner.

11:11, By faith Sarah <u>received power</u> to conceive and she bore a child when she was past the age.

11:17, By faith Abraham offered up Isaac, his only son, when tested. <u>Faith brings obedience</u>.

11:19, By faith he <u>concluded God was able</u> to raise him from the dead.

11:20-21, Faith prompted blessings.

11:22, By faith Joseph <u>confidently knew</u> the people of Israel would leave Egypt. So, he gave instructions concerning his bones.

11:23, By faith Moses was hidden for three months by his parents for his protection.

11:24, Faith enabled Moses to <u>choose God's will</u>.

11:25, Faith enables us to <u>endure affliction</u> rather than enjoy the passing pleasures of sin.

11:27, By faith Moses <u>left Egypt not being afraid</u> of the anger of the king. He endured as seeing Him who is invisible.

11:28, By faith he kept the Passover and the sprinkling of blood so the destroyer of the first born would not touch them.

11:29, Faith <u>opened the way</u> through the Red Sea on dry land.

11:30, By faith the walls of Jericho fell.

11:31, By faith Rahab the prostitute <u>was not destroyed</u> because she provided a way of escape for the spies.

11:33, By faith kingdoms were subdued, justice established, promises were obtained, and faith closed the mouth of lions.

11:34, Faith quenched the power of fire. Faith provided an escape from the edge of the sword. Made men strong out of weakness (sparked courage in them). Made them mighty in war and unbeatable. Faith put foreign armies to flight.

11:35, Faith raised the dead of mothers. Yet faith enabled others to endure torture refusing to accept release.

11:36, By faith others endured the trial of mocking and scourging, and chains and imprisonment.

11:37, By faith they endured being stoned to death and being sawn in two. They endured luring with tempting offers to renounce their faith. They were put to death by the sword. They wandered about in sheepskins and goatskins being destitute, afflicted, and tormented.

11:38, They wandered in deserts, mountains, dens, and caves.

11:39, Through faith they were able to obtain a good testimony and yet they did not receive the fulfillment of what was promised because God had us in mind and had something better for us so that they would not be made perfect apart from us.

James 1:2-4, "My brethren, count it all joy when you fall into various trials, knowing that the testing of your faith produces patience. But let patience have its perfect work, that you may be perfect and complete, lacking nothing."

Sin

"If you can't be free from sin until you die then Jesus isn't your savior, death is."

Georgian Banov

Please look up and read the following Scriptures for yourself in their entirety. Some of what is written is only in part.

Romans 6, please read the whole chapter. I will share some examples of what you will find.

Romans 6:2, "How shall we who died to sin live any longer in it?"

Romans 6:6, 'Knowing this, that our old man was crucified with Him, that the body of sin might be done away with, that we should no longer be slaves of sin."

Romans 6:7, "For he who has died has been freed from sin."

Romans 6:11, "Likewise you also, reckon yourselves to be dead indeed to sin, but alive to God in Christ Jesus our Lord."

Romans 6:14, "For sin shall not have dominion over you, for you are not under the law but under grace."

Romans 6:18, "And having been set free from sin, you became salves of righteousness."

Romans 6:22, "But now having been set free from sin, and having become slaves of God, you have your fruit to holiness, and the end, everlasting life."

Romans 8:2, "For the law of the Spirit of life in Christ Jesus has made me free from the law of sin and death."

1 Corinthians 15:33-34, "... Awake to righteousness, and do not sin."

2 Corinthians 5:15, "and He died for all, that those who live should no

longer live for themselves, but for Him who died for them and rose again."

Galatians 5:1, "<u>Stand fast therefore in the liberty</u> by which Christ has made us free, and do not be entangled again with a yoke of bondage."

Galatians 5:16, "I say then; Walk in the Spirit and you shall not fulfill the lust of the flesh."

Galatians 5:24, "And those who are Christ's have crucified the flesh with its passions and desires."

Philippians 2:14-15, "... that you may become blameless (Greek; faultless) and harmless (Greek; unmixed, innocent)."

Colossians 1:19-24, Please read.

Colossians 3:3-5, "For <u>you died</u>, and your life is hidden with Christ in God..." (Please read in its entirety).

1 Thessalonians 5:22, "Abstain from every form of evil."

2 Timothy 2:19, "... Let everyone who names the name of Christ depart from iniquity."

James 4:7, "Therefore submit to God. Resist the devil and he will flee from you."

1 Peter 1:15-16, "But as He who called you is holy (Greek; sacred, physically pure, morally blameless, saint), you also <u>be holy in all your conduct</u>..."

1 Peter 2:21-25, We are to follow Jesus' steps: <u>who committed no sin</u> ... <u>we having died to sin</u>, might live for righteousness. (Please read in its entirety).

1 Peter 4:1-2, For he who has suffered in the flesh <u>has ceased from sin</u>. No longer live in the flesh. (Please read in its entirety).

2 Peter 1:3-11, Vs 3, God has given to us ALL things pertaining to life and godliness. Vs 4, we are partakers of the divine nature having escaped the corruption that is in the world. Vs 5-9 we are given a list we are to abound in. Vs 10, If you do these things <u>you will NEVER stumble</u>. (Please read in its entirety).

2 Peter 3:14, "... be found without spot and blameless."

1 John 2:1, "My little children, these things I write to you, so that you may not sin. And if anyone sins, we have an Advocate with the Father, Jesus Christ the righteous."

1 John 2:6, "He who says he abides in Him ought himself also to <u>walk just as He walked</u>."

1 John 3:3-10 "... Whoever abides in Him does not sin." (Please read in its entirety).

1 John 4:17, "... As He is so are we in this world." (Please read in its entirety).

Jude 24, "Now to Him who is able to keep you from stumbling, and to present you faultless before the presence of His glory with exceeding joy.'

John 5:14, "... See, you have been made well. Sin no more, lest a worse thing come upon you."

John 8:11, "... Neither do I condemn you; go and sin no more."

John 8:34-36, "... whoever commits sin is a slave of sin. And a slave does not abide in the house forever, but a son abides forever. Therefore, if the Son makes you free, you are free indeed."

Galatians 2:20 (KJV), "I am crucified with Christ: nevertheless I live; yet not I, but <u>Christ liveth in me</u>: and the life which I now live in the flesh <u>I live by the faith of the Son of God</u>, who loved me, and gave Himself for me." (Christ in me does not want to sin. Christ in me does not sin.)

Proverbs 3:7, "Do not be wise in your own eyes; fear the LORD and depart from evil."

Proverbs 8:13, "The fear of the LORD is to hate evil; Pride and arrogance and the evil way and the perverse mouth I hate."

Proverbs 16:6, "In mercy and truth Atonement is provided for iniquity; and by the fear of the LORD one departs from evil."

Acknowledgements

BACK IN 2013 Holy Spirit showed me I would be writing a book. This is God's idea. This has always been His plan. This is His gifting. This is His book. Lord, I give You all glory, honor, and praise. Holy Spirit thank You for Your Words, Your guidance, Your Love, Your patience with me, in learning how to live the crucified life in Christ Jesus and then being able to put it in writing. I am eternally grateful for the work You have done in my life and producing a book out of it to help others become free. You have my eternal gratitude, Love, and life. You are worthy!

There are a few other acknowledgments I would like to give.

To Dan Mohler, for the countless hours of teaching I have listened to over the last 4 years (since 2019). Holy Spirit has used you to change my life and inspire this book to what it is today. I knew since 2013 the book God wanted me to write was a book about transformation, but God knew I needed to understand a whole lot more about it and become this life before I could pen it. God used you, Dan, in my life for this reason, and I am eternally grateful for your life lived as the example of what transformation is. Of what being like Christ really looks like. Thank you!

To Steven Hogwood, God has used you in my life to help get this book written, published, and out there. I am eternally grateful for your obedience to the Lord. For following Him in what was your part in this whole endeavor. I am incredibly thankful for your support in every way and for your friendship. You have been a rock of encouragement for me. Thank you!

To ALL my family and friends who have always been nothing but supportive and encouraging. It was like the days of Noah. In 2013, "I'm writing a book!" As years went on... "where's the book?" "It's coming!" Years later "when is the book going to get here?" "I don't know. But it's coming!" It didn't quite take 120 years to write, but it felt like it! The difference is you believed the book was coming. Your faith in what the Lord had given me to do has been a blessing in my life. You have always believed and have never once thought I was crazy. Well at least you never made it known to my face if you did (smile). All your prayers have been priceless to me! All your support during this entire journey of my life thus far and in making this book possible has been such an encouragement to me, that words do not suffice. I am eternally grateful to **ALL** of you, and I Love you all greatly and deeply! Thank you!

The author is a girl who said "yes" to the Lord's call. Who was given instruction to write a book and so she did. Who was given a desire for the bride of Christ, to help prepare us for our wedding day that is approaching. Who was given a mission to help disciple the church in what the words of Jesus saying, "Follow Me" really mean. She grows more in Love with Him with each day that passes. Jesus is the air she breathes, her Bread of Life, her Living Water, her everything. She cannot live without Him. Her desire is for everyone to know Him, and to have this kind of relationship with Him.

Index